THE MASSIVE

"ONE OF THE BOLDEST AND SMARTEST BOOKS TO DROP IN 2012."

—COMICBOOKRESOURCES.COM

"Awesome. Brilliant. Brian Wood has one hell of an imagination. Every issue he expands the landscape. He could write this story for years. I'd buy it, too. A unique book. Just get it already."

—iFanboy.com

"IT'S A DENSE, CHALLENGING COMIC AND I MEAN THAT IN THE BEST POSSIBLE WAY."

—BLEEDINGCOOL.COM

"*The Massive* hits the mark in terms of the hype built up for the title, delivering a great read. Even those who aren't interested in ecological collapse or environmentalism can enjoy the book because of the stellar writing of Wood, coupled with the beautiful and fitting art of Donaldson and Stewart."

—EGMNow.com

"WE'VE BEEN PSYCHED FOR *DMZ* AUTHOR BRIAN WOOD'S NEXT BIG END-OF-THE-WORLD PROJECT *THE MASSIVE* FOR A SPELL NOW."

—IO9.COM

"Despite being a huge fan of Brian Wood's series *DMZ*, it's difficult to feel too choked up about its recent conclusion. That's because *The Massive* is doing an excellent job serving as a spiritual sequel to *DMZ*."

—IGN.com

"THE PRIMARY JOB OF A FIRST ISSUE IS TO HOOK THE READER, AND *THE MASSIVE* #1 DOES EXACTLY THAT."

—*PASTE*

"A post-apocalyptic story done right."

—Uproxx.com

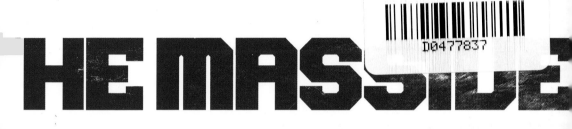

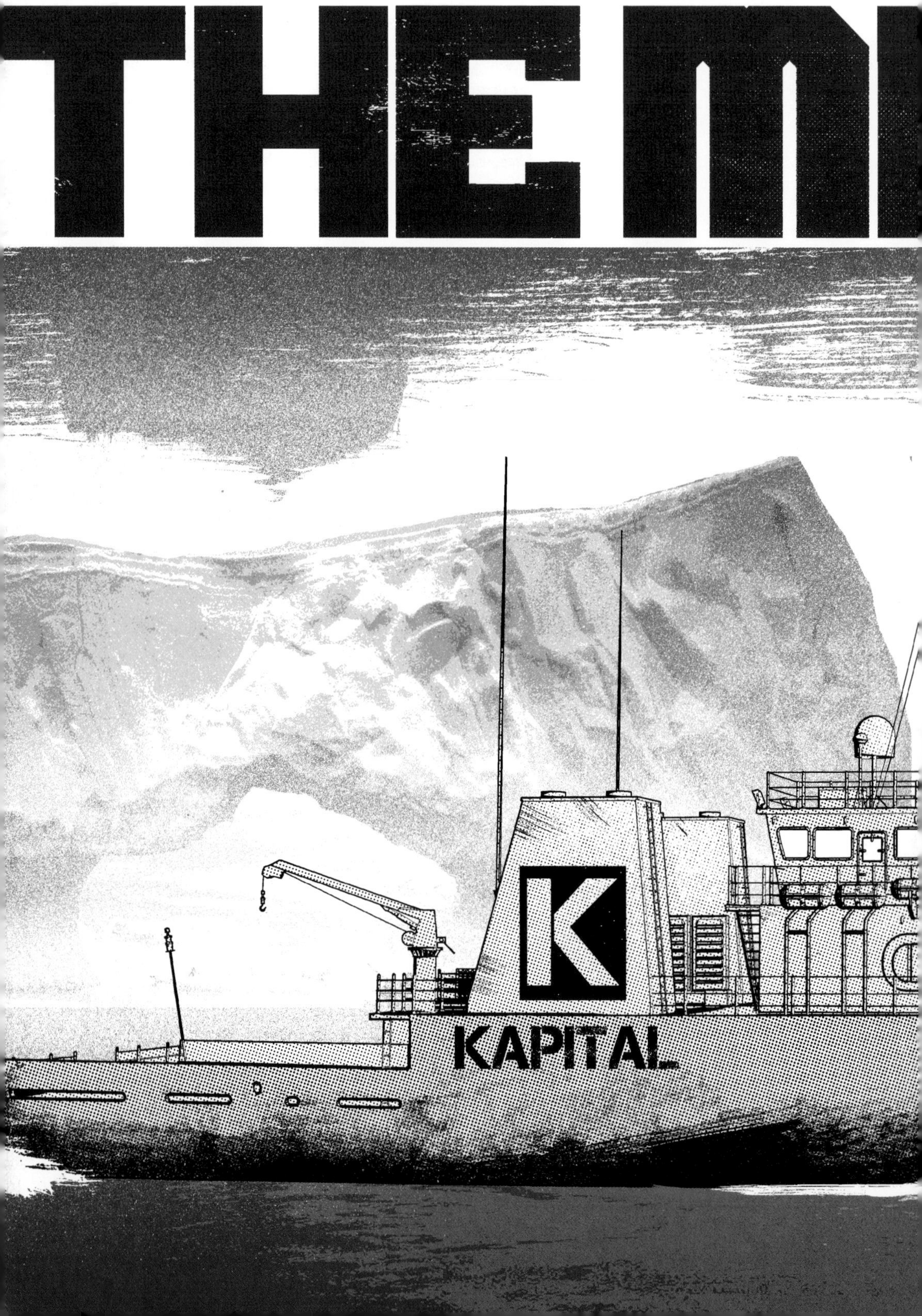
THE M
K
KAPITAL

BLACK PACIFIC

BRIAN WOOD
STORY

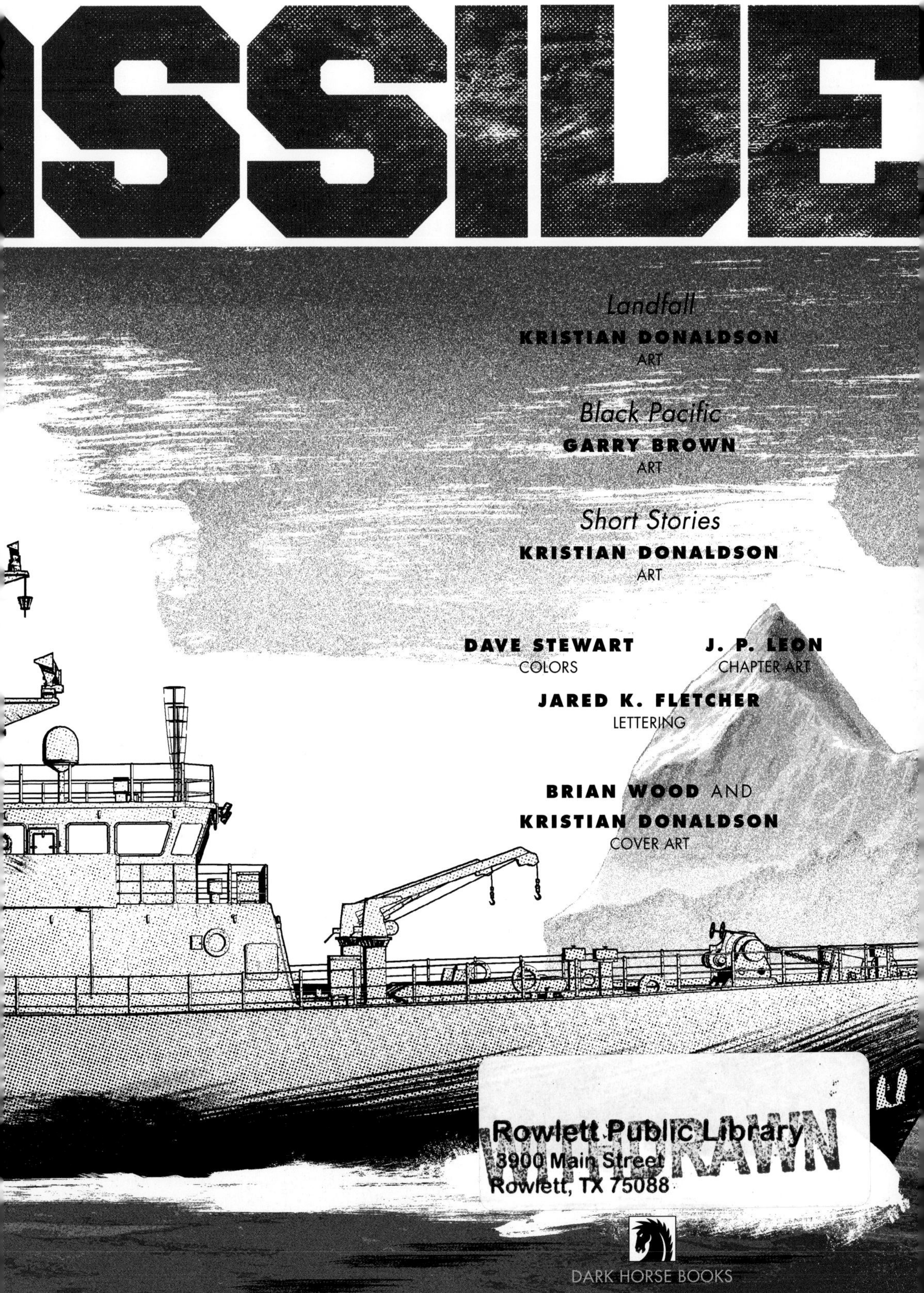

Landfall
KRISTIAN DONALDSON
ART

Black Pacific
GARRY BROWN
ART

Short Stories
KRISTIAN DONALDSON
ART

DAVE STEWART
COLORS

J. P. LEON
CHAPTER ART

JARED K. FLETCHER
LETTERING

BRIAN WOOD AND
KRISTIAN DONALDSON
COVER ART

DARK HORSE BOOKS

MIKE RICHARDSON
PRESIDENT & PUBLISHER

SIERRA HAHN
EDITOR

JIM GIBBONS
ASSISTANT EDITOR

JUSTIN COUCH
COLLECTION DESIGNER

Special thanks to the Wood family: Meredith,
Audrey, and Ian. Also, Emi Yonemura,
Leo Fernandez, Will Dennis, Esther Walker,
the Wanamaker family, Zeus Comics,
Tim Doyle, Nick Derington, David Marques,
Allison Baker, and Chris Roberson.

Published by **DARK HORSE BOOKS**
A division of Dark Horse Comics, Inc.
10956 SE Main Street, Milwaukie, OR 97222

DARKHORSE.COM

First edition: March 2013
ISBN 978-1-61655-132-2

3 5 7 9 10 8 6 4

To find a comics shop in your area,
call the Comic Shop Locator Service toll-free at (888) 266-4226.

Neil Hankerson Executive Vice President · Tom Weddle Chief Financial Officer · Randy Stradley Vice President of Publishing · Michael Martens Vice President of Book Trade Sales · Anita Nelson Vice President of Business Affairs · Scott Allie Editor in Chief · Matt Parkinson Vice President of Marketing · David Scroggy Vice President of Product Development · Dale LaFountain Vice President of Information Technology · Darlene Vogel Senior Director of Print, Design, and Production · Ken Lizzi General Counsel · Davey Estrada Editorial Director · Chris Warner Senior Books Editor · Diana Schutz Executive Editor · Cary Grazzini Director of Print and Development · Lia Ribacchi Art Director · Cara Niece Director of Scheduling · Tim Wiesch Director of International Licensing · Mark Bernardi Director of Digital Publishing

This volume reprints the comic-book series *The Massive* #1–#6 from Dark Horse Comics, as well as material originally published in *Dark Horse Presents* #8–#10.

LIFE AFTER THE APOCALYPSE
JAMAIS CASCIO

Here's the secret of *The Massive*: the "end of the world" isn't. It's just the beginning of what's next.

"End of the world" dramas are popular on both screen and paper, especially in the midst of economically or politically difficult times. As bad as things seem now, they tell us, they could be a lot worse. Most such stories depict, with almost pornographic glee, the details of things falling apart, the center no longer holding, and not-so-mere anarchy loosed upon the world—even as they leave the question of what comes afterward as an exercise for the viewer or reader. And when they do take us to the day after, they are almost invariably simplistic tales of grim survival, a dwindling group of PTSD victims trying to make it to the next food cache before the zombies, aliens, or viruses catch up. But neither of these narrative paradigms ultimately has much lasting weight: in the end, these stories are meant only to remind us to be satisfied with our lives as they are now.

The Massive gives us a different, and essentially unique, take on the story of the end of the world. It doesn't revel in destruction; when scenes describing the planetary crisis show up, they make clear that this was a true disaster, not a disaster movie. Millions have died, in dirty, tragic, and decidedly noncinematic ways. Instead, *The Massive* is a story of the necessity of resilience. While it leads us through the catastrophic aftermath of the Crash, we soon see that survival here is not the purpose in and of itself—it's survival with the hope of making things better, even while recognizing that the old world's legacies (in materials and ideologies) yet remain.

But it's a *hope* of making things better, not a guarantee: Arkady's rooftop of shark fins should underscore that point. The old ways will fight to retain a stranglehold on civilization, no matter how pathological their effects. While Ninth Wave reminds us that this isn't the only option, it too has to contend with a world coping with collapse. Compromises are inevitable—but compromise isn't the same as surrender.

The (perhaps intended) irony here is that nearly all of the fictional disasters posited as part of the year-long Crash parallel the kinds of real-world problems we could very well see over the course of the next century, even absent a Crash. Rising seas, lack of access to basic necessities, collapsing transportation and economic networks—all frighteningly possible, albeit spread over the course of years and decades, not weeks and months, due to the complex effects of a catastrophically disrupted global climate. In our world, Ninth Wave would be fighting the same kinds of fights, but in the world of *The Massive*—with the Crash—the problems can't be waved away as something for future generations to worry about.

The Massive doesn't explicitly pin the blame for the Crash on anthropogenic climate change; the cause(s) remain a mystery, and may or may not be revealed as the series goes on. But whether or not humans are at fault, this is the new normal, not a momentary problem cleaned up by the next issue. Rebuilding has to happen within this context—but it will happen.

With the world of *The Massive*, Brian Wood has captured a too-little-noticed slice of reality: in the wake of a catastrophe, the acts of heroes and villains happen amidst the masses simply trying to regain a sense of normalcy. Those of us who work to figure out how to prevent or adapt to dramatic environmental and technological crises need to bear this reality in mind.

I keep with me a small illustration of this fact. My grandfather left me a set of photos taken during his time in World War II, and one image in the collection has particular resonance, a reminder of the nature of resilience. In it, a group of four Belgian women wash their laundry in the flooded rubble of a bombed-out railway. It's a quiet scene, almost prosaic, but one which captures an essential truth: even in the midst of horror and conflict, our lives continue. The story doesn't end, even if the world does.

Selected by *Foreign Policy* magazine as one of their Top 100 Global Thinkers, Jamais Cascio specializes in the design and creation of plausible scenarios of the future. His work has appeared in the *Atlantic* and *Foreign Policy*, among others, and he has been featured in a variety of future-oriented television programs. Cascio speaks about future possibilities around the world, at venues including the National Academy of Sciences and TED. Cascio is currently a Distinguished Fellow at the Institute for the Future. In 2003, he cofounded the award-winning environmental website WorldChanging.com, and now blogs at *Open the Future*.

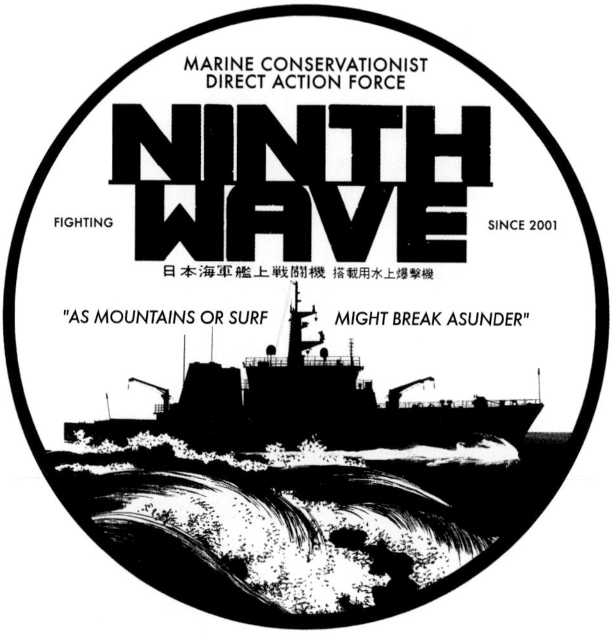
MARINE CONSERVATIONIST
DIRECT ACTION FORCE
NINTH
WAVE
FIGHTING
SINCE 2001
日本海軍艦上戦闘機 搭載用水上爆撃機
"AS MOUNTAINS OR SURF
MIGHT BREAK ASUNDER"

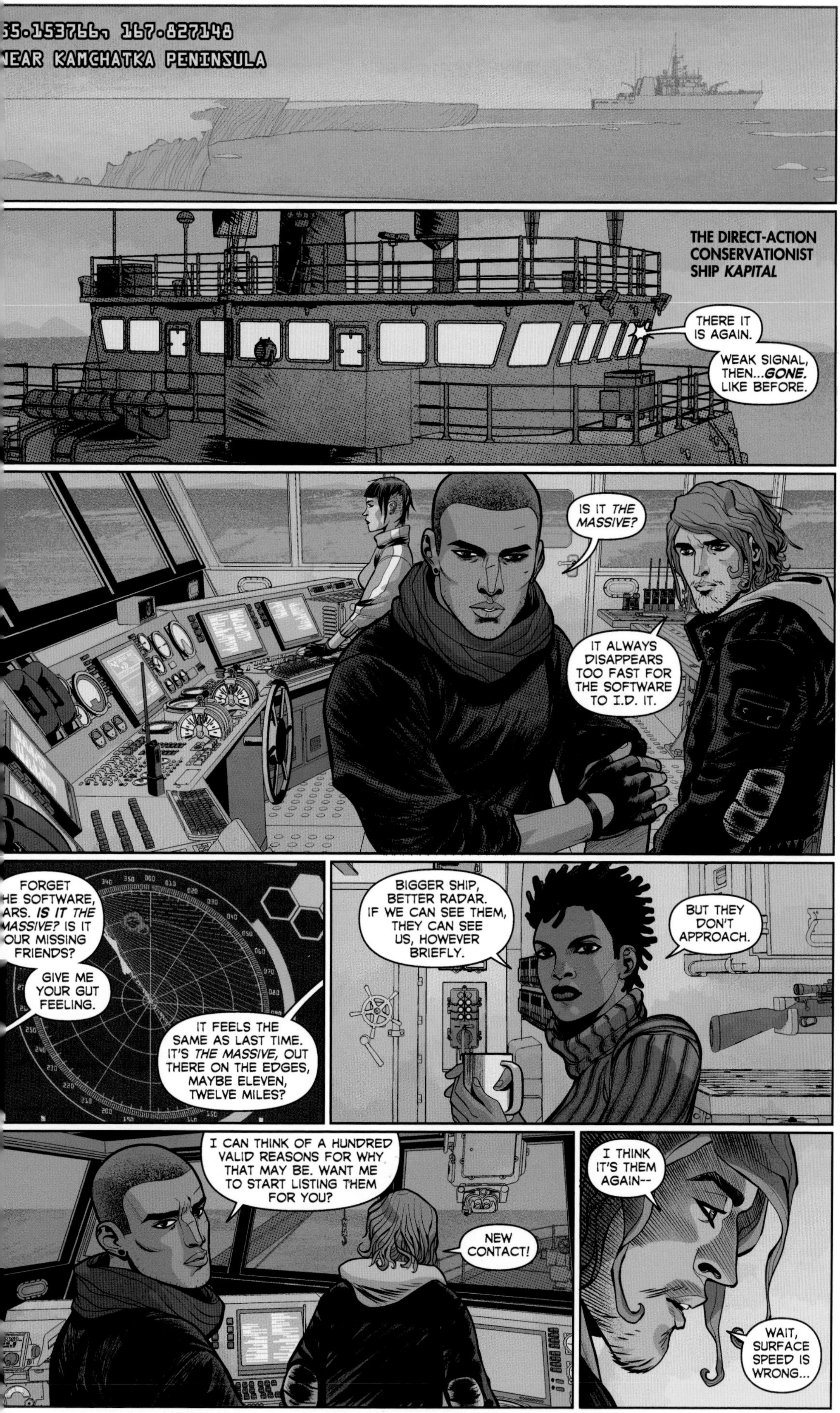
55.153766, 167.827148
NEAR KAMCHATKA PENINSULA
THE DIRECT-ACTION CONSERVATIONIST SHIP *KAPITAL*
THERE IT IS AGAIN.
WEAK SIGNAL, THEN...*GONE.* LIKE BEFORE.
IS IT *THE MASSIVE?*
IT ALWAYS DISAPPEARS TOO FAST FOR THE SOFTWARE TO I.D. IT.
FORGET THE SOFTWARE, ARS. *IS IT THE MASSIVE?* IS IT OUR MISSING FRIENDS?
GIVE ME YOUR GUT FEELING.
IT FEELS THE SAME AS LAST TIME. IT'S *THE MASSIVE,* OUT THERE ON THE EDGES, MAYBE ELEVEN, TWELVE MILES?
BIGGER SHIP, BETTER RADAR. IF WE CAN SEE THEM, THEY CAN SEE US, HOWEVER BRIEFLY.
BUT THEY DON'T APPROACH.
I CAN THINK OF A HUNDRED VALID REASONS FOR WHY THAT MAY BE. WANT ME TO START LISTING THEM FOR YOU?
NEW CONTACT!
I THINK IT'S THEM AGAIN--
WAIT, SURFACE SPEED IS WRONG...

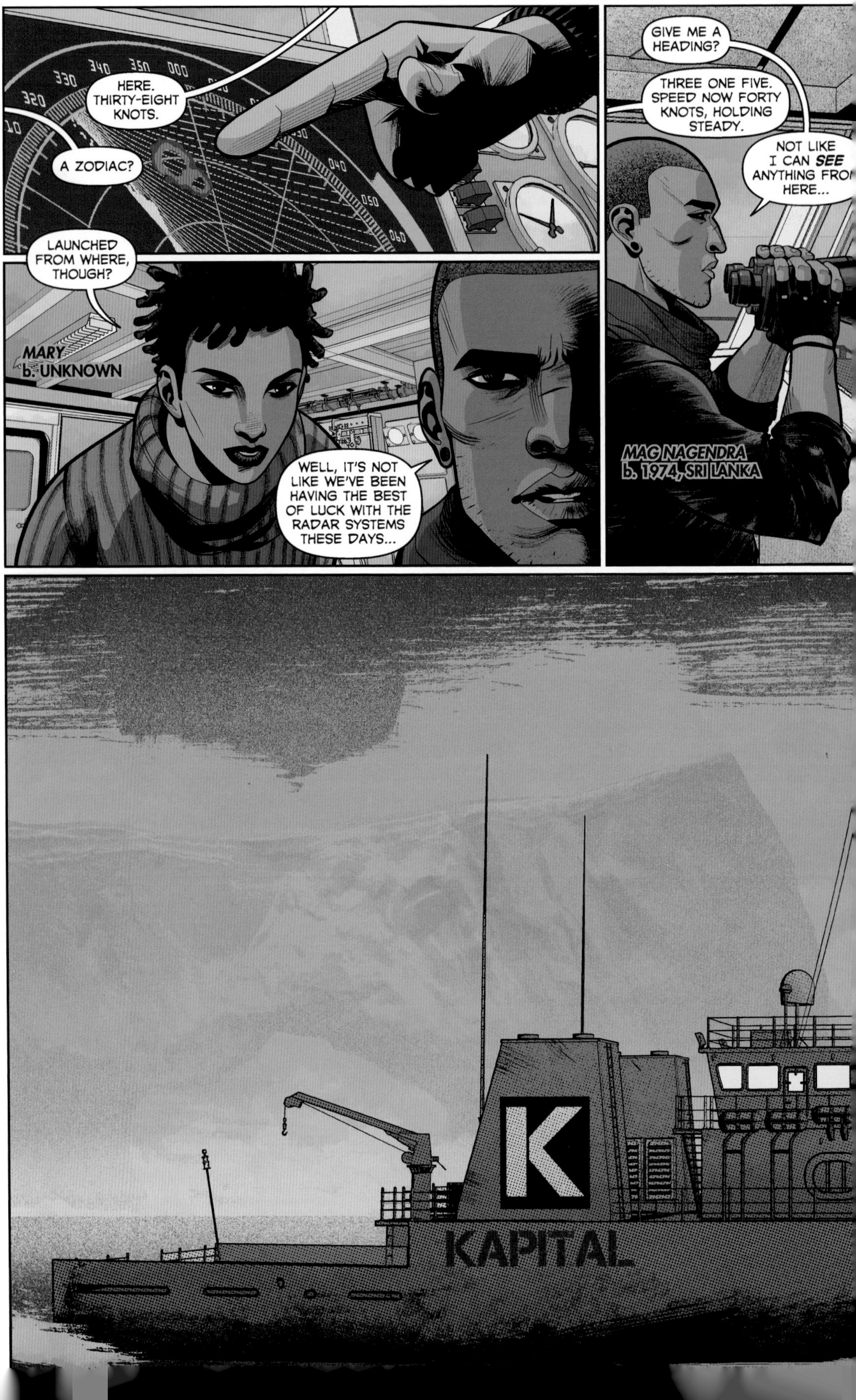

A ZODIAC?
HERE. THIRTY-EIGHT KNOTS.
GIVE ME A HEADING?
THREE ONE FIVE. SPEED NOW FORTY KNOTS, HOLDING STEADY.
NOT LIKE I CAN SEE ANYTHING FROM HERE...
LAUNCHED FROM WHERE, THOUGH?
MARY
b. UNKNOWN
WELL, IT'S NOT LIKE WE'VE BEEN HAVING THE BEST OF LUCK WITH THE RADAR SYSTEMS THESE DAYS...
MAG NAGENDRA
b. 1974, SRI LANKA
KAPITAL

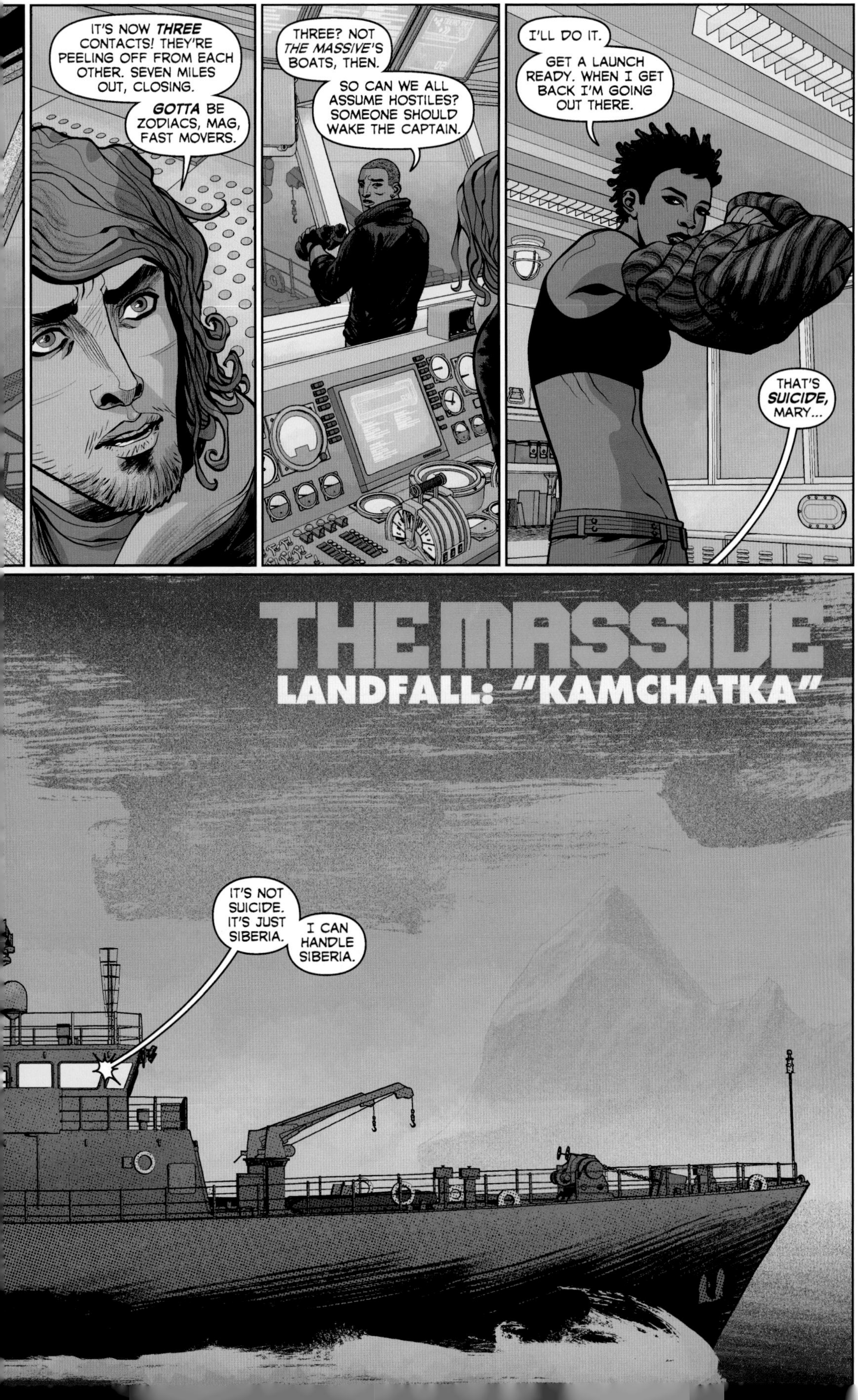
IT'S NOW THREE CONTACTS! THEY'RE PEELING OFF FROM EACH OTHER. SEVEN MILES OUT, CLOSING.
GOTTA BE ZODIACS, MAG, FAST MOVERS.
THREE? NOT THE MASSIVE'S BOATS, THEN.
SO CAN WE ALL ASSUME HOSTILES? SOMEONE SHOULD WAKE THE CAPTAIN.
I'LL DO IT.
GET A LAUNCH READY. WHEN I GET BACK I'M GOING OUT THERE.
THAT'S SUICIDE, MARY...
THE MASSIVE
LANDFALL: "KAMCHATKA"
IT'S NOT SUICIDE. IT'S JUST SIBERIA.
I CAN HANDLE SIBERIA.

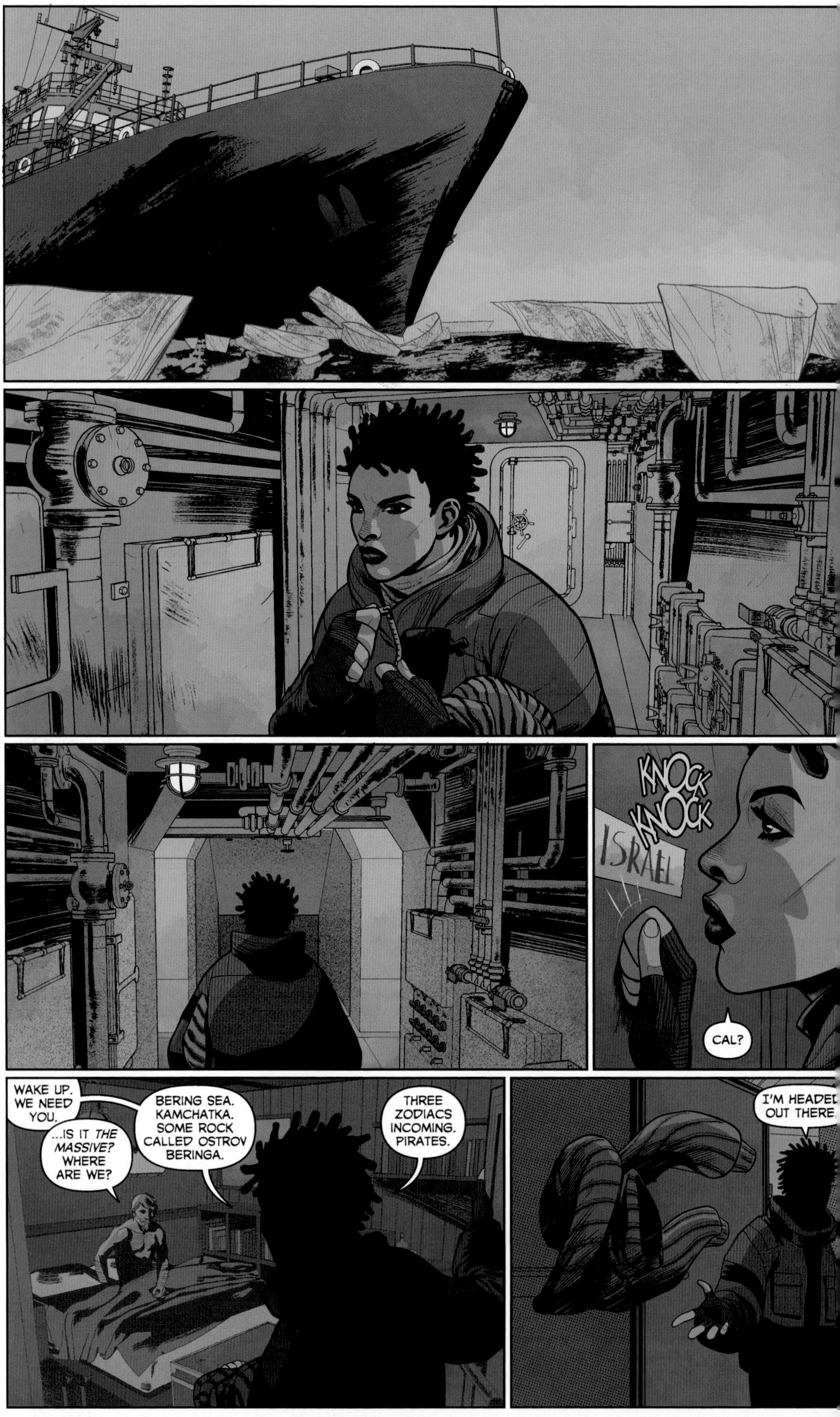
KNOCK KNOCK
ISRAEL
CAL?
WAKE UP. WE NEED YOU.
...IS IT THE MASSIVE? WHERE ARE WE?
BERING SEA. KAMCHATKA. SOME ROCK CALLED OSTROV BERINGA.
THREE ZODIACS INCOMING. PIRATES.
I'M HEADED OUT THERE.

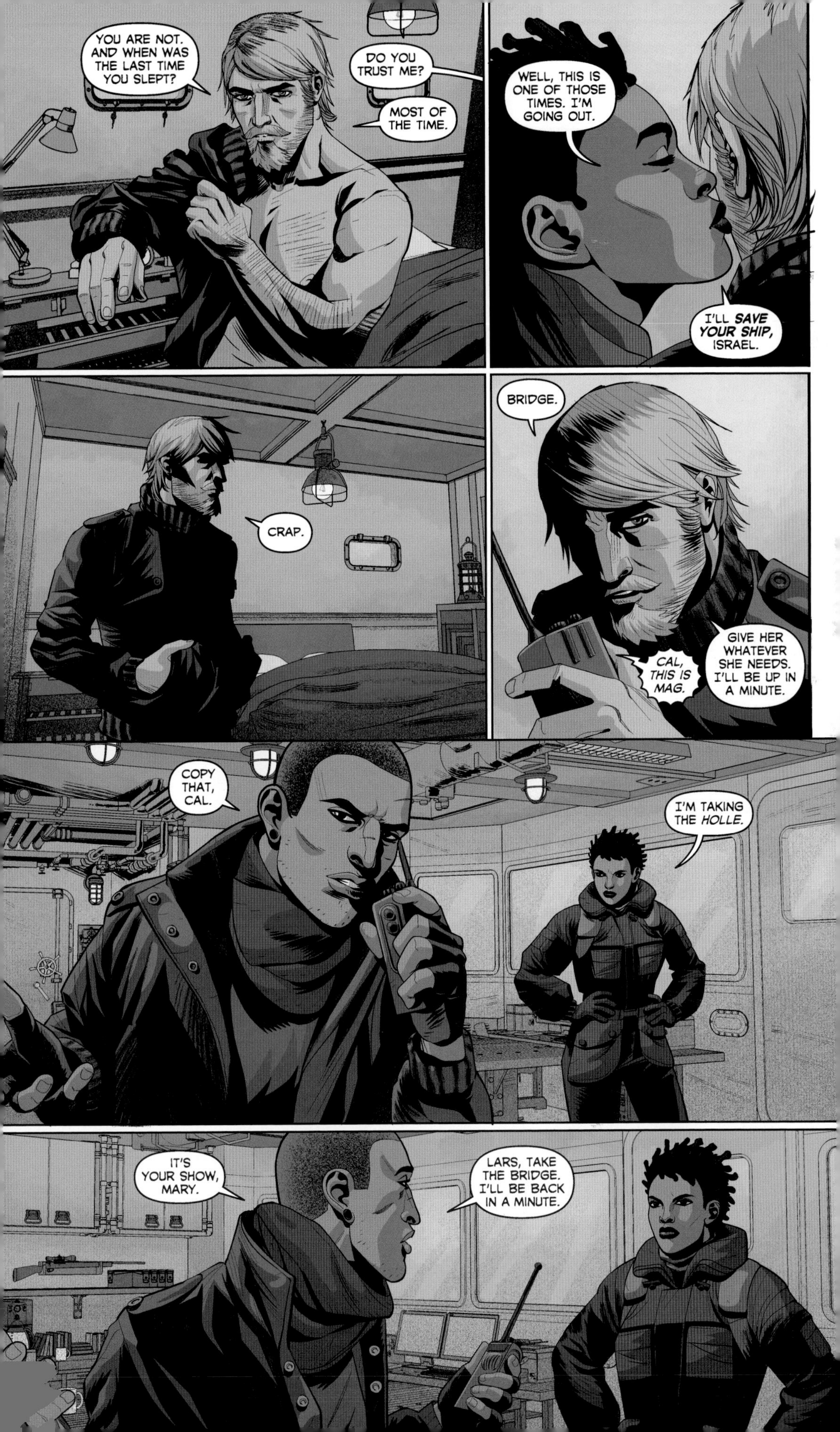
YOU ARE NOT. AND WHEN WAS THE LAST TIME YOU SLEPT?
DO YOU TRUST ME?
MOST OF THE TIME.
WELL, THIS IS ONE OF THOSE TIMES. I'M GOING OUT.
I'LL *SAVE YOUR SHIP,* ISRAEL.
CRAP.
BRIDGE.
CAL, THIS IS MAG.
GIVE HER WHATEVER SHE NEEDS. I'LL BE UP IN A MINUTE.
COPY THAT, CAL.
I'M TAKING THE *HOLLE.*
IT'S YOUR SHOW, MARY.
LARS, TAKE THE BRIDGE. I'LL BE BACK IN A MINUTE.

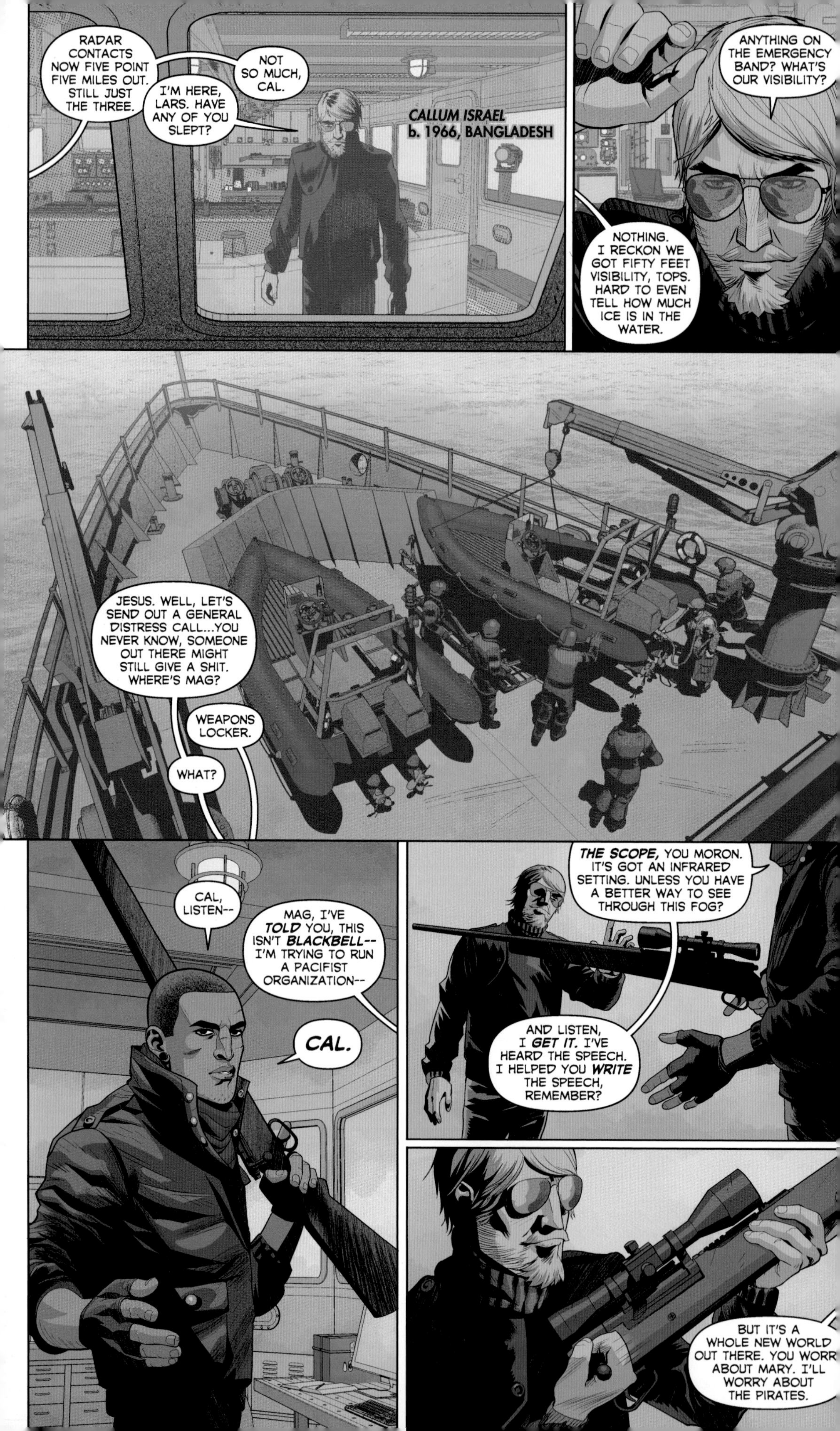

RADAR CONTACTS NOW FIVE POINT FIVE MILES OUT. STILL JUST THE THREE.
NOT SO MUCH, CAL.
I'M HERE, LARS. HAVE ANY OF YOU SLEPT?
CALLUM ISRAEL
b. 1966, BANGLADESH
ANYTHING ON THE EMERGENCY BAND? WHAT'S OUR VISIBILITY?
NOTHING. I RECKON WE GOT FIFTY FEET VISIBILITY, TOPS. HARD TO EVEN TELL HOW MUCH ICE IS IN THE WATER.
JESUS. WELL, LET'S SEND OUT A GENERAL DISTRESS CALL...YOU NEVER KNOW, SOMEONE OUT THERE MIGHT STILL GIVE A SHIT. WHERE'S MAG?
WEAPONS LOCKER.
WHAT?
CAL, LISTEN--
MAG, I'VE TOLD YOU, THIS ISN'T BLACKBELL-- I'M TRYING TO RUN A PACIFIST ORGANIZATION--
CAL.
THE SCOPE, YOU MORON. IT'S GOT AN INFRARED SETTING. UNLESS YOU HAVE A BETTER WAY TO SEE THROUGH THIS FOG?
AND LISTEN, I GET IT. I'VE HEARD THE SPEECH. I HELPED YOU WRITE THE SPEECH, REMEMBER?
BUT IT'S A WHOLE NEW WORLD OUT THERE. YOU WORR ABOUT MARY. I'LL WORRY ABOUT THE PIRATES.

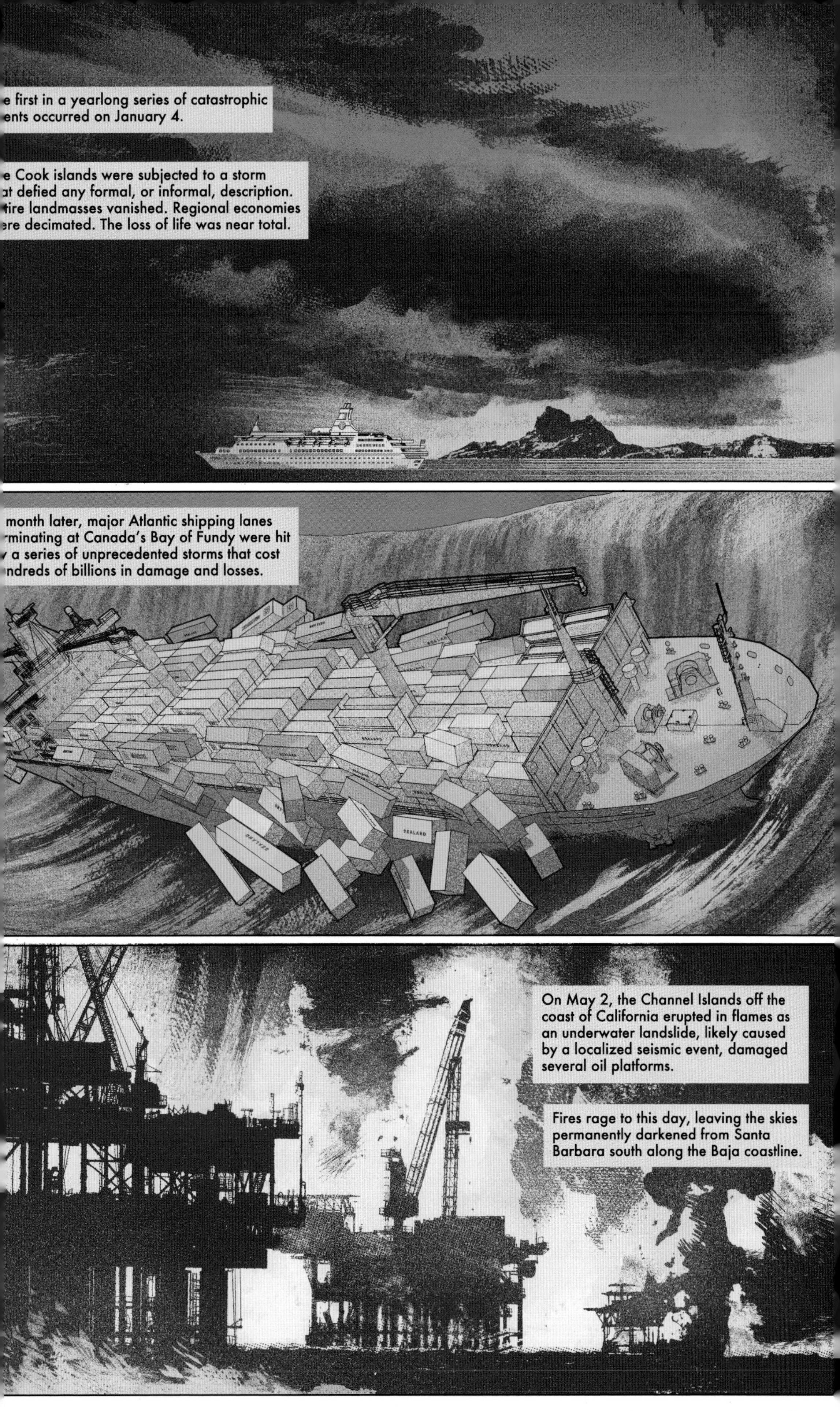
e first in a yearlong series of catastrophic
ents occurred on January 4.
e Cook islands were subjected to a storm
at defied any formal, or informal, description.
tire landmasses vanished. Regional economies
ere decimated. The loss of life was near total.
month later, major Atlantic shipping lanes
rminating at Canada's Bay of Fundy were hit
a series of unprecedented storms that cost
ndreds of billions in damage and losses.
On May 2, the Channel Islands off the
coast of California erupted in flames as
an underwater landslide, likely caused
by a localized seismic event, damaged
several oil platforms.
Fires rage to this day, leaving the skies
permanently darkened from Santa
Barbara south along the Baja coastline.

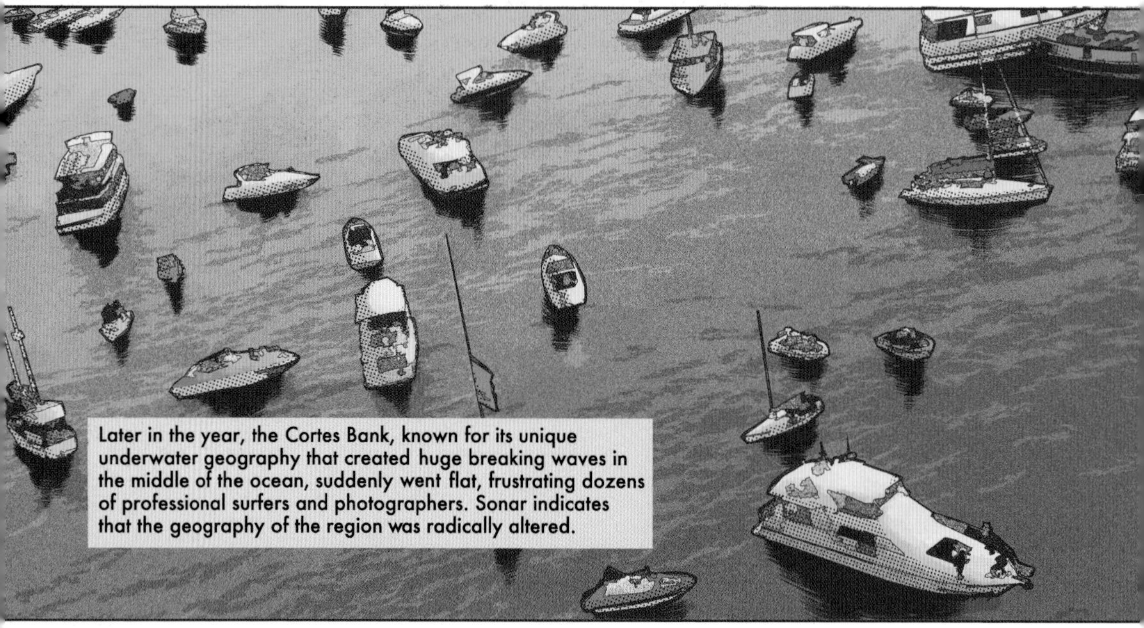
Later in the year, the Cortes Bank, known for its unique underwater geography that created huge breaking waves in the middle of the ocean, suddenly went flat, frustrating dozens of professional surfers and photographers. Sonar indicates that the geography of the region was radically altered.

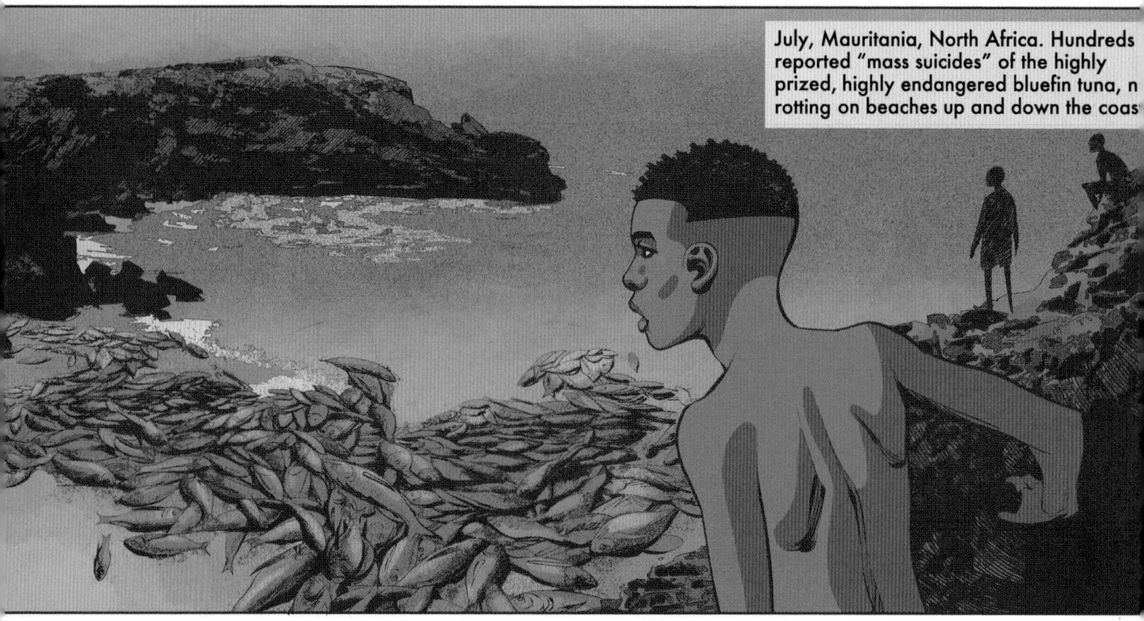
July, Mauritania, North Africa. Hundreds reported "mass suicides" of the highly prized, highly endangered bluefin tuna, n rotting on beaches up and down the coas

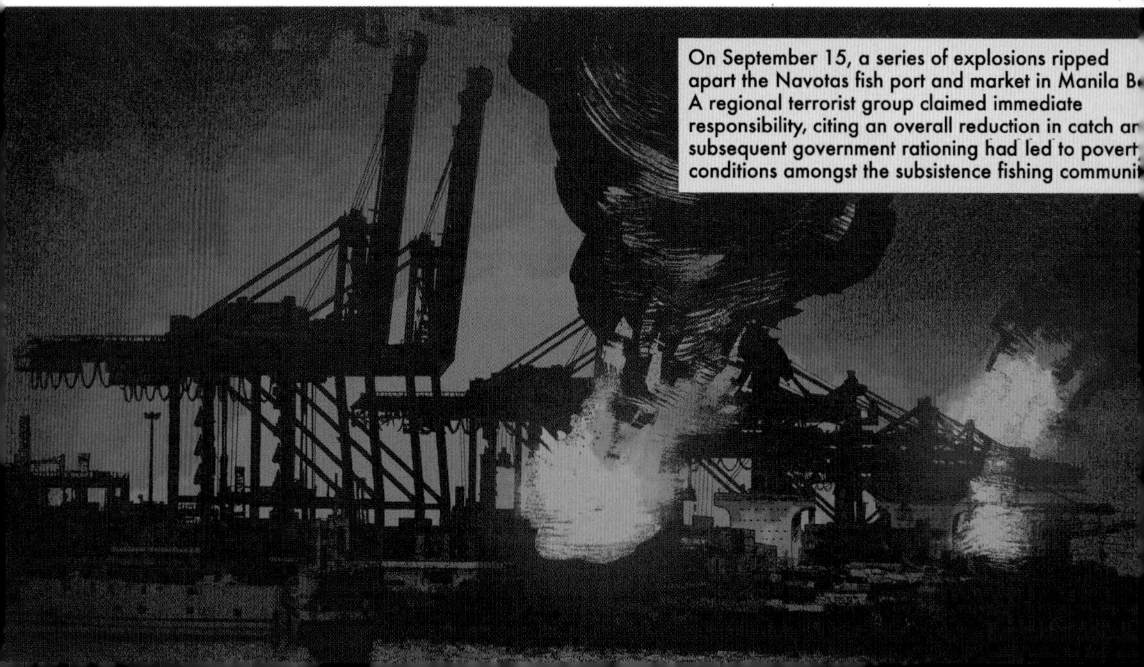
On September 15, a series of explosions ripped apart the Navotas fish port and market in Manila B A regional terrorist group claimed immediate responsibility, citing an overall reduction in catch an subsequent government rationing had led to povert conditions amongst the subsistence fishing communi

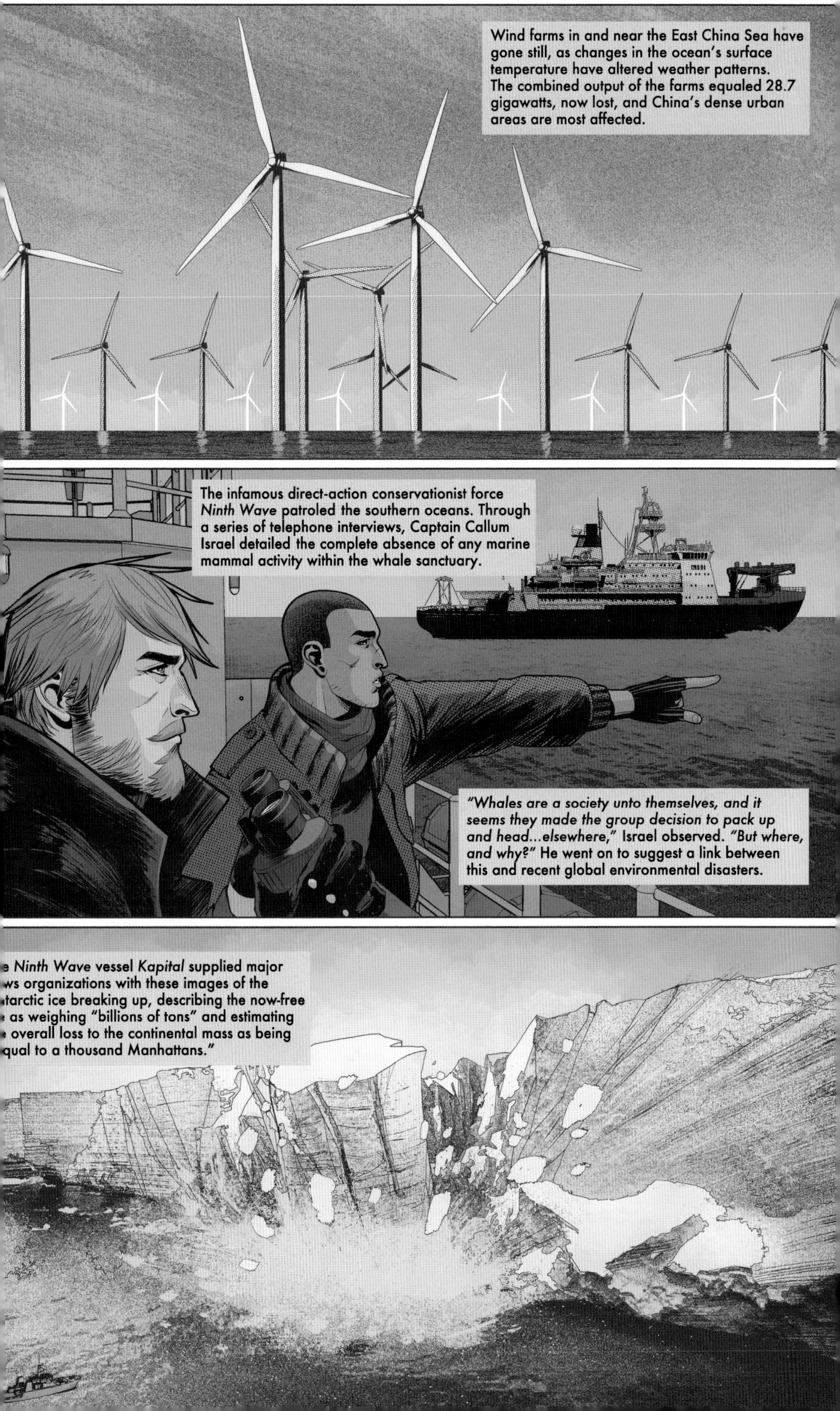

Wind farms in and near the East China Sea have gone still, as changes in the ocean's surface temperature have altered weather patterns. The combined output of the farms equaled 28.7 gigawatts, now lost, and China's dense urban areas are most affected.
The infamous direct-action conservationist force *Ninth Wave* patroled the southern oceans. Through a series of telephone interviews, Captain Callum Israel detailed the complete absence of any marine mammal activity within the whale sanctuary.
"Whales are a society unto themselves, and it seems they made the group decision to pack up and head...elsewhere," Israel observed. *"But where, and why?"* He went on to suggest a link between this and recent global environmental disasters.
e *Ninth Wave* vessel *Kapital* supplied major ws organizations with these images of the tarctic ice breaking up, describing the now-free e as weighing "billions of tons" and estimating e overall loss to the continental mass as being qual to a thousand Manhattans."

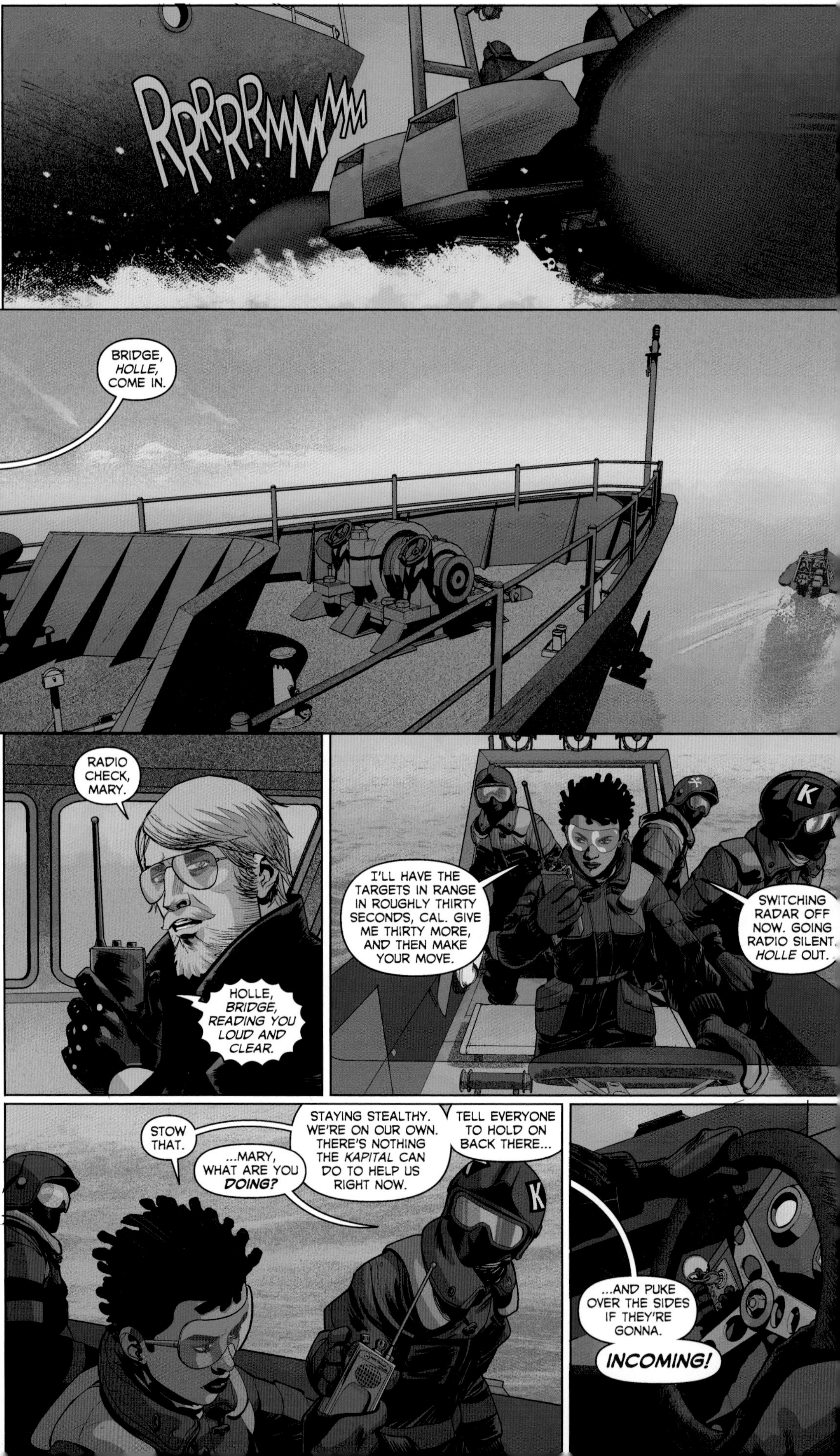
RRRRMMMMM
BRIDGE, HOLLE, COME IN.
RADIO CHECK, MARY.
HOLLE, BRIDGE, READING YOU LOUD AND CLEAR.
I'LL HAVE THE TARGETS IN RANGE IN ROUGHLY THIRTY SECONDS, CAL. GIVE ME THIRTY MORE, AND THEN MAKE YOUR MOVE.
SWITCHING RADAR OFF NOW. GOING RADIO SILENT. HOLLE OUT.
STOW THAT.
...MARY, WHAT ARE YOU DOING?
STAYING STEALTHY. WE'RE ON OUR OWN. THERE'S NOTHING THE KAPITAL CAN DO TO HELP US RIGHT NOW.
TELL EVERYONE TO HOLD ON BACK THERE...
...AND PUKE OVER THE SIDES IF THEY'RE GONNA.
INCOMING!

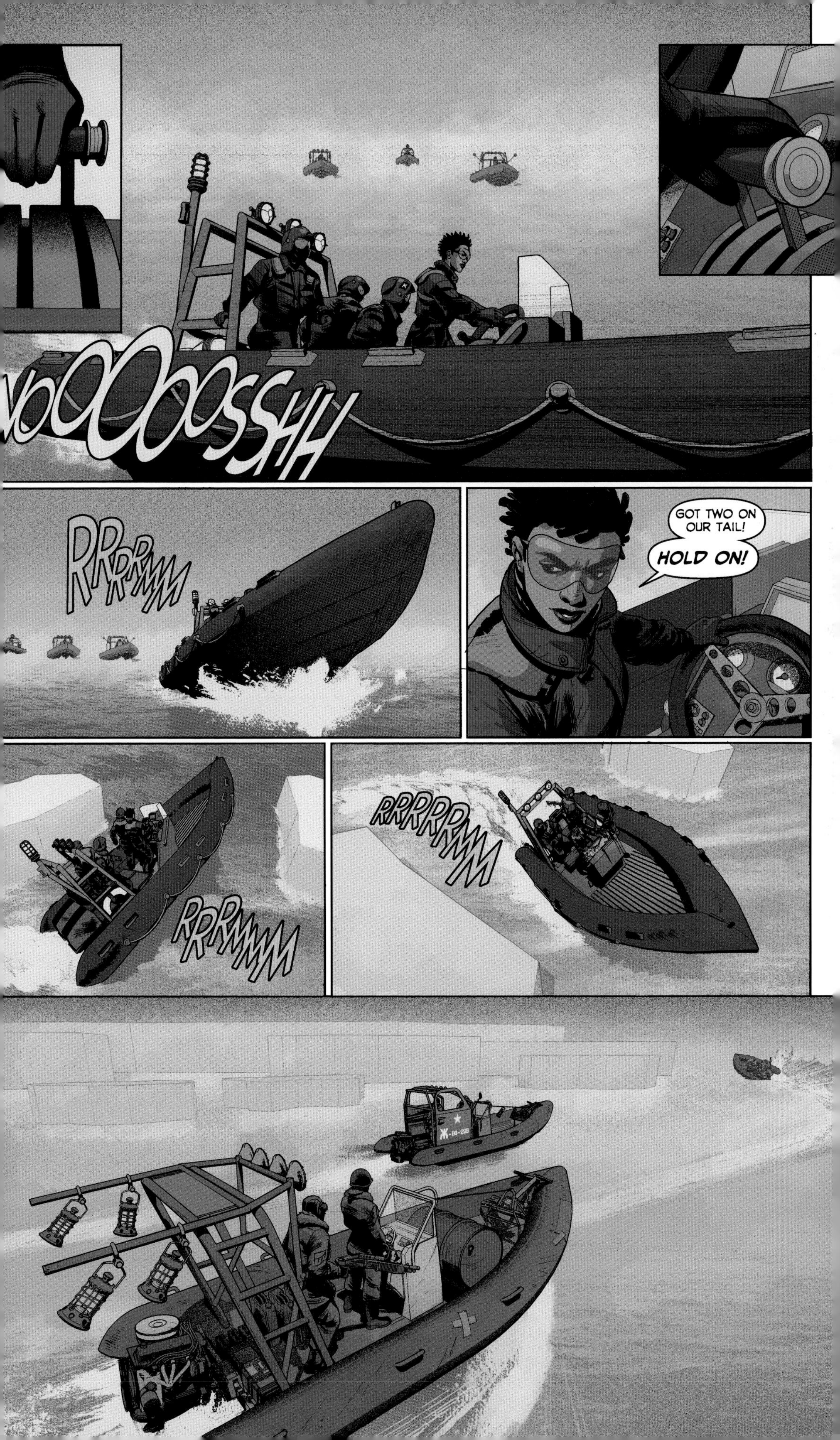
VOOOOOSSHH
RRRRRMM
GOT TWO ON OUR TAIL!
HOLD ON!
RRRMMM
RRRRRRMM

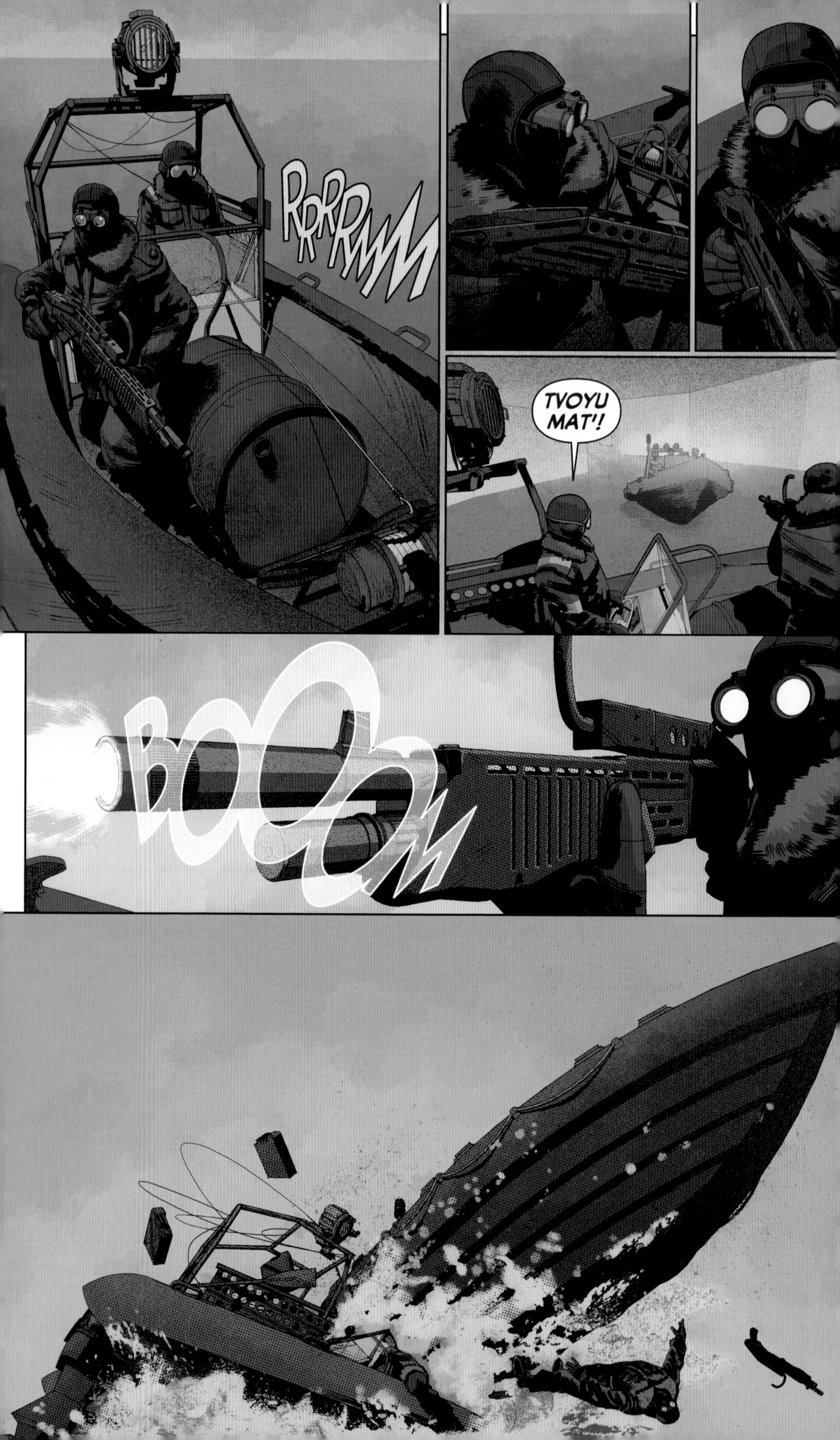
RRRRMM
TVOYU MAT'!
BOOOOM

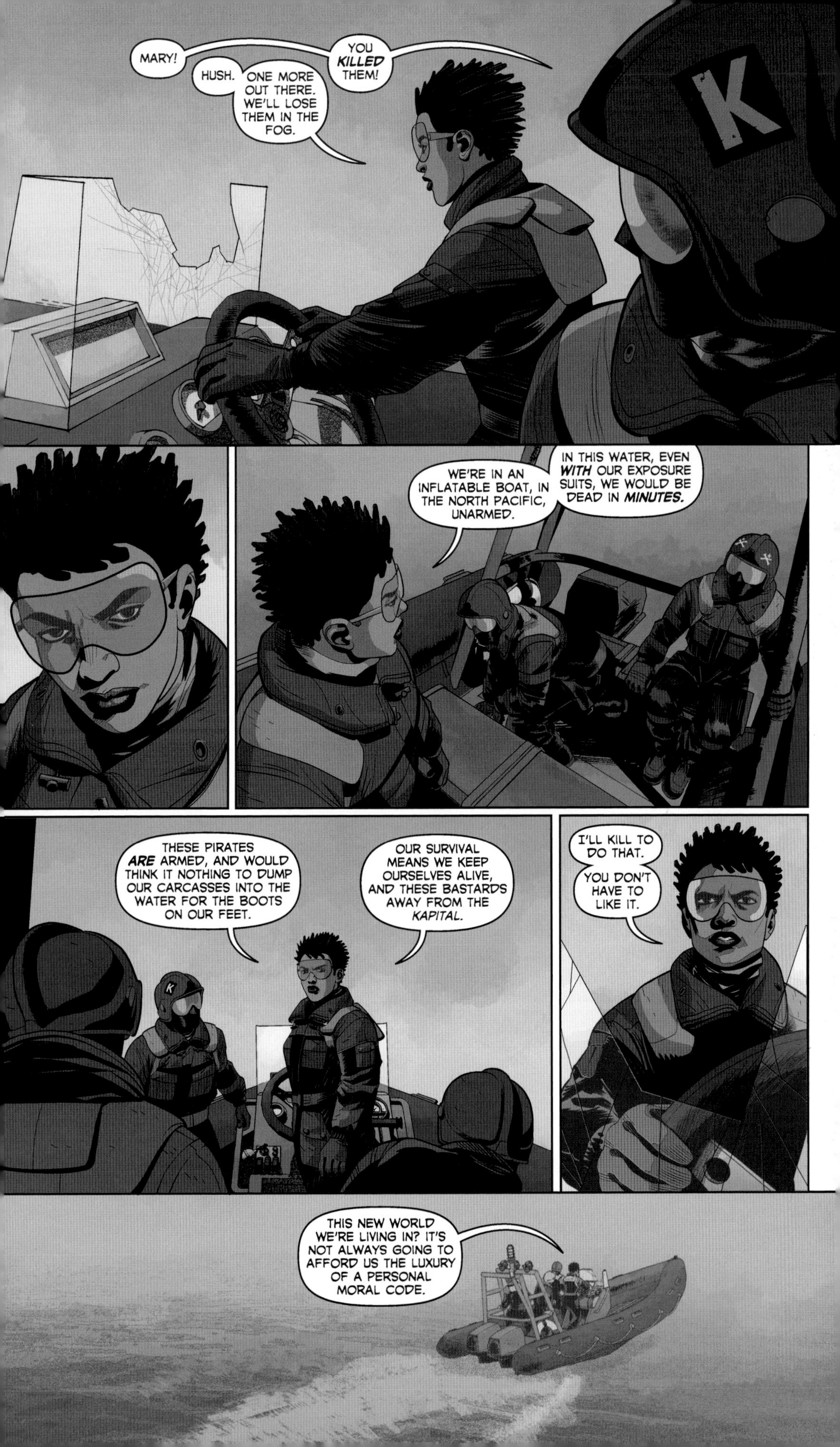

MARY!
YOU *KILLED* THEM!
HUSH.
ONE MORE OUT THERE. WE'LL LOSE THEM IN THE FOG.
WE'RE IN AN INFLATABLE BOAT, IN THE NORTH PACIFIC, UNARMED.
IN THIS WATER, EVEN *WITH* OUR EXPOSURE SUITS, WE WOULD BE DEAD IN *MINUTES.*
THESE PIRATES *ARE* ARMED, AND WOULD THINK IT NOTHING TO DUMP OUR CARCASSES INTO THE WATER FOR THE BOOTS ON OUR FEET.
OUR SURVIVAL MEANS WE KEEP OURSELVES ALIVE, AND THESE BASTARDS AWAY FROM THE *KAPITAL.*
I'LL KILL TO DO THAT.
YOU DON'T HAVE TO LIKE IT.
THIS NEW WORLD WE'RE LIVING IN? IT'S NOT ALWAYS GOING TO AFFORD US THE LUXURY OF A PERSONAL MORAL CODE.

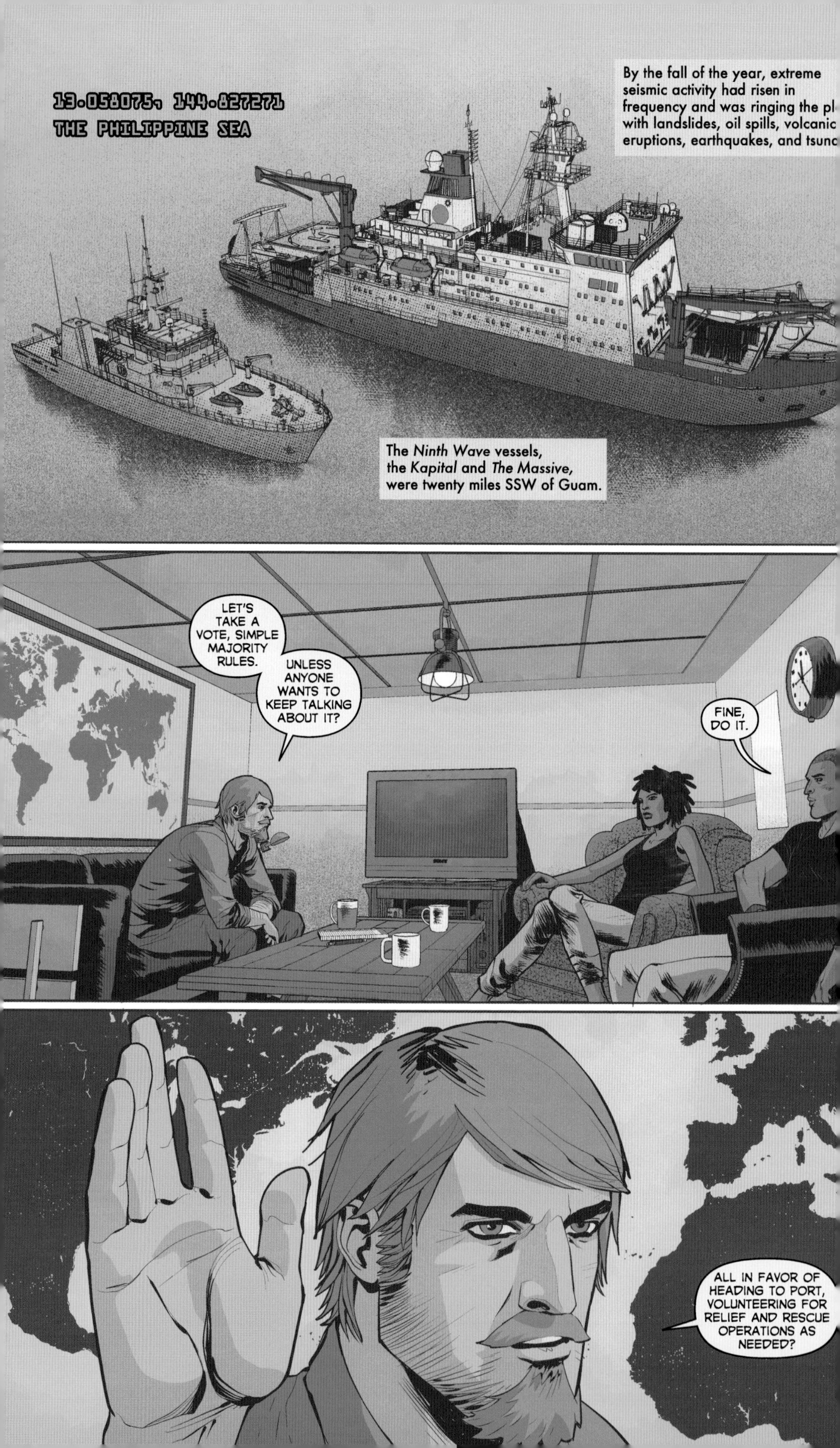
13.058075, 144.827271
THE PHILIPPINE SEA
By the fall of the year, extreme seismic activity had risen in frequency and was ringing the pl with landslides, oil spills, volcanic eruptions, earthquakes, and tsunc
The *Ninth Wave* vessels, the *Kapital* and *The Massive*, were twenty miles SSW of Guam.
LET'S TAKE A VOTE, SIMPLE MAJORITY RULES.
UNLESS ANYONE WANTS TO KEEP TALKING ABOUT IT?
FINE, DO IT.
ALL IN FAVOR OF HEADING TO PORT, VOLUNTEERING FOR RELIEF AND RESCUE OPERATIONS AS NEEDED?

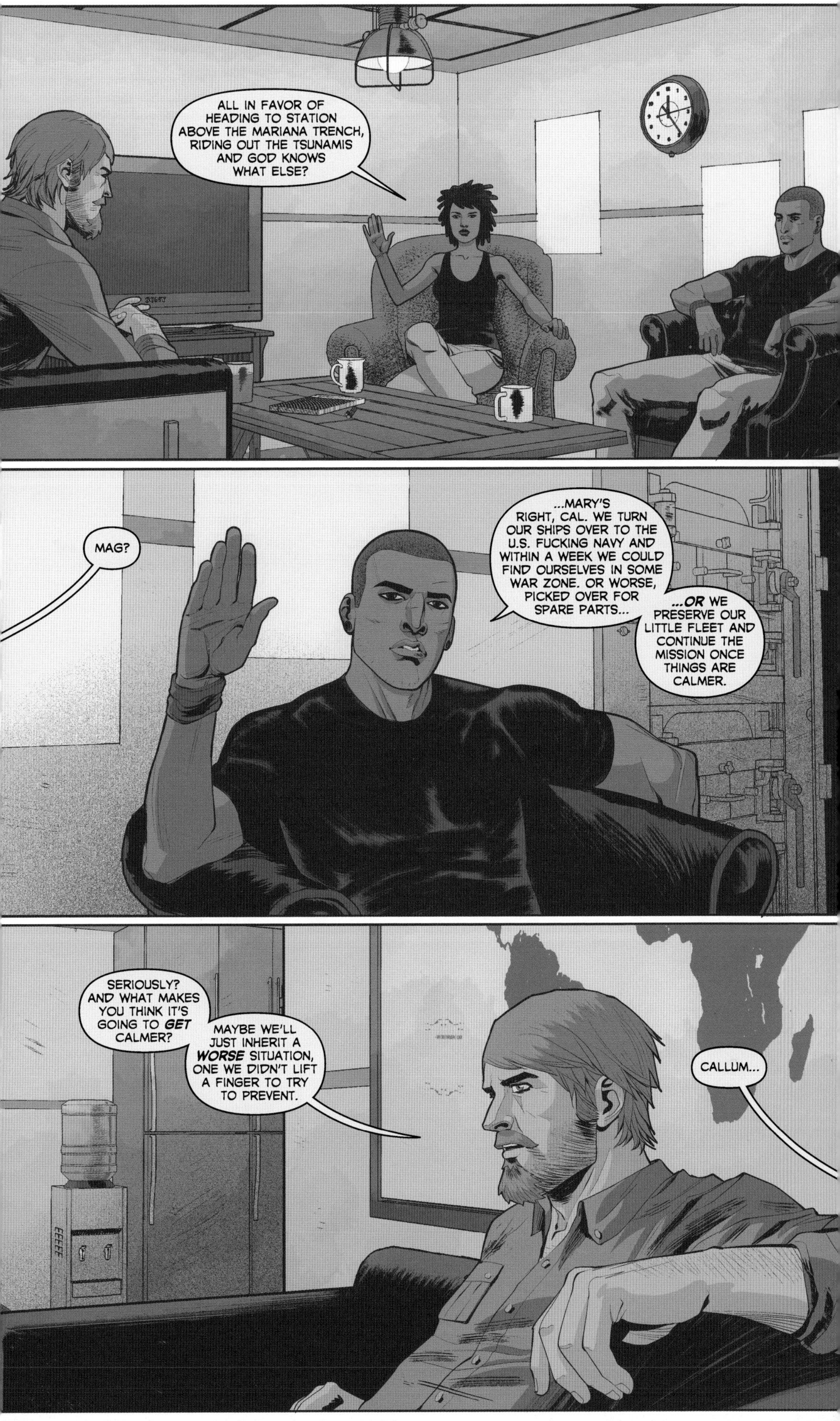
ALL IN FAVOR OF HEADING TO STATION ABOVE THE MARIANA TRENCH, RIDING OUT THE TSUNAMIS AND GOD KNOWS WHAT ELSE?
MAG?
...MARY'S RIGHT, CAL. WE TURN OUR SHIPS OVER TO THE U.S. FUCKING NAVY AND WITHIN A WEEK WE COULD FIND OURSELVES IN SOME WAR ZONE. OR WORSE, PICKED OVER FOR SPARE PARTS...
...OR WE PRESERVE OUR LITTLE FLEET AND CONTINUE THE MISSION ONCE THINGS ARE CALMER.
SERIOUSLY? AND WHAT MAKES YOU THINK IT'S GOING TO GET CALMER?
MAYBE WE'LL JUST INHERIT A WORSE SITUATION, ONE WE DIDN'T LIFT A FINGER TO TRY TO PREVENT.
CALLUM...

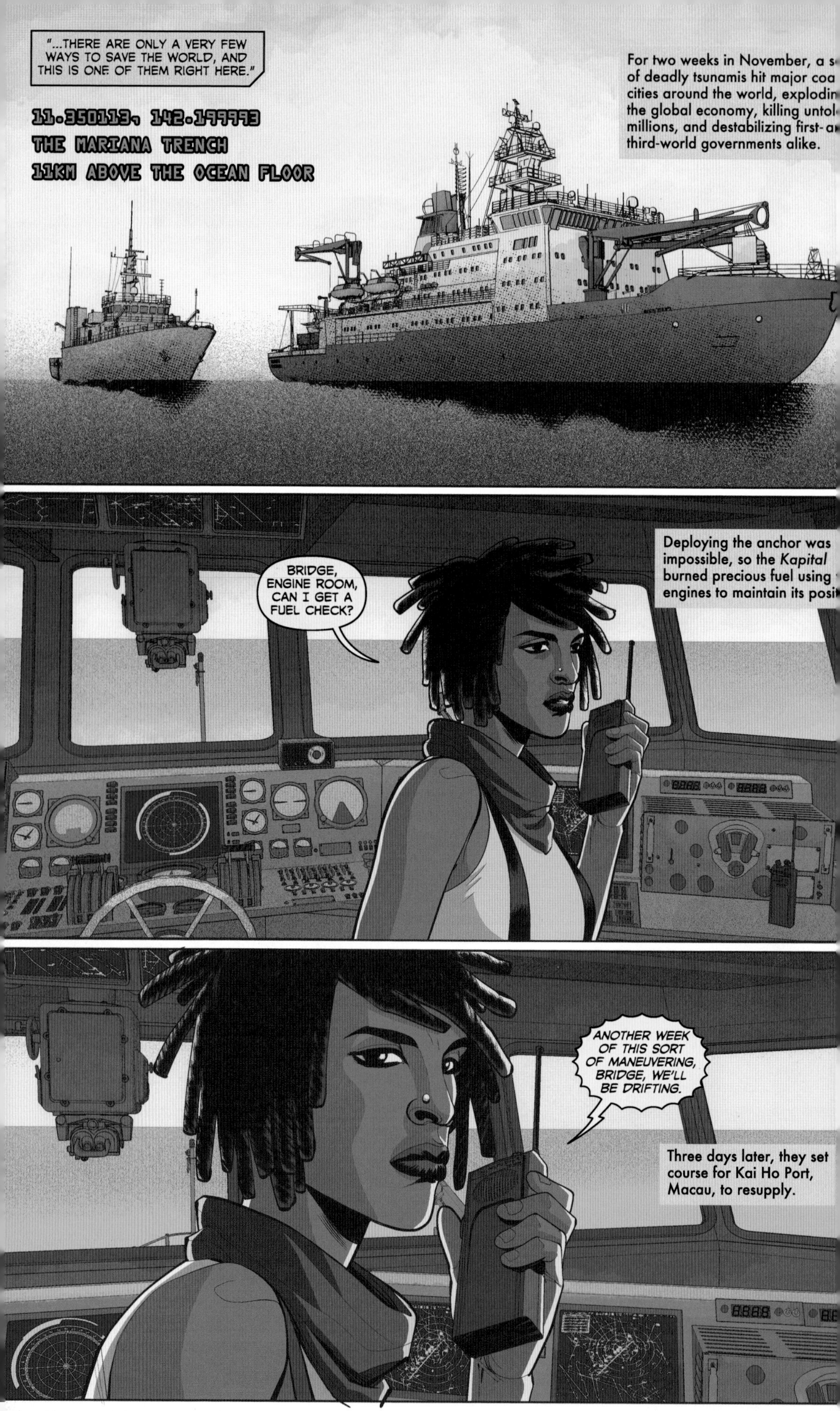
"...THERE ARE ONLY A VERY FEW WAYS TO SAVE THE WORLD, AND THIS IS ONE OF THEM RIGHT HERE."
11.350113, 142.199993
THE MARIANA TRENCH
11KM ABOVE THE OCEAN FLOOR
For two weeks in November, a s of deadly tsunamis hit major coa cities around the world, explodin the global economy, killing untol millions, and destabilizing first- a third-world governments alike.
Deploying the anchor was impossible, so the Kapital burned precious fuel using engines to maintain its posi
BRIDGE, ENGINE ROOM, CAN I GET A FUEL CHECK?
ANOTHER WEEK OF THIS SORT OF MANEUVERING, BRIDGE, WE'LL BE DRIFTING.
Three days later, they set course for Kai Ho Port, Macau, to resupply.

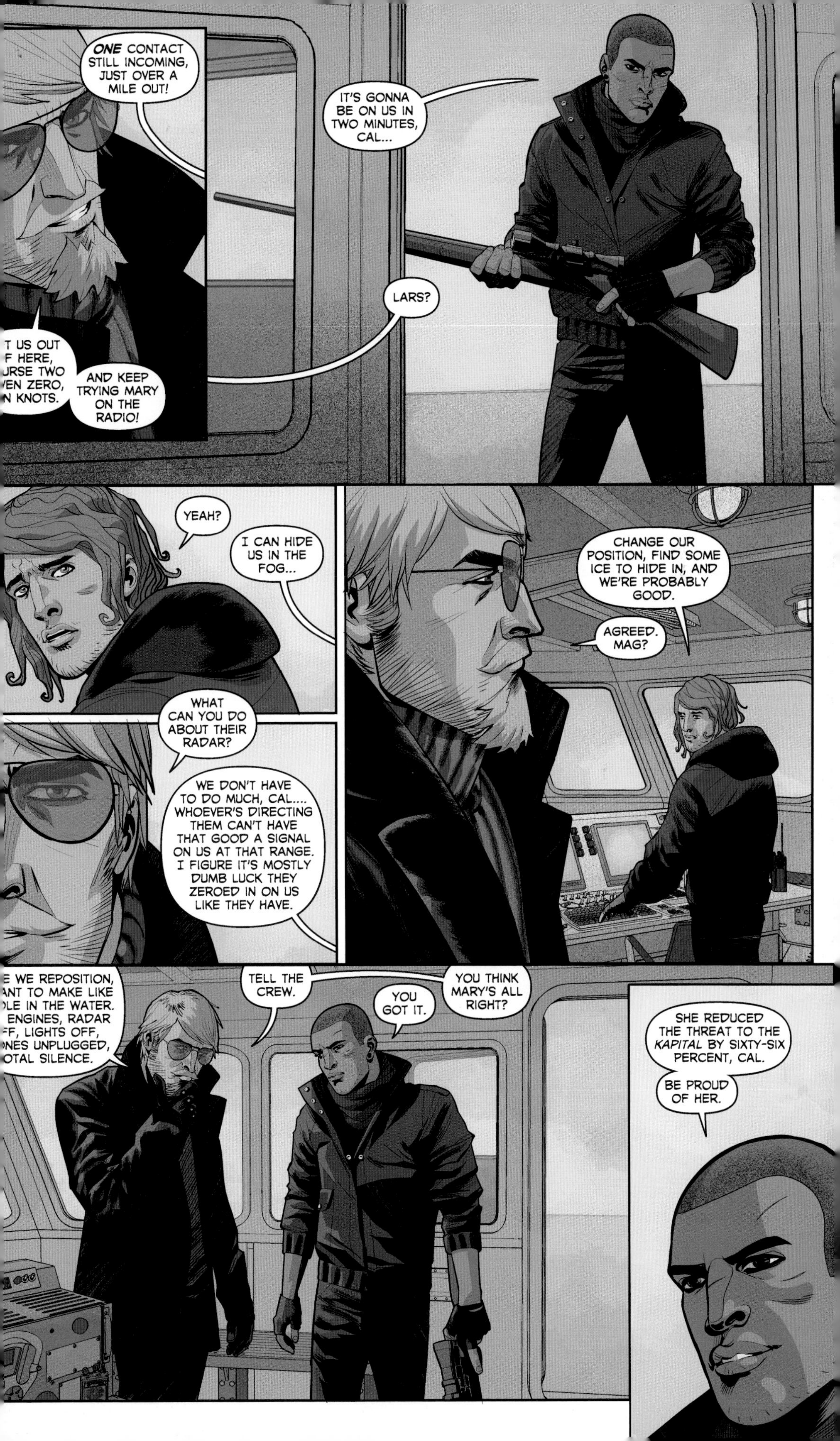
ONE CONTACT STILL INCOMING, JUST OVER A MILE OUT!
IT'S GONNA BE ON US IN TWO MINUTES, CAL...
LARS?
T US OUT F HERE, URSE TWO VEN ZERO, N KNOTS.
AND KEEP TRYING MARY ON THE RADIO!
YEAH?
I CAN HIDE US IN THE FOG...
CHANGE OUR POSITION, FIND SOME ICE TO HIDE IN, AND WE'RE PROBABLY GOOD.
AGREED. MAG?
WHAT CAN YOU DO ABOUT THEIR RADAR?
WE DON'T HAVE TO DO MUCH, CAL.... WHOEVER'S DIRECTING THEM CAN'T HAVE THAT GOOD A SIGNAL ON US AT THAT RANGE. I FIGURE IT'S MOSTLY DUMB LUCK THEY ZEROED IN ON US LIKE THEY HAVE.
E WE REPOSITION, ANT TO MAKE LIKE OLE IN THE WATER. ENGINES, RADAR FF, LIGHTS OFF, ONES UNPLUGGED, OTAL SILENCE.
TELL THE CREW.
YOU GOT IT.
YOU THINK MARY'S ALL RIGHT?
SHE REDUCED THE THREAT TO THE *KAPITAL* BY SIXTY-SIX PERCENT, CAL.
BE PROUD OF HER.

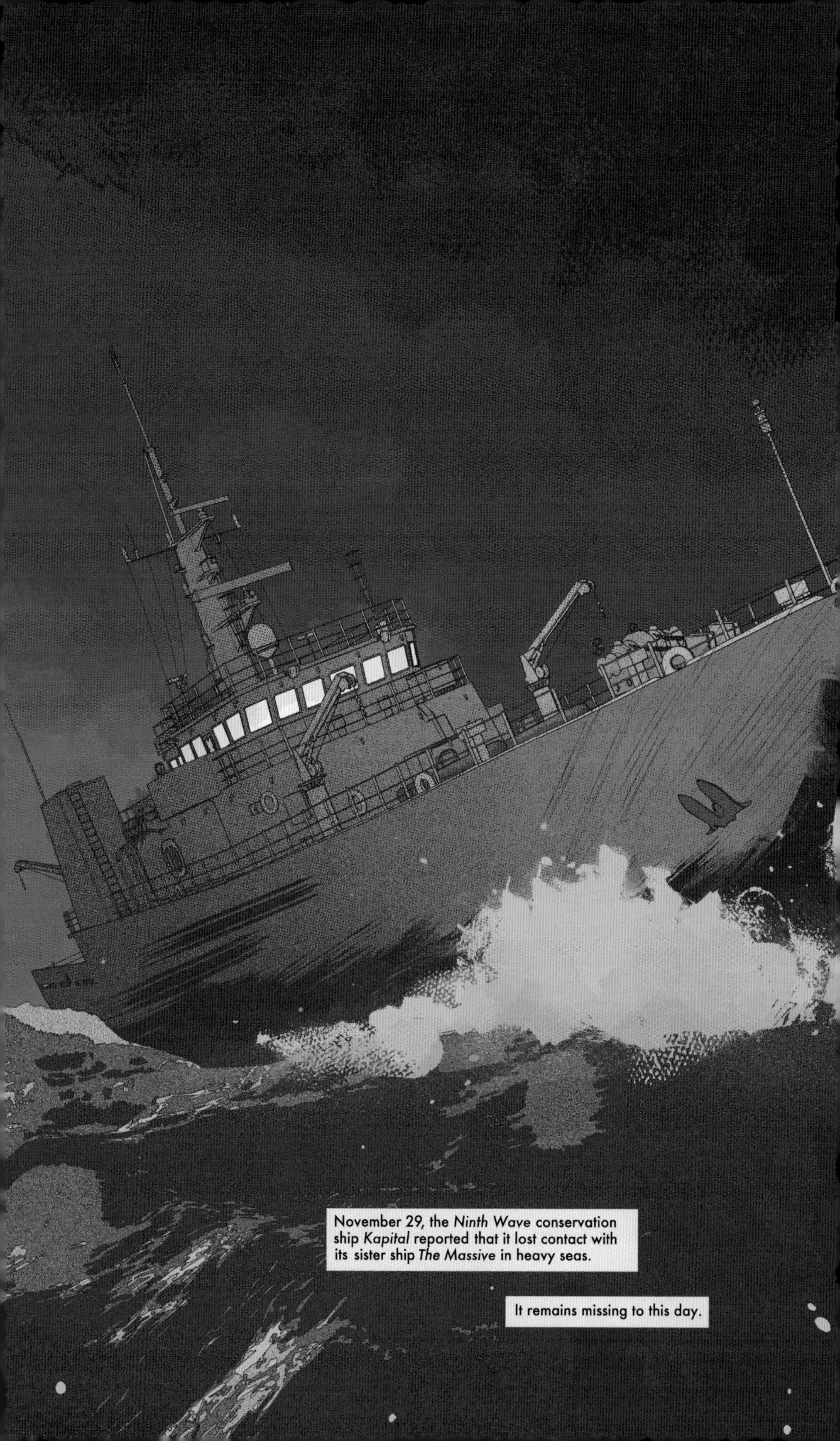
November 29, the *Ninth Wave* conservation ship *Kapital* reported that it lost contact with its sister ship *The Massive* in heavy seas.
It remains missing to this day.

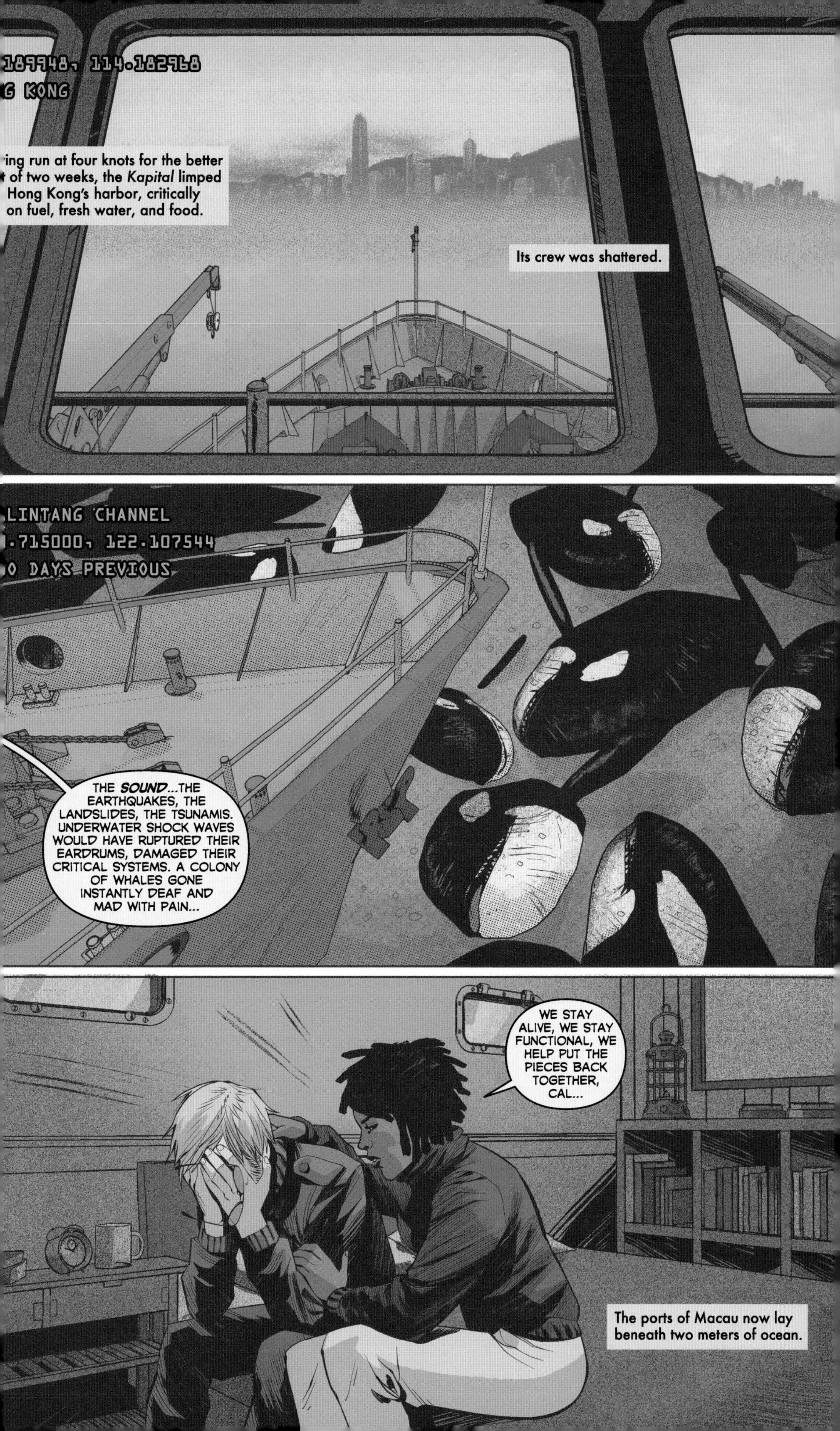
189948, 114.182968
G KONG
ing run at four knots for the better of two weeks, the Kapital limped Hong Kong's harbor, critically on fuel, fresh water, and food.
Its crew was shattered.
LINTANG CHANNEL
.715000, 122.107544
0 DAYS PREVIOUS
THE SOUND...THE EARTHQUAKES, THE LANDSLIDES, THE TSUNAMIS. UNDERWATER SHOCK WAVES WOULD HAVE RUPTURED THEIR EARDRUMS, DAMAGED THEIR CRITICAL SYSTEMS. A COLONY OF WHALES GONE INSTANTLY DEAF AND MAD WITH PAIN...
WE STAY ALIVE, WE STAY FUNCTIONAL, WE HELP PUT THE PIECES BACK TOGETHER, CAL...
The ports of Macau now lay beneath two meters of ocean.

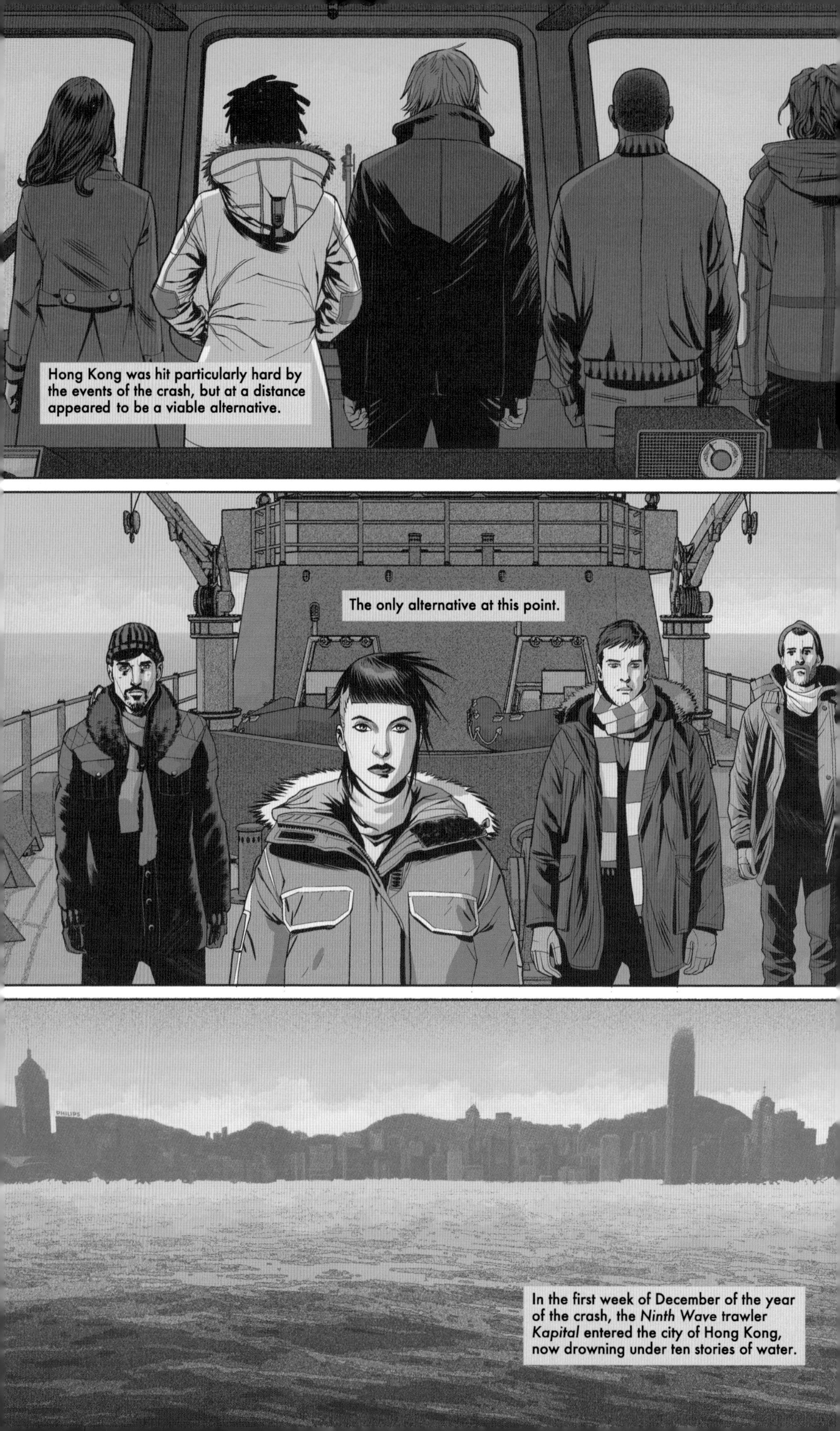
Hong Kong was hit particularly hard by the events of the crash, but at a distance appeared to be a viable alternative.
The only alternative at this point.
PHILIPS
In the first week of December of the year of the crash, the *Ninth Wave* trawler *Kapital* entered the city of Hong Kong, now drowning under ten stories of water.

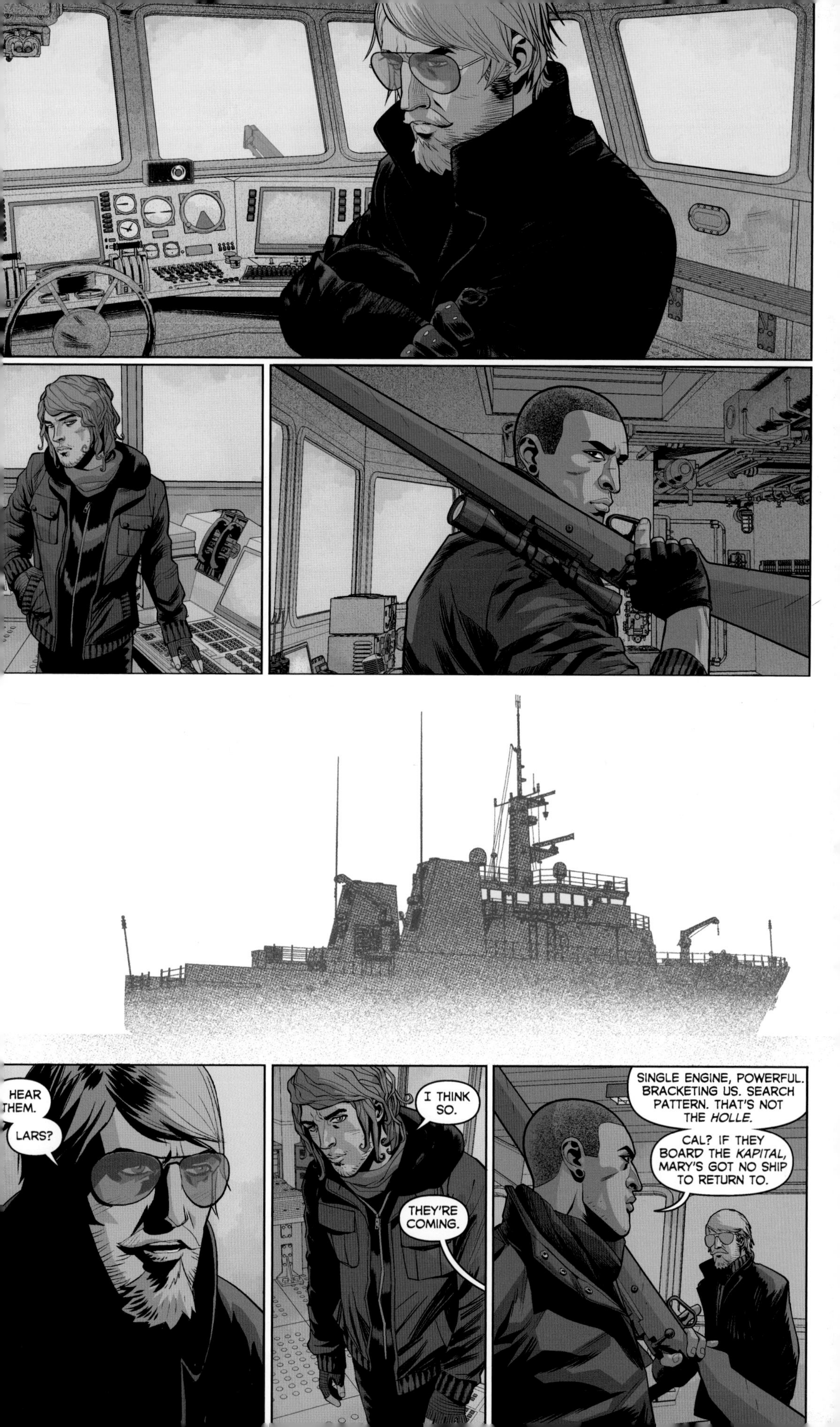
HEAR THEM.
LARS?
I THINK SO.
THEY'RE COMING.
SINGLE ENGINE, POWERFUL. BRACKETING US. SEARCH PATTERN. THAT'S NOT THE *HOLLE*.
CAL? IF THEY BOARD THE *KAPITAL*, MARY'S GOT NO SHIP TO RETURN TO.

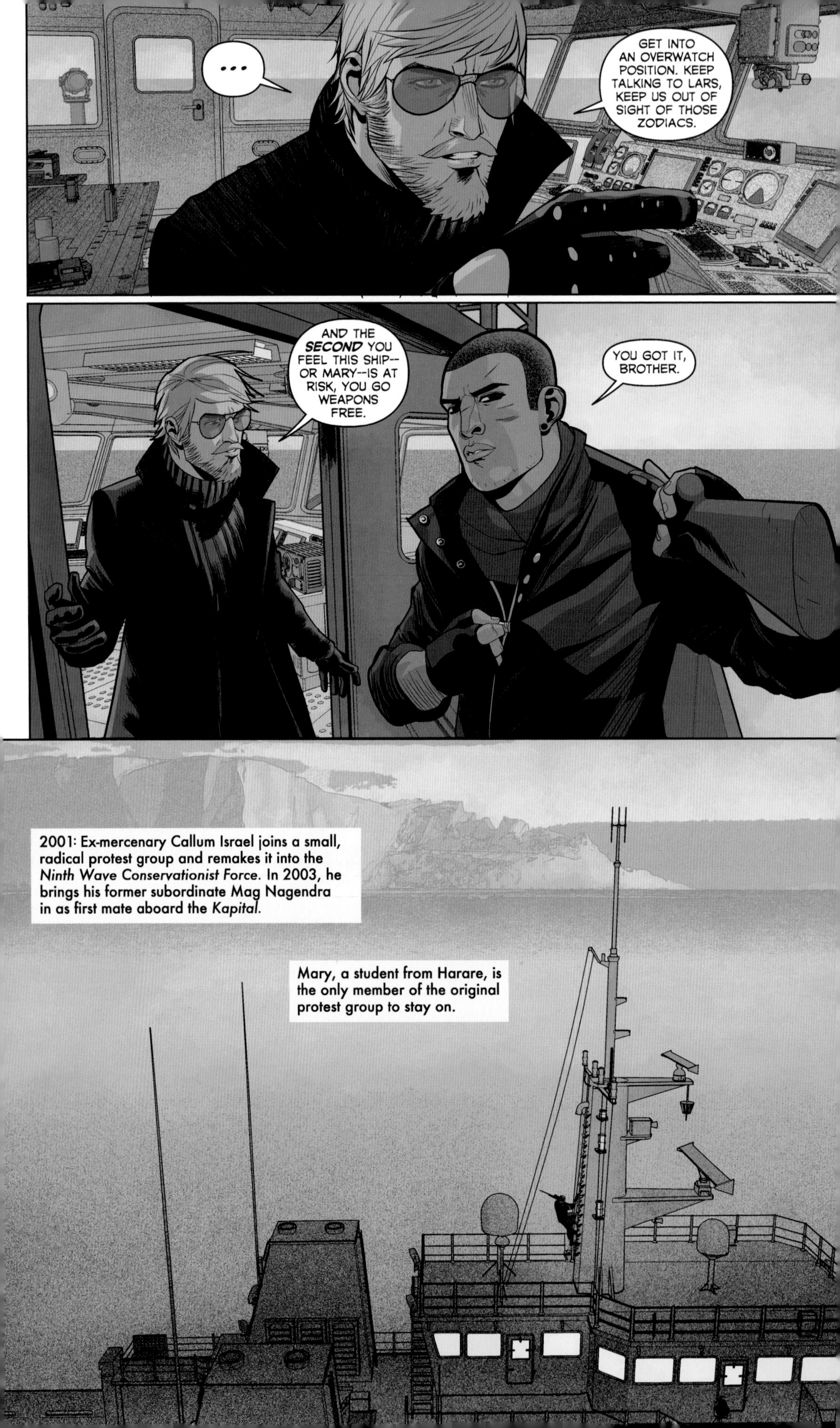
...
GET INTO AN OVERWATCH POSITION. KEEP TALKING TO LARS, KEEP US OUT OF SIGHT OF THOSE ZODIACS.
AND THE SECOND YOU FEEL THIS SHIP--OR MARY--IS AT RISK, YOU GO WEAPONS FREE.
YOU GOT IT, BROTHER.
2001: Ex-mercenary Callum Israel joins a small, radical protest group and remakes it into the Ninth Wave Conservationist Force. In 2003, he brings his former subordinate Mag Nagendra in as first mate aboard the Kapital.
Mary, a student from Harare, is the only member of the original protest group to stay on.

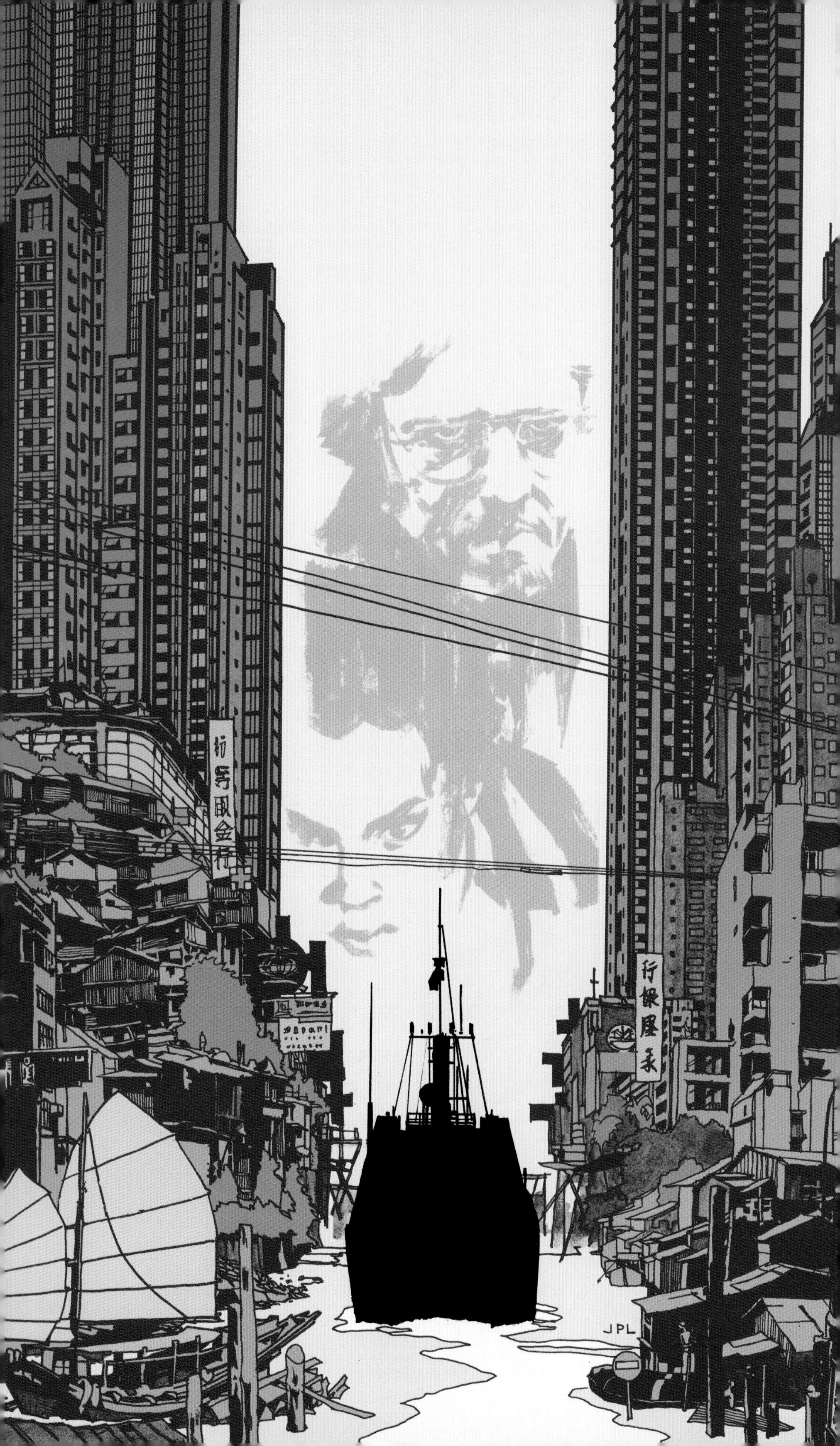
JPL

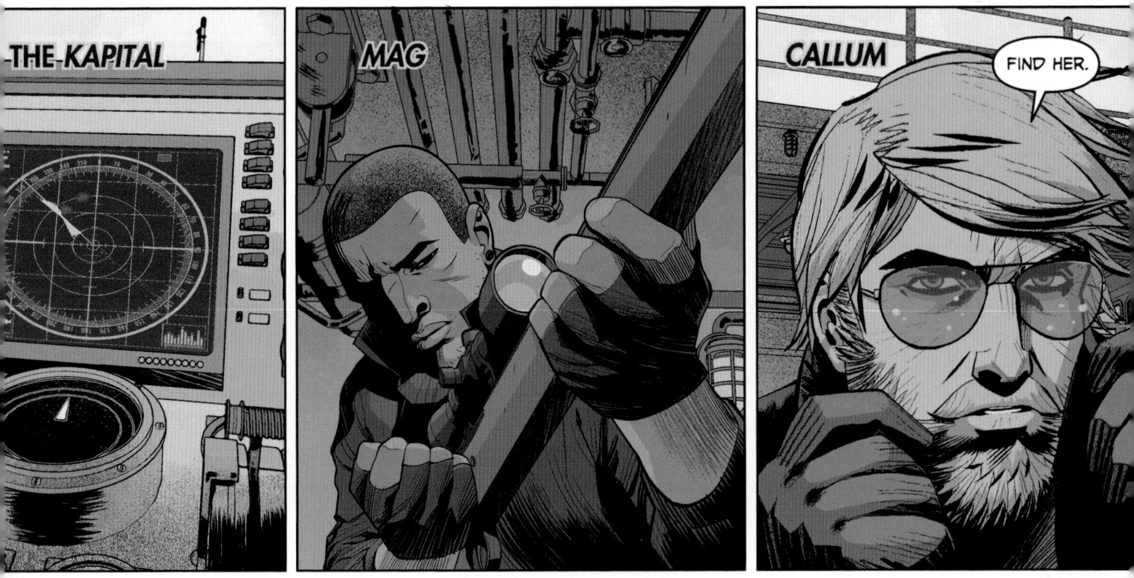
THE KAPITAL
MAG
CALLUM
FIND HER.

In the months following the Crash--a global eco-socio-environmental cataclysm that sent the world into chaos--the direct-action conservationist ship *Kapital* searches the world's oceans for *The Massive*, its missing sister ship.

Off the coast of Russia, the *Kapital* hides in dense fog from marauding Siberian pirates. Mary, and several more of the crew, are out in a zodiac fast-attack boat attempting to lure the pirates away.

55.153766, 167.827148
NEAR KAMCHATKA PENINSULA
THE BERING SEA

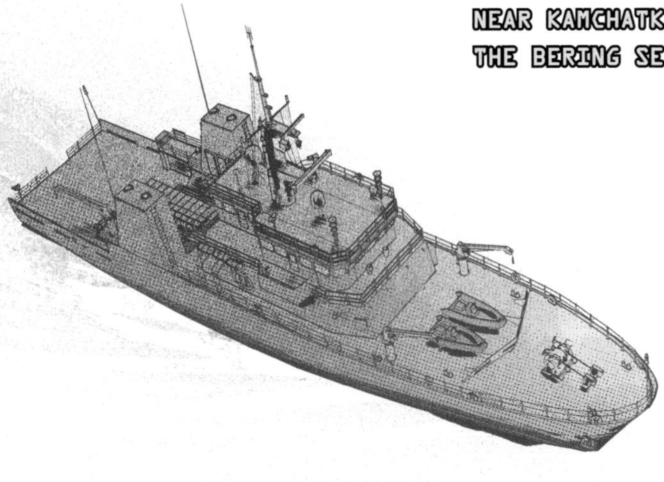

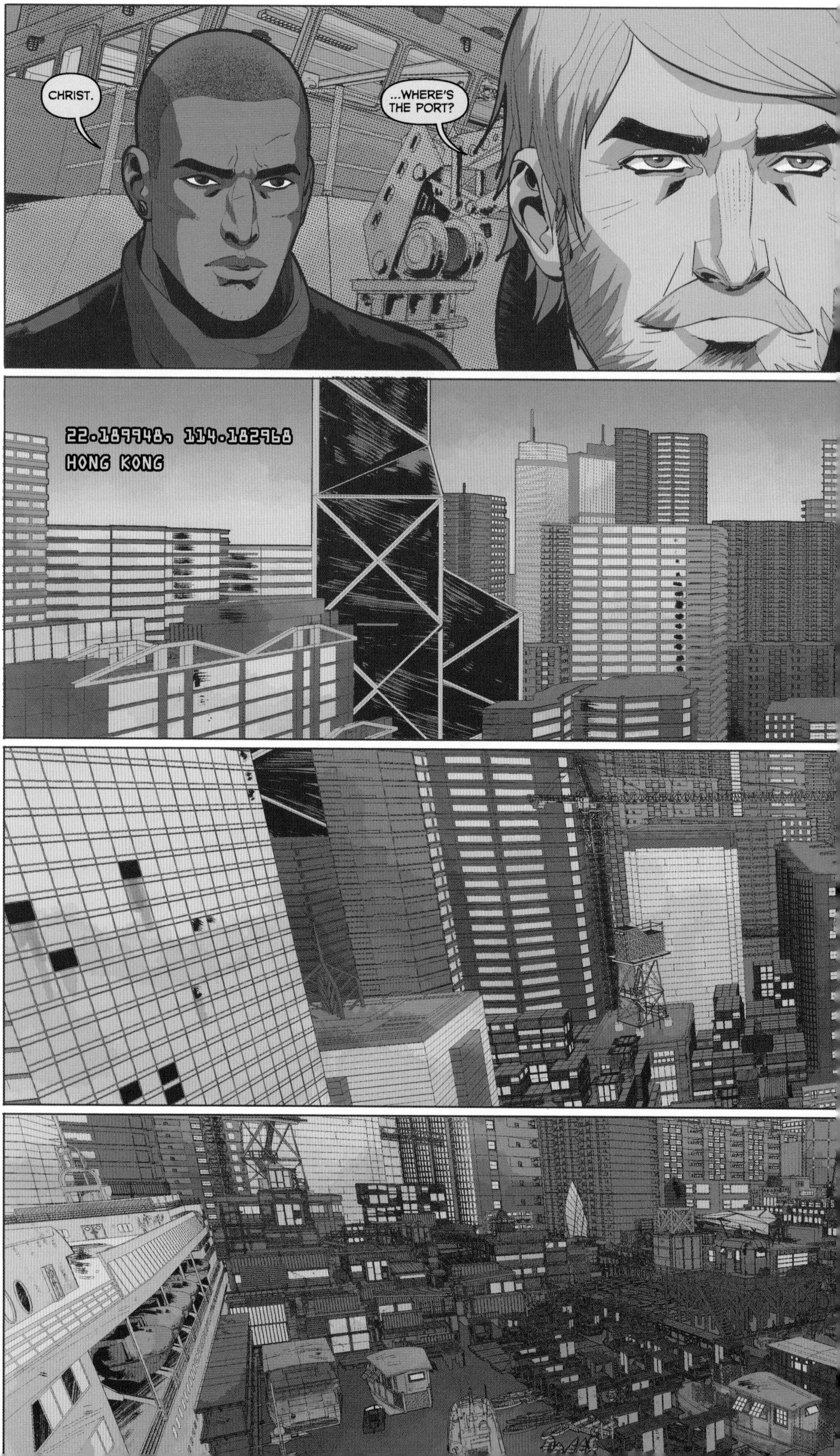
CHRIST.
...WHERE'S THE PORT?
22.189948, 114.182968
HONG KONG

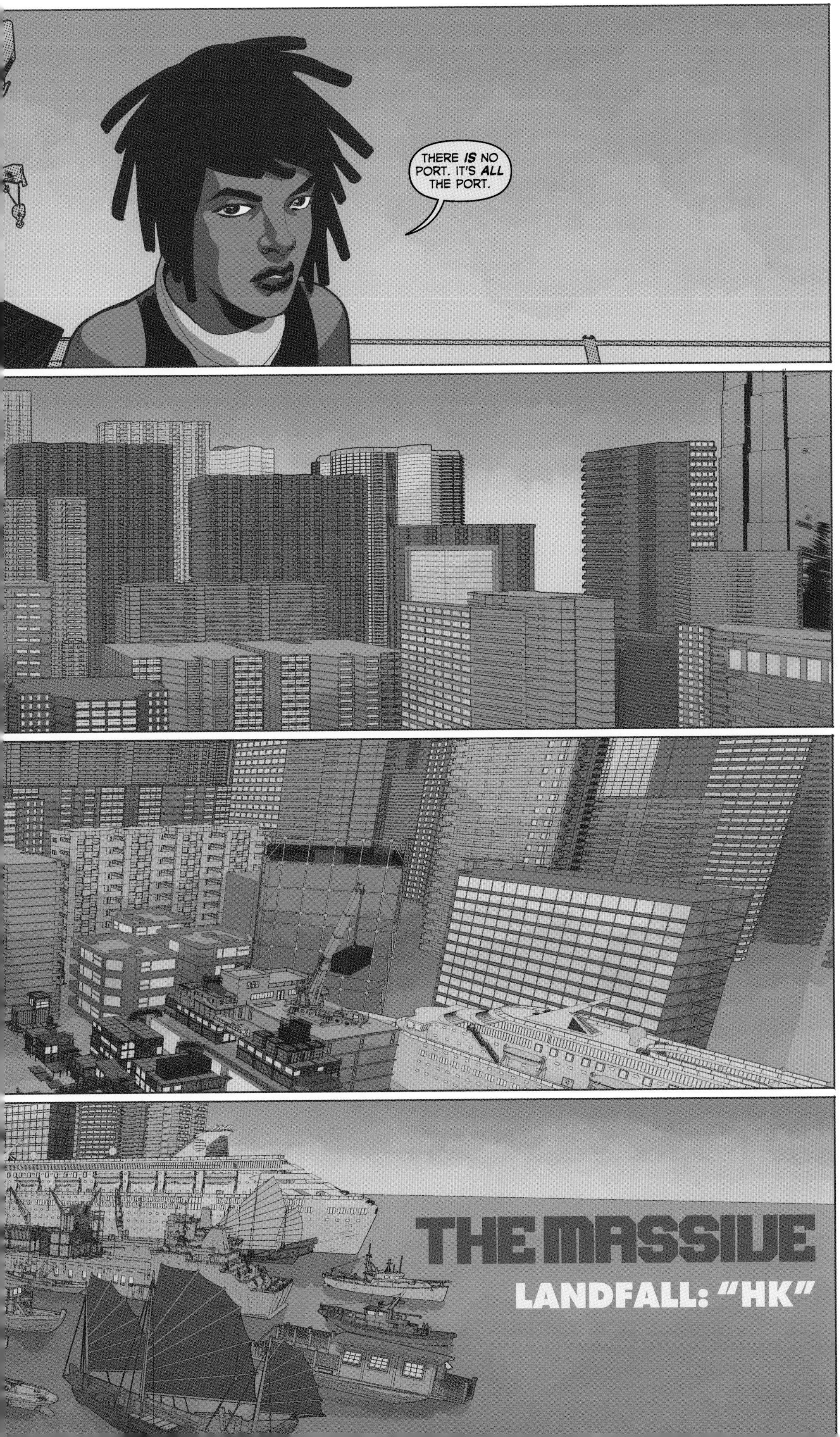
THERE IS NO PORT. IT'S ALL THE PORT.
THE MASSIVE
LANDFALL: "HK"

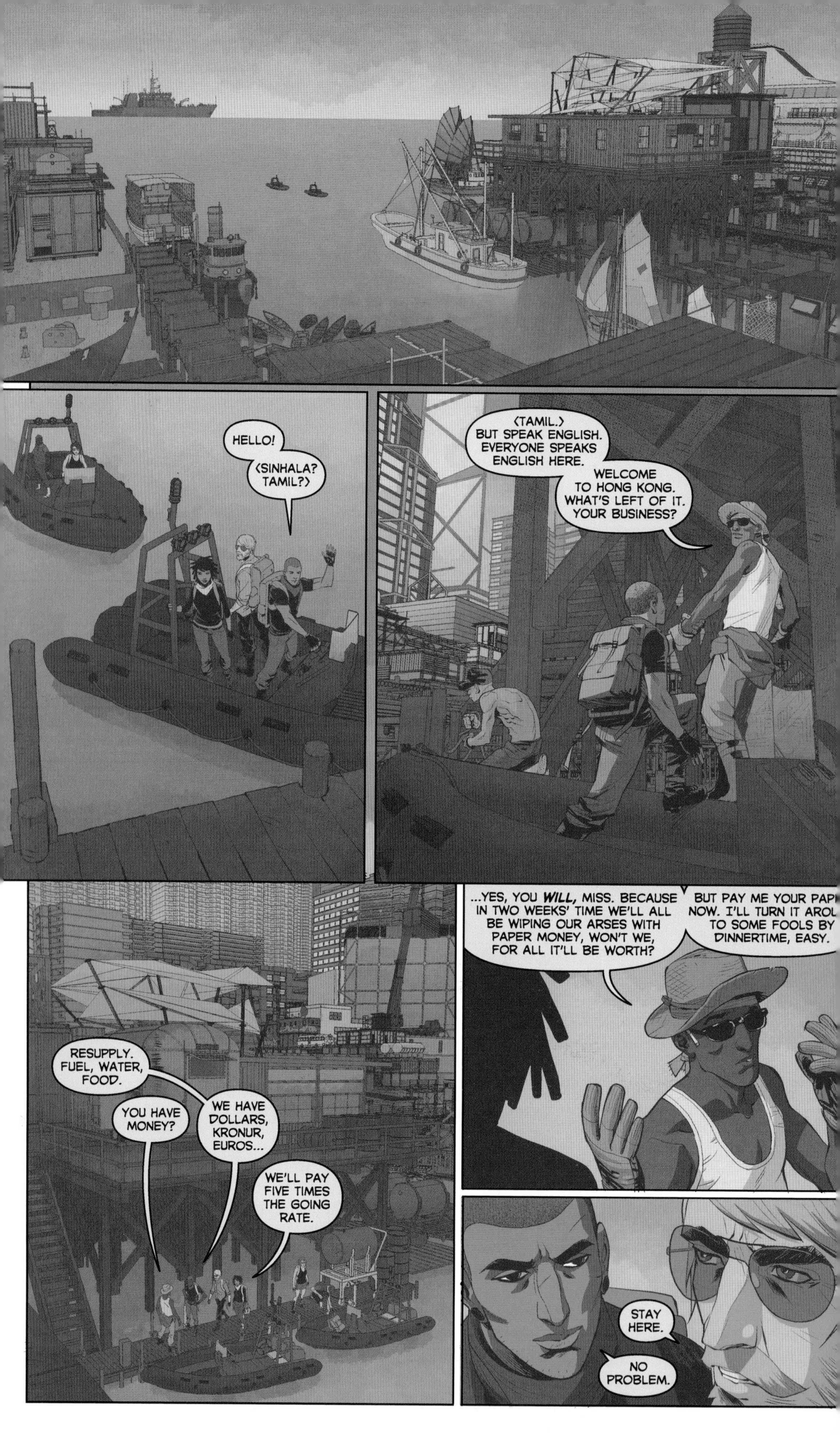
HELLO!
⟨SINHALA? TAMIL?⟩
⟨TAMIL.⟩ BUT SPEAK ENGLISH. EVERYONE SPEAKS ENGLISH HERE.
WELCOME TO HONG KONG. WHAT'S LEFT OF IT. YOUR BUSINESS?
RESUPPLY. FUEL, WATER, FOOD.
YOU HAVE MONEY?
WE HAVE DOLLARS, KRONUR, EUROS...
WE'LL PAY FIVE TIMES THE GOING RATE.
...YES, YOU *WILL*, MISS. BECAUSE IN TWO WEEKS' TIME WE'LL ALL BE WIPING OUR ARSES WITH PAPER MONEY, WON'T WE, FOR ALL IT'LL BE WORTH?
BUT PAY ME YOUR PAP
NOW. I'LL TURN IT ARO
TO SOME FOOLS BY
DINNERTIME, EASY.
STAY HERE.
NO PROBLEM.

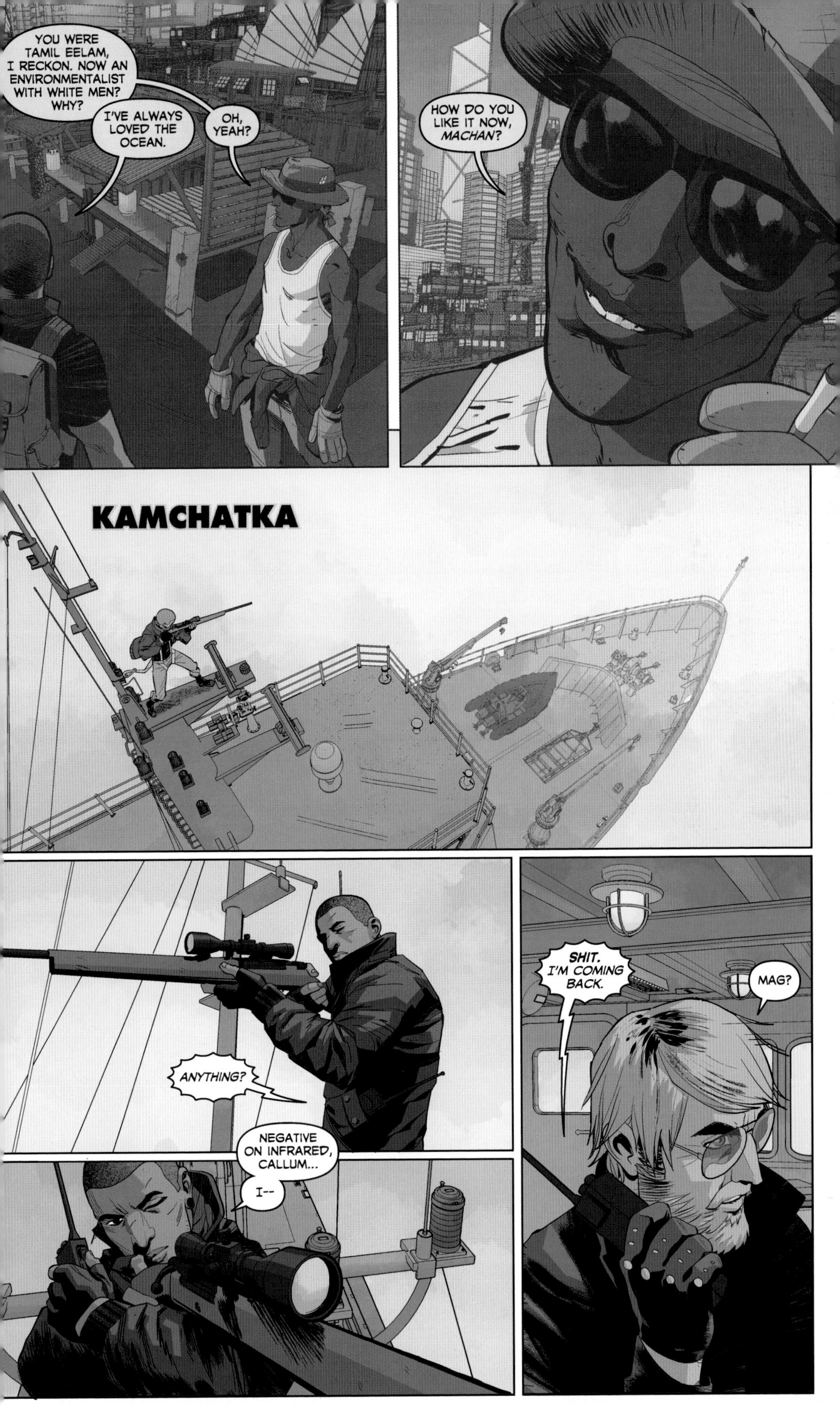
YOU WERE TAMIL EELAM, I RECKON. NOW AN ENVIRONMENTALIST WITH WHITE MEN? WHY?
I'VE ALWAYS LOVED THE OCEAN.
OH, YEAH?
HOW DO YOU LIKE IT NOW, *MACHAN*?
KAMCHATKA
ANYTHING?
NEGATIVE ON INFRARED, CALLUM...
I--
SHIT. I'M COMING BACK.
MAG?

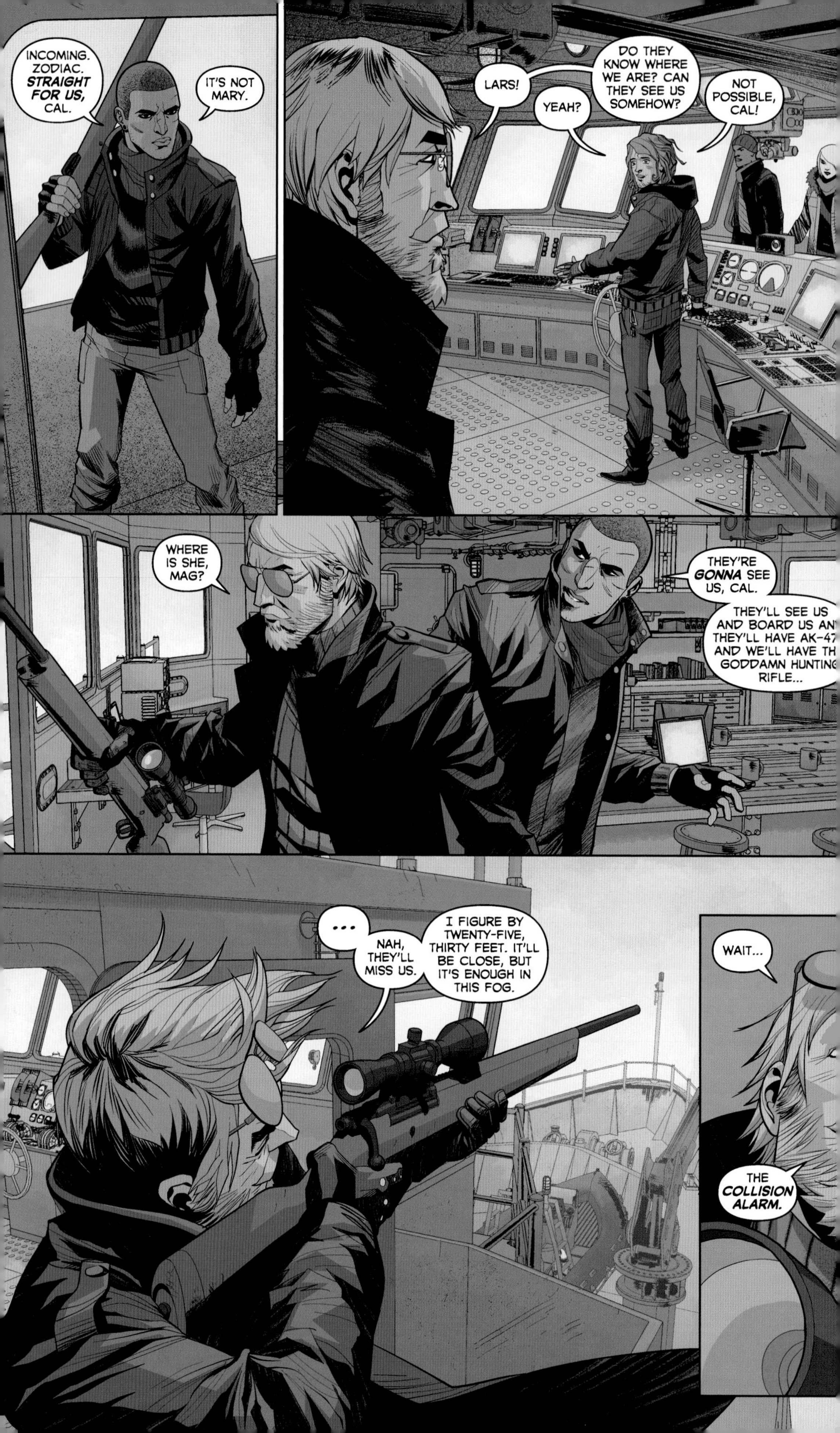
INCOMING. ZODIAC. **STRAIGHT FOR US,** CAL.
IT'S NOT MARY.
LARS!
YEAH?
DO THEY KNOW WHERE WE ARE? CAN THEY SEE US SOMEHOW?
NOT POSSIBLE, CAL!
WHERE IS SHE, MAG?
THEY'RE ***GONNA*** SEE US, CAL.
THEY'LL SEE US AND BOARD US AN' THEY'LL HAVE AK-47 AND WE'LL HAVE TH GODDAMN HUNTING RIFLE...
...
NAH, THEY'LL MISS US.
I FIGURE BY TWENTY-FIVE, THIRTY FEET. IT'LL BE CLOSE, BUT IT'S ENOUGH IN THIS FOG.
WAIT...
THE ***COLLISION ALARM.***

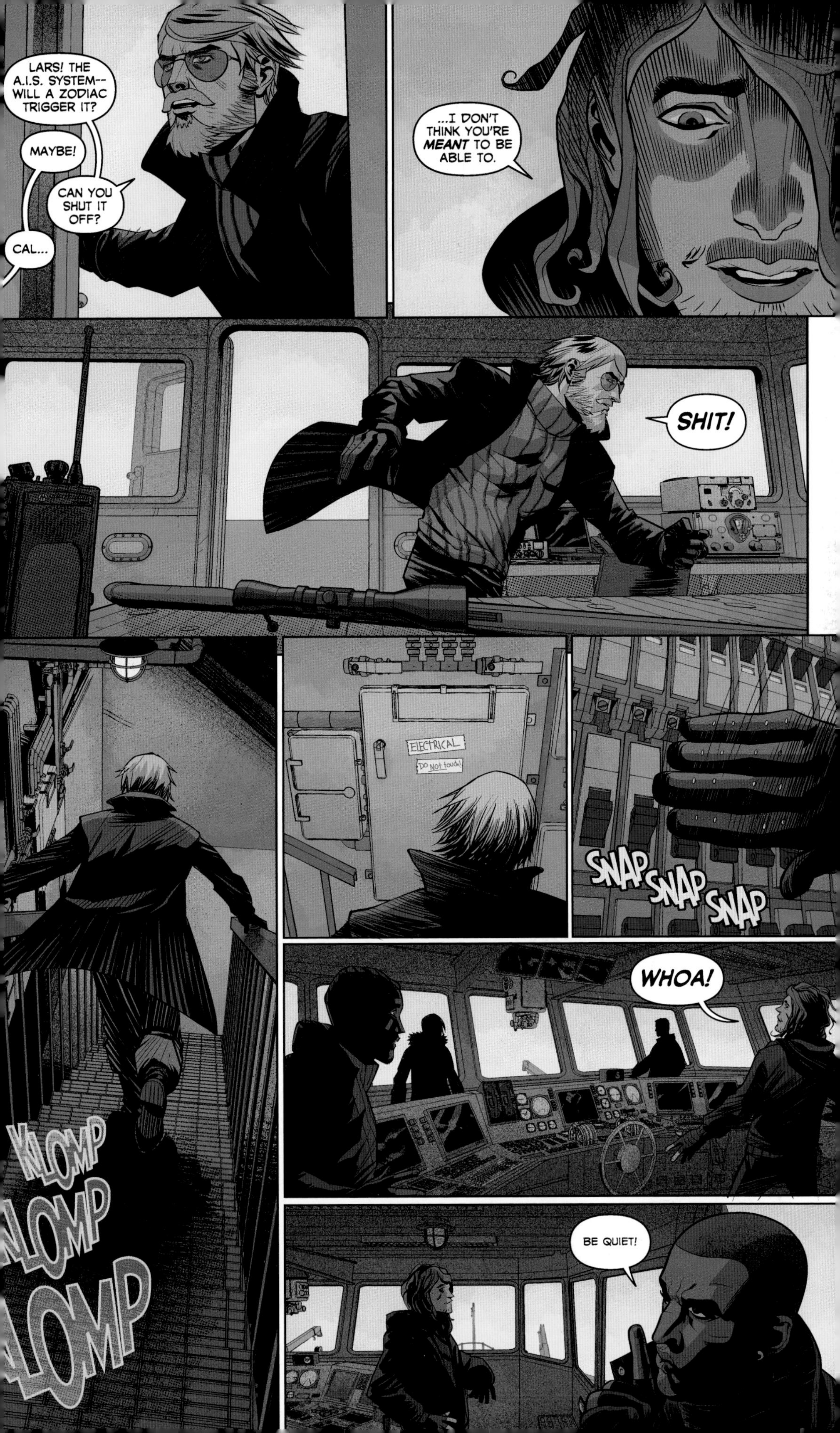
LARS! THE A.I.S. SYSTEM-- WILL A ZODIAC TRIGGER IT?
MAYBE!
CAN YOU SHUT IT OFF?
CAL...
...I DON'T THINK YOU'RE MEANT TO BE ABLE TO.
SHIT!
KLOMP
KLOMP
KLOMP
ELECTRICAL
DO NOT TOUCH!
SNAP SNAP SNAP
WHOA!
BE QUIET!

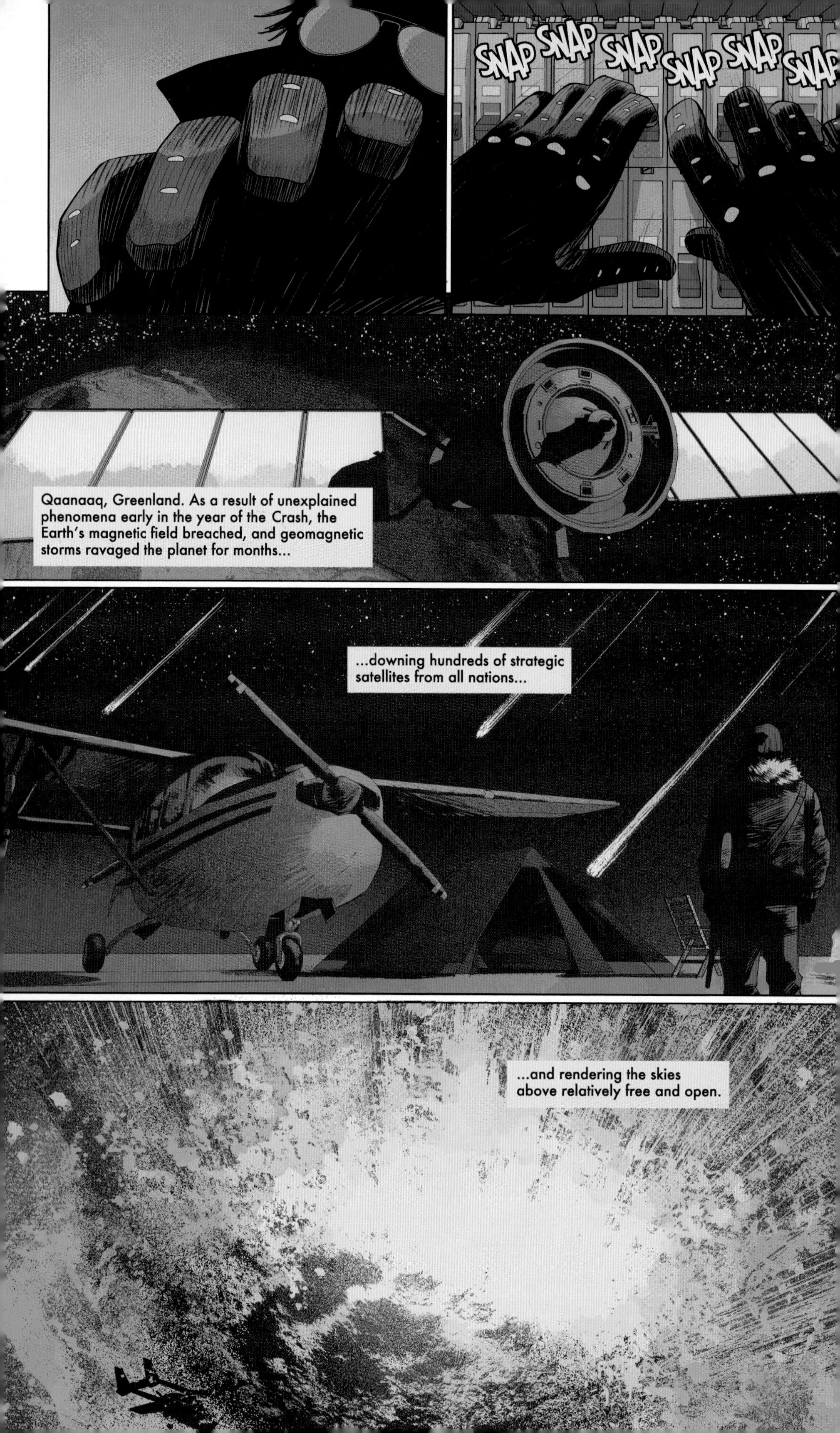
SNAP SNAP SNAP SNAP SNAP SNAP
Qaanaaq, Greenland. As a result of unexplained phenomena early in the year of the Crash, the Earth's magnetic field breached, and geomagnetic storms ravaged the planet for months...
...downing hundreds of strategic satellites from all nations...
...and rendering the skies above relatively free and open.

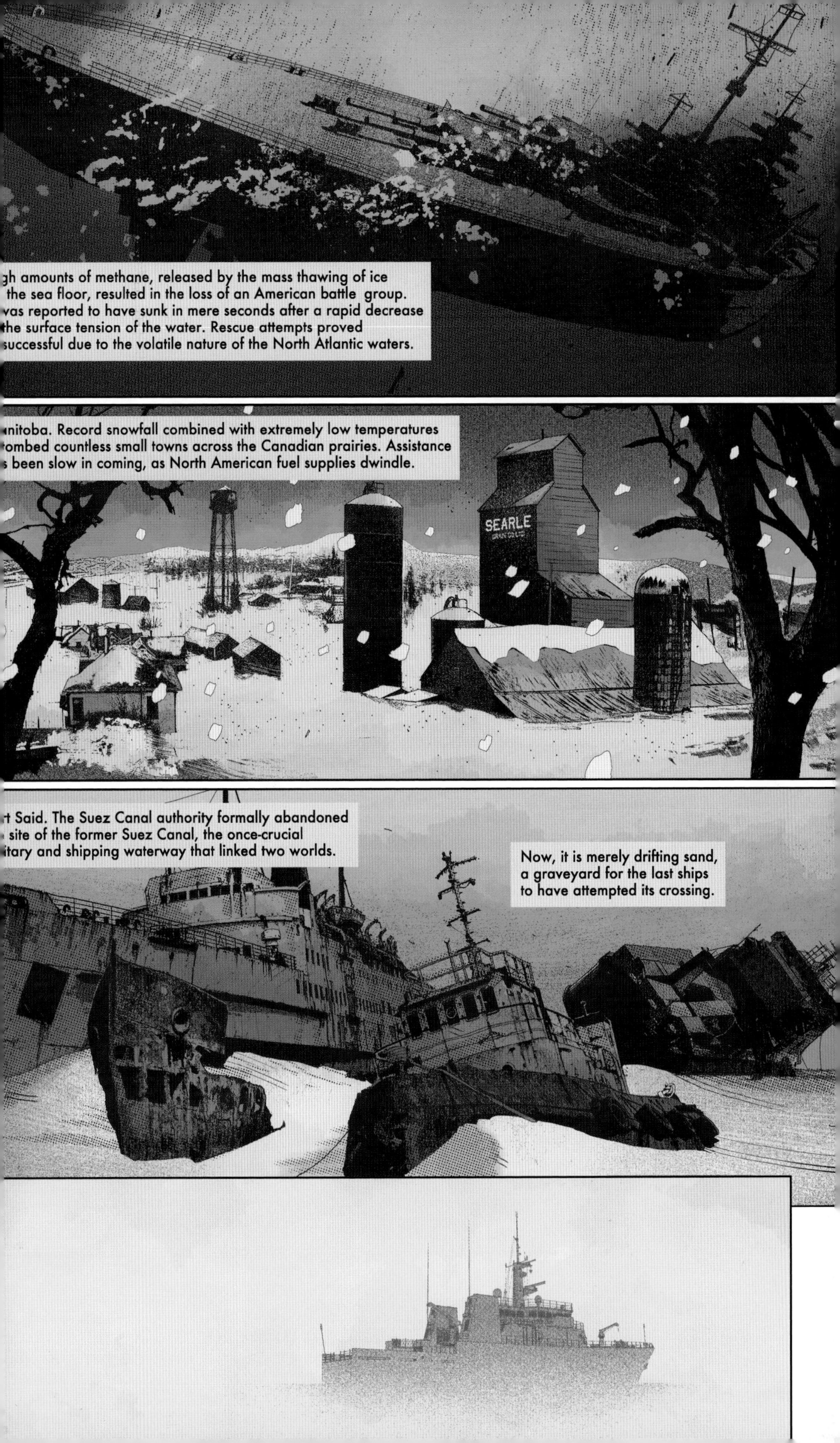
gh amounts of methane, released by the mass thawing of ice
the sea floor, resulted in the loss of an American battle group.
vas reported to have sunk in mere seconds after a rapid decrease
the surface tension of the water. Rescue attempts proved
successful due to the volatile nature of the North Atlantic waters.
nitoba. Record snowfall combined with extremely low temperatures
ombed countless small towns across the Canadian prairies. Assistance
been slow in coming, as North American fuel supplies dwindle.
SEARLE
t Said. The Suez Canal authority formally abandoned
site of the former Suez Canal, the once-crucial
itary and shipping waterway that linked two worlds.
Now, it is merely drifting sand,
a graveyard for the last ships
to have attempted its crossing.

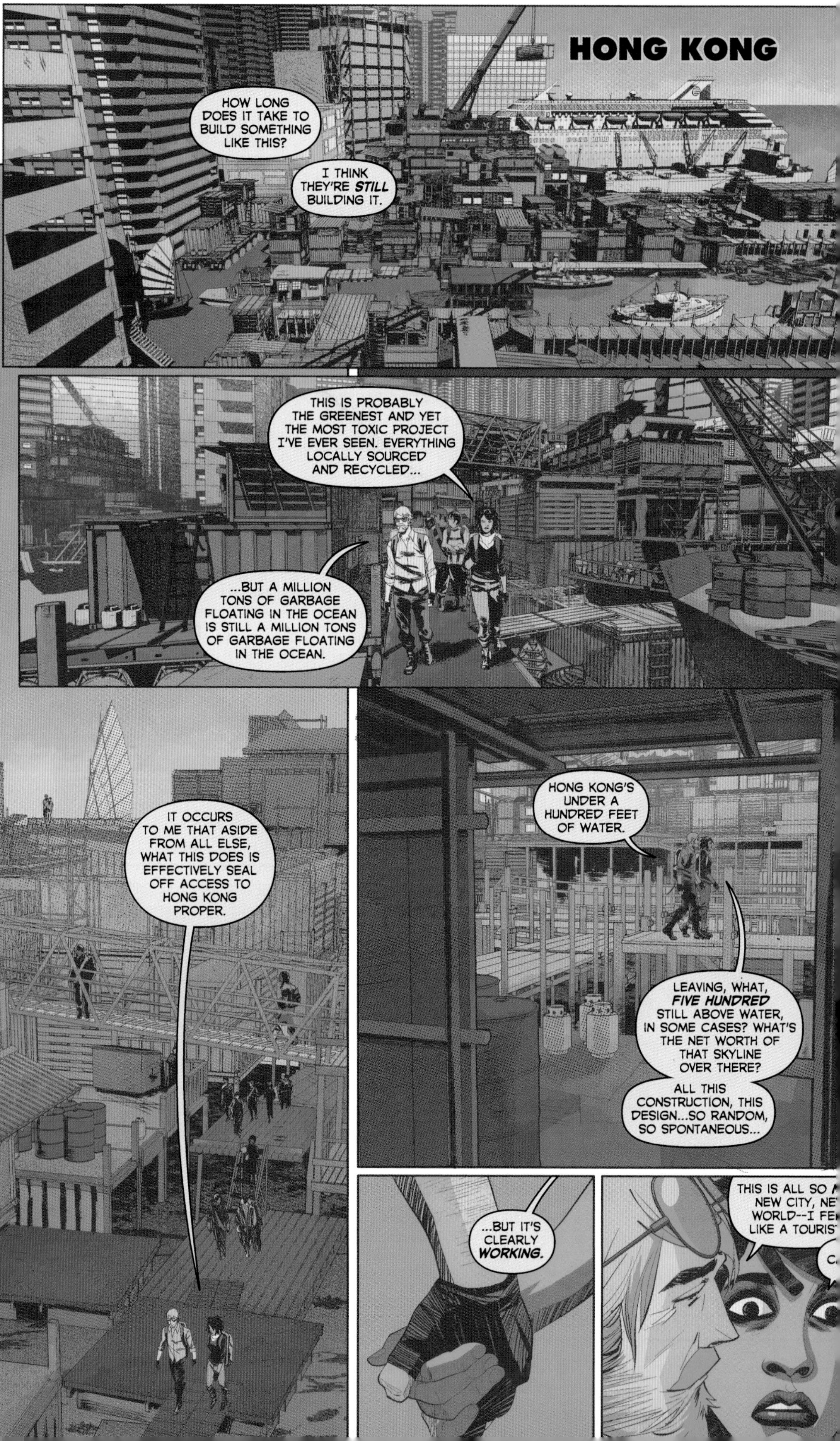
HONG KONG
HOW LONG DOES IT TAKE TO BUILD SOMETHING LIKE THIS?
I THINK THEY'RE *STILL* BUILDING IT.
THIS IS PROBABLY THE GREENEST AND YET THE MOST TOXIC PROJECT I'VE EVER SEEN. EVERYTHING LOCALLY SOURCED AND RECYCLED...
...BUT A MILLION TONS OF GARBAGE FLOATING IN THE OCEAN IS STILL A MILLION TONS OF GARBAGE FLOATING IN THE OCEAN.
IT OCCURS TO ME THAT ASIDE FROM ALL ELSE, WHAT THIS DOES IS EFFECTIVELY SEAL OFF ACCESS TO HONG KONG PROPER.
HONG KONG'S UNDER A HUNDRED FEET OF WATER.
LEAVING, WHAT, *FIVE HUNDRED* STILL ABOVE WATER, IN SOME CASES? WHAT'S THE NET WORTH OF THAT SKYLINE OVER THERE?
ALL THIS CONSTRUCTION, THIS DESIGN...SO RANDOM, SO SPONTANEOUS...
...BUT IT'S CLEARLY *WORKING.*
THIS IS ALL SO
NEW CITY,
WORLD--I
LIKE A

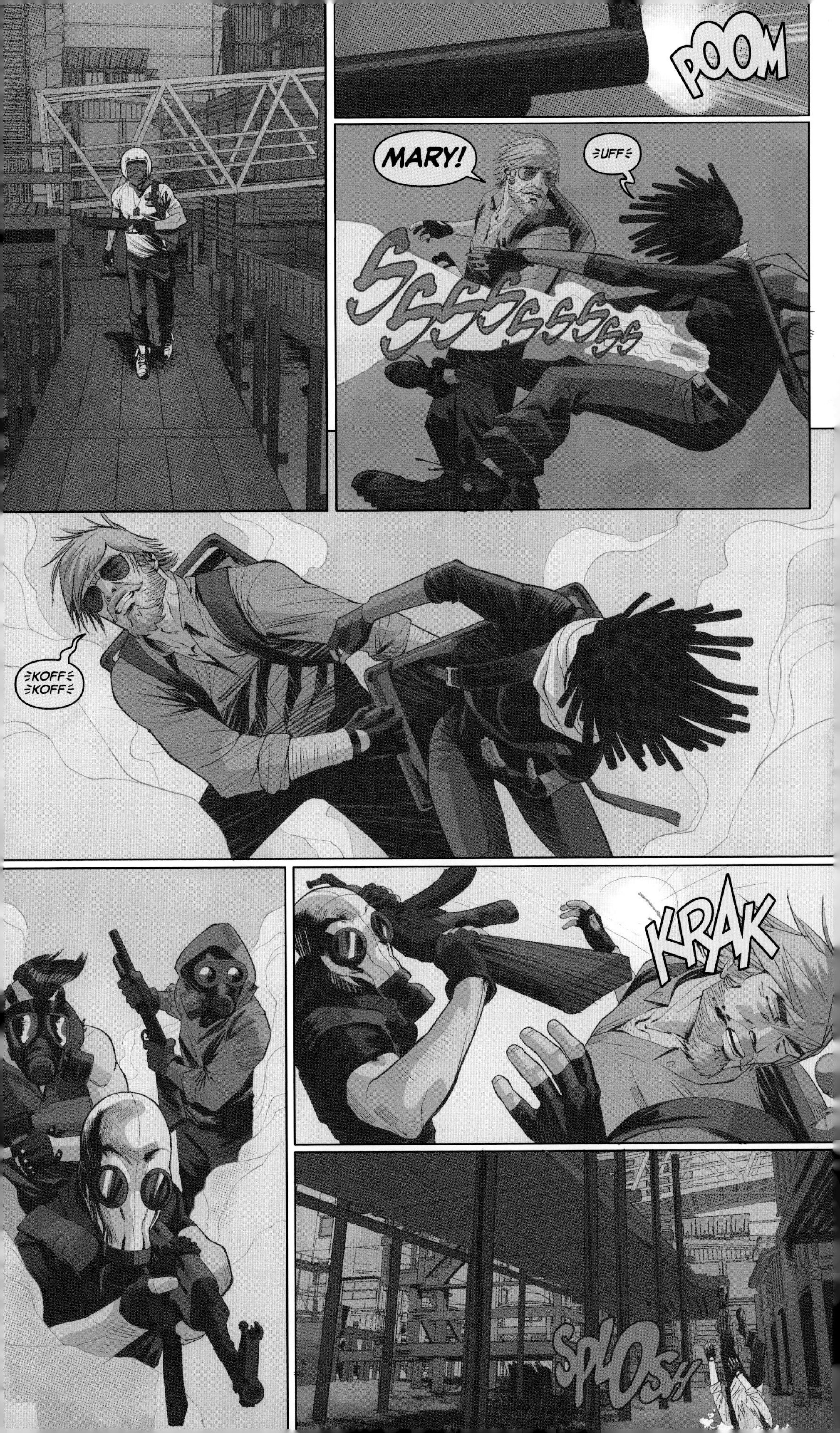
POOM
MARY!
UFF
SSSSSSSSSS
KOFF KOFF
KRAK
SPLOSH

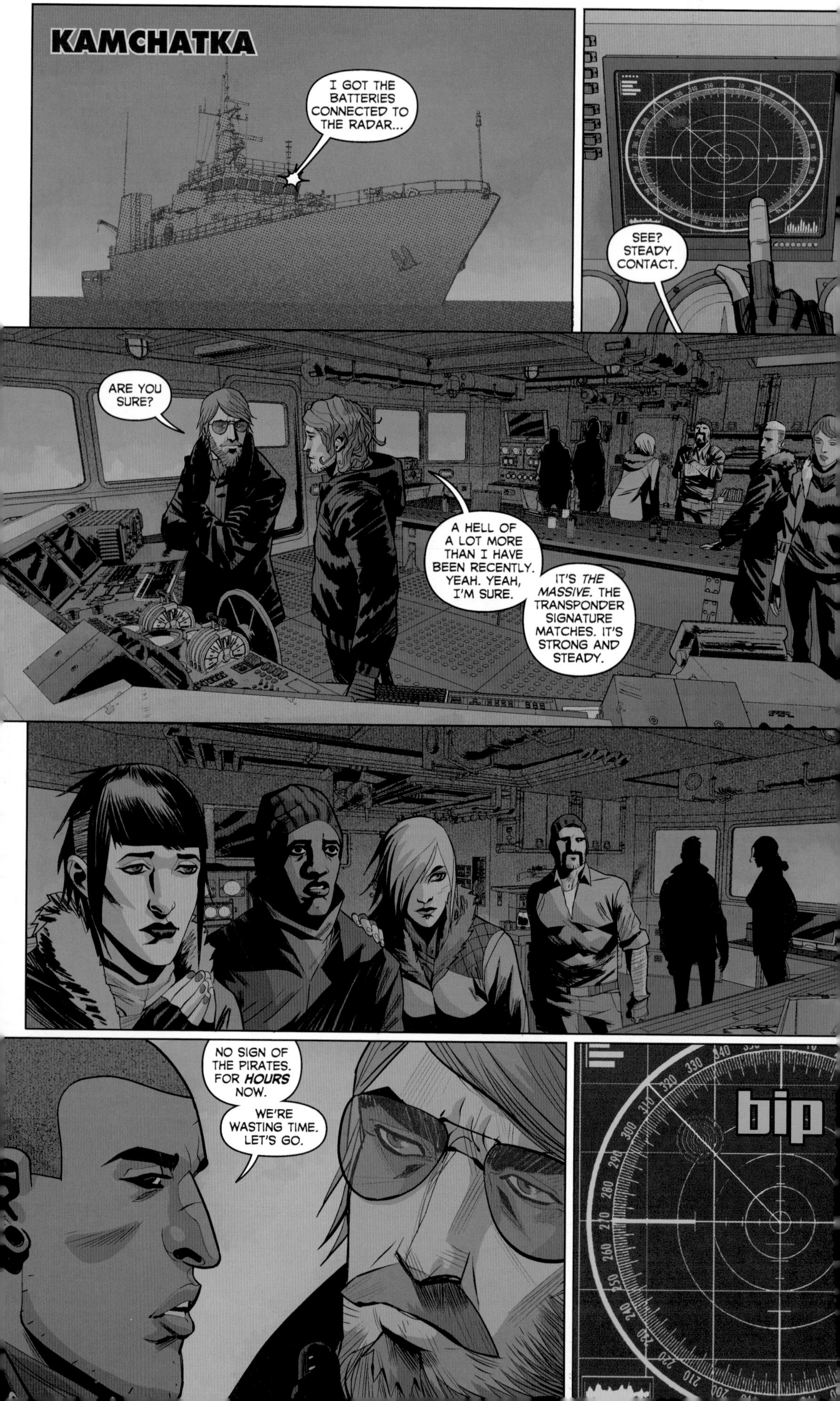
KAMCHATKA
I GOT THE BATTERIES CONNECTED TO THE RADAR...
SEE? STEADY CONTACT.
ARE YOU SURE?
A HELL OF A LOT MORE THAN I HAVE BEEN RECENTLY. YEAH. YEAH, I'M SURE.
IT'S *THE MASSIVE.* THE TRANSPONDER SIGNATURE MATCHES. IT'S STRONG AND STEADY.
NO SIGN OF THE PIRATES. FOR ***HOURS*** NOW.
WE'RE WASTING TIME. LET'S GO.
bip

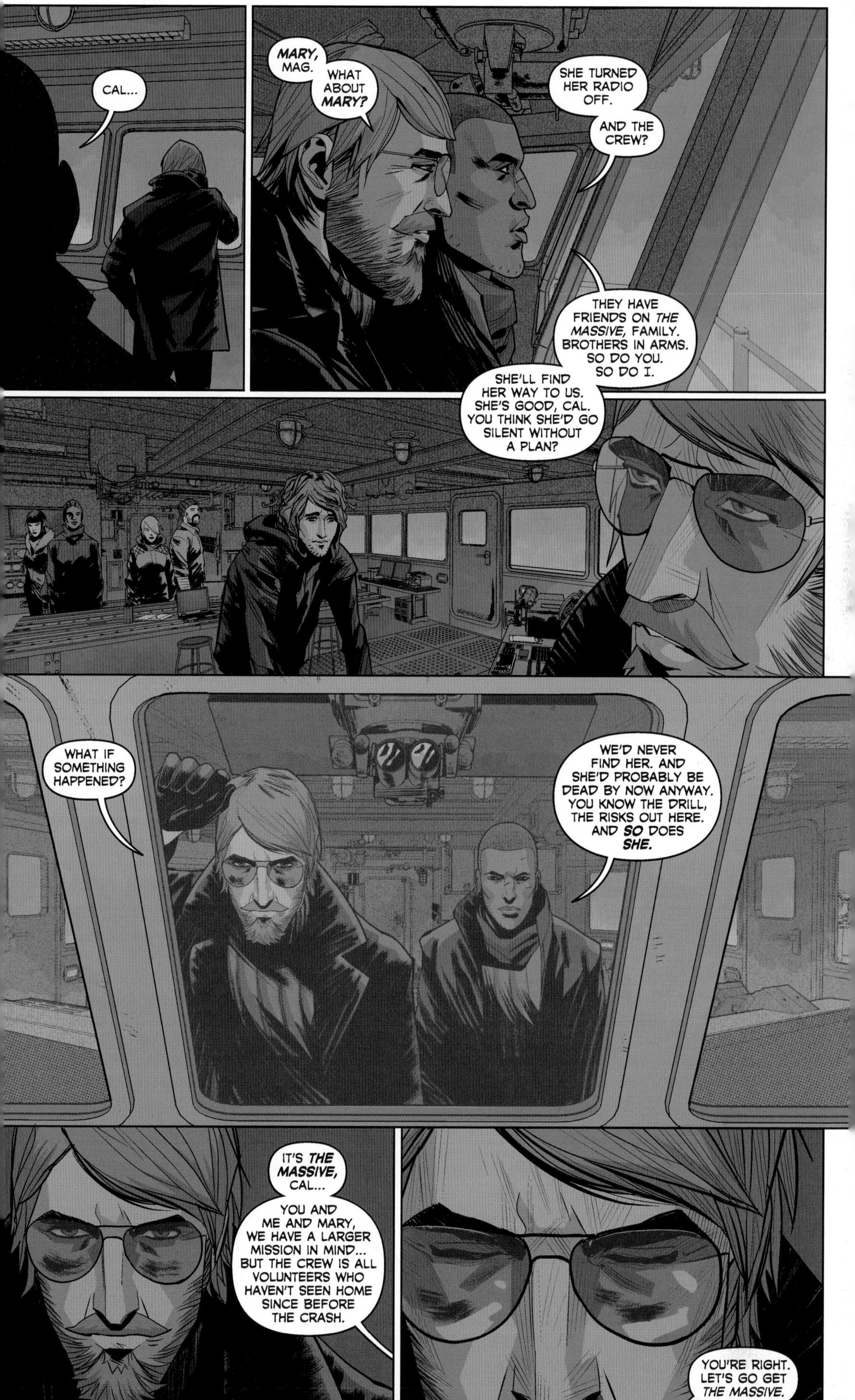
CAL...
MARY, MAG.
WHAT ABOUT MARY?
SHE TURNED HER RADIO OFF.
AND THE CREW?
THEY HAVE FRIENDS ON THE MASSIVE, FAMILY. BROTHERS IN ARMS. SO DO YOU. SO DO I.
SHE'LL FIND HER WAY TO US. SHE'S GOOD, CAL. YOU THINK SHE'D GO SILENT WITHOUT A PLAN?
WHAT IF SOMETHING HAPPENED?
WE'D NEVER FIND HER. AND SHE'D PROBABLY BE DEAD BY NOW ANYWAY. YOU KNOW THE DRILL, THE RISKS OUT HERE. AND SO DOES SHE.
IT'S THE MASSIVE, CAL...
YOU AND ME AND MARY, WE HAVE A LARGER MISSION IN MIND... BUT THE CREW IS ALL VOLUNTEERS WHO HAVEN'T SEEN HOME SINCE BEFORE THE CRASH.
YOU'RE RIGHT. LET'S GO GET THE MASSIVE.

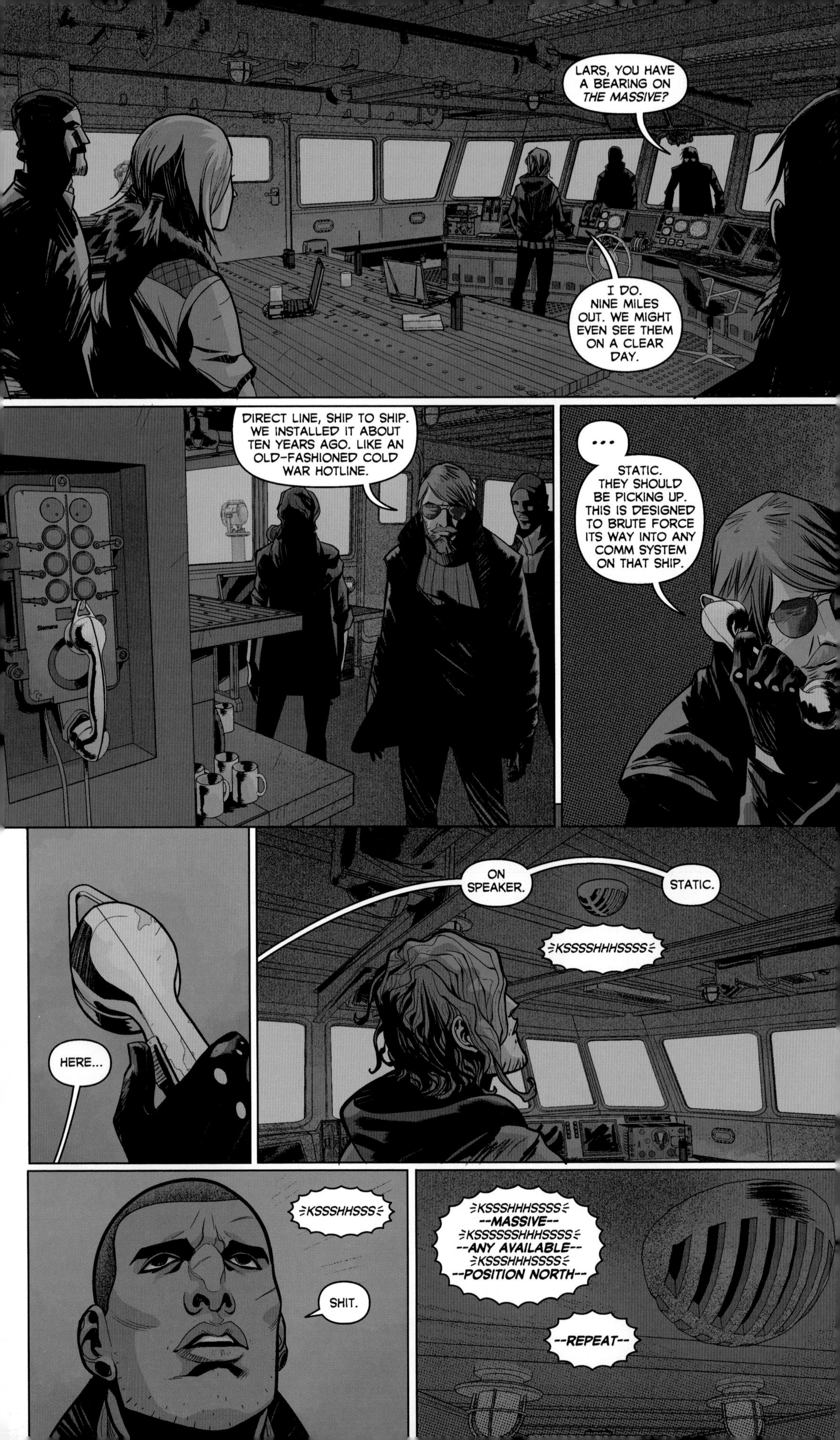
LARS, YOU HAVE A BEARING ON *THE MASSIVE?*
I DO. NINE MILES OUT. WE MIGHT EVEN SEE THEM ON A CLEAR DAY.
DIRECT LINE, SHIP TO SHIP. WE INSTALLED IT ABOUT TEN YEARS AGO. LIKE AN OLD-FASHIONED COLD WAR HOTLINE.
...
STATIC. THEY SHOULD BE PICKING UP. THIS IS DESIGNED TO BRUTE FORCE ITS WAY INTO ANY COMM SYSTEM ON THAT SHIP.
HERE...
ON SPEAKER.
STATIC.
KSSSSHHHSSSS
KSSSHHSSS
SHIT.
KSSSHHHSSSS
--MASSIVE--
KSSSSSSHHHSSSS
--ANY AVAILABLE--
KSSSHHHSSSS
--POSITION NORTH--
--REPEAT--

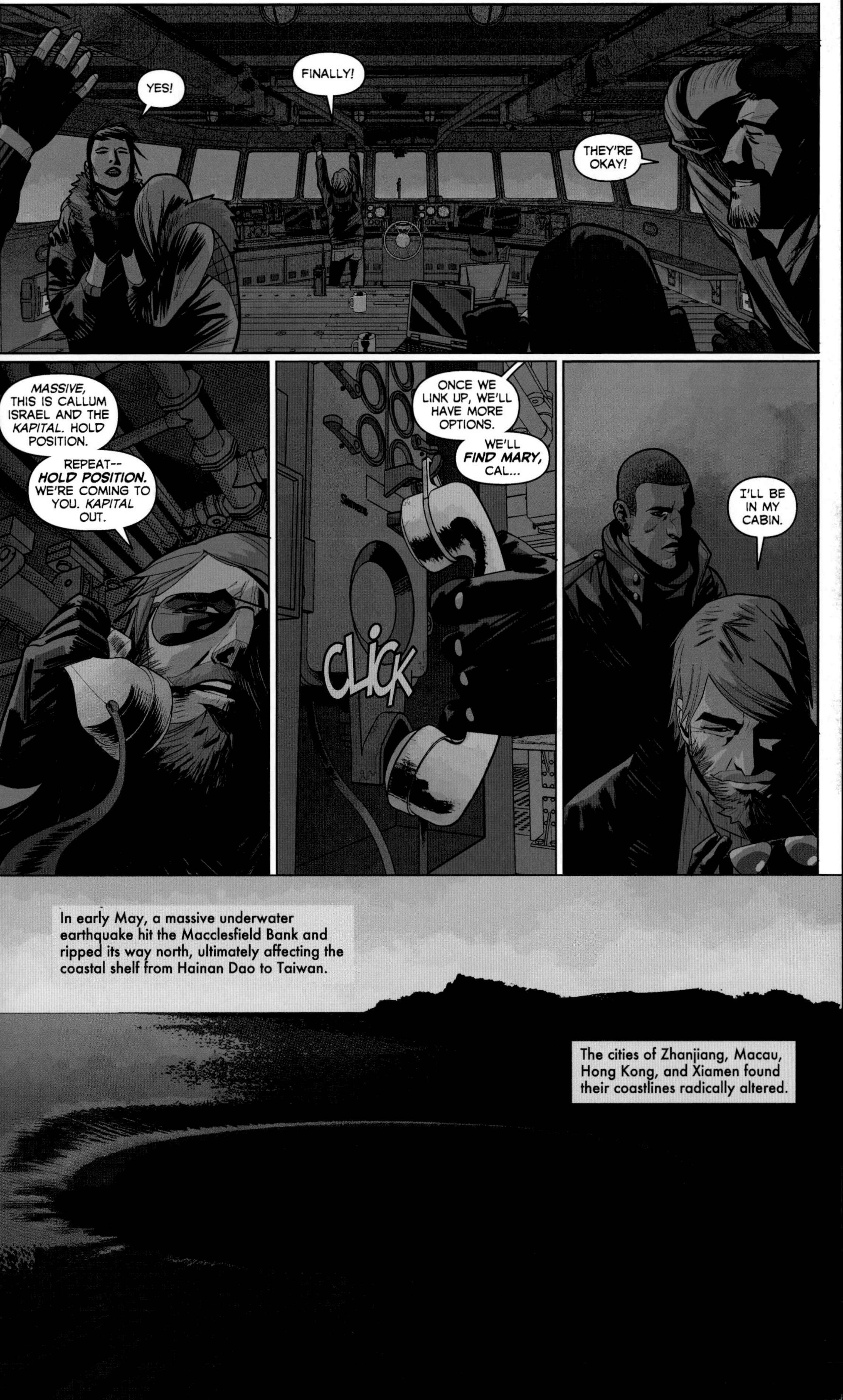
YES!
FINALLY!
THEY'RE OKAY!
MASSIVE, THIS IS CALLUM ISRAEL AND THE *KAPITAL.* HOLD POSITION.
REPEAT-- **HOLD POSITION.** WE'RE COMING TO YOU. *KAPITAL* OUT.
ONCE WE LINK UP, WE'LL HAVE MORE OPTIONS.
WE'LL **FIND MARY,** CAL...
CLICK
I'LL BE IN MY CABIN.
In early May, a massive underwater earthquake hit the Macclesfield Bank and ripped its way north, ultimately affecting the coastal shelf from Hainan Dao to Taiwan.
The cities of Zhanjiang, Macau, Hong Kong, and Xiamen found their coastlines radically altered.

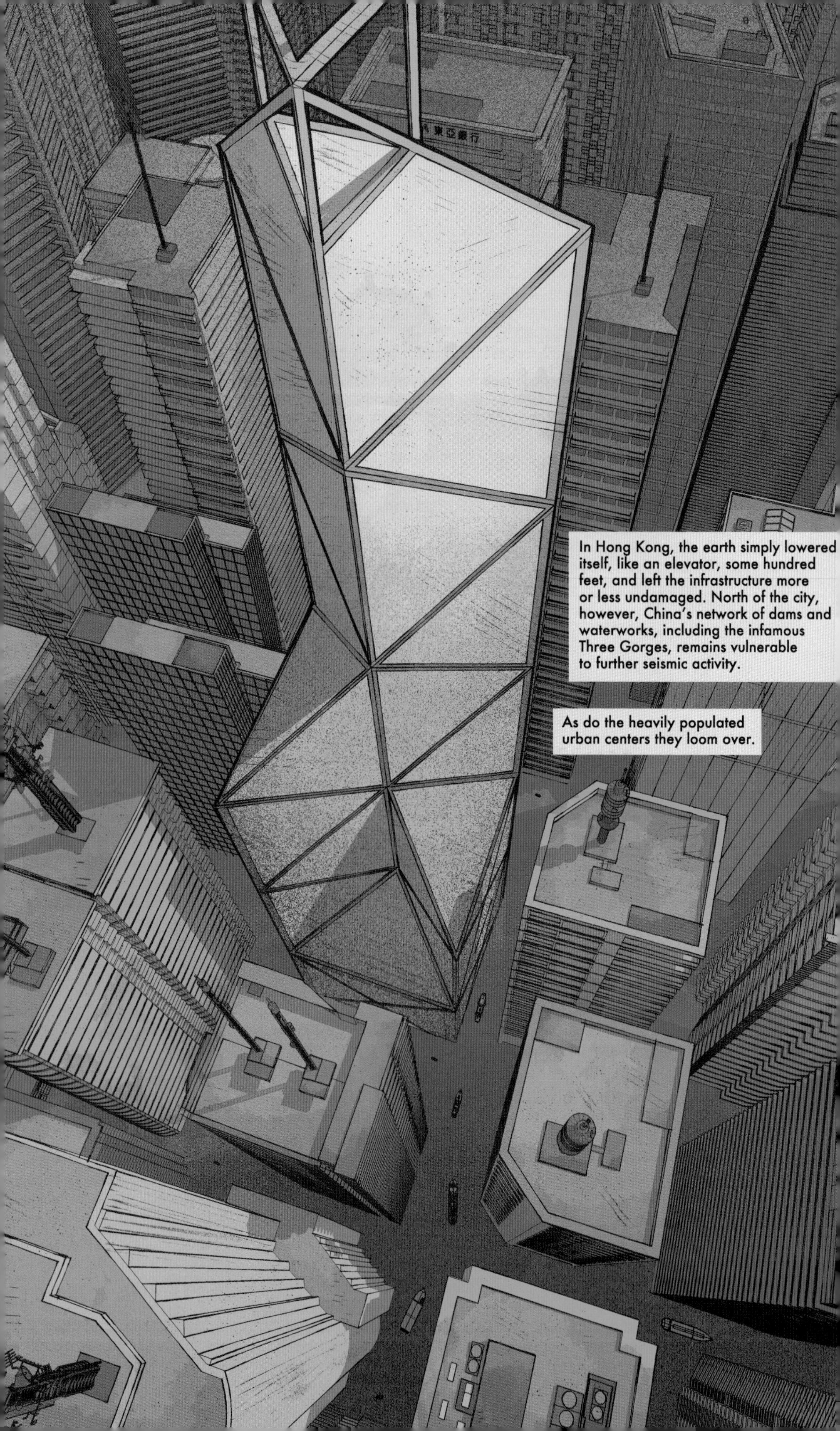
In Hong Kong, the earth simply lowered itself, like an elevator, some hundred feet, and left the infrastructure more or less undamaged. North of the city, however, China's network of dams and waterworks, including the infamous Three Gorges, remains vulnerable to further seismic activity.
As do the heavily populated urban centers they loom over.

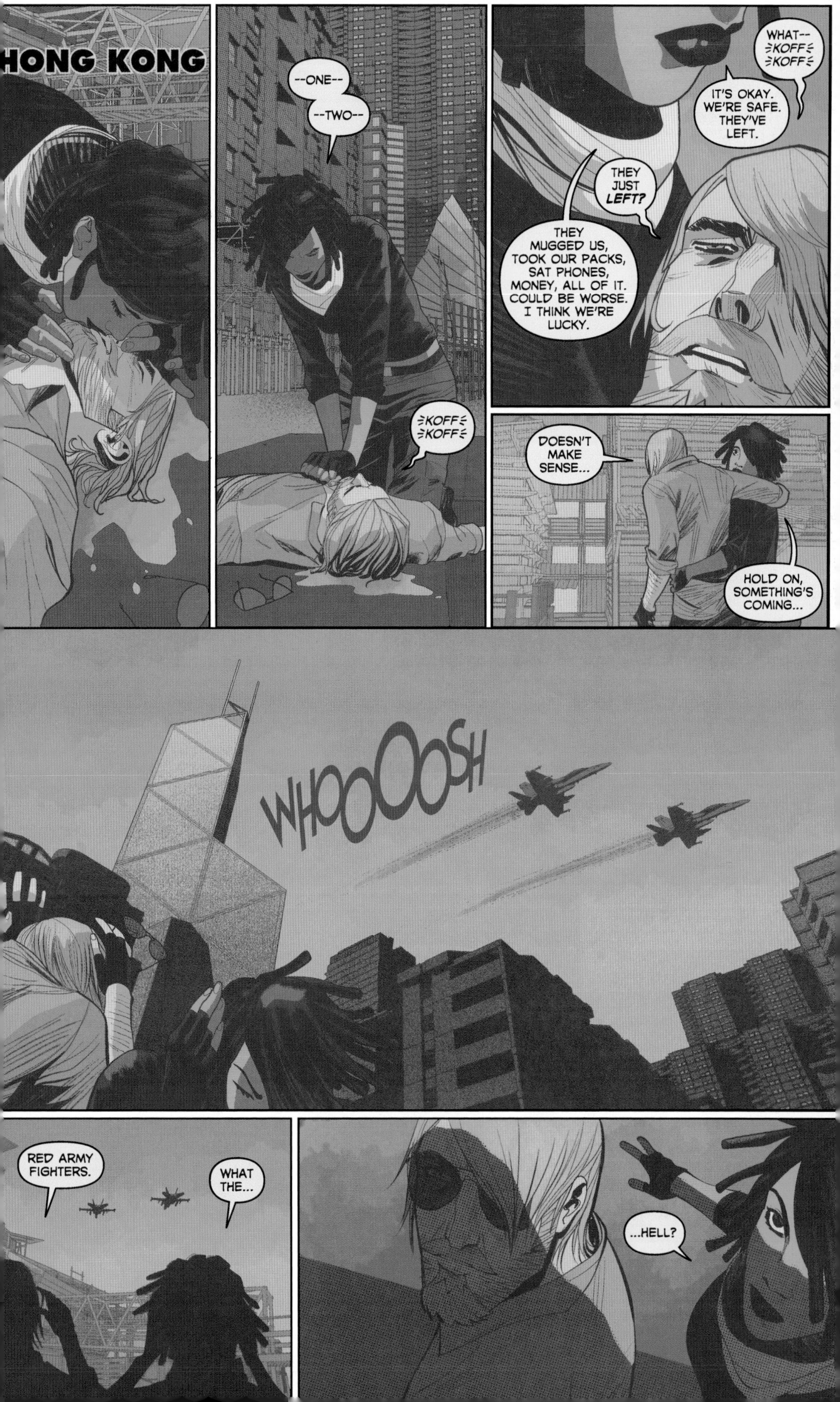
HONG KONG
--ONE--
--TWO--
KOFF KOFF
WHAT-- KOFF KOFF
IT'S OKAY. WE'RE SAFE. THEY'VE LEFT.
THEY JUST LEFT?
THEY MUGGED US, TOOK OUR PACKS, SAT PHONES, MONEY, ALL OF IT. COULD BE WORSE. I THINK WE'RE LUCKY.
DOESN'T MAKE SENSE...
HOLD ON, SOMETHING'S COMING...
WHOOOOSH
RED ARMY FIGHTERS.
WHAT THE...
...HELL?

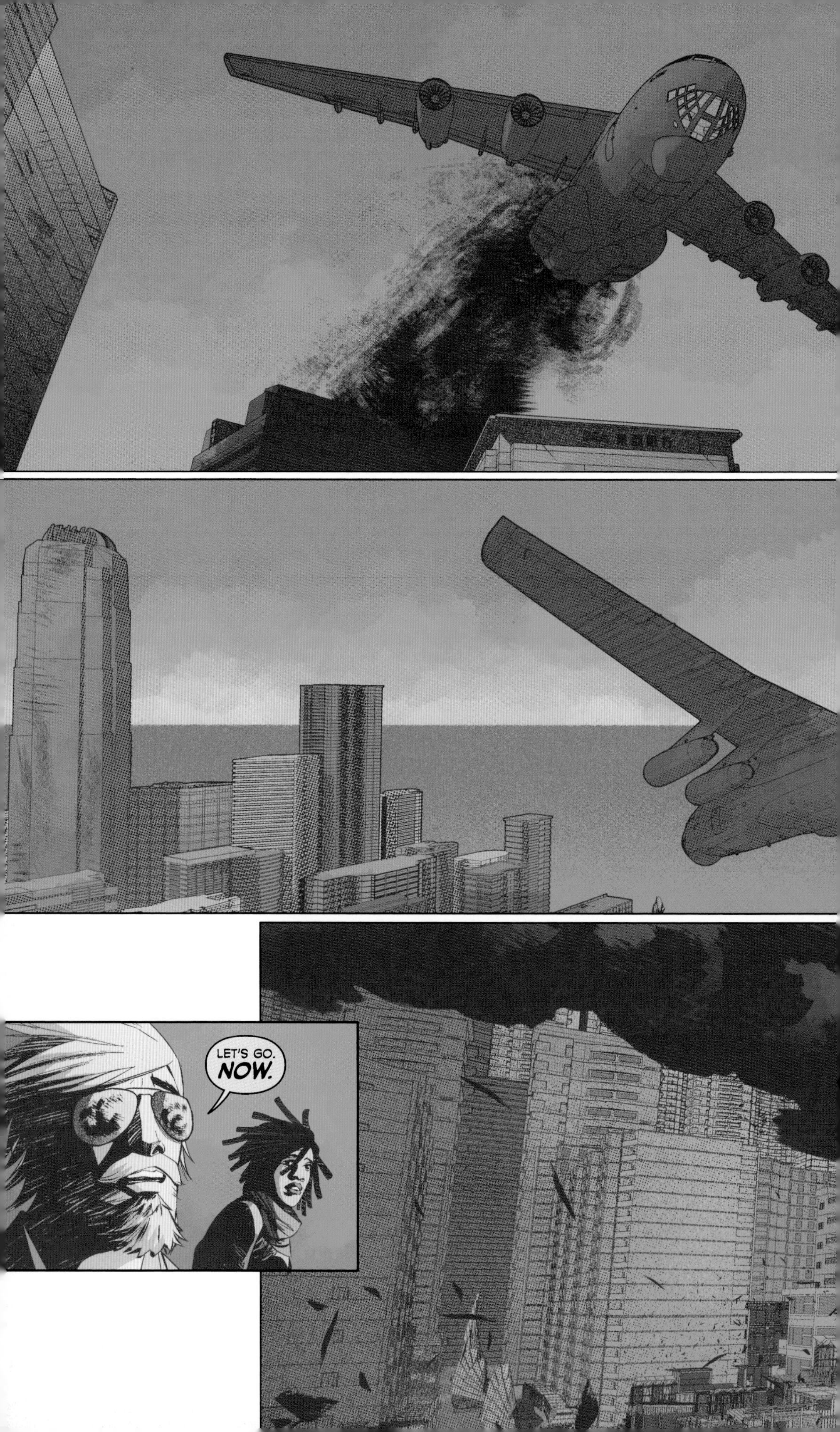
LET'S GO. NOW.

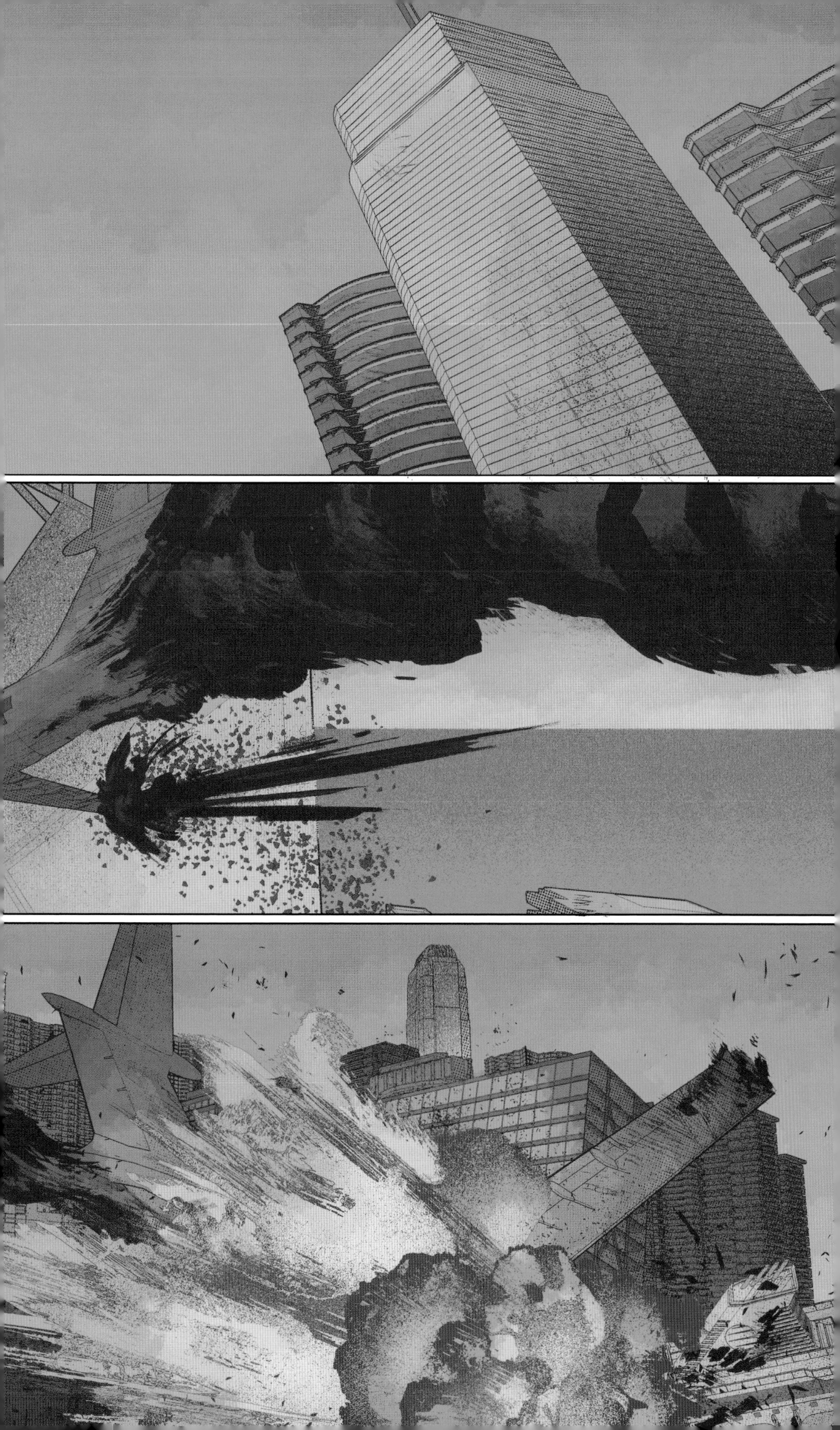

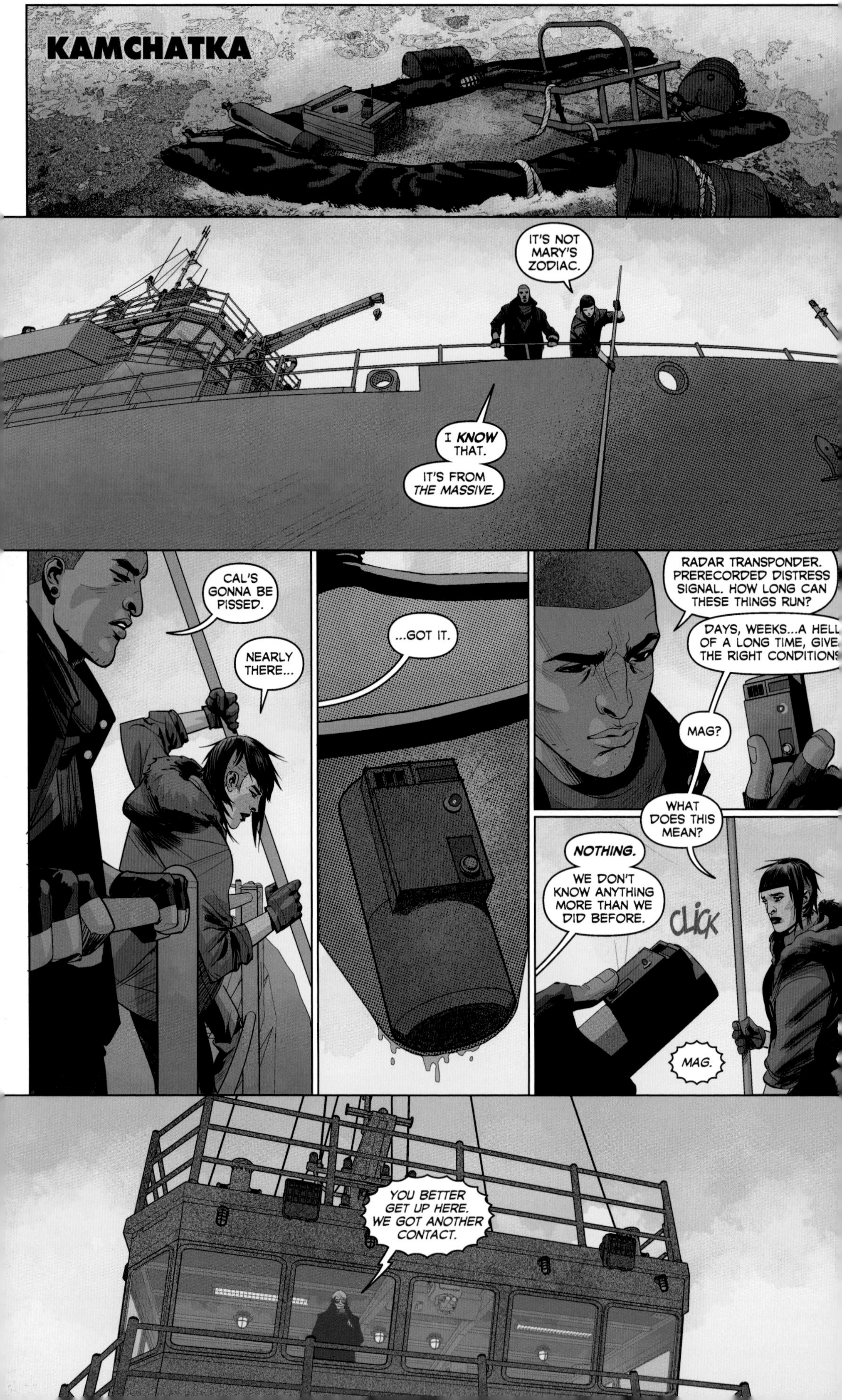
KAMCHATKA
IT'S NOT MARY'S ZODIAC.
I KNOW THAT.
IT'S FROM THE MASSIVE.
CAL'S GONNA BE PISSED.
NEARLY THERE...
...GOT IT.
RADAR TRANSPONDER. PRERECORDED DISTRESS SIGNAL. HOW LONG CAN THESE THINGS RUN?
DAYS, WEEKS...A HELL OF A LONG TIME, GIVE THE RIGHT CONDITIONS
MAG?
WHAT DOES THIS MEAN?
NOTHING.
WE DON'T KNOW ANYTHING MORE THAN WE DID BEFORE.
CLICK
MAG.
YOU BETTER GET UP HERE. WE GOT ANOTHER CONTACT.

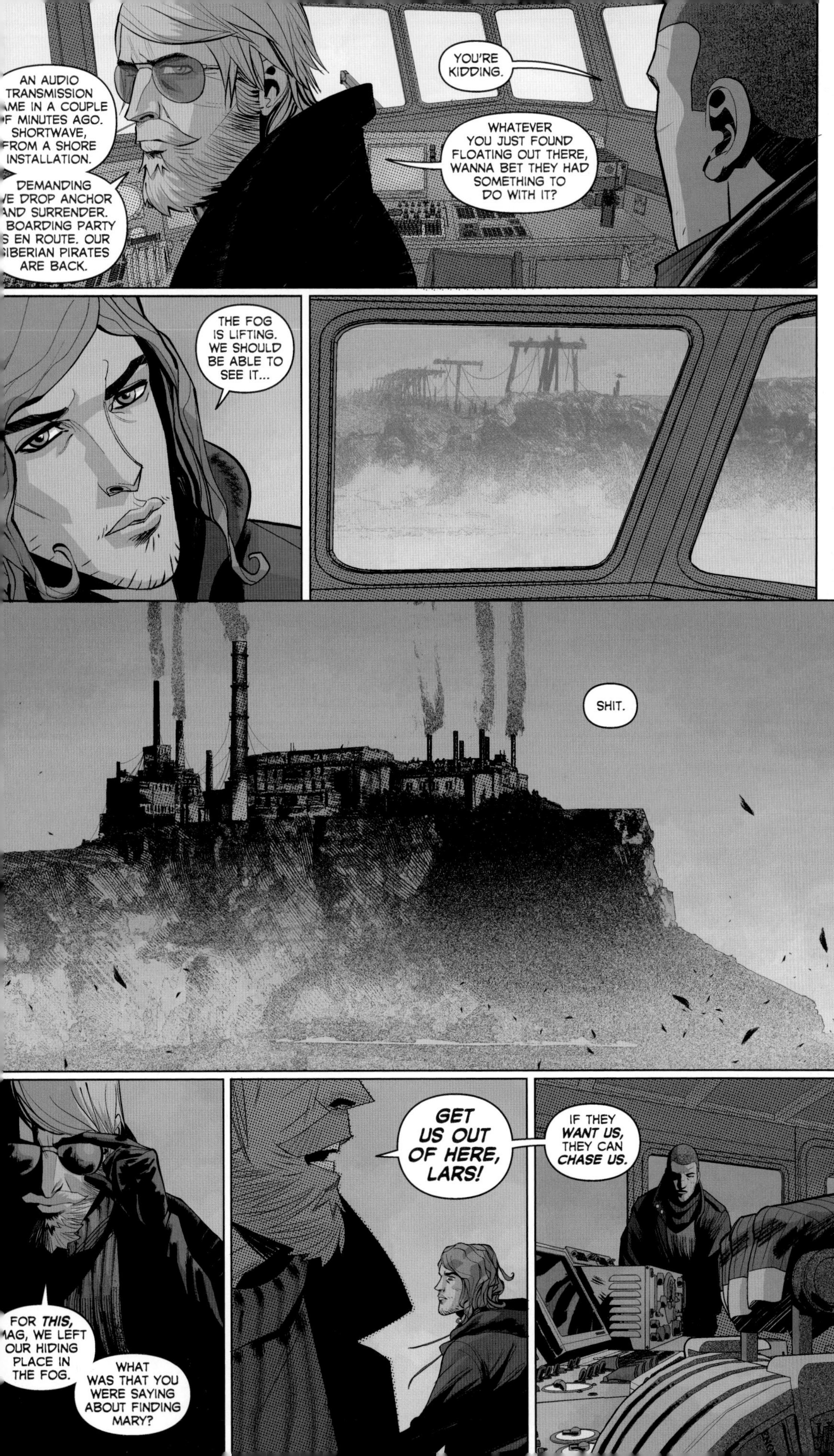
AN AUDIO TRANSMISSION
AME IN A COUPLE
F MINUTES AGO. SHORTWAVE, FROM A SHORE INSTALLATION.
DEMANDING
E DROP ANCHOR
AND SURRENDER.
BOARDING PARTY
S EN ROUTE. OUR
IBERIAN PIRATES ARE BACK.
YOU'RE KIDDING.
WHATEVER YOU JUST FOUND FLOATING OUT THERE, WANNA BET THEY HAD SOMETHING TO DO WITH IT?
THE FOG IS LIFTING. WE SHOULD BE ABLE TO SEE IT...
SHIT.
FOR *THIS,*
AG, WE LEFT OUR HIDING PLACE IN THE FOG.
WHAT WAS THAT YOU WERE SAYING ABOUT FINDING MARY?
GET US OUT OF HERE, LARS!
IF THEY *WANT US,* THEY CAN *CHASE US.*

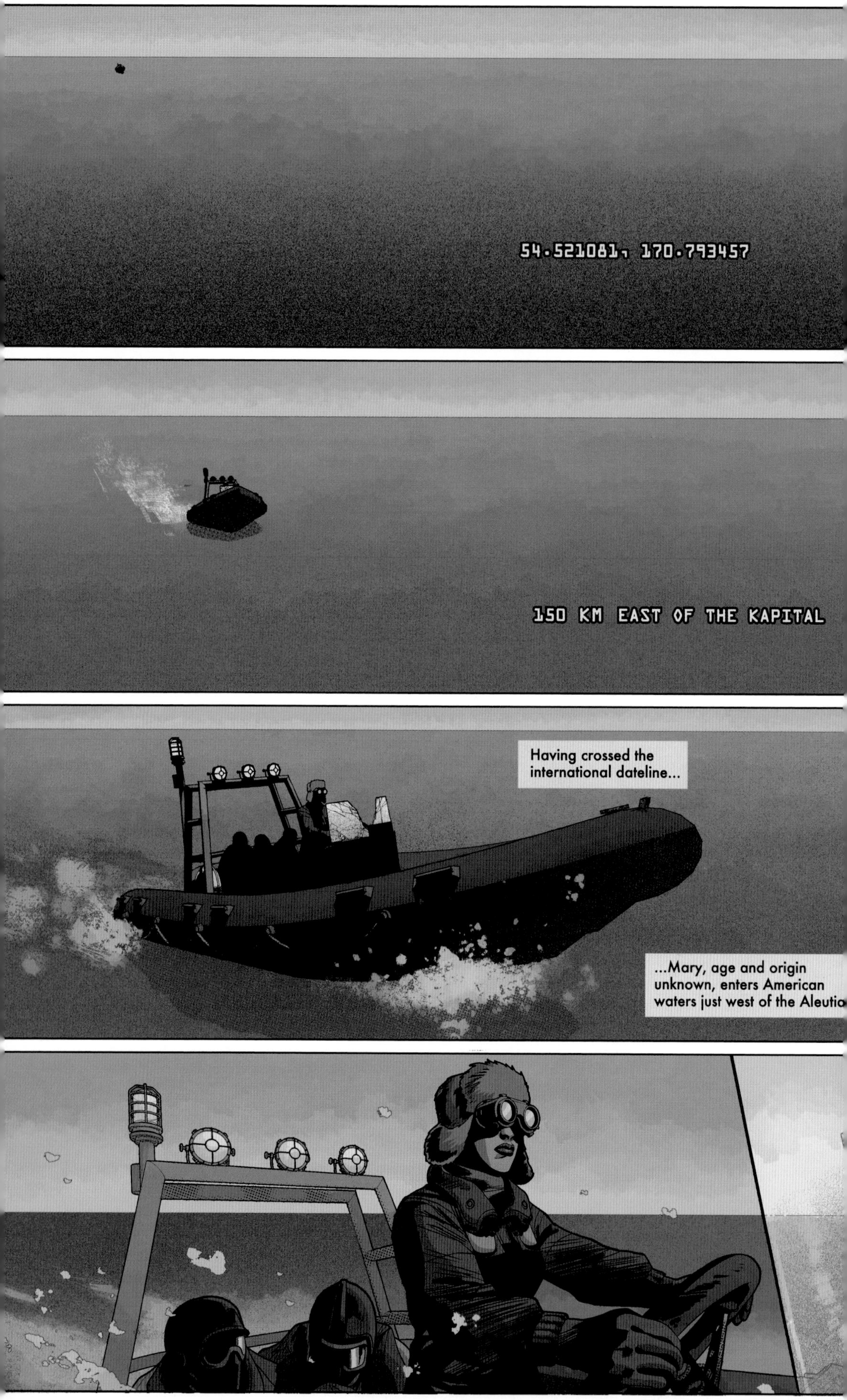

54.521081, 170.793457
150 KM EAST OF THE KAPITAL
Having crossed the international dateline...
...Mary, age and origin unknown, enters American waters just west of the Aleutia

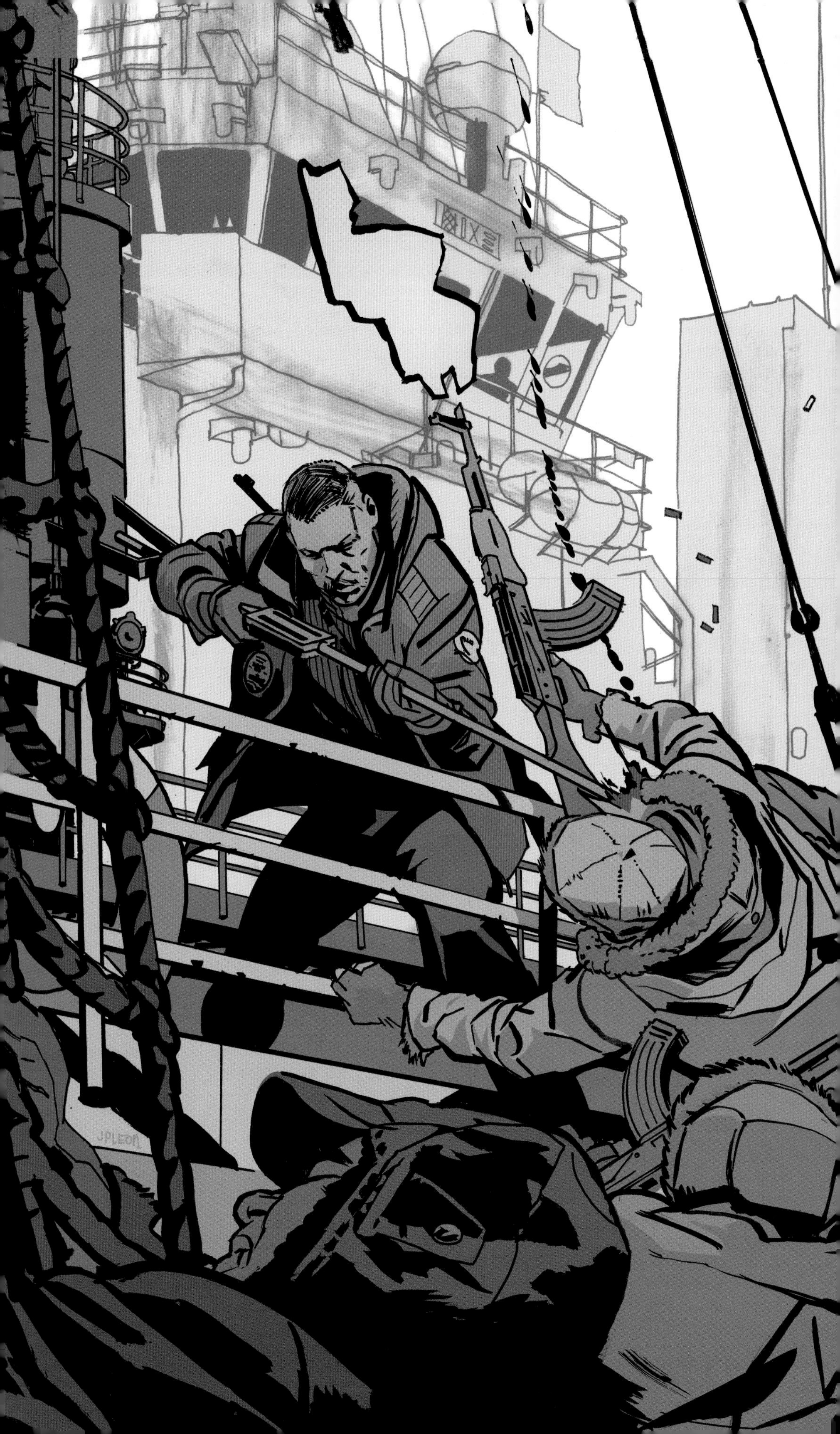
JPLEON

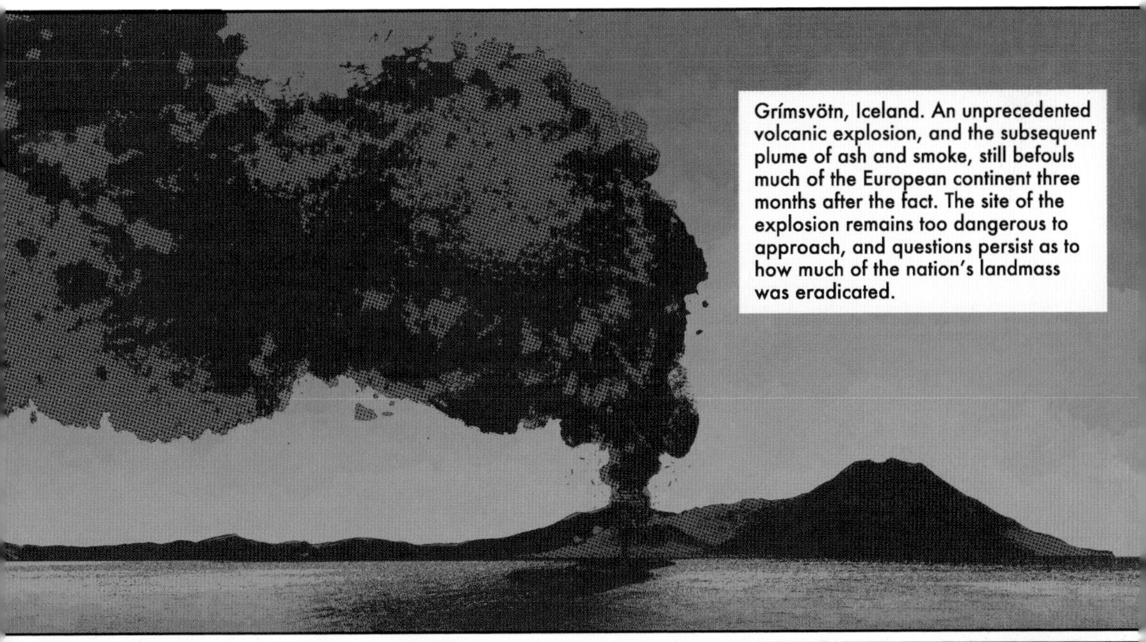
Grímsvötn, Iceland. An unprecedented volcanic explosion, and the subsequent plume of ash and smoke, still befouls much of the European continent three months after the fact. The site of the explosion remains too dangerous to approach, and questions persist as to how much of the nation's landmass was eradicated.

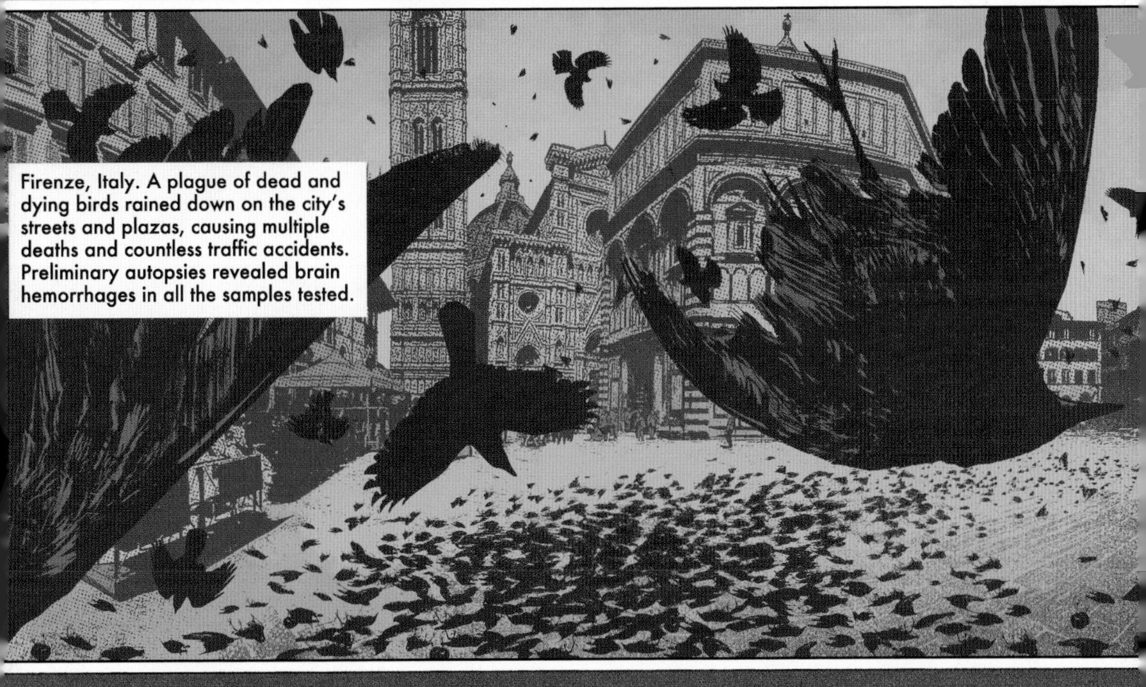
Firenze, Italy. A plague of dead and dying birds rained down on the city's streets and plazas, causing multiple deaths and countless traffic accidents. Preliminary autopsies revealed brain hemorrhages in all the samples tested.

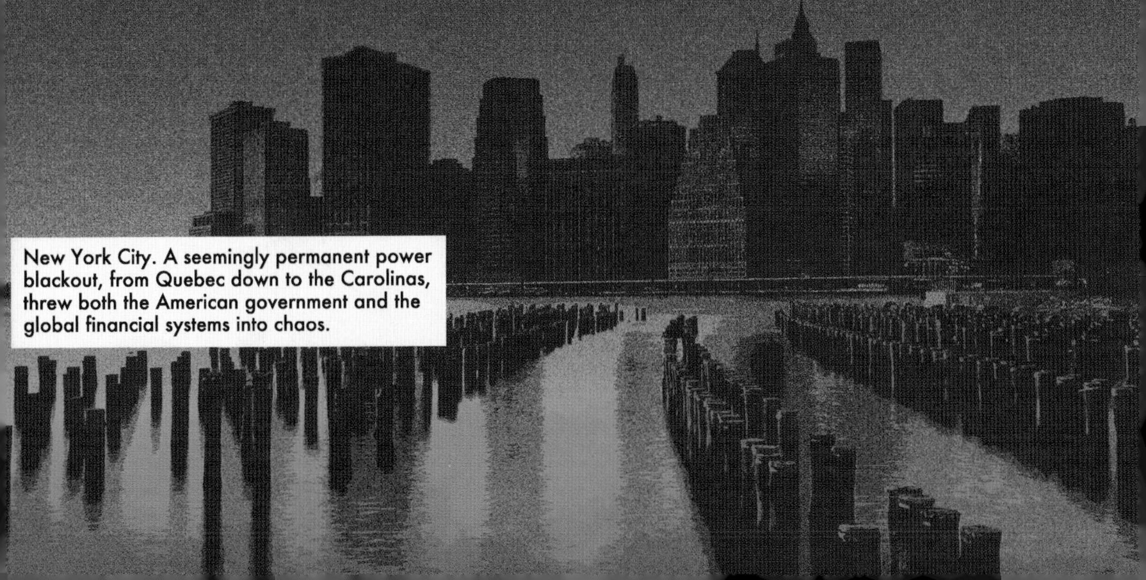
New York City. A seemingly permanent power blackout, from Quebec down to the Carolinas, threw both the American government and the global financial systems into chaos.

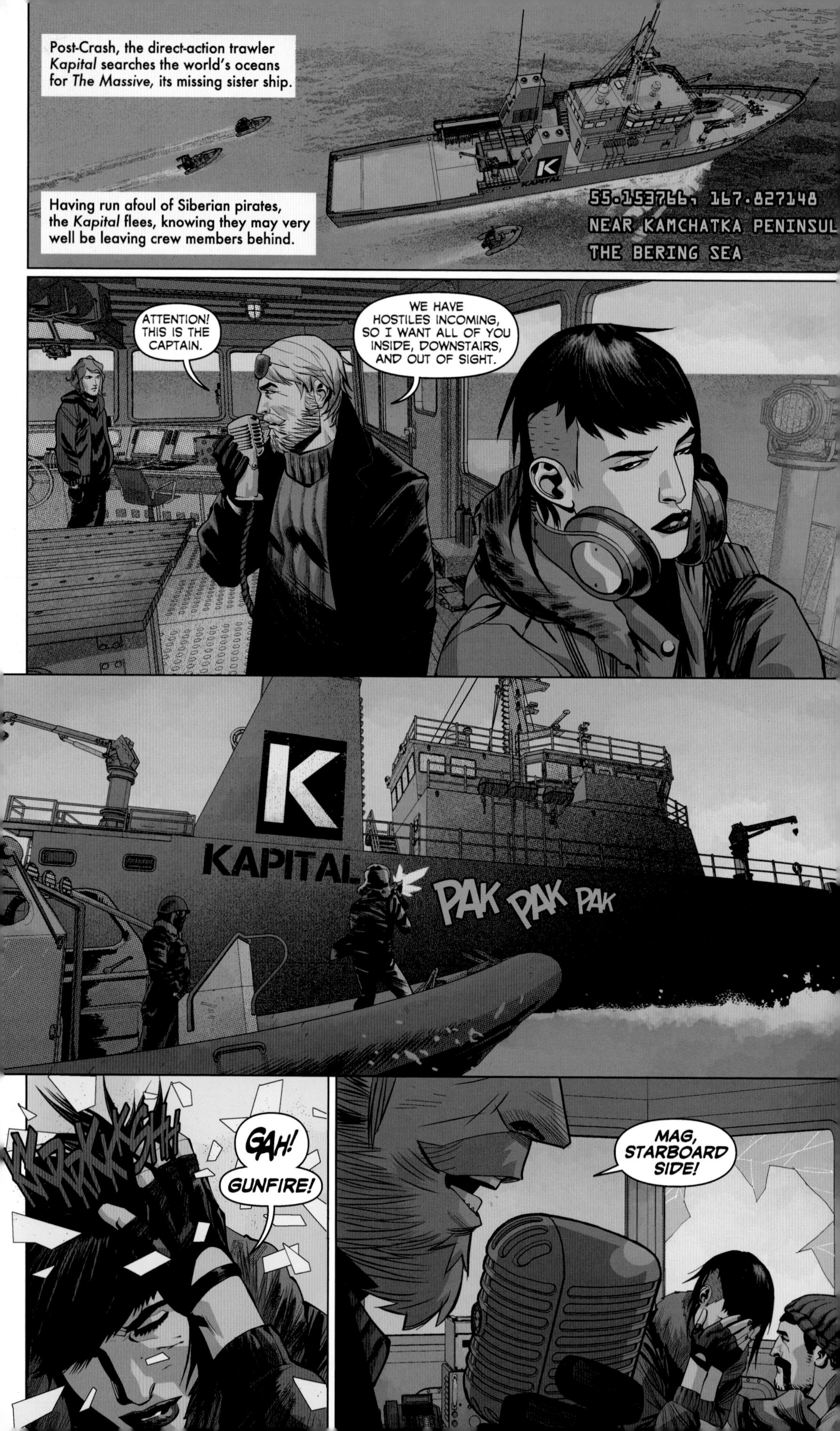

Post-Crash, the direct-action trawler *Kapital* searches the world's oceans for *The Massive*, its missing sister ship.
Having run afoul of Siberian pirates, the *Kapital* flees, knowing they may very well be leaving crew members behind.
55.153766, 167.827148
NEAR KAMCHATKA PENINSUL
THE BERING SEA
ATTENTION! THIS IS THE CAPTAIN.
WE HAVE HOSTILES INCOMING, SO I WANT ALL OF YOU INSIDE, DOWNSTAIRS, AND OUT OF SIGHT.
KAPITAL
PAK PAK PAK
GAH!
GUNFIRE!
MAG, STARBOARD SIDE!

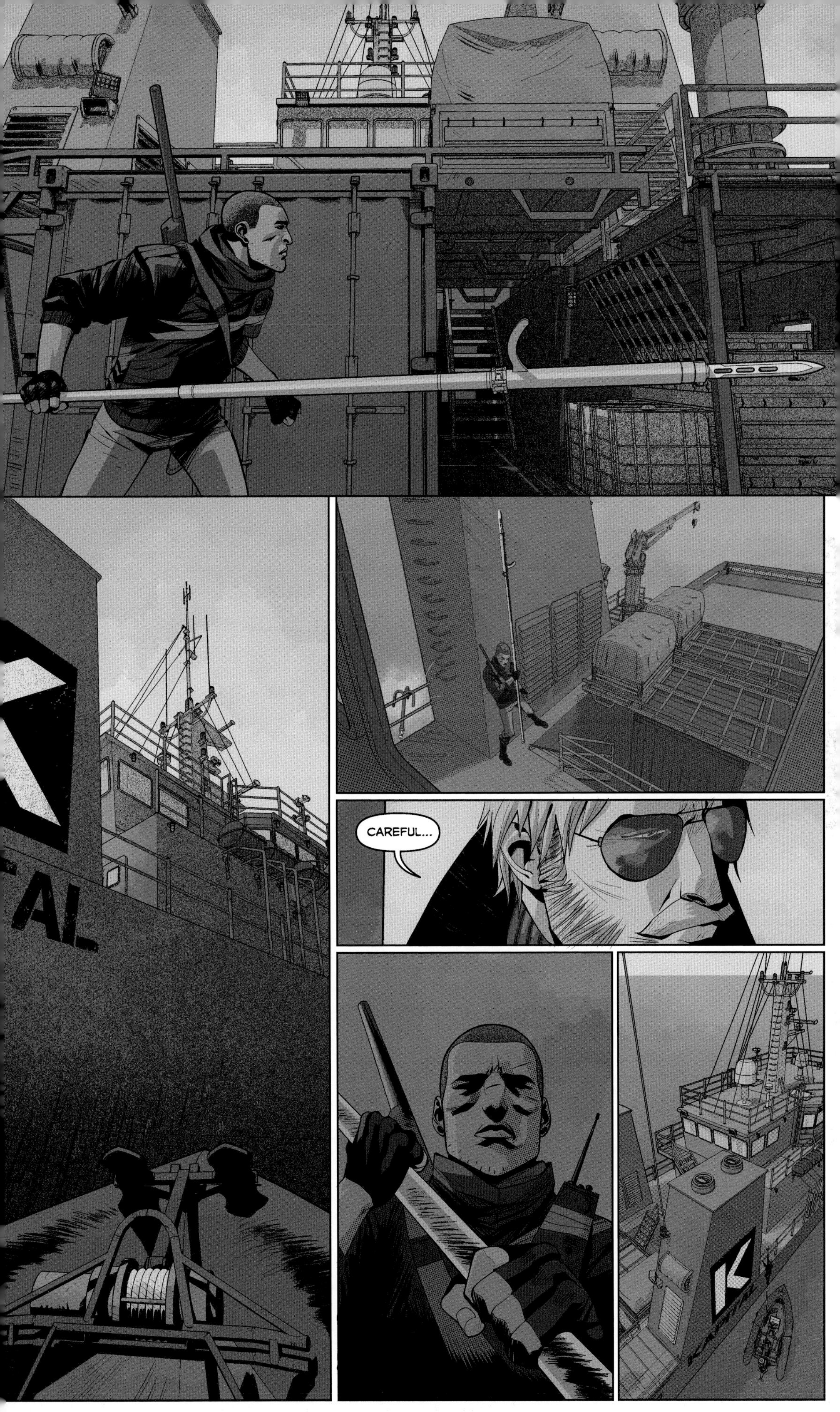
CAREFUL...

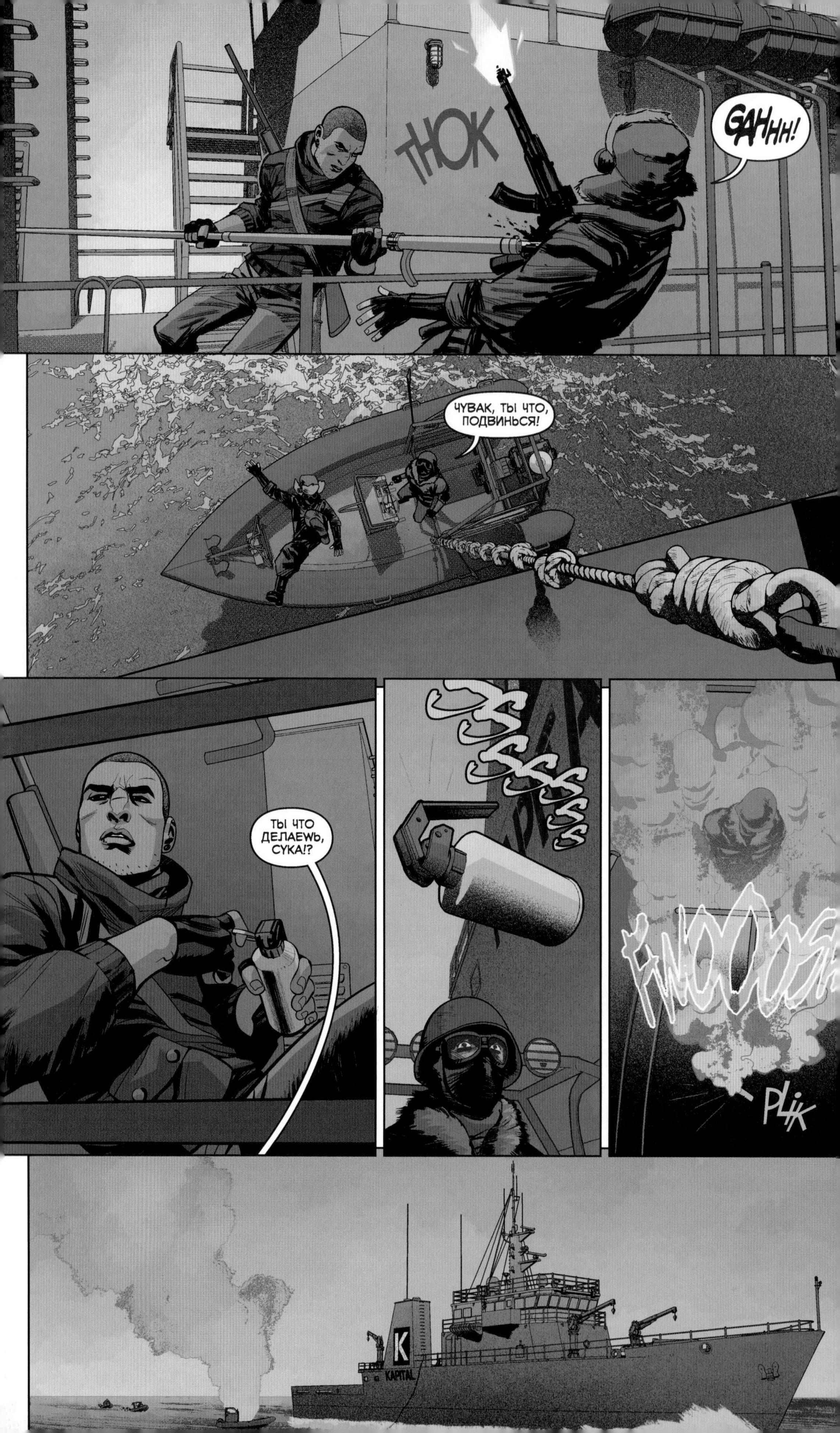
THOK
GAHHH!
ЧУВАК, ТЫ ЧТО, ПОДВИНЬСЯ!
ТЫ ЧТО ДЕЛАЕШЬ, СУКА!?
PLIK
KAPITAL

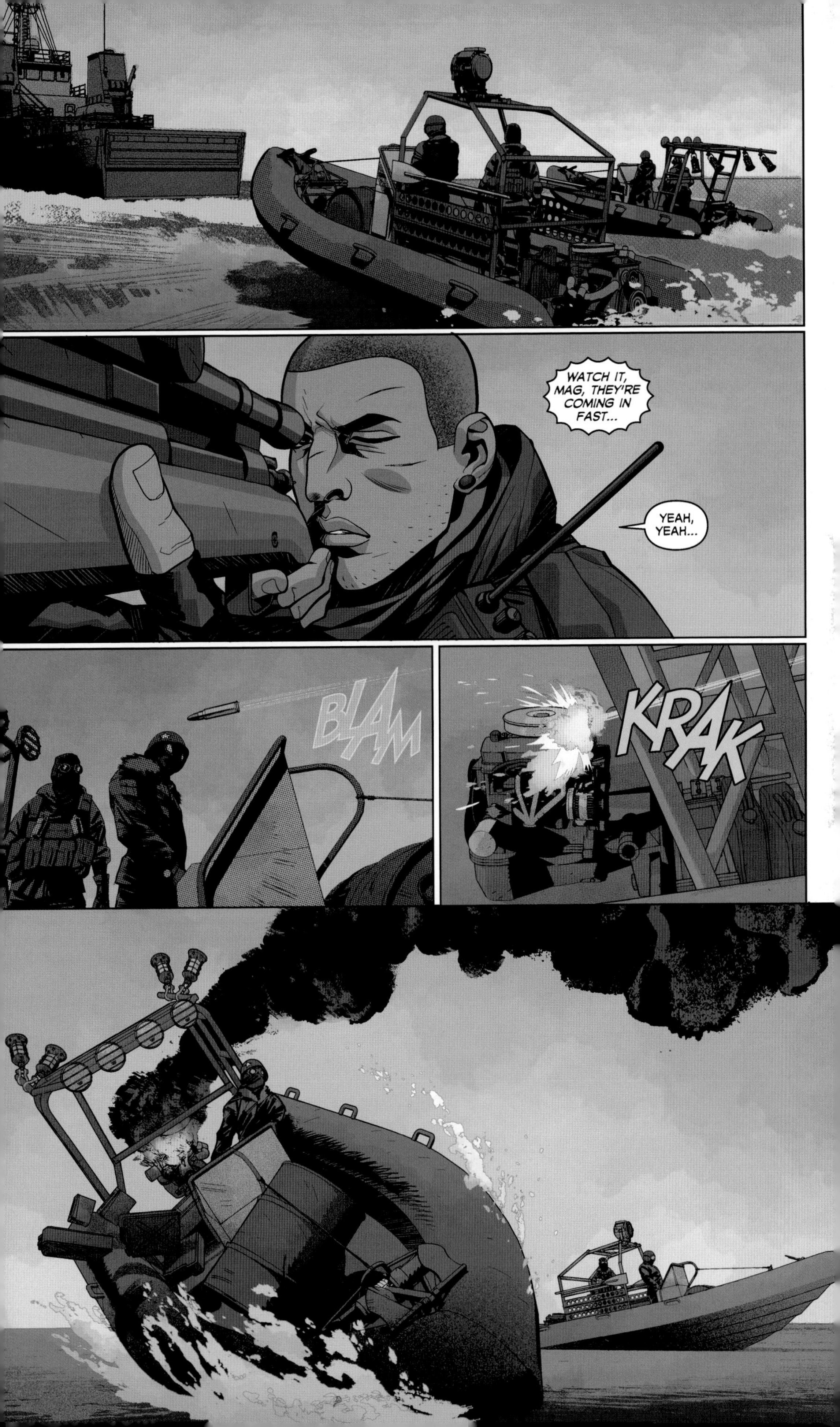
WATCH IT, MAG, THEY'RE COMING IN FAST...
YEAH, YEAH...
BLAM
KRAK

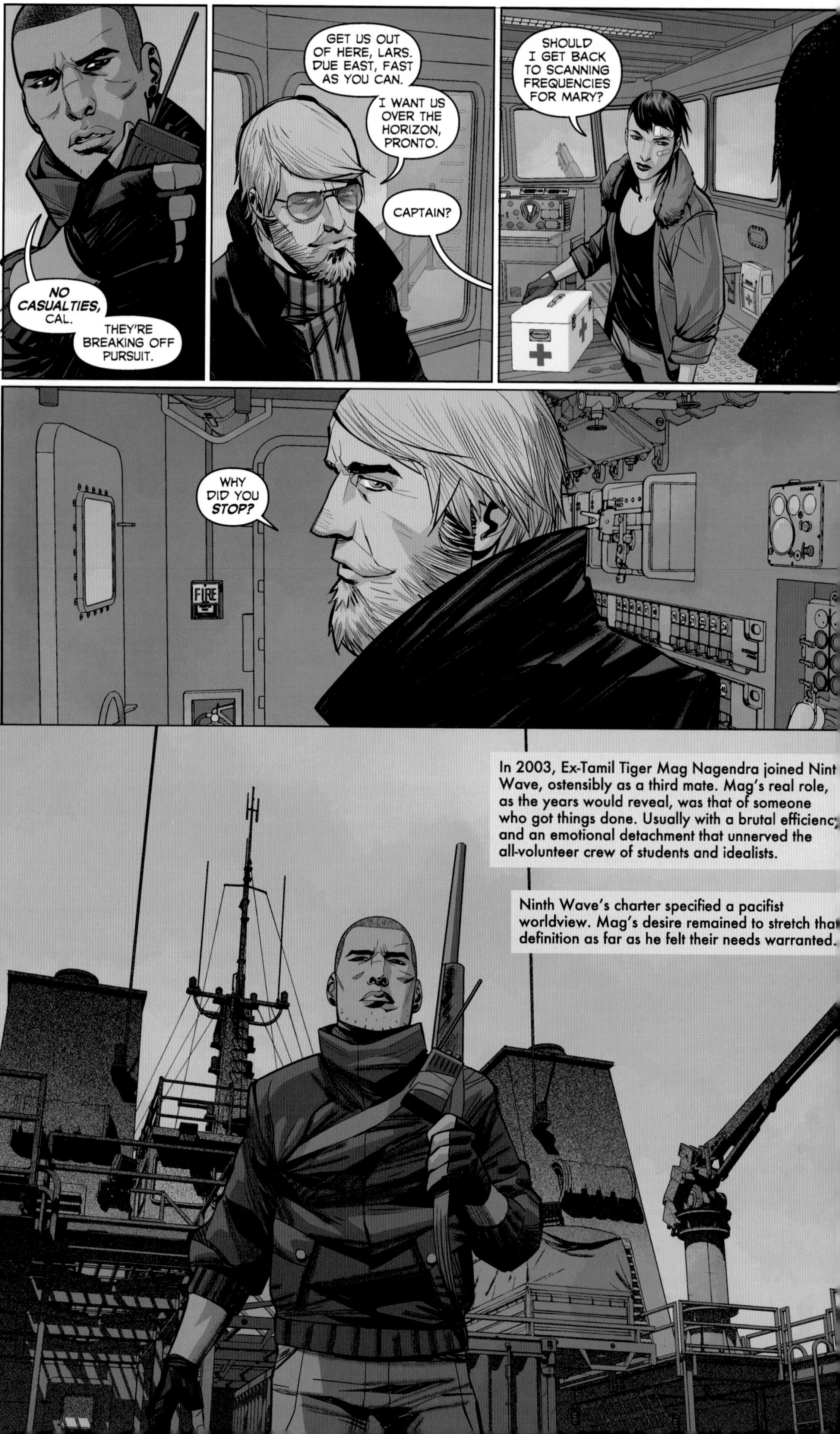

NO CASUALTIES, CAL.
THEY'RE BREAKING OFF PURSUIT.
GET US OUT OF HERE, LARS. DUE EAST, FAST AS YOU CAN.
I WANT US OVER THE HORIZON, PRONTO.
CAPTAIN?
SHOULD I GET BACK TO SCANNING FREQUENCIES FOR MARY?
WHY DID YOU STOP?
FIRE
In 2003, Ex-Tamil Tiger Mag Nagendra joined Ninth Wave, ostensibly as a third mate. Mag's real role, as the years would reveal, was that of someone who got things done. Usually with a brutal efficiency and an emotional detachment that unnerved the all-volunteer crew of students and idealists.
Ninth Wave's charter specified a pacifist worldview. Mag's desire remained to stretch that definition as far as he felt their needs warranted.

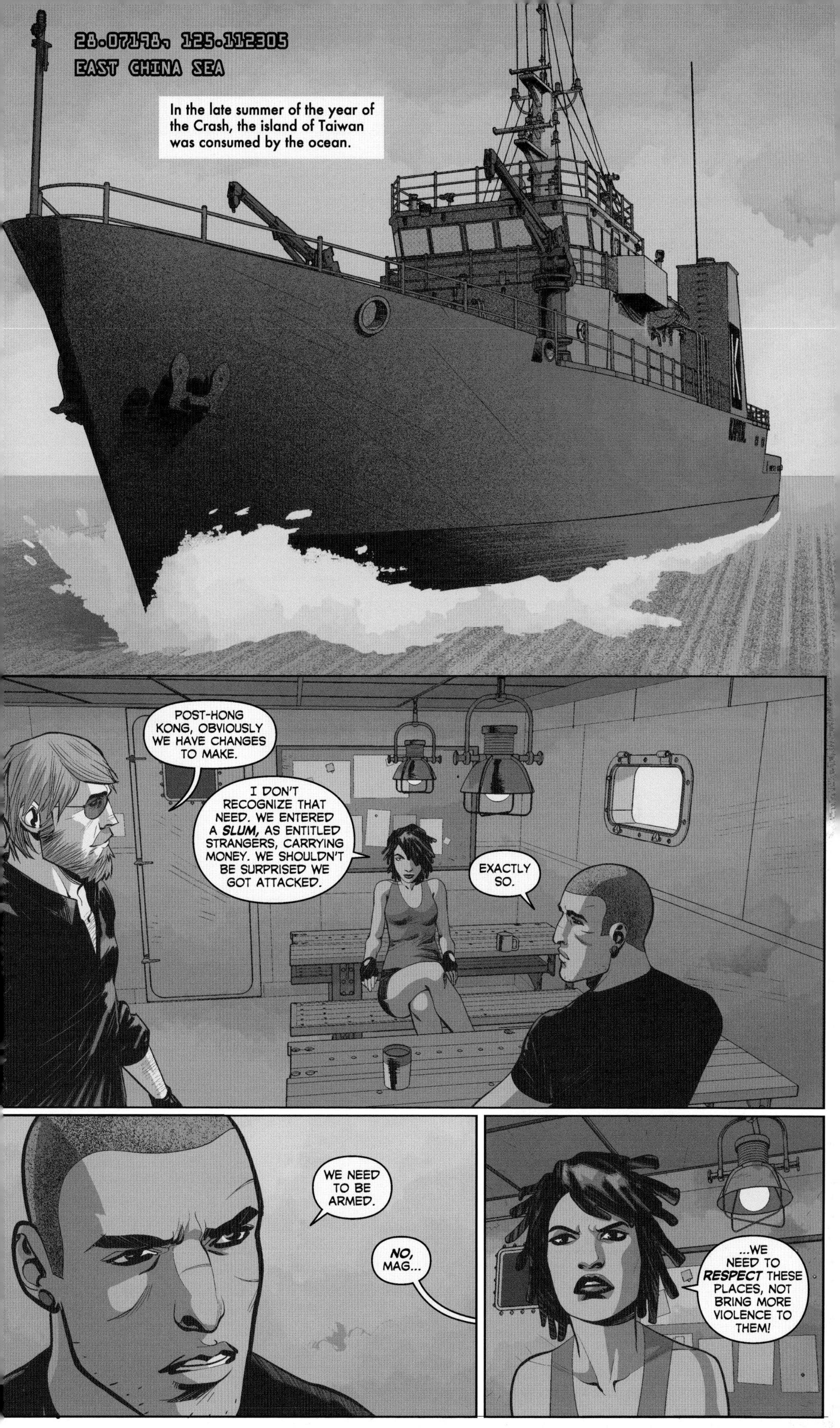

28.07198, 125.112305
EAST CHINA SEA
In the late summer of the year of the Crash, the island of Taiwan was consumed by the ocean.
POST-HONG KONG, OBVIOUSLY WE HAVE CHANGES TO MAKE.
I DON'T RECOGNIZE THAT NEED. WE ENTERED A *SLUM,* AS ENTITLED STRANGERS, CARRYING MONEY. WE SHOULDN'T BE SURPRISED WE GOT ATTACKED.
EXACTLY SO.
WE NEED TO BE ARMED.
NO, MAG...
...WE NEED TO *RESPECT* THESE PLACES, NOT BRING MORE VIOLENCE TO THEM!

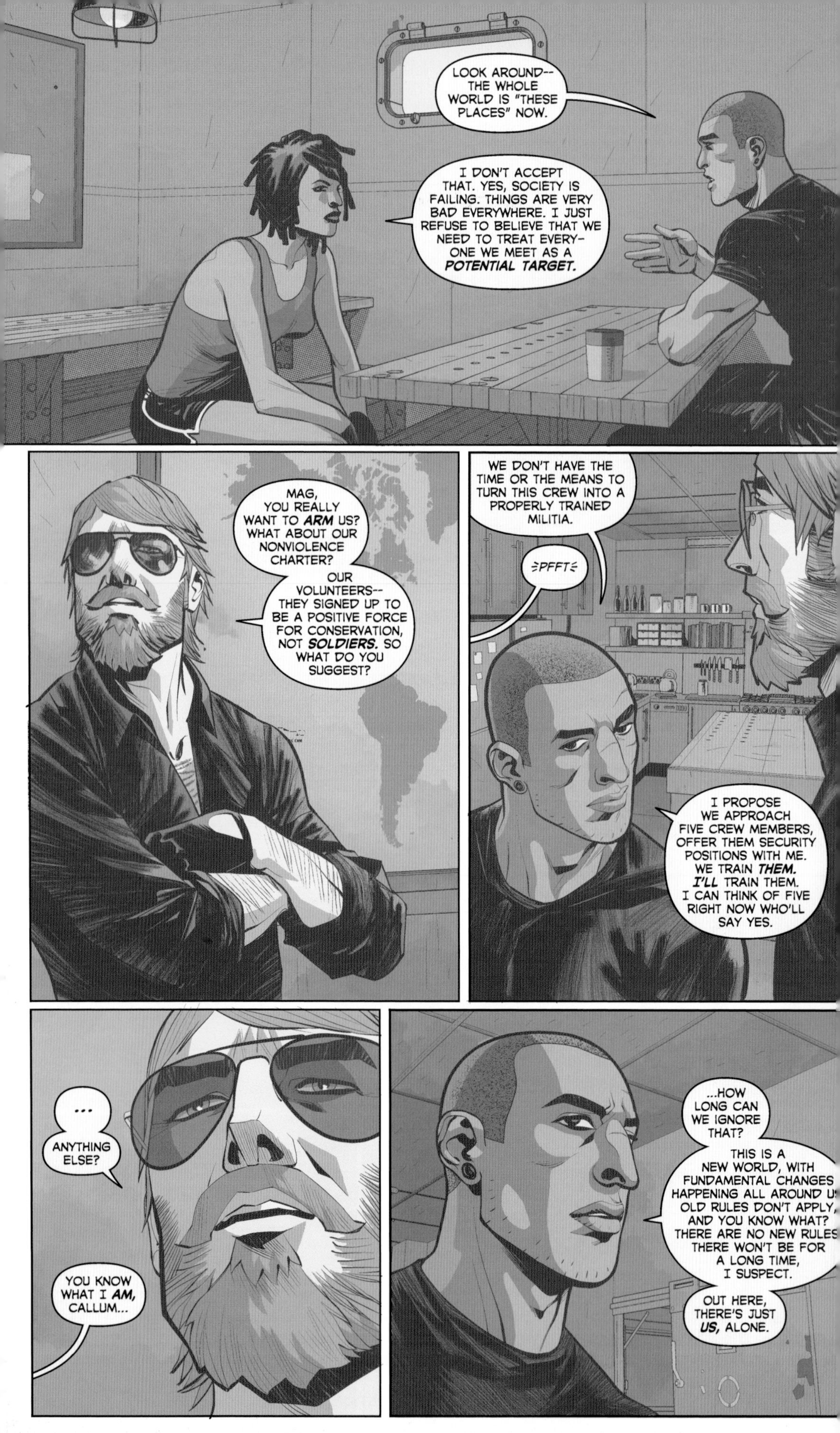
LOOK AROUND-- THE WHOLE WORLD IS "THESE PLACES" NOW.
I DON'T ACCEPT THAT. YES, SOCIETY IS FAILING. THINGS ARE VERY BAD EVERYWHERE. I JUST REFUSE TO BELIEVE THAT WE NEED TO TREAT EVERY-ONE WE MEET AS A POTENTIAL TARGET.
MAG, YOU REALLY WANT TO ARM US? WHAT ABOUT OUR NONVIOLENCE CHARTER?
OUR VOLUNTEERS-- THEY SIGNED UP TO BE A POSITIVE FORCE FOR CONSERVATION, NOT SOLDIERS. SO WHAT DO YOU SUGGEST?
WE DON'T HAVE THE TIME OR THE MEANS TO TURN THIS CREW INTO A PROPERLY TRAINED MILITIA.
PFFT
I PROPOSE WE APPROACH FIVE CREW MEMBERS, OFFER THEM SECURITY POSITIONS WITH ME. WE TRAIN THEM. I'LL TRAIN THEM. I CAN THINK OF FIVE RIGHT NOW WHO'LL SAY YES.
...
ANYTHING ELSE?
YOU KNOW WHAT I AM, CALLUM...
...HOW LONG CAN WE IGNORE THAT?
THIS IS A NEW WORLD, WITH FUNDAMENTAL CHANGES HAPPENING ALL AROUND US. OLD RULES DON'T APPLY, AND YOU KNOW WHAT? THERE ARE NO NEW RULES. THERE WON'T BE FOR A LONG TIME, I SUSPECT.
OUT HERE, THERE'S JUST US, ALONE.

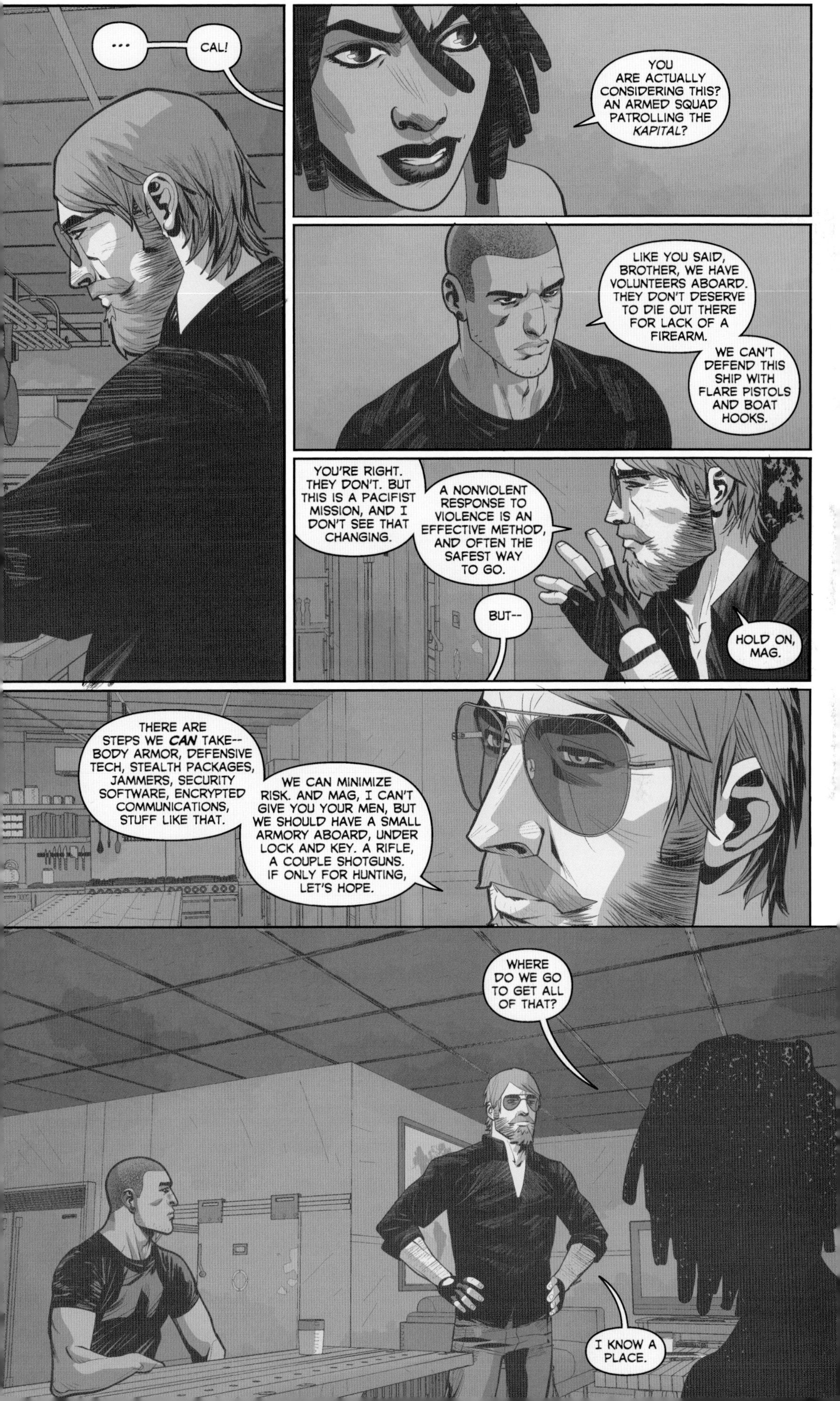
...
CAL!
YOU ARE ACTUALLY CONSIDERING THIS? AN ARMED SQUAD PATROLLING THE *KAPITAL*?
LIKE YOU SAID, BROTHER, WE HAVE VOLUNTEERS ABOARD. THEY DON'T DESERVE TO DIE OUT THERE FOR LACK OF A FIREARM.
WE CAN'T DEFEND THIS SHIP WITH FLARE PISTOLS AND BOAT HOOKS.
YOU'RE RIGHT. THEY DON'T. BUT THIS IS A PACIFIST MISSION, AND I DON'T SEE THAT CHANGING.
A NONVIOLENT RESPONSE TO VIOLENCE IS AN EFFECTIVE METHOD, AND OFTEN THE SAFEST WAY TO GO.
BUT--
HOLD ON, MAG.
THERE ARE STEPS WE ***CAN*** TAKE--BODY ARMOR, DEFENSIVE TECH, STEALTH PACKAGES, JAMMERS, SECURITY SOFTWARE, ENCRYPTED COMMUNICATIONS, STUFF LIKE THAT.
WE CAN MINIMIZE RISK. AND MAG, I CAN'T GIVE YOU YOUR MEN, BUT WE SHOULD HAVE A SMALL ARMORY ABOARD, UNDER LOCK AND KEY. A RIFLE, A COUPLE SHOTGUNS. IF ONLY FOR HUNTING, LET'S HOPE.
WHERE DO WE GO TO GET ALL OF THAT?
I KNOW A PLACE.

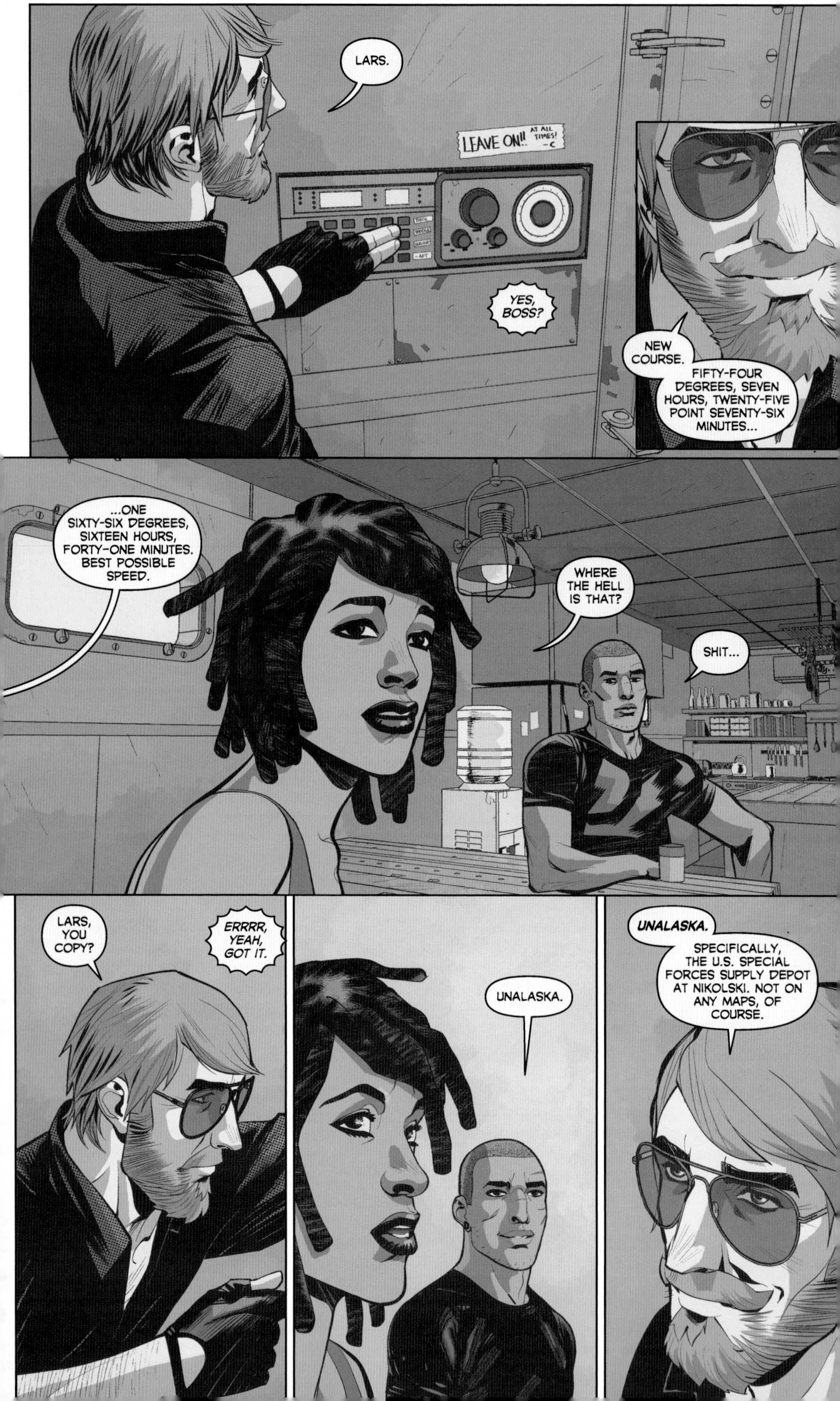
LARS.
LEAVE ON!! AT ALL TIMES! -C
YES, BOSS?
NEW COURSE.
FIFTY-FOUR DEGREES, SEVEN HOURS, TWENTY-FIVE POINT SEVENTY-SIX MINUTES...
...ONE SIXTY-SIX DEGREES, SIXTEEN HOURS, FORTY-ONE MINUTES. BEST POSSIBLE SPEED.
WHERE THE HELL IS THAT?
SHIT...
LARS, YOU COPY?
ERRRR, YEAH, GOT IT.
UNALASKA.
UNALASKA.
SPECIFICALLY, THE U.S. SPECIAL FORCES SUPPLY DEPOT AT NIKOLSKI. NOT ON ANY MAPS, OF COURSE.

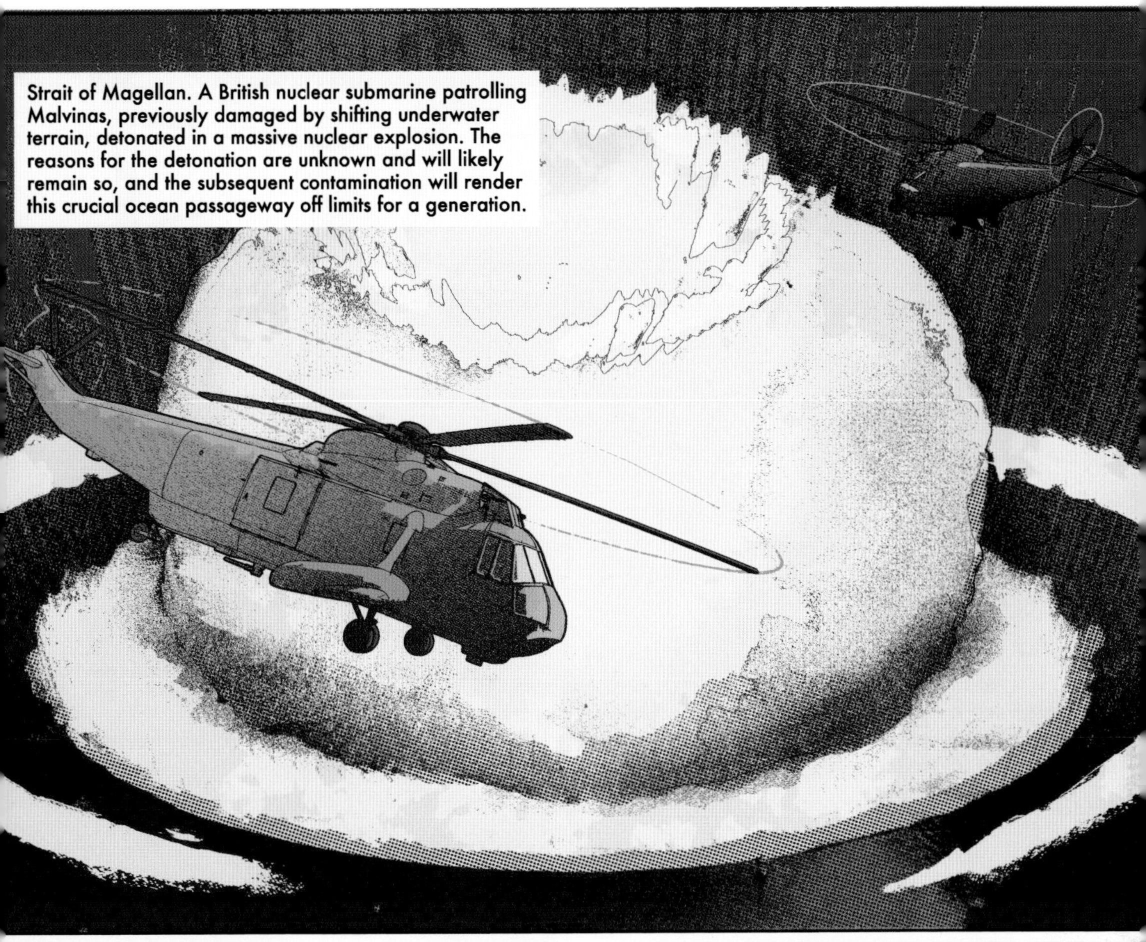
Strait of Magellan. A British nuclear submarine patrolling Malvinas, previously damaged by shifting underwater terrain, detonated in a massive nuclear explosion. The reasons for the detonation are unknown and will likely remain so, and the subsequent contamination will render this crucial ocean passageway off limits for a generation.

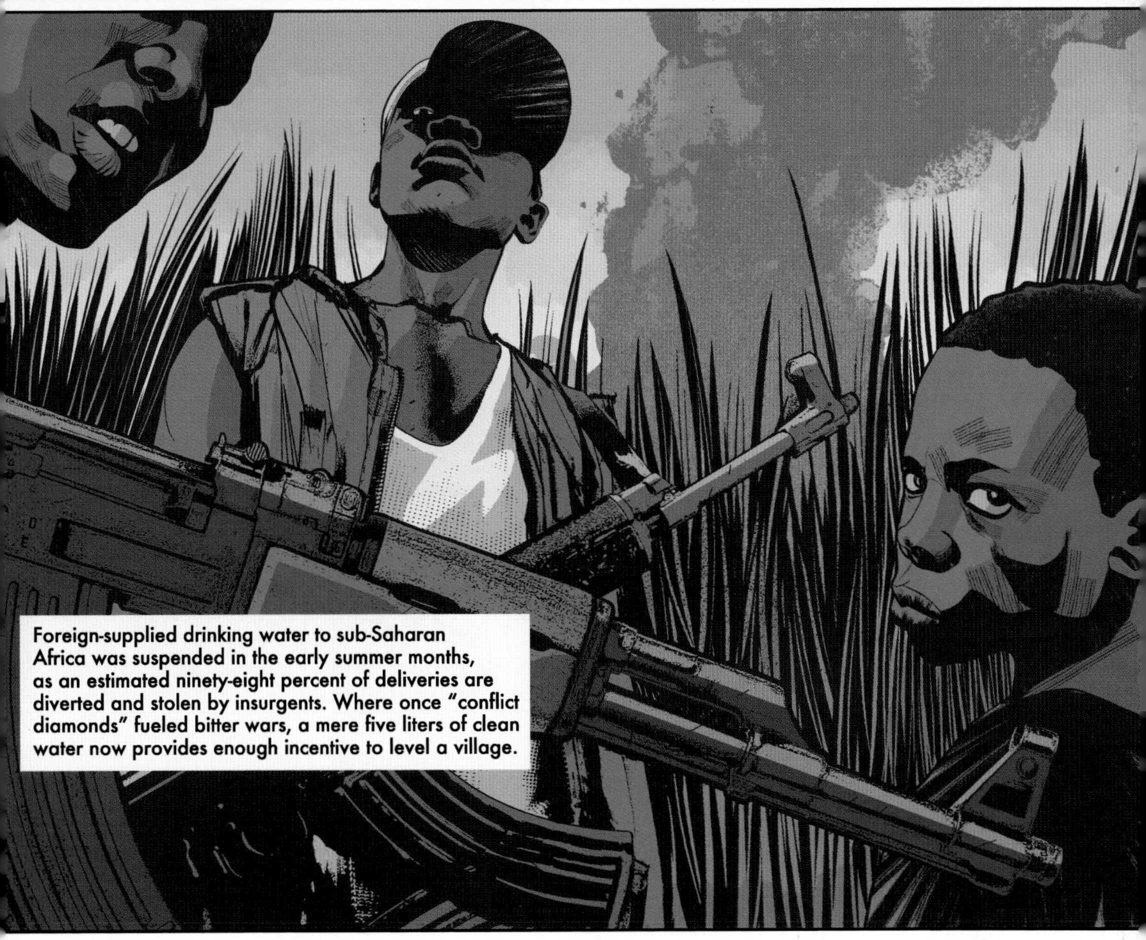
Foreign-supplied drinking water to sub-Saharan Africa was suspended in the early summer months, as an estimated ninety-eight percent of deliveries are diverted and stolen by insurgents. Where once "conflict diamonds" fueled bitter wars, a mere five liters of clean water now provides enough incentive to level a village.

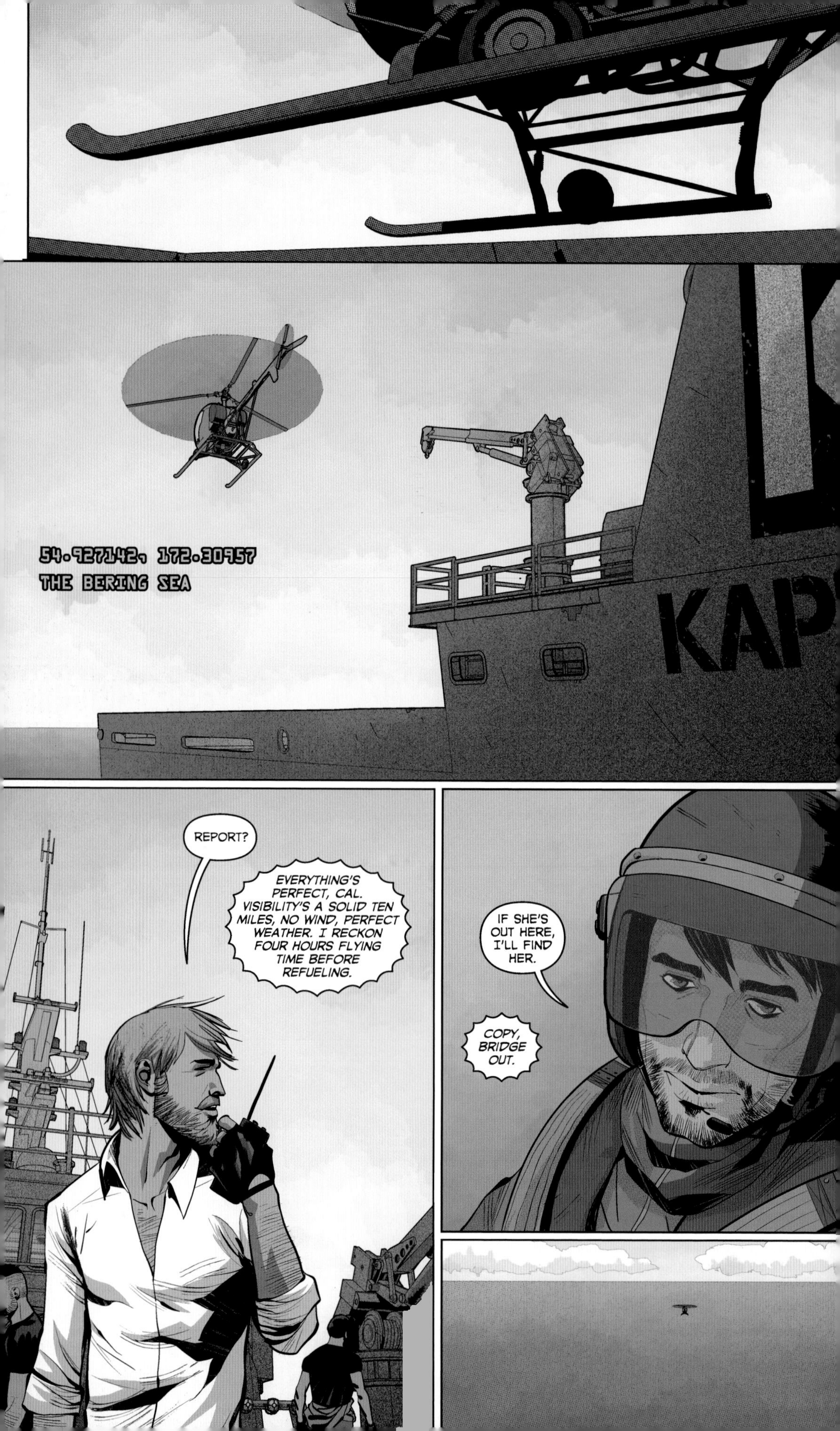

54.927142, 172.30957
THE BERING SEA
KAP
REPORT?
EVERYTHING'S PERFECT, CAL. VISIBILITY'S A SOLID TEN MILES, NO WIND, PERFECT WEATHER. I RECKON FOUR HOURS FLYING TIME BEFORE REFUELING.
IF SHE'S OUT HERE, I'LL FIND HER.
COPY, BRIDGE OUT.

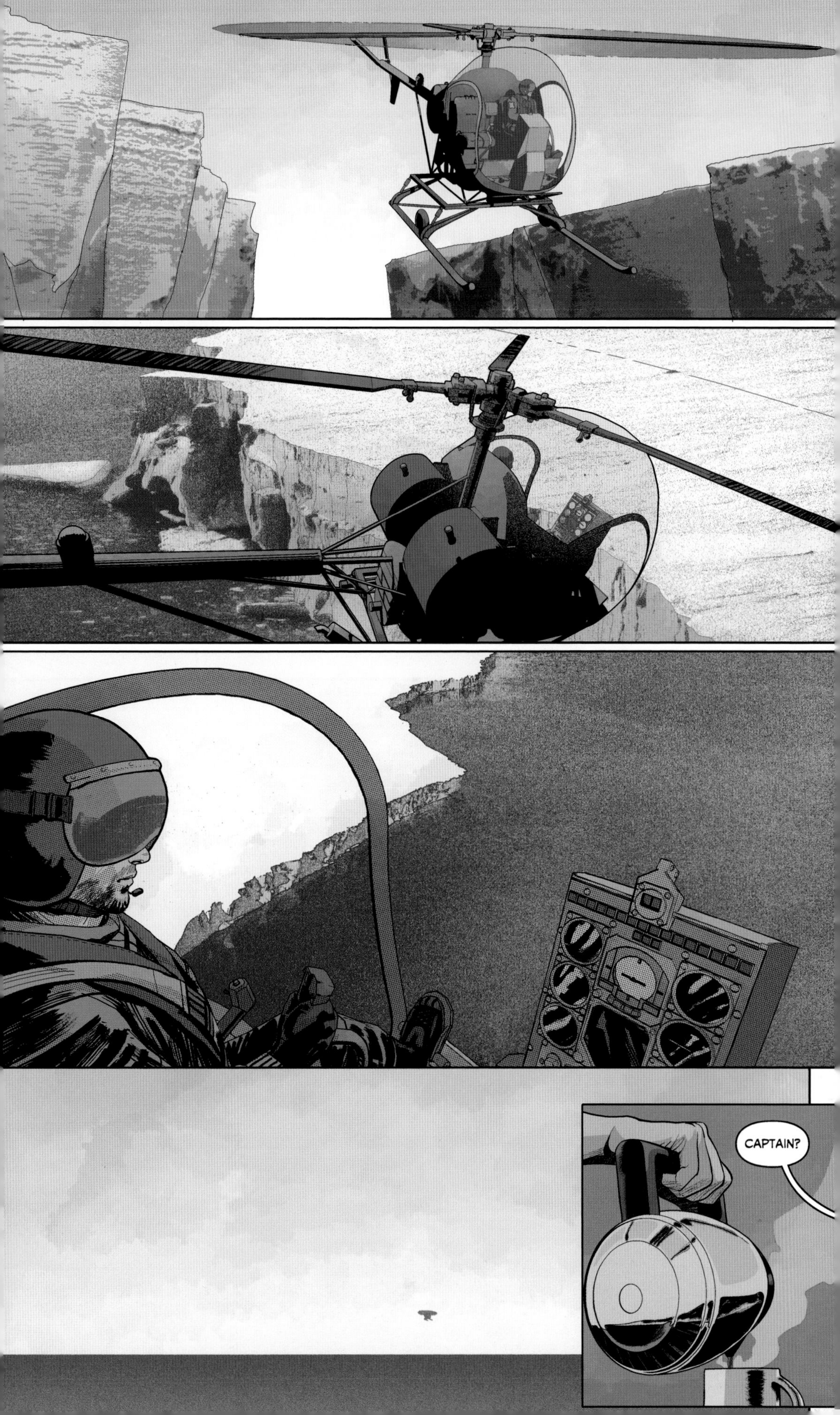
CAPTAIN?

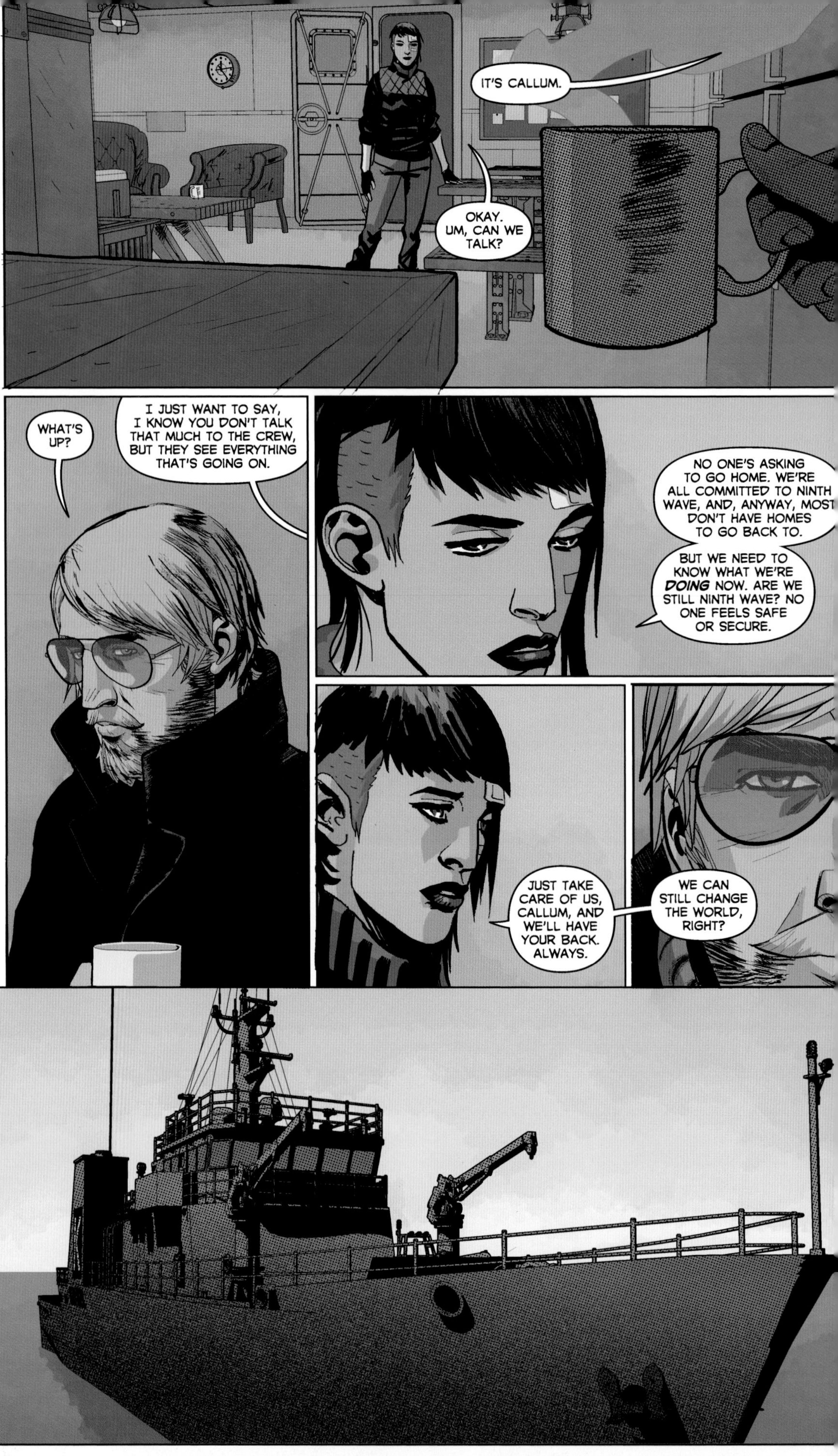
IT'S CALLUM.
OKAY. UM, CAN WE TALK?
WHAT'S UP?
I JUST WANT TO SAY, I KNOW YOU DON'T TALK THAT MUCH TO THE CREW, BUT THEY SEE EVERYTHING THAT'S GOING ON.
NO ONE'S ASKING TO GO HOME. WE'RE ALL COMMITTED TO NINTH WAVE, AND, ANYWAY, MOST DON'T HAVE HOMES TO GO BACK TO.
BUT WE NEED TO KNOW WHAT WE'RE *DOING* NOW. ARE WE STILL NINTH WAVE? NO ONE FEELS SAFE OR SECURE.
JUST TAKE CARE OF US, CALLUM, AND WE'LL HAVE YOUR BACK. ALWAYS.
WE CAN STILL CHANGE THE WORLD, RIGHT?

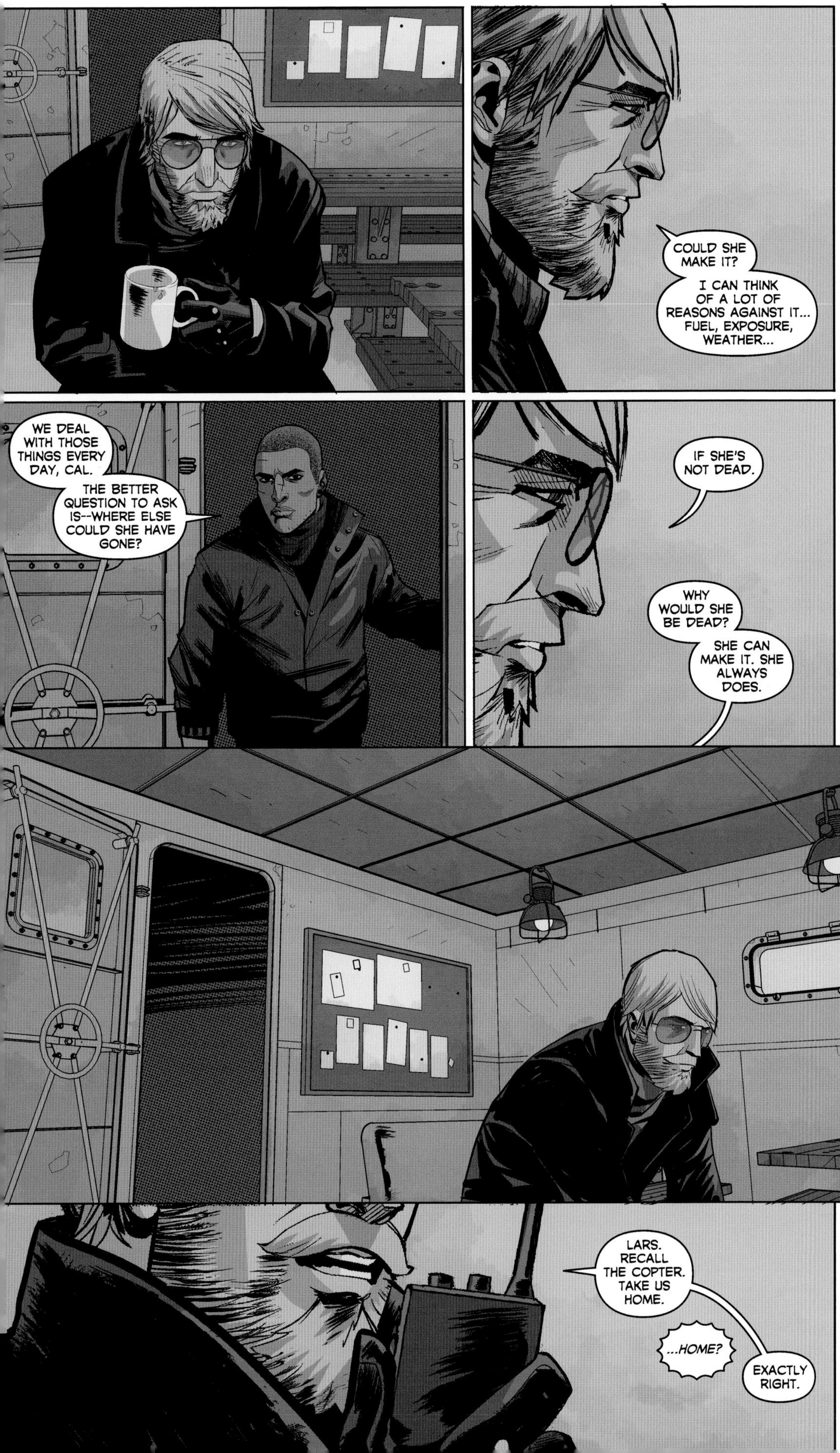
COULD SHE MAKE IT?
I CAN THINK OF A LOT OF REASONS AGAINST IT... FUEL, EXPOSURE, WEATHER...
WE DEAL WITH THOSE THINGS EVERY DAY, CAL.
THE BETTER QUESTION TO ASK IS--WHERE ELSE COULD SHE HAVE GONE?
IF SHE'S NOT DEAD.
WHY WOULD SHE BE DEAD?
SHE CAN MAKE IT. SHE ALWAYS DOES.
LARS. RECALL THE COPTER. TAKE US HOME.
...HOME?
EXACTLY RIGHT.

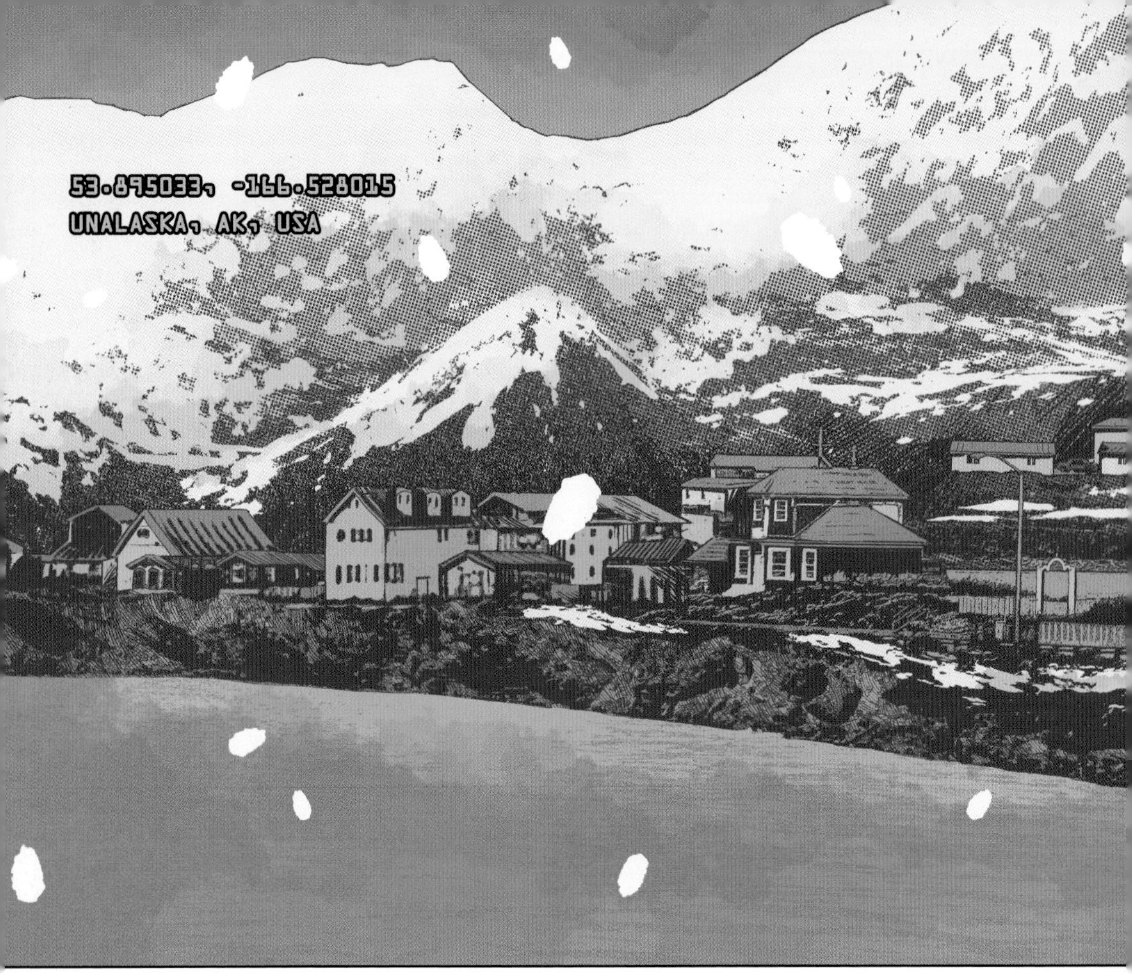
53.895033, -166.528015
UNALASKA, AK, USA

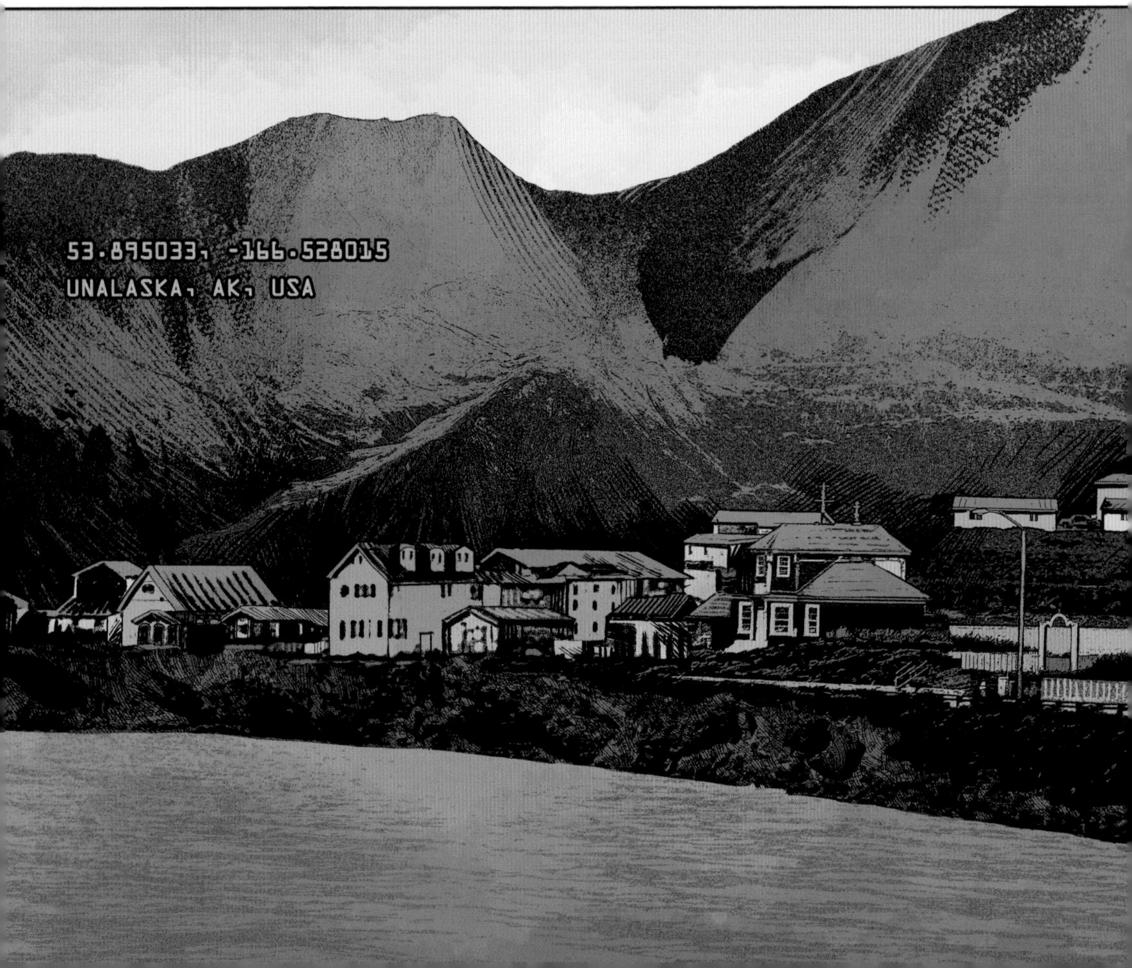
53.895033, -166.528015
UNALASKA, AK, USA

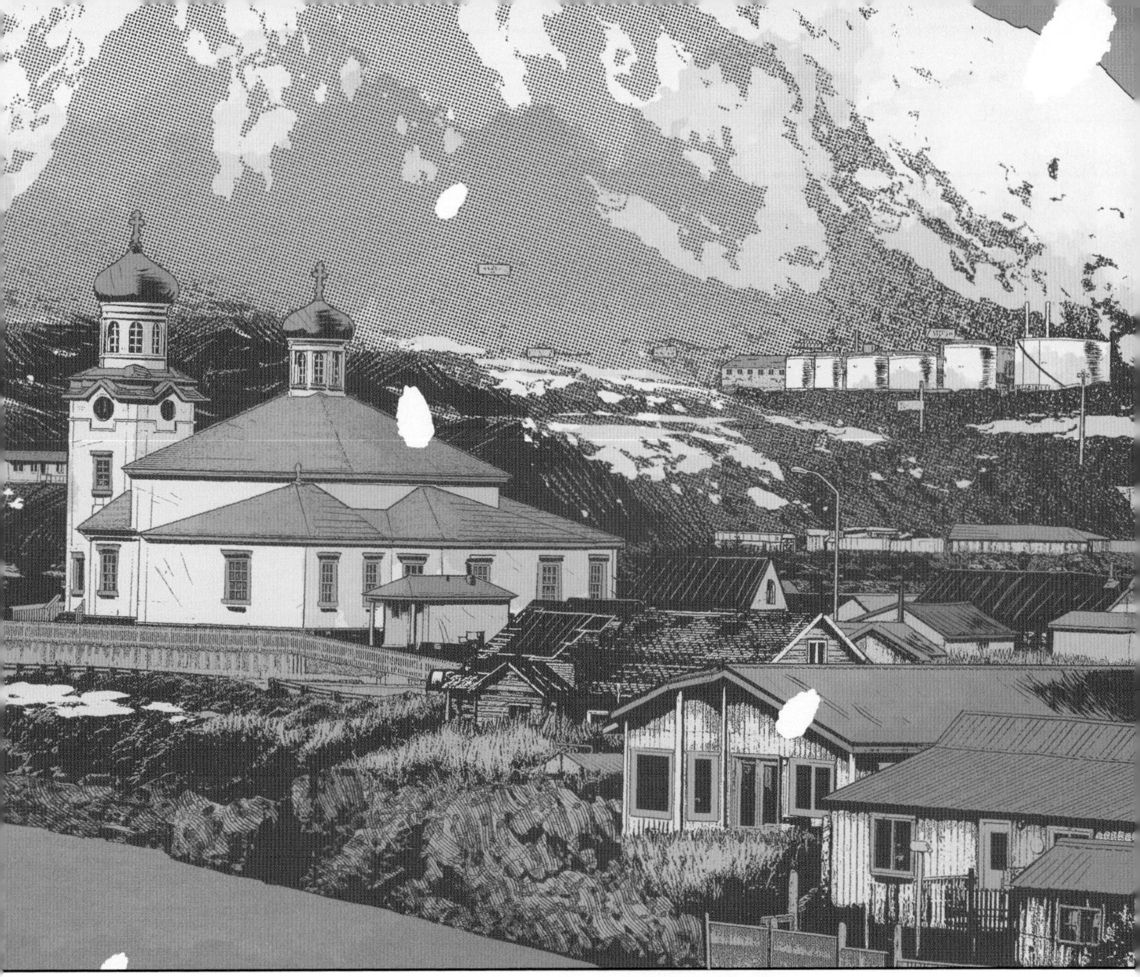
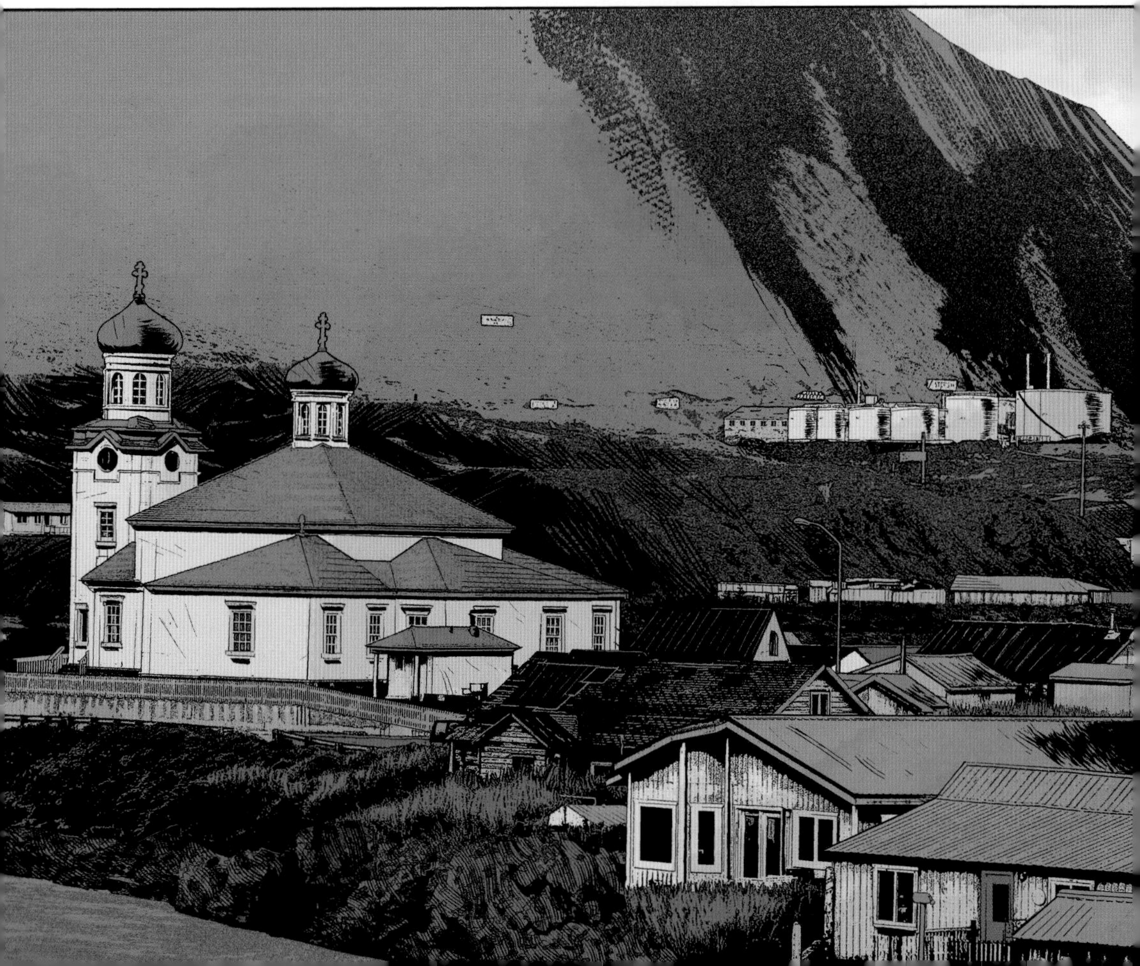

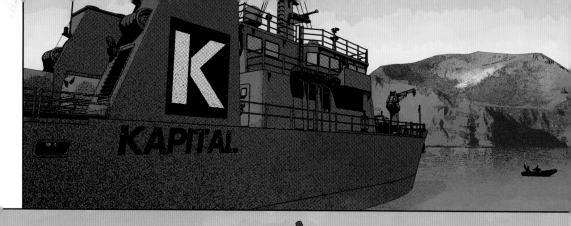

Following weeks of silence, the direct-action group Ninth Wave, currently operating in the Northern Pacific, issued a statement to the world press.

"We are fully functional, and don't see our core mission as changing in a significant way," founder Callum Israel wrote. "Ninth Wave has always been about aggressively challenging abuses of the environment--in particular, protecting the oceans and those who rely upon them.

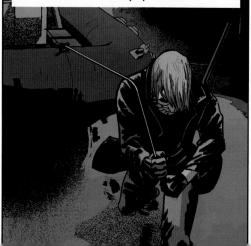

"Looking at that mission statement broadly, very little has in fact changed. I believe our oceans are at their most vulnerable right now.

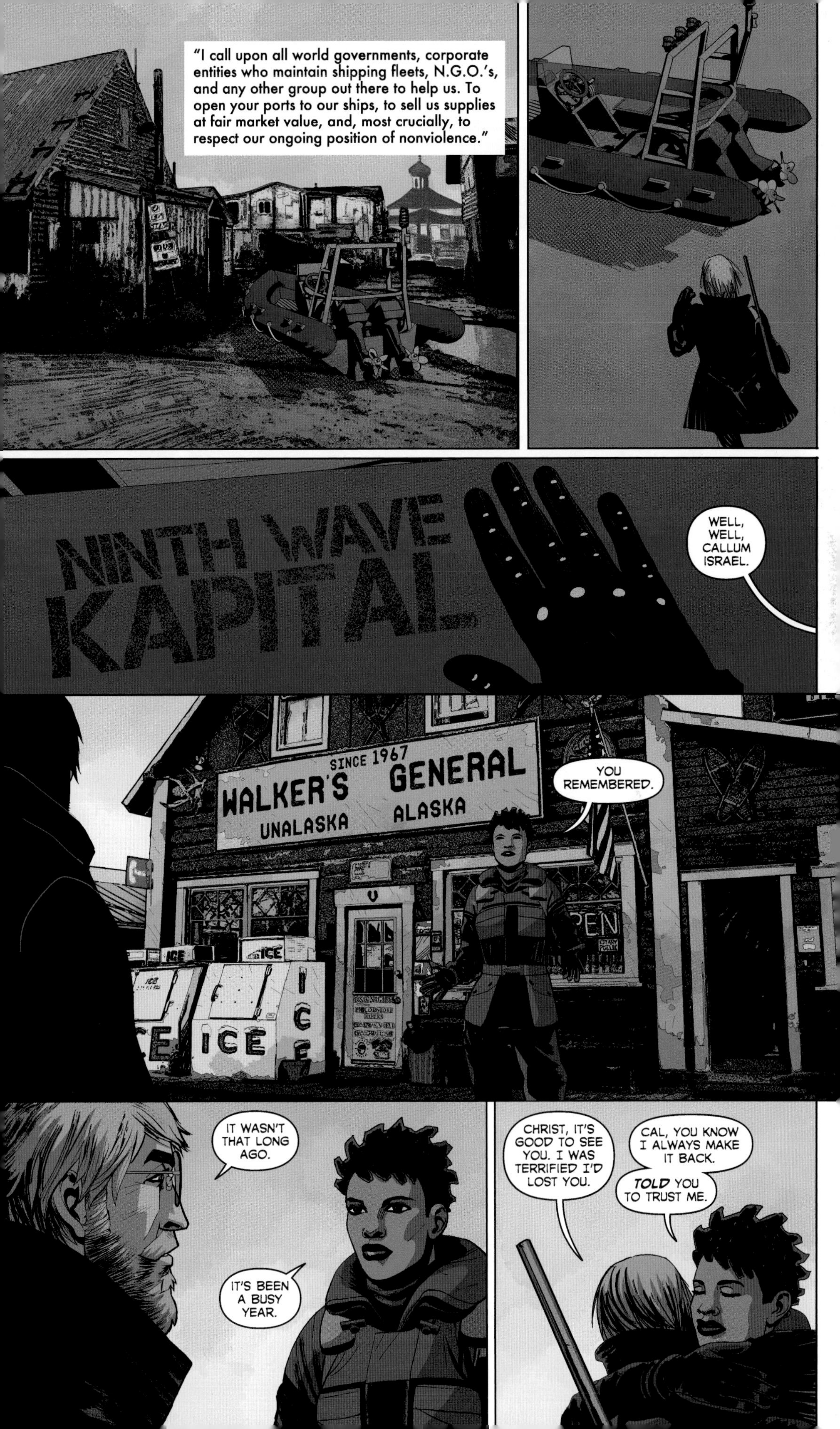
"I call upon all world governments, corporate entities who maintain shipping fleets, N.G.O.'s, and any other group out there to help us. To open your ports to our ships, to sell us supplies at fair market value, and, most crucially, to respect our ongoing position of nonviolence."
NINTH WAVE KAPITAL
WELL, WELL, CALLUM ISRAEL.
SINCE 1967
WALKER'S GENERAL
UNALASKA ALASKA
YOU REMEMBERED.
ICE
ICE
ICE
IT WASN'T THAT LONG AGO.
IT'S BEEN A BUSY YEAR.
CHRIST, IT'S GOOD TO SEE YOU. I WAS TERRIFIED I'D LOST YOU.
CAL, YOU KNOW I ALWAYS MAKE IT BACK.
TOLD YOU TO TRUST ME.

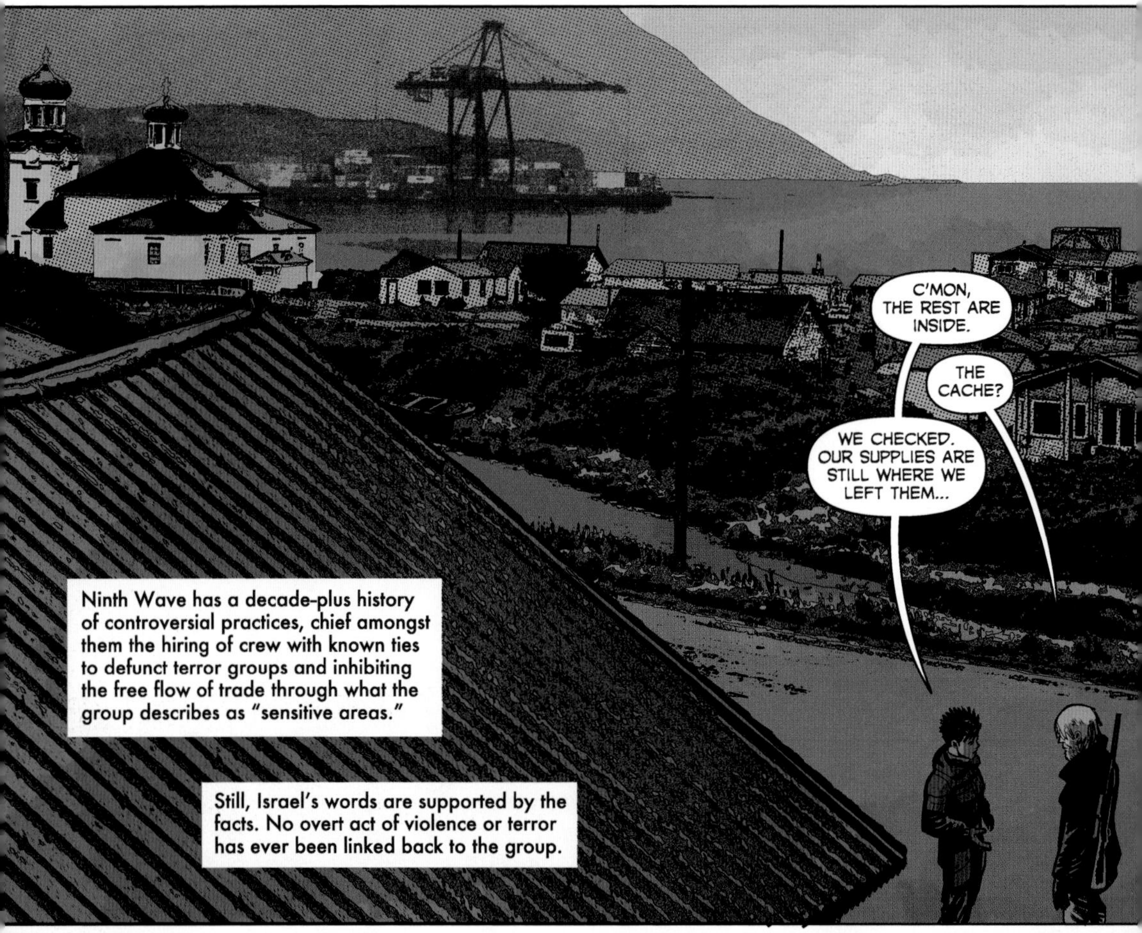
C'MON, THE REST ARE INSIDE.
THE CACHE?
WE CHECKED. OUR SUPPLIES ARE STILL WHERE WE LEFT THEM...
Ninth Wave has a decade-plus history of controversial practices, chief amongst them the hiring of crew with known ties to defunct terror groups and inhibiting the free flow of trade through what the group describes as "sensitive areas."
Still, Israel's words are supported by the facts. No overt act of violence or terror has ever been linked back to the group.

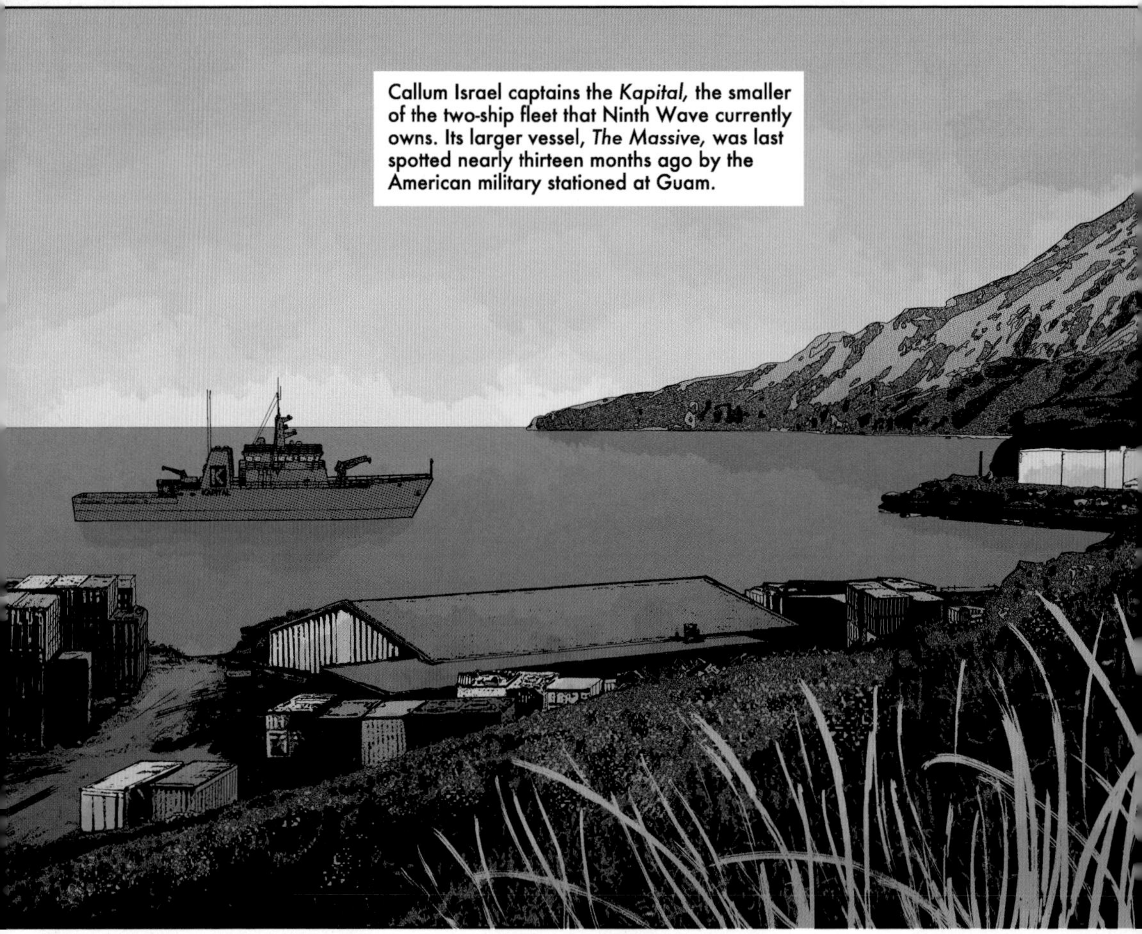
Callum Israel captains the *Kapital,* the smaller of the two-ship fleet that Ninth Wave currently owns. Its larger vessel, *The Massive,* was last spotted nearly thirteen months ago by the American military stationed at Guam.

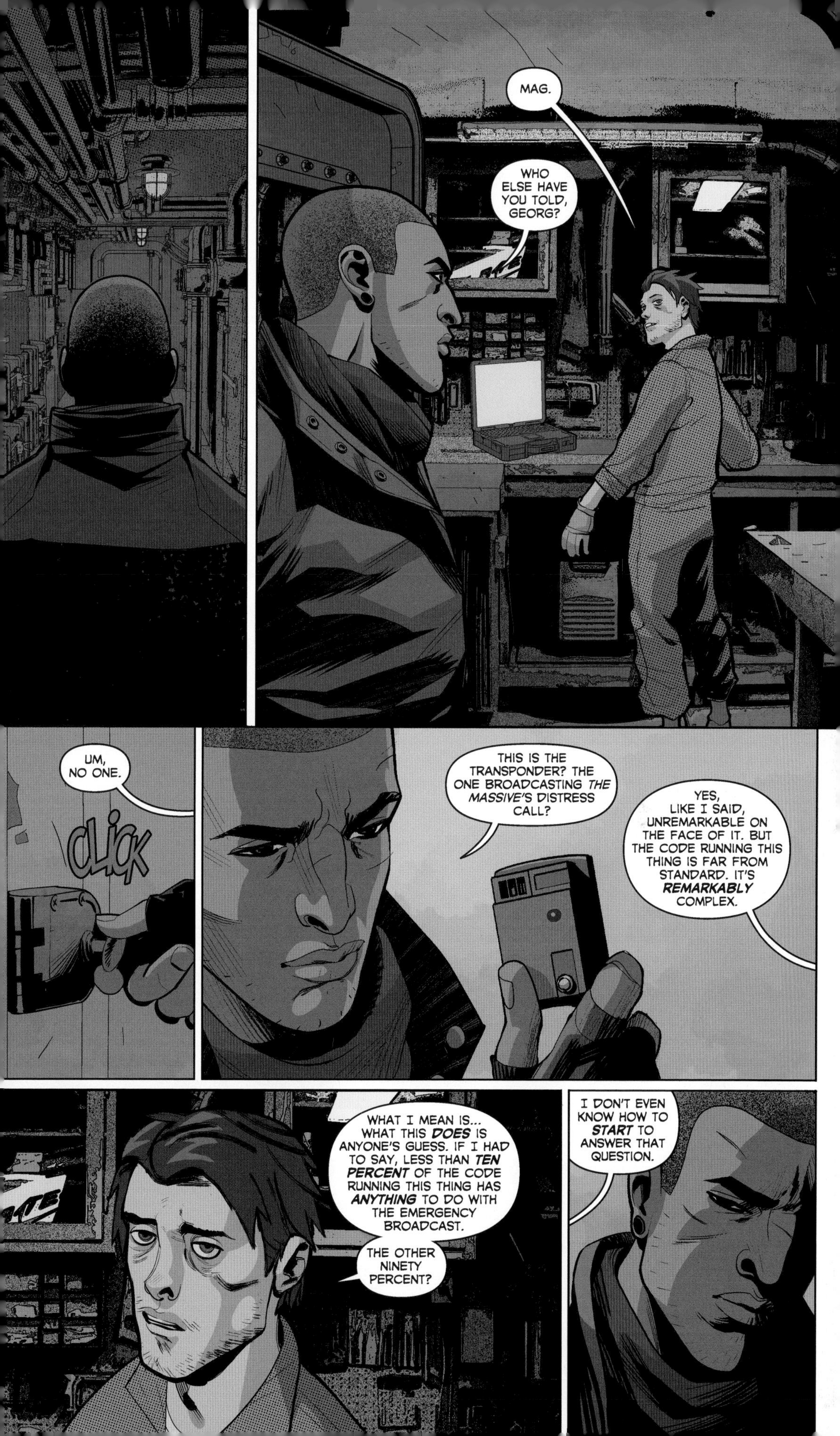

MAG.
WHO ELSE HAVE YOU TOLD, GEORG?
UM, NO ONE.
CLICK
THIS IS THE TRANSPONDER? THE ONE BROADCASTING *THE MASSIVE*'S DISTRESS CALL?
YES, LIKE I SAID, UNREMARKABLE ON THE FACE OF IT. BUT THE CODE RUNNING THIS THING IS FAR FROM STANDARD. IT'S ***REMARKABLY*** COMPLEX.
WHAT I MEAN IS... WHAT THIS ***DOES*** IS ANYONE'S GUESS. IF I HAD TO SAY, LESS THAN ***TEN PERCENT*** OF THE CODE RUNNING THIS THING HAS ***ANYTHING*** TO DO WITH THE EMERGENCY BROADCAST.
THE OTHER NINETY PERCENT?
I DON'T EVEN KNOW HOW TO ***START*** TO ANSWER THAT QUESTION.

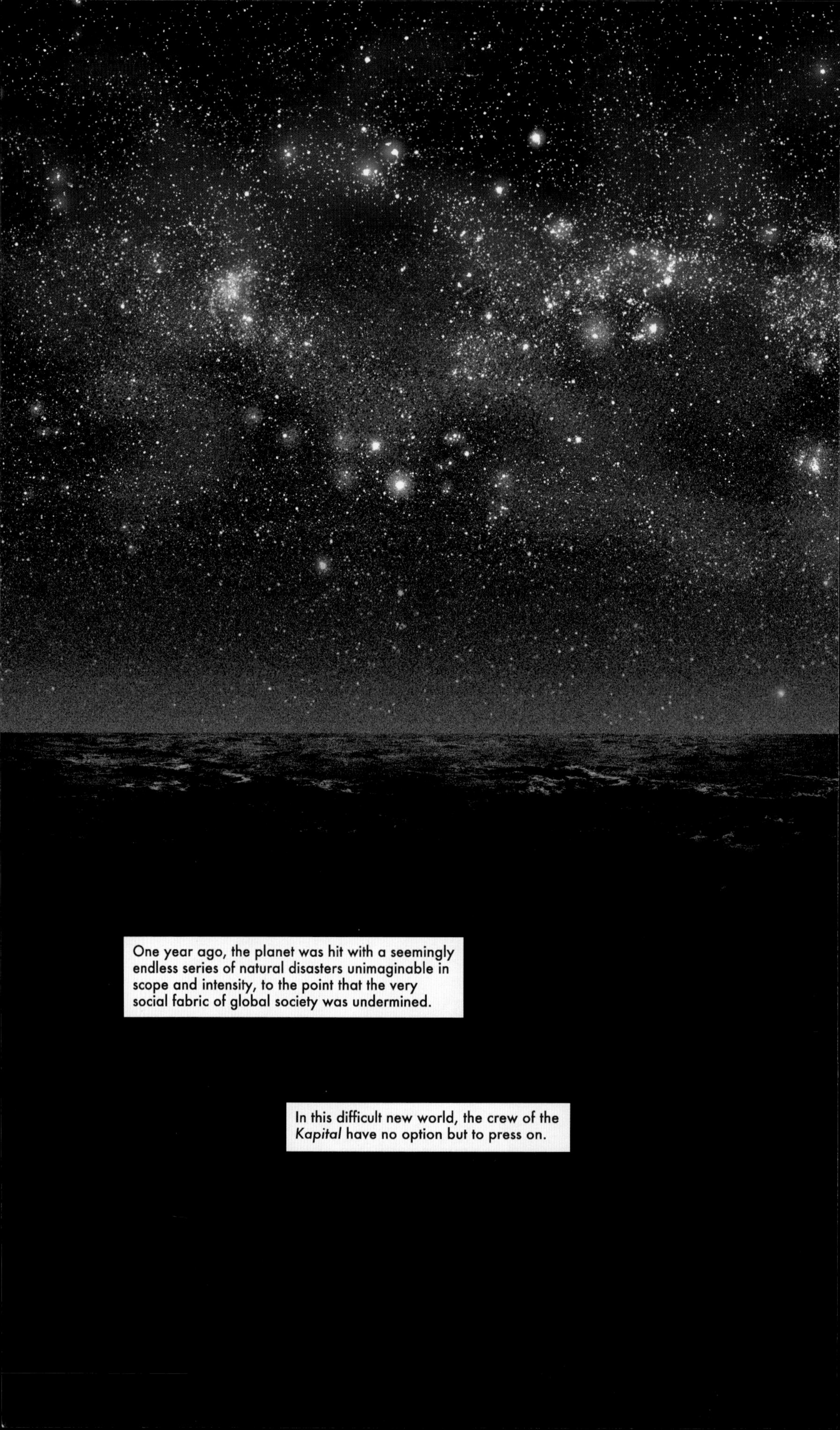
One year ago, the planet was hit with a seemingly endless series of natural disasters unimaginable in scope and intensity, to the point that the very social fabric of global society was undermined.
In this difficult new world, the crew of the *Kapital* have no option but to press on.

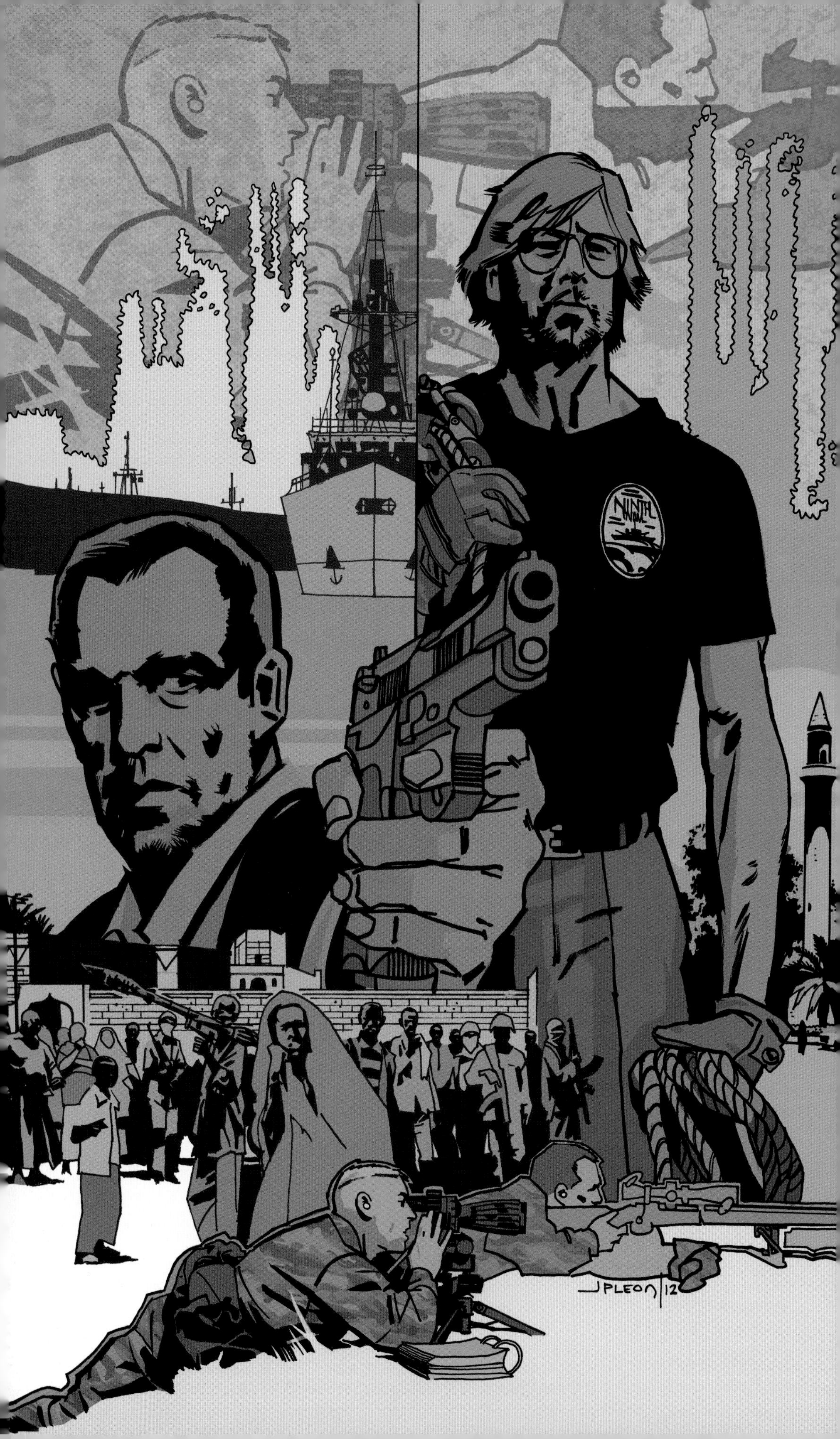
NINTH WAVE
JPLEON 12

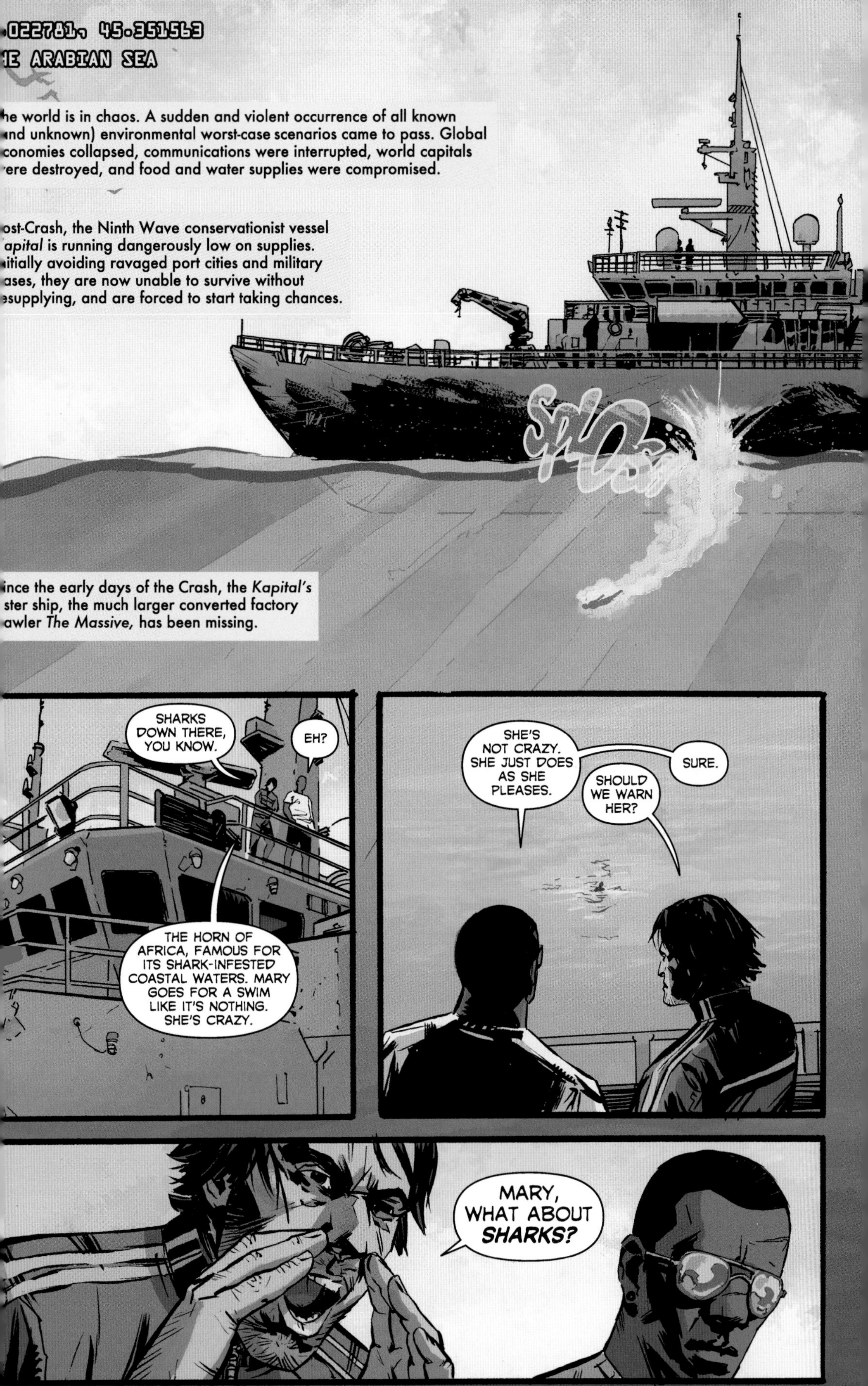

.022781, 45.351563
HE ARABIAN SEA
he world is in chaos. A sudden and violent occurrence of all known
ind unknown) environmental worst-case scenarios came to pass. Global
conomies collapsed, communications were interrupted, world capitals
ere destroyed, and food and water supplies were compromised.
ost-Crash, the Ninth Wave conservationist vessel
apital is running dangerously low on supplies.
itially avoiding ravaged port cities and military
ases, they are now unable to survive without
esupplying, and are forced to start taking chances.
SPLOOSH
ince the early days of the Crash, the Kapital's
ster ship, the much larger converted factory
awler The Massive, has been missing.
SHARKS DOWN THERE, YOU KNOW.
EH?
THE HORN OF AFRICA, FAMOUS FOR ITS SHARK-INFESTED COASTAL WATERS. MARY GOES FOR A SWIM LIKE IT'S NOTHING. SHE'S CRAZY.
SHE'S NOT CRAZY. SHE JUST DOES AS SHE PLEASES.
SURE.
SHOULD WE WARN HER?
MARY, WHAT ABOUT SHARKS?

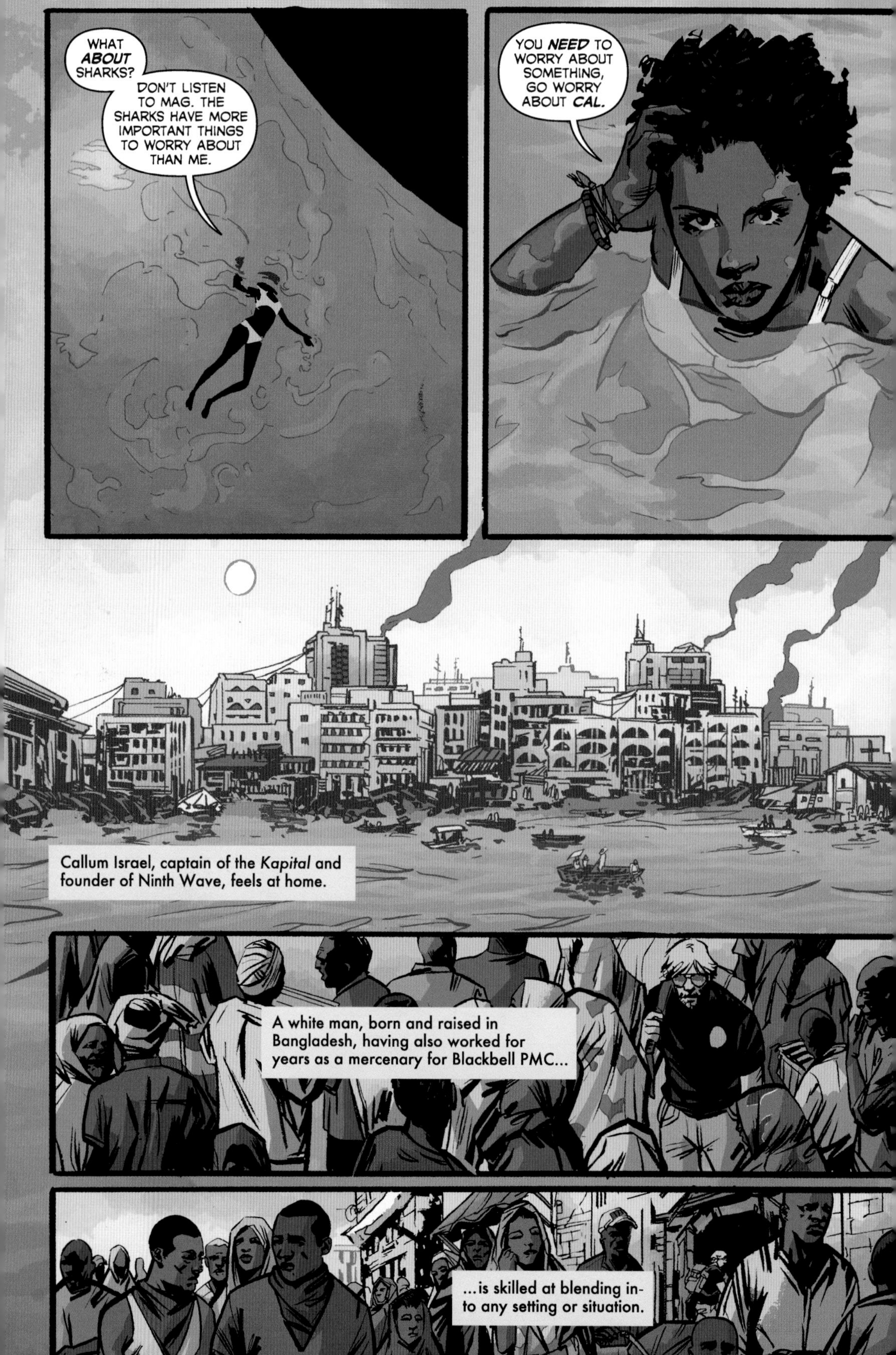
WHAT *ABOUT* SHARKS?
DON'T LISTEN TO MAG. THE SHARKS HAVE MORE IMPORTANT THINGS TO WORRY ABOUT THAN ME.
YOU *NEED* TO WORRY ABOUT SOMETHING, GO WORRY ABOUT *CAL.*
Callum Israel, captain of the *Kapital* and founder of Ninth Wave, feels at home.
A white man, born and raised in Bangladesh, having also worked for years as a mercenary for Blackbell PMC...
...is skilled at blending into any setting or situation.

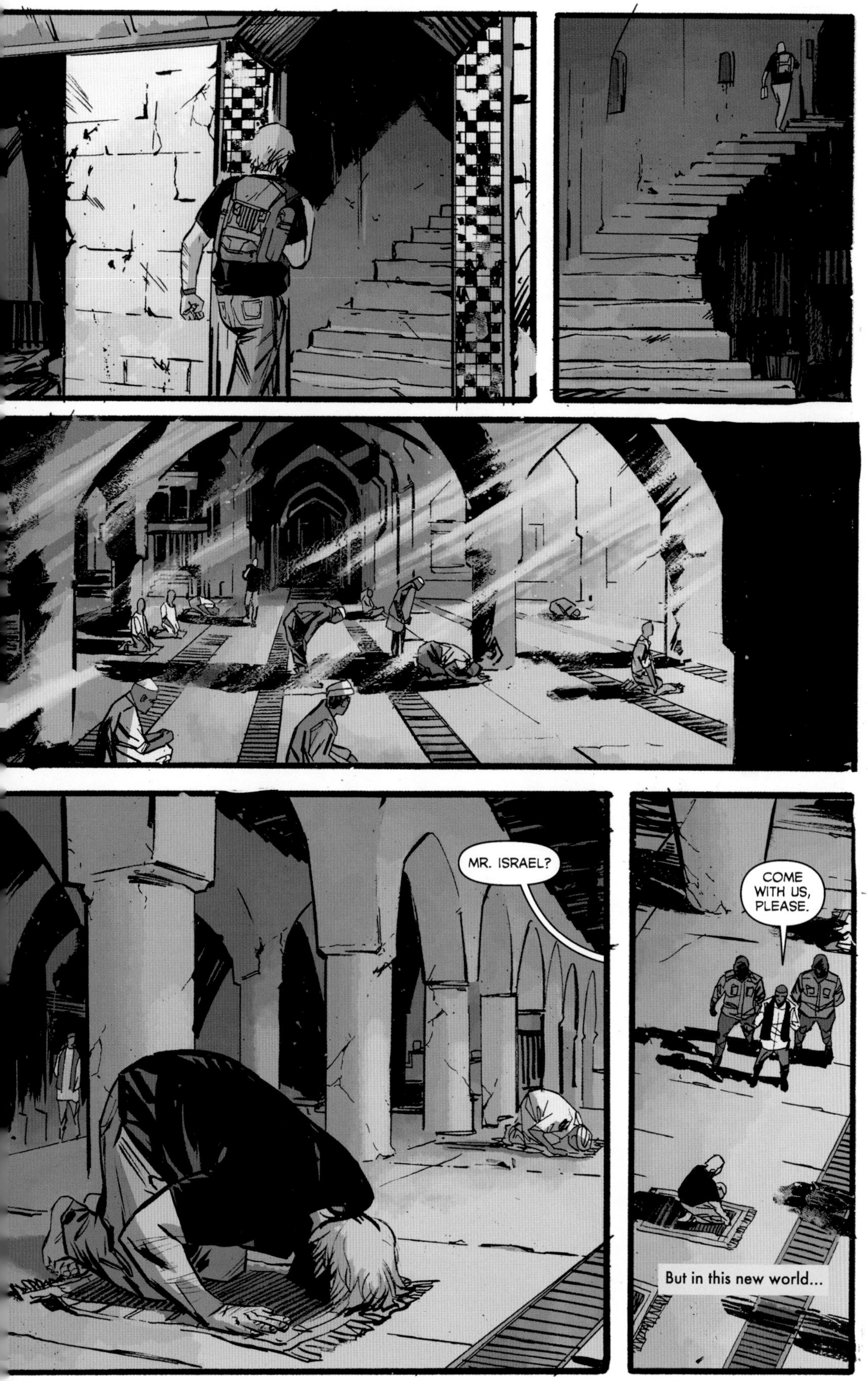
MR. ISRAEL?
COME WITH US, PLEASE.
But in this new world...

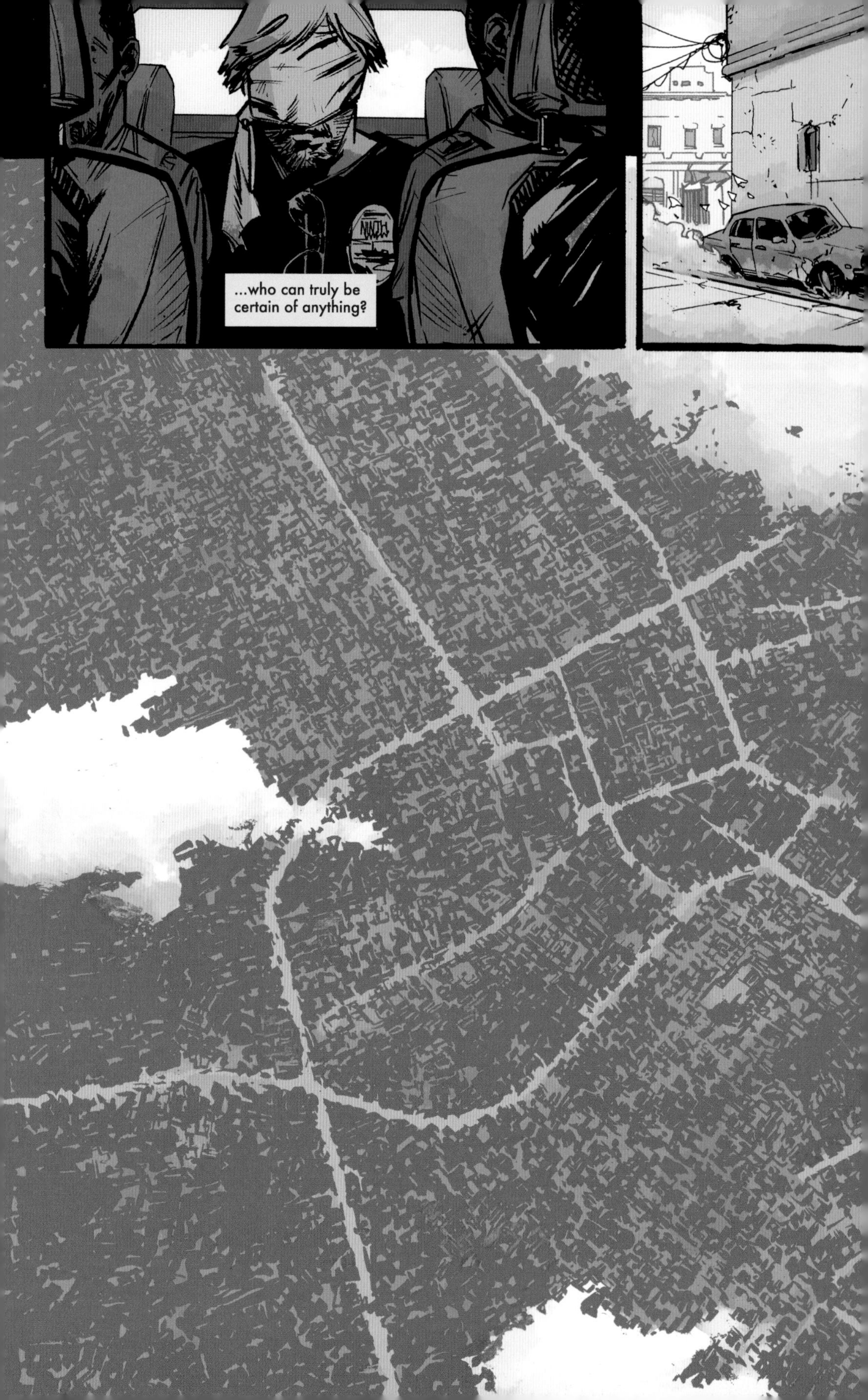
...who can truly be certain of anything?

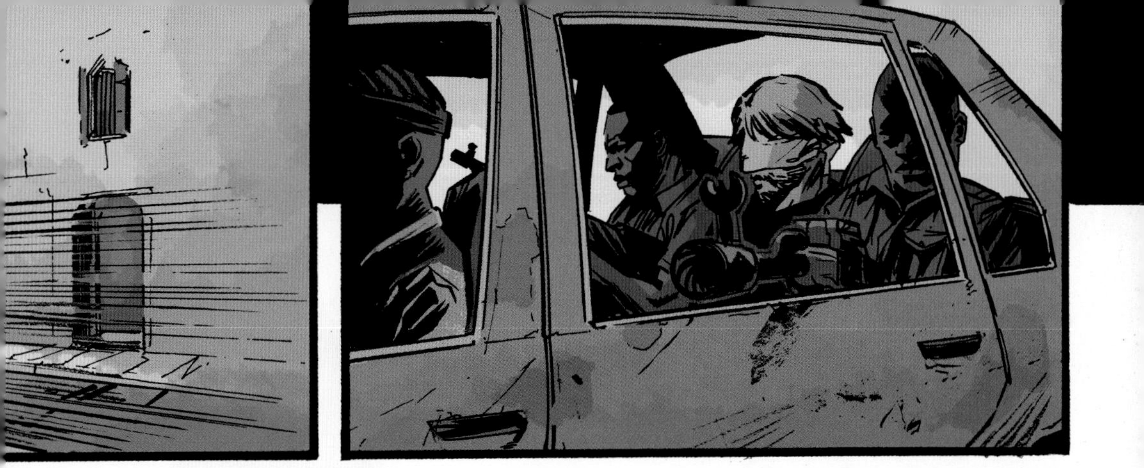

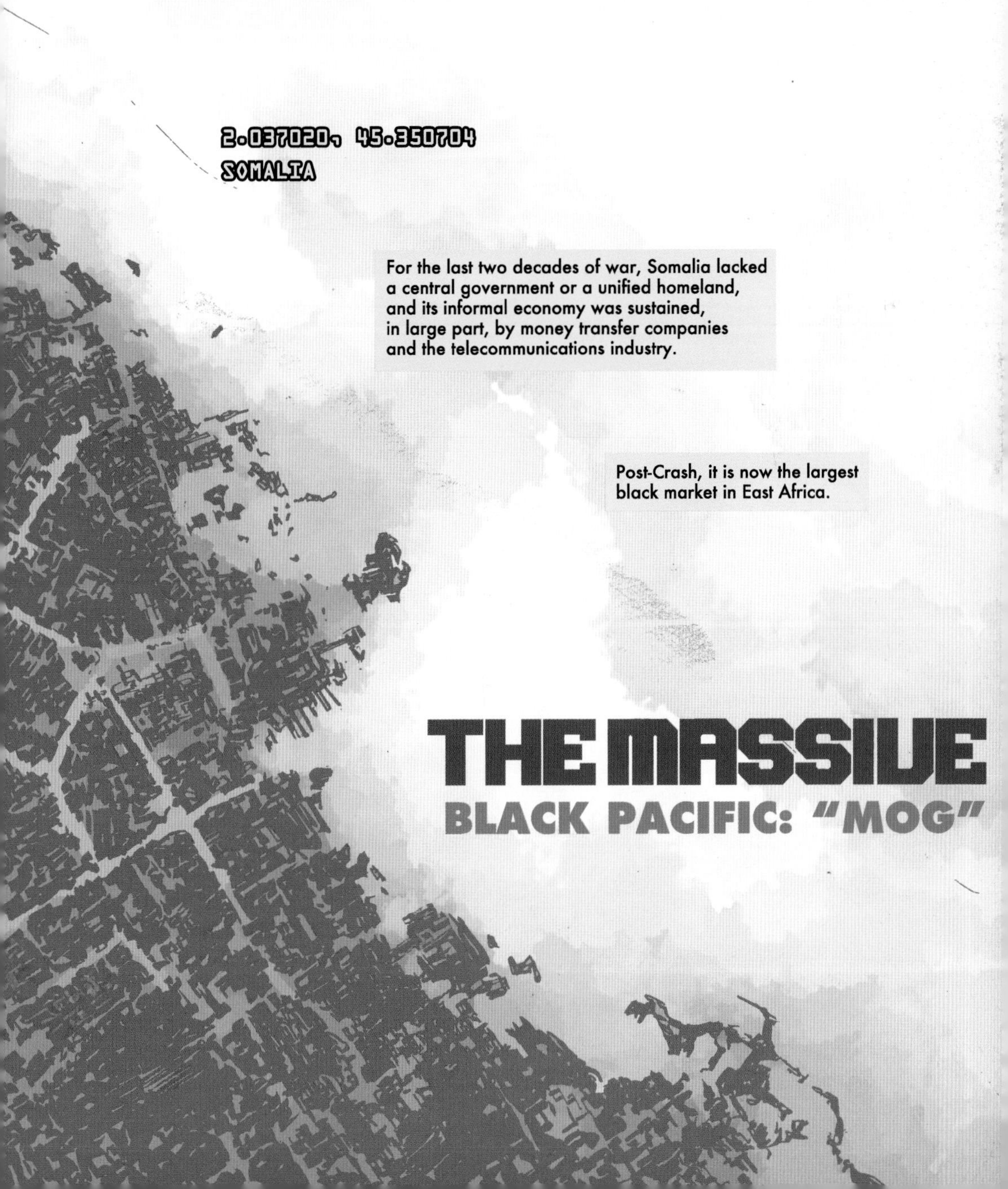
2.037020, 45.350704
SOMALIA
For the last two decades of war, Somalia lacked a central government or a unified homeland, and its informal economy was sustained, in large part, by money transfer companies and the telecommunications industry.
Post-Crash, it is now the largest black market in East Africa.
THE MASSIVE
BLACK PACIFIC: "MOG"

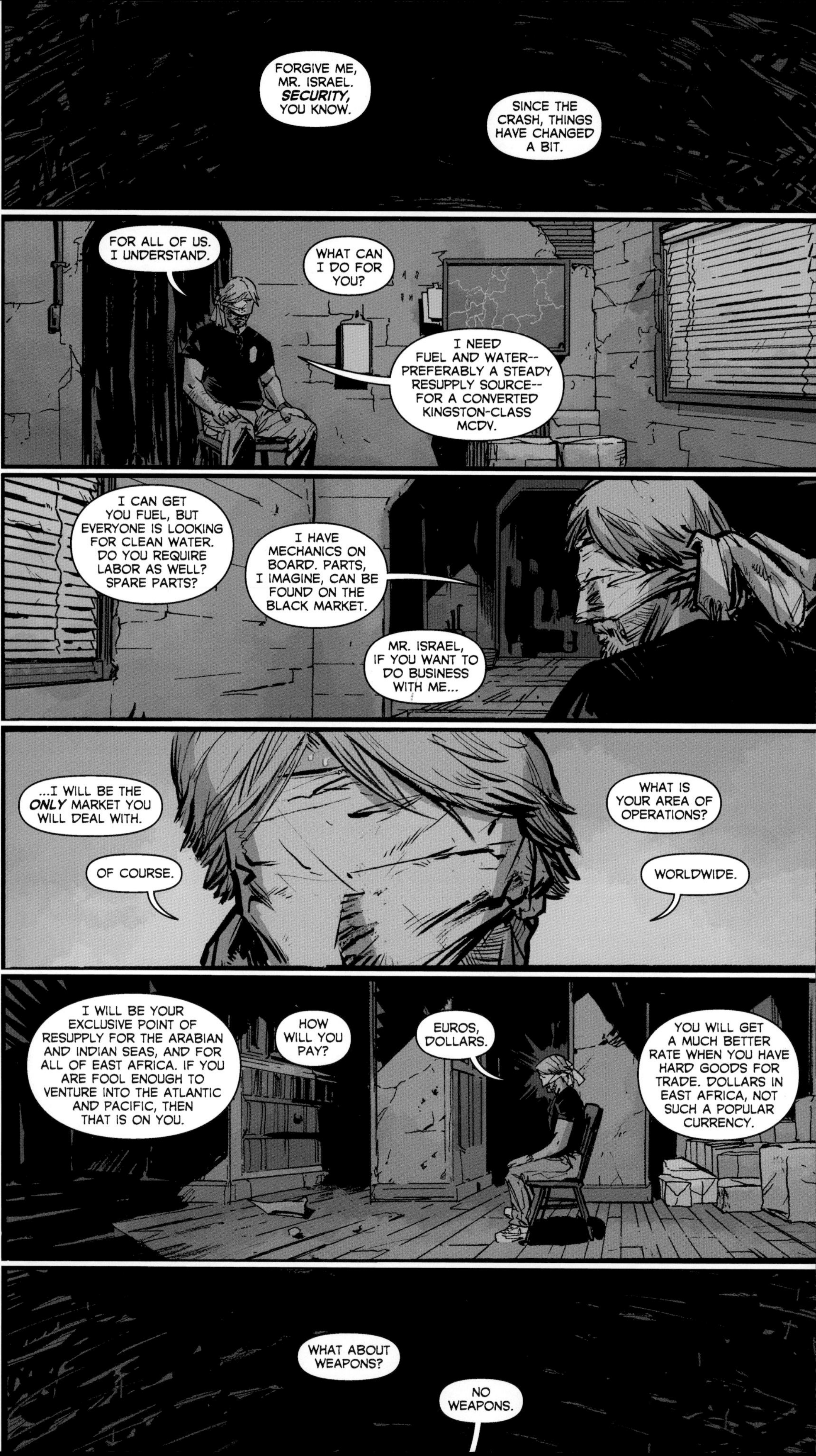
FORGIVE ME, MR. ISRAEL. SECURITY, YOU KNOW.
SINCE THE CRASH, THINGS HAVE CHANGED A BIT.
FOR ALL OF US. I UNDERSTAND.
WHAT CAN I DO FOR YOU?
I NEED FUEL AND WATER-- PREFERABLY A STEADY RESUPPLY SOURCE-- FOR A CONVERTED KINGSTON-CLASS MCDV.
I CAN GET YOU FUEL, BUT EVERYONE IS LOOKING FOR CLEAN WATER. DO YOU REQUIRE LABOR AS WELL? SPARE PARTS?
I HAVE MECHANICS ON BOARD. PARTS, I IMAGINE, CAN BE FOUND ON THE BLACK MARKET.
MR. ISRAEL, IF YOU WANT TO DO BUSINESS WITH ME...
...I WILL BE THE ONLY MARKET YOU WILL DEAL WITH.
OF COURSE.
WHAT IS YOUR AREA OF OPERATIONS?
WORLDWIDE.
I WILL BE YOUR EXCLUSIVE POINT OF RESUPPLY FOR THE ARABIAN AND INDIAN SEAS, AND FOR ALL OF EAST AFRICA. IF YOU ARE FOOL ENOUGH TO VENTURE INTO THE ATLANTIC AND PACIFIC, THEN THAT IS ON YOU.
HOW WILL YOU PAY?
EUROS, DOLLARS.
YOU WILL GET A MUCH BETTER RATE WHEN YOU HAVE HARD GOODS FOR TRADE. DOLLARS IN EAST AFRICA, NOT SUCH A POPULAR CURRENCY.
WHAT ABOUT WEAPONS?
NO WEAPONS.

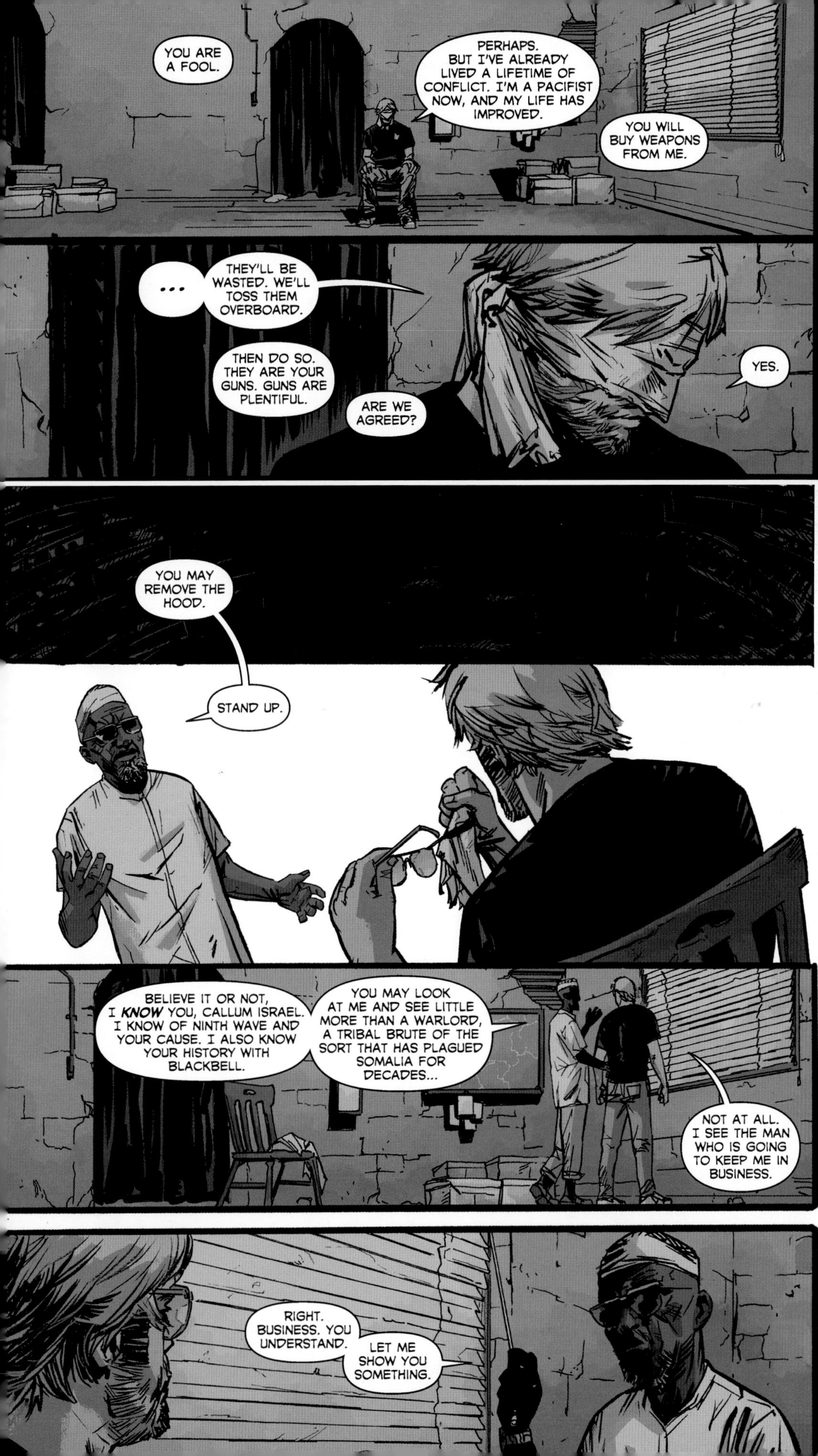
YOU ARE A FOOL.
PERHAPS. BUT I'VE ALREADY LIVED A LIFETIME OF CONFLICT. I'M A PACIFIST NOW, AND MY LIFE HAS IMPROVED.
YOU WILL BUY WEAPONS FROM ME.
...
THEY'LL BE WASTED. WE'LL TOSS THEM OVERBOARD.
THEN DO SO. THEY ARE YOUR GUNS. GUNS ARE PLENTIFUL.
ARE WE AGREED?
YES.
YOU MAY REMOVE THE HOOD.
STAND UP.
BELIEVE IT OR NOT, I ***KNOW*** YOU, CALLUM ISRAEL. I KNOW OF NINTH WAVE AND YOUR CAUSE. I ALSO KNOW YOUR HISTORY WITH BLACKBELL.
YOU MAY LOOK AT ME AND SEE LITTLE MORE THAN A WARLORD, A TRIBAL BRUTE OF THE SORT THAT HAS PLAGUED SOMALIA FOR DECADES...
NOT AT ALL. I SEE THE MAN WHO IS GOING TO KEEP ME IN BUSINESS.
RIGHT. BUSINESS. YOU UNDERSTAND.
LET ME SHOW YOU SOMETHING.

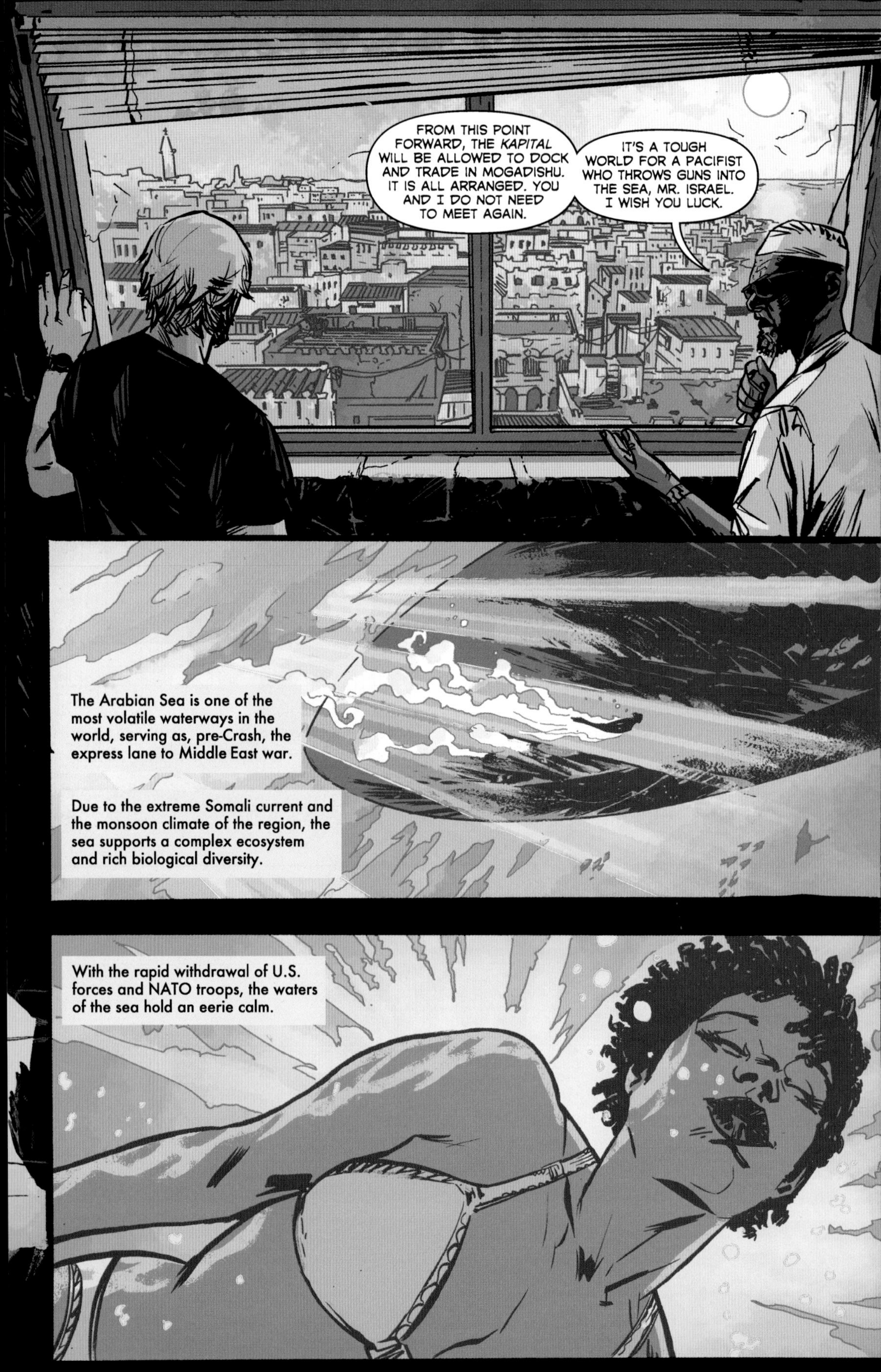
FROM THIS POINT FORWARD, THE *KAPITAL* WILL BE ALLOWED TO DOCK AND TRADE IN MOGADISHU. IT IS ALL ARRANGED. YOU AND I DO NOT NEED TO MEET AGAIN.
IT'S A TOUGH WORLD FOR A PACIFIST WHO THROWS GUNS INTO THE SEA, MR. ISRAEL. I WISH YOU LUCK.
The Arabian Sea is one of the most volatile waterways in the world, serving as, pre-Crash, the express lane to Middle East war.
Due to the extreme Somali current and the monsoon climate of the region, the sea supports a complex ecosystem and rich biological diversity.
With the rapid withdrawal of U.S. forces and NATO troops, the waters of the sea hold an eerie calm.

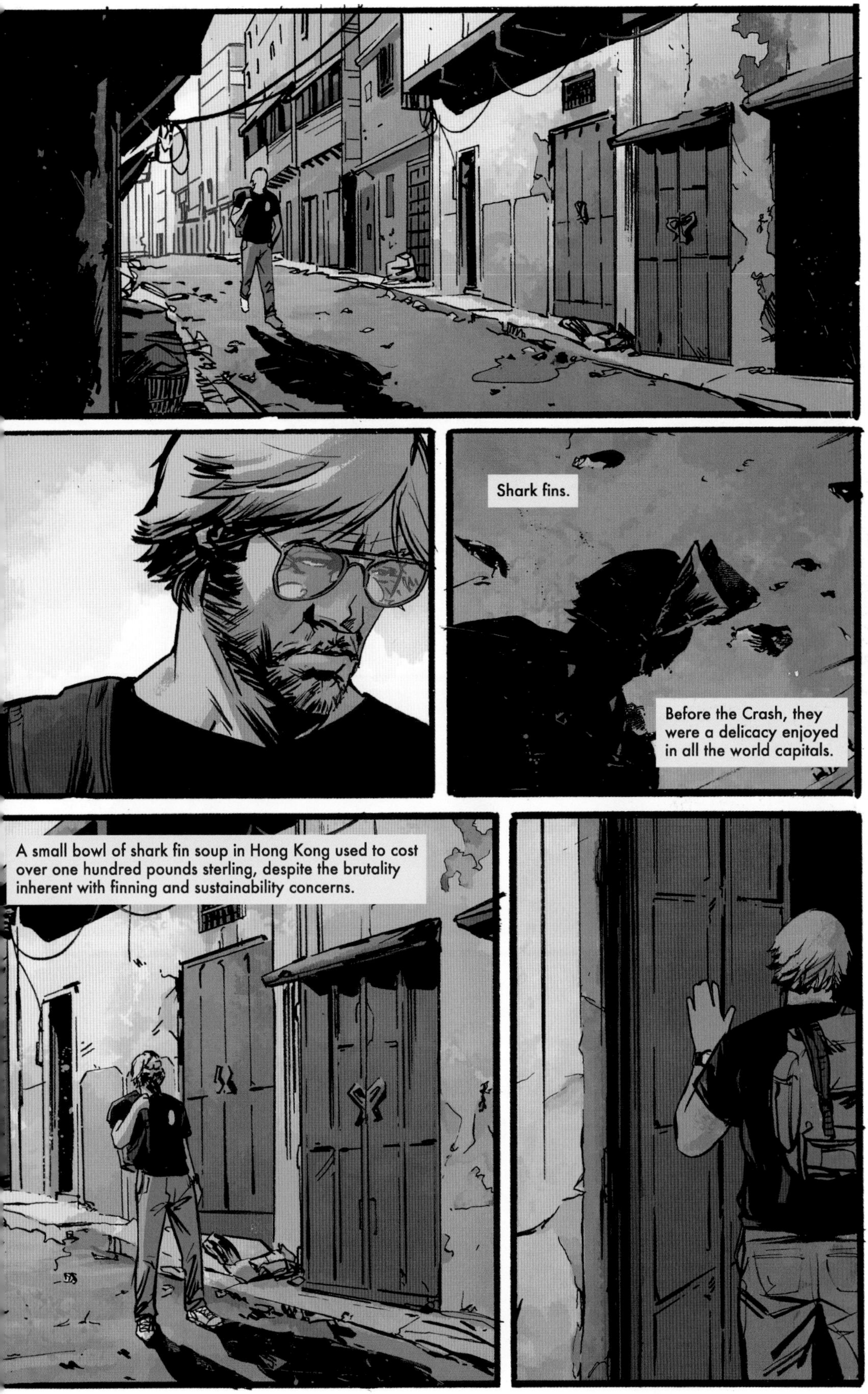
Shark fins.
Before the Crash, they were a delicacy enjoyed in all the world capitals.
A small bowl of shark fin soup in Hong Kong used to cost over one hundred pounds sterling, despite the brutality inherent with finning and sustainability concerns.

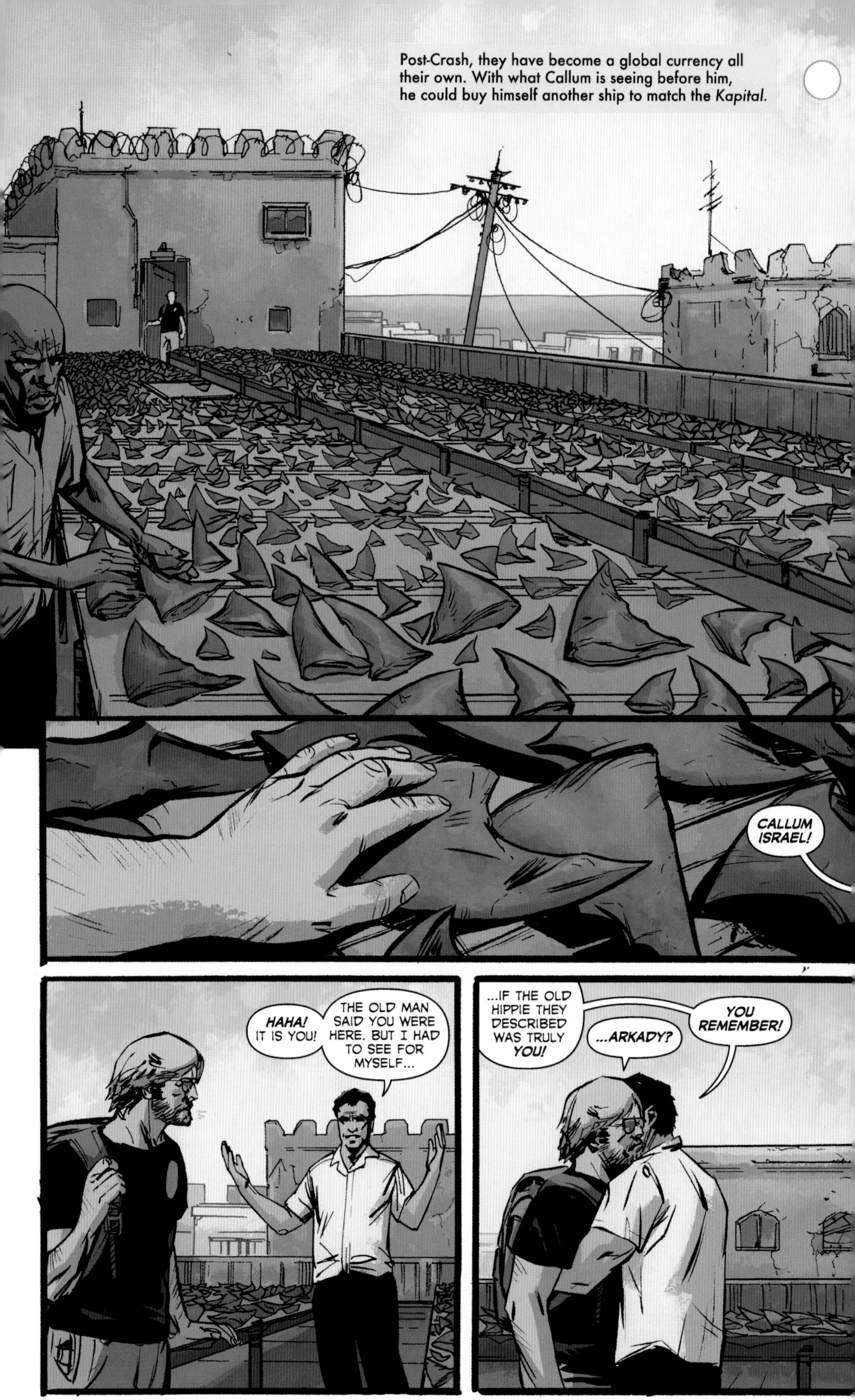
Post-Crash, they have become a global currency all their own. With what Callum is seeing before him, he could buy himself another ship to match the *Kapital*.
CALLUM ISRAEL!
HAHA! IT IS YOU!
THE OLD MAN SAID YOU WERE HERE. BUT I HAD TO SEE FOR MYSELF...
...IF THE OLD HIPPIE THEY DESCRIBED WAS TRULY YOU!
...ARKADY?
YOU REMEMBER!

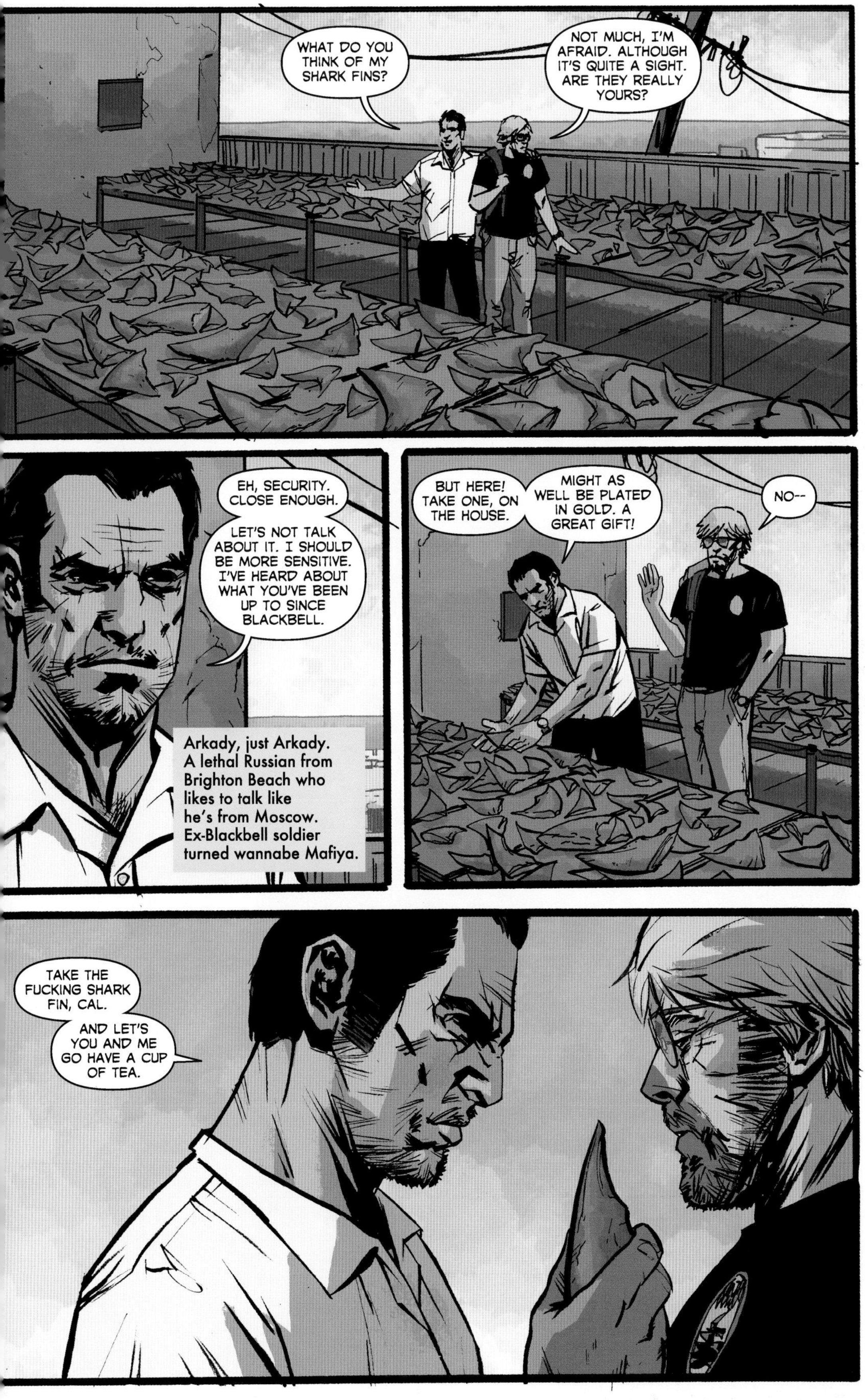
WHAT DO YOU THINK OF MY SHARK FINS?
NOT MUCH, I'M AFRAID. ALTHOUGH IT'S QUITE A SIGHT. ARE THEY REALLY YOURS?
EH, SECURITY. CLOSE ENOUGH.
LET'S NOT TALK ABOUT IT. I SHOULD BE MORE SENSITIVE. I'VE HEARD ABOUT WHAT YOU'VE BEEN UP TO SINCE BLACKBELL.
Arkady, just Arkady. A lethal Russian from Brighton Beach who likes to talk like he's from Moscow. Ex-Blackbell soldier turned wannabe Mafiya.
BUT HERE! TAKE ONE, ON THE HOUSE.
MIGHT AS WELL BE PLATED IN GOLD. A GREAT GIFT!
NO--
TAKE THE FUCKING SHARK FIN, CAL.
AND LET'S YOU AND ME GO HAVE A CUP OF TEA.

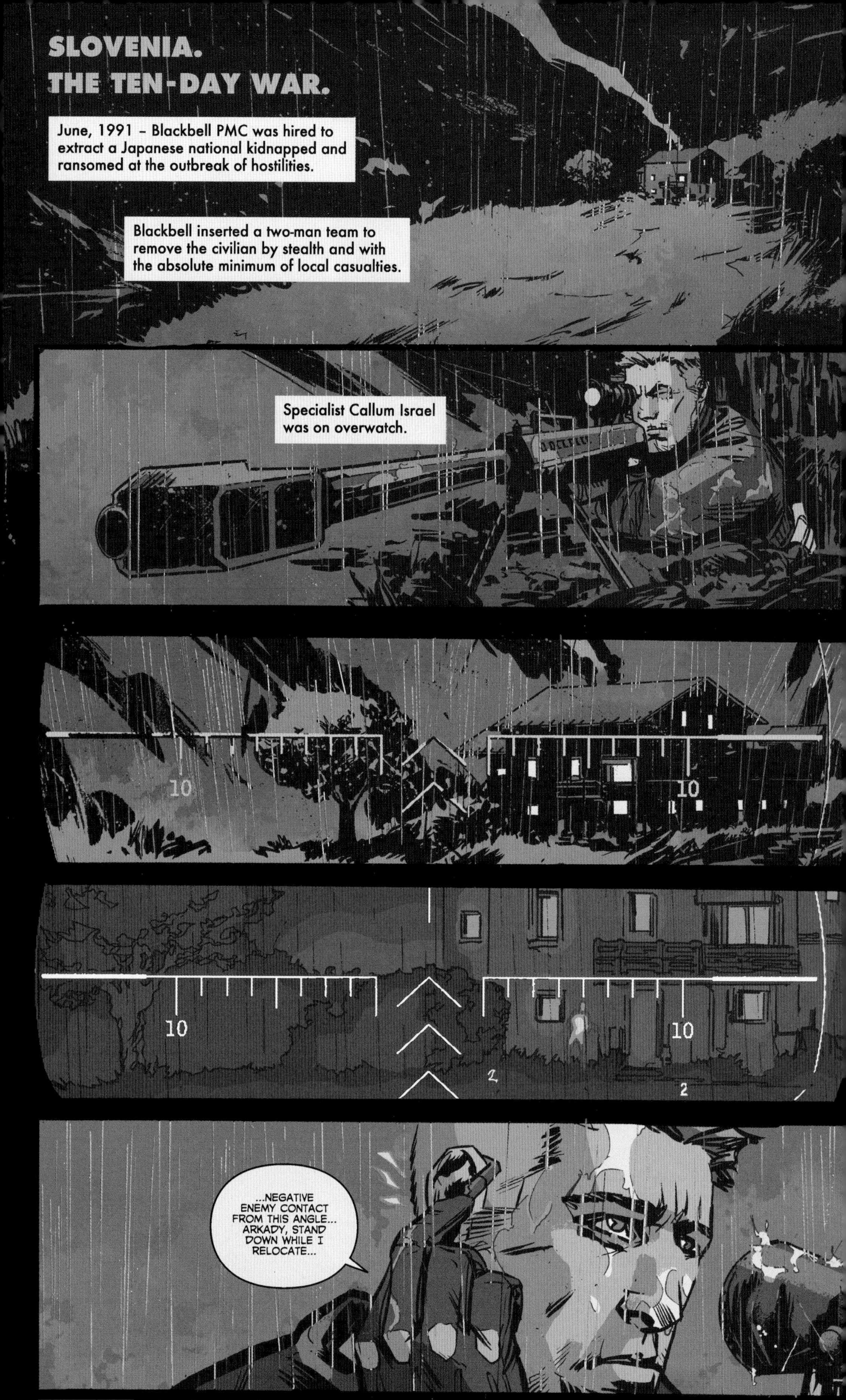
SLOVENIA.
THE TEN-DAY WAR.
June, 1991 – Blackbell PMC was hired to extract a Japanese national kidnapped and ransomed at the outbreak of hostilities.
Blackbell inserted a two-man team to remove the civilian by stealth and with the absolute minimum of local casualties.
Specialist Callum Israel was on overwatch.
10
10
10
10
2
2
...NEGATIVE ENEMY CONTACT FROM THIS ANGLE... ARKADY, STAND DOWN WHILE I RELOCATE...

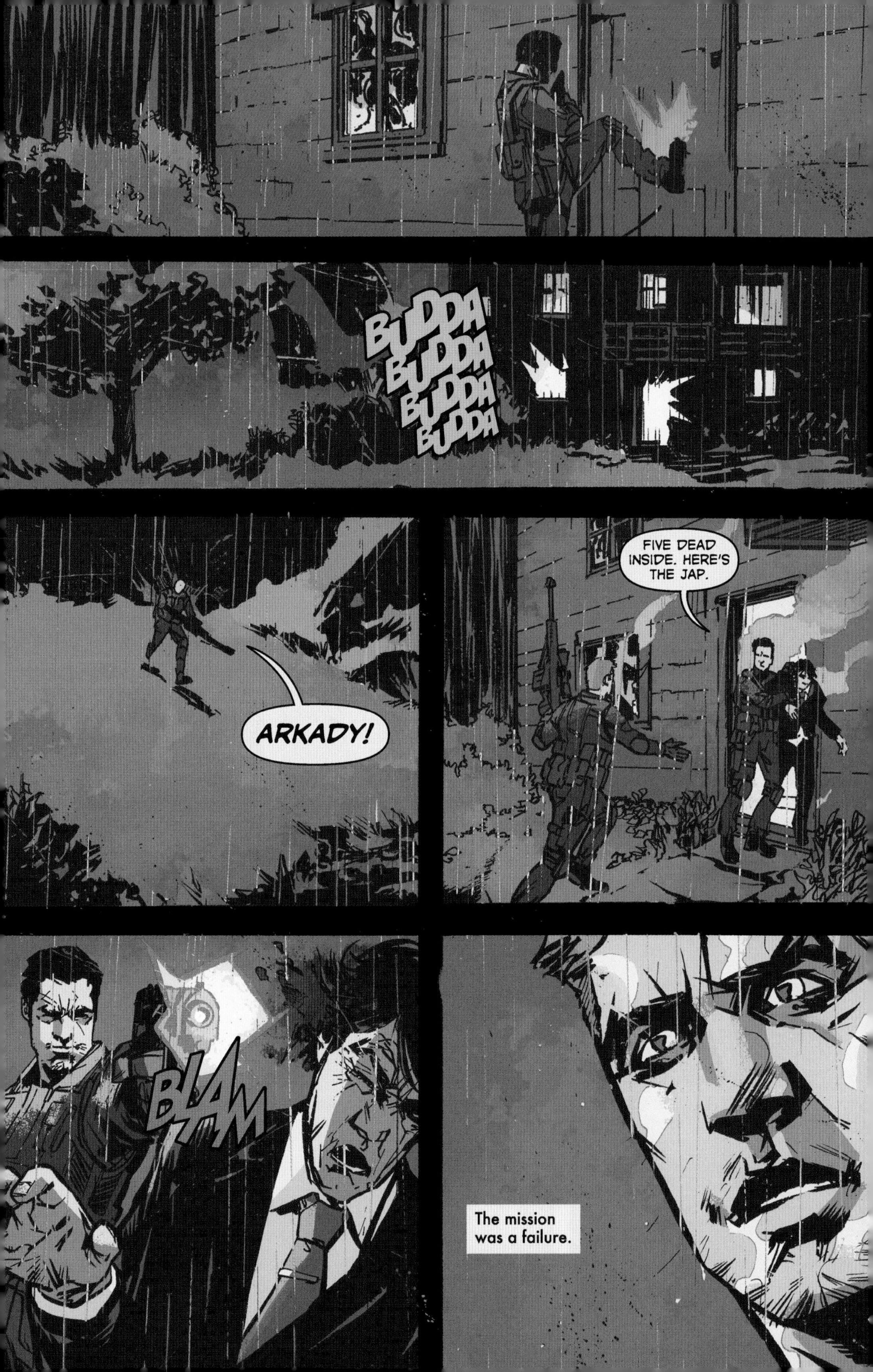
BUDDA
BUDDA
BUDDA
BUDDA
ARKADY!
FIVE DEAD INSIDE. HERE'S THE JAP.
BLAM
The mission was a failure.

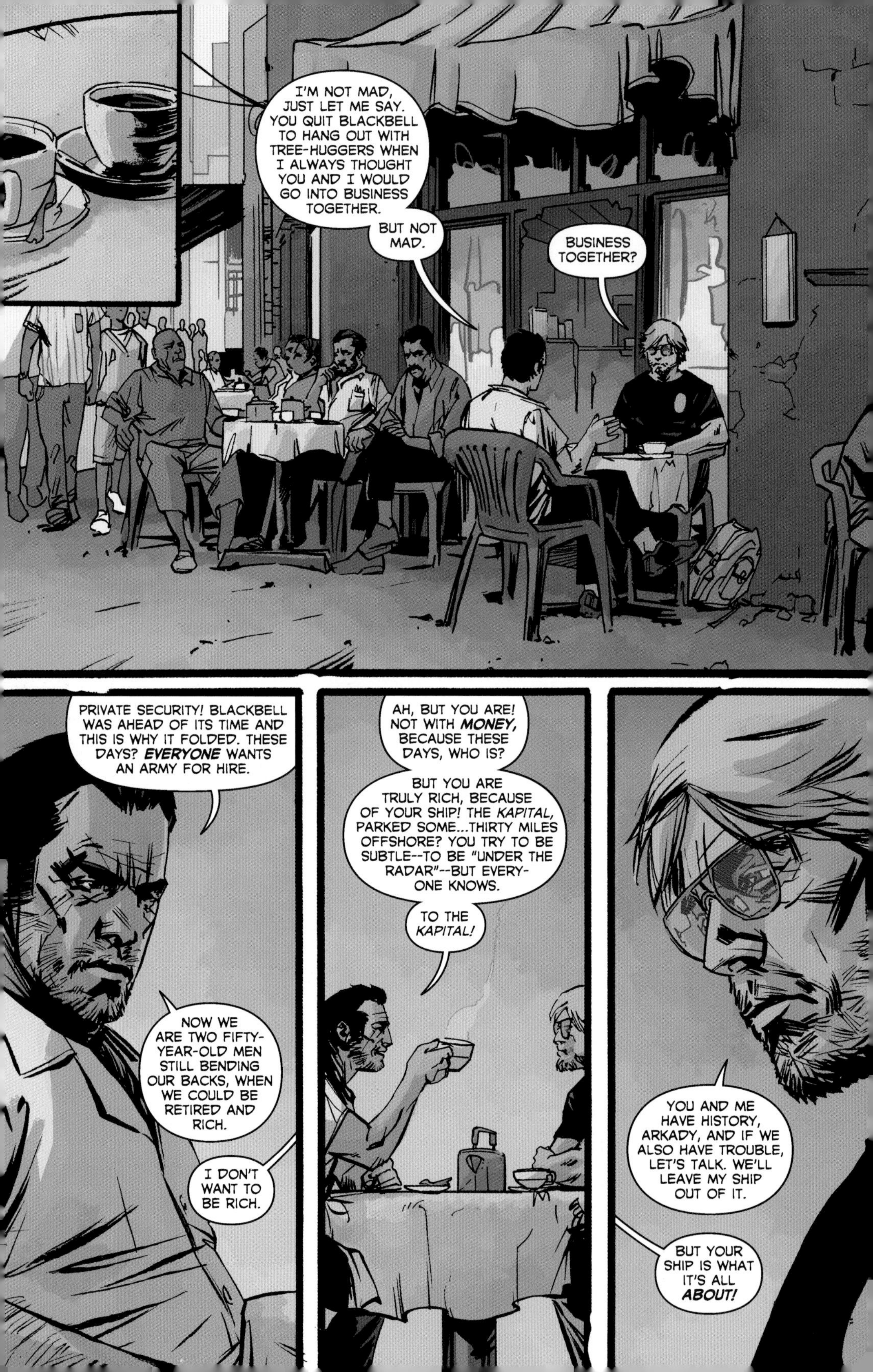
I'M NOT MAD, JUST LET ME SAY. YOU QUIT BLACKBELL TO HANG OUT WITH TREE-HUGGERS WHEN I ALWAYS THOUGHT YOU AND I WOULD GO INTO BUSINESS TOGETHER.
BUT NOT MAD.
BUSINESS TOGETHER?
PRIVATE SECURITY! BLACKBELL WAS AHEAD OF ITS TIME AND THIS IS WHY IT FOLDED. THESE DAYS? *EVERYONE* WANTS AN ARMY FOR HIRE.
NOW WE ARE TWO FIFTY-YEAR-OLD MEN STILL BENDING OUR BACKS, WHEN WE COULD BE RETIRED AND RICH.
I DON'T WANT TO BE RICH.
AH, BUT YOU ARE! NOT WITH *MONEY,* BECAUSE THESE DAYS, WHO IS?
BUT YOU ARE TRULY RICH, BECAUSE OF YOUR SHIP! THE *KAPITAL,* PARKED SOME...THIRTY MILES OFFSHORE? YOU TRY TO BE SUBTLE--TO BE "UNDER THE RADAR"--BUT EVERY-ONE KNOWS.
TO THE *KAPITAL!*
YOU AND ME HAVE HISTORY, ARKADY, AND IF WE ALSO HAVE TROUBLE, LET'S TALK. WE'LL LEAVE MY SHIP OUT OF IT.
BUT YOUR SHIP IS WHAT IT'S ALL ***ABOUT!***

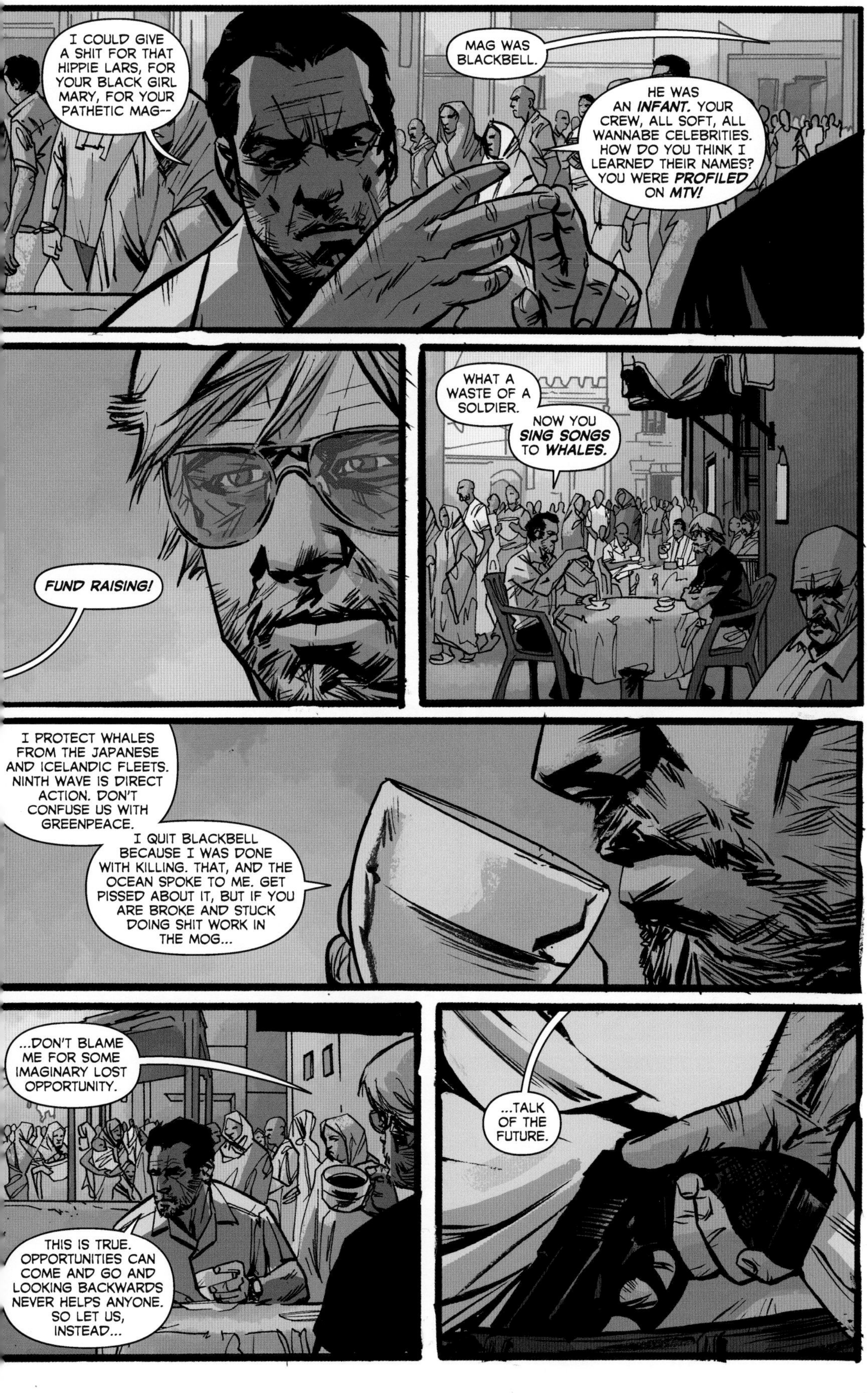
I COULD GIVE A SHIT FOR THAT HIPPIE LARS, FOR YOUR BLACK GIRL MARY, FOR YOUR PATHETIC MAG--
MAG WAS BLACKBELL.
HE WAS AN INFANT. YOUR CREW, ALL SOFT, ALL WANNABE CELEBRITIES. HOW DO YOU THINK I LEARNED THEIR NAMES? YOU WERE PROFILED ON MTV!
FUND RAISING!
WHAT A WASTE OF A SOLDIER.
NOW YOU SING SONGS TO WHALES.
I PROTECT WHALES FROM THE JAPANESE AND ICELANDIC FLEETS. NINTH WAVE IS DIRECT ACTION. DON'T CONFUSE US WITH GREENPEACE.
I QUIT BLACKBELL BECAUSE I WAS DONE WITH KILLING. THAT, AND THE OCEAN SPOKE TO ME. GET PISSED ABOUT IT, BUT IF YOU ARE BROKE AND STUCK DOING SHIT WORK IN THE MOG...
...DON'T BLAME ME FOR SOME IMAGINARY LOST OPPORTUNITY.
THIS IS TRUE. OPPORTUNITIES CAN COME AND GO AND LOOKING BACKWARDS NEVER HELPS ANYONE. SO LET US, INSTEAD...
...TALK OF THE FUTURE.

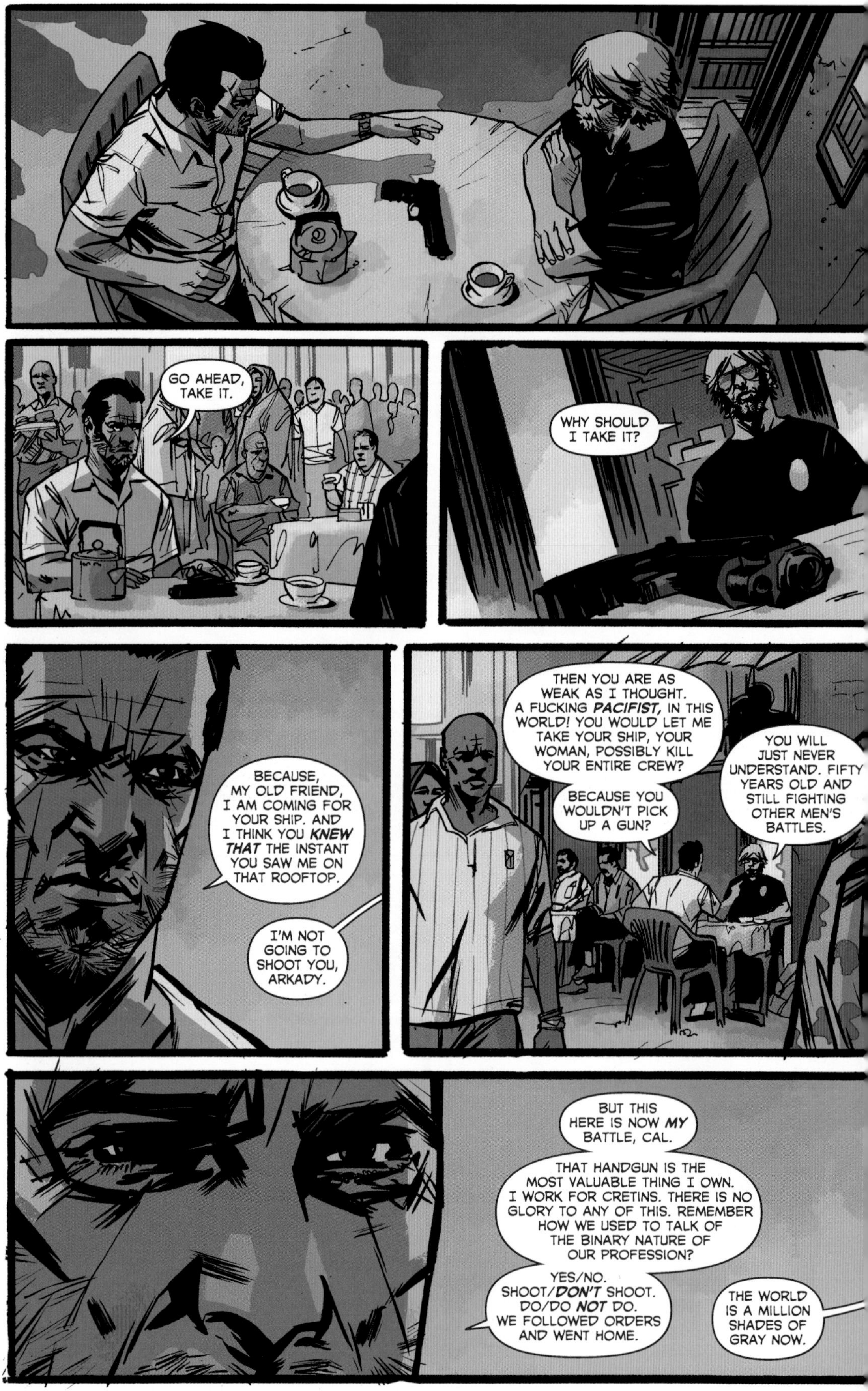

GO AHEAD, TAKE IT.
WHY SHOULD I TAKE IT?
BECAUSE, MY OLD FRIEND, I AM COMING FOR YOUR SHIP. AND I THINK YOU KNEW THAT THE INSTANT YOU SAW ME ON THAT ROOFTOP.
I'M NOT GOING TO SHOOT YOU, ARKADY.
THEN YOU ARE AS WEAK AS I THOUGHT. A FUCKING PACIFIST, IN THIS WORLD! YOU WOULD LET ME TAKE YOUR SHIP, YOUR WOMAN, POSSIBLY KILL YOUR ENTIRE CREW?
BECAUSE YOU WOULDN'T PICK UP A GUN?
YOU WILL JUST NEVER UNDERSTAND. FIFTY YEARS OLD AND STILL FIGHTING OTHER MEN'S BATTLES.
BUT THIS HERE IS NOW MY BATTLE, CAL.
THAT HANDGUN IS THE MOST VALUABLE THING I OWN. I WORK FOR CRETINS. THERE IS NO GLORY TO ANY OF THIS. REMEMBER HOW WE USED TO TALK OF THE BINARY NATURE OF OUR PROFESSION?
YES/NO. SHOOT/DON'T SHOOT. DO/DO NOT DO. WE FOLLOWED ORDERS AND WENT HOME.
THE WORLD IS A MILLION SHADES OF GRAY NOW.

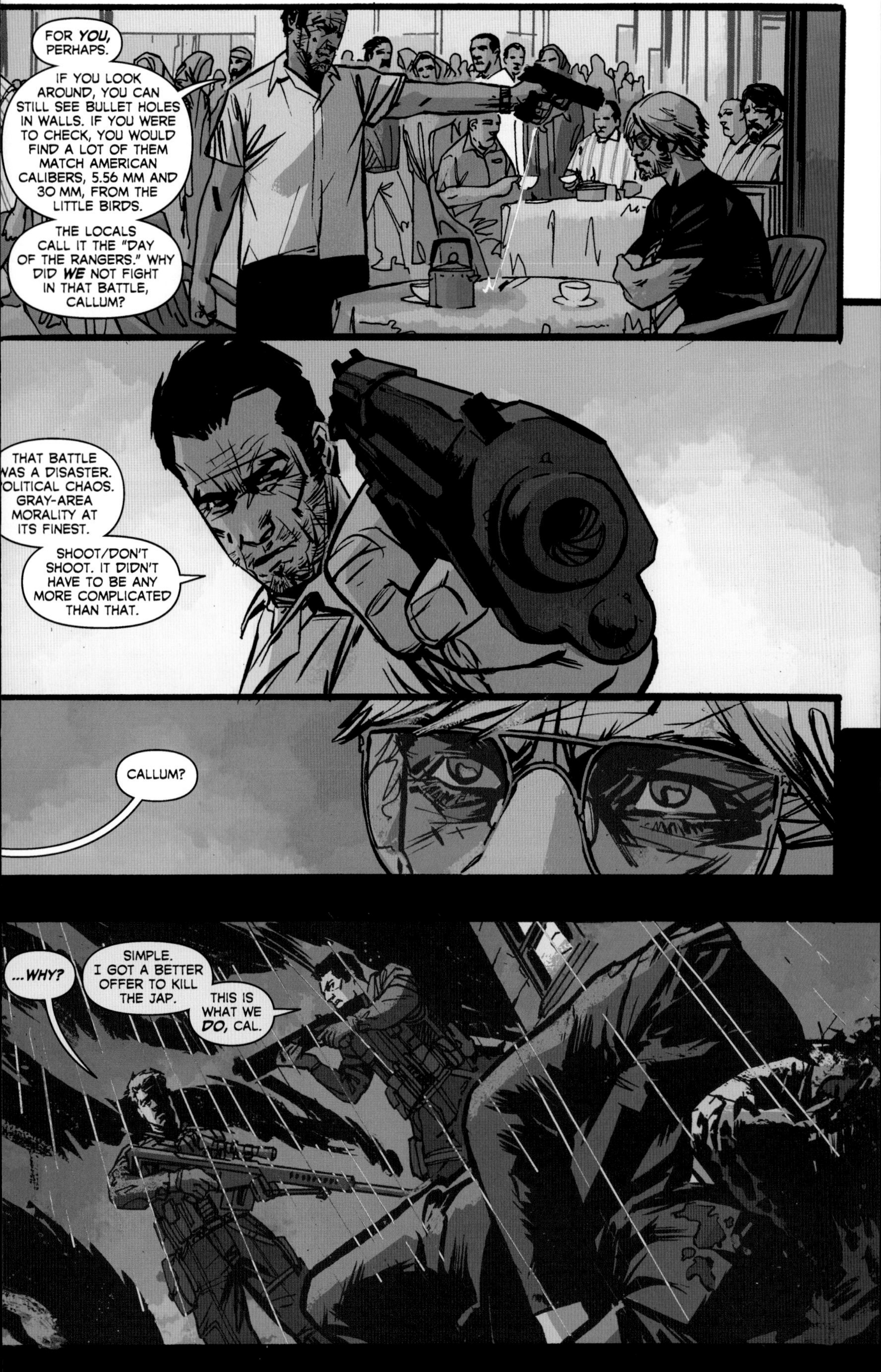
FOR *YOU,* PERHAPS.
IF YOU LOOK AROUND, YOU CAN STILL SEE BULLET HOLES IN WALLS. IF YOU WERE TO CHECK, YOU WOULD FIND A LOT OF THEM MATCH AMERICAN CALIBERS, 5.56 MM AND 30 MM, FROM THE LITTLE BIRDS.
THE LOCALS CALL IT THE "DAY OF THE RANGERS." WHY DID ***WE*** NOT FIGHT IN THAT BATTLE, CALLUM?
THAT BATTLE WAS A DISASTER. OLITICAL CHAOS. GRAY-AREA MORALITY AT ITS FINEST.
SHOOT/DON'T SHOOT. IT DIDN'T HAVE TO BE ANY MORE COMPLICATED THAN THAT.
CALLUM?
...WHY?
SIMPLE. I GOT A BETTER OFFER TO KILL THE JAP.
THIS IS WHAT WE *DO,* CAL.

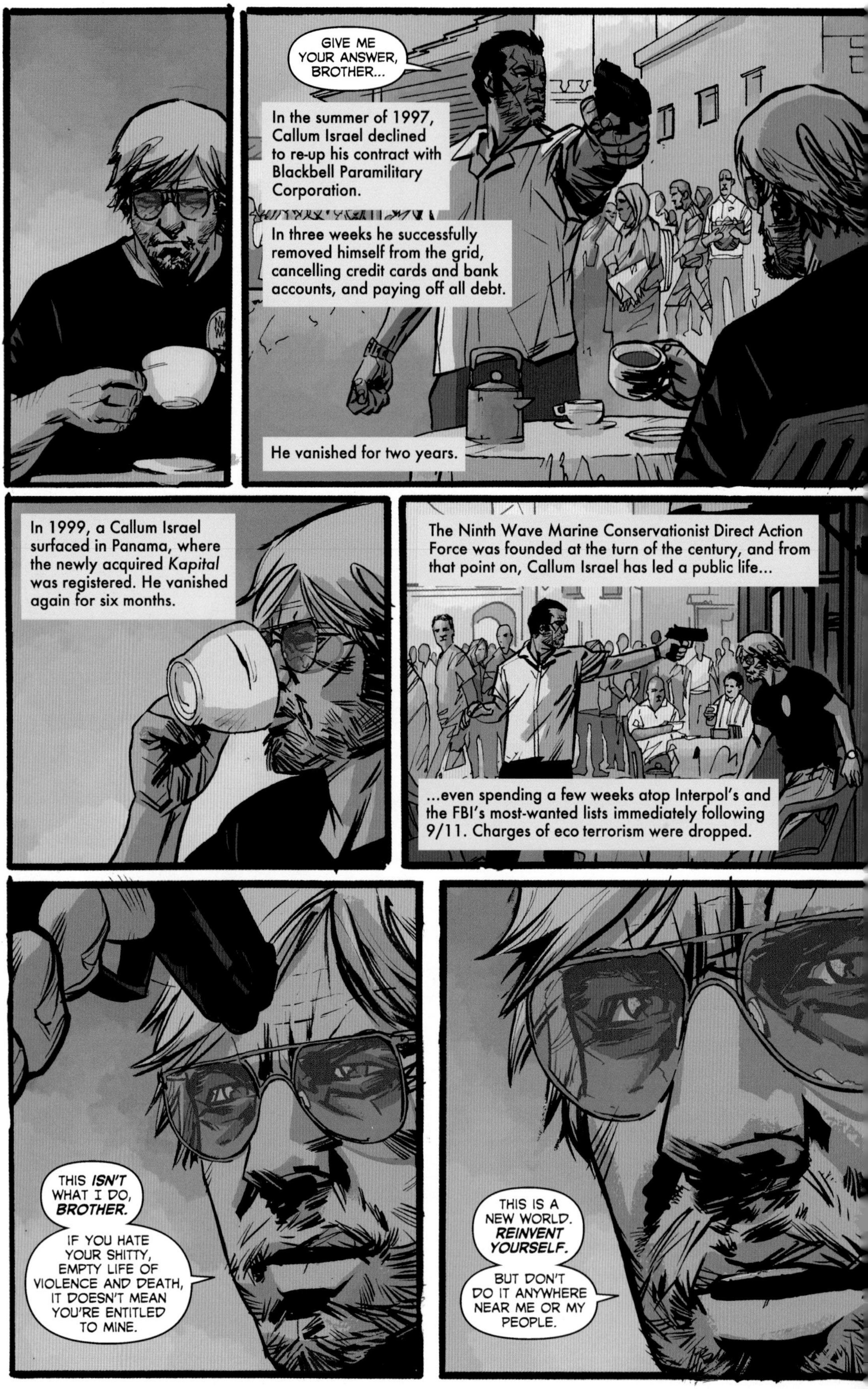
GIVE ME YOUR ANSWER, BROTHER...
In the summer of 1997, Callum Israel declined to re-up his contract with Blackbell Paramilitary Corporation.
In three weeks he successfully removed himself from the grid, cancelling credit cards and bank accounts, and paying off all debt.
He vanished for two years.
In 1999, a Callum Israel surfaced in Panama, where the newly acquired *Kapital* was registered. He vanished again for six months.
The Ninth Wave Marine Conservationist Direct Action Force was founded at the turn of the century, and from that point on, Callum Israel has led a public life...
...even spending a few weeks atop Interpol's and the FBI's most-wanted lists immediately following 9/11. Charges of eco terrorism were dropped.
THIS ***ISN'T*** WHAT I DO, ***BROTHER.***
IF YOU HATE YOUR SHITTY, EMPTY LIFE OF VIOLENCE AND DEATH, IT DOESN'T MEAN YOU'RE ENTITLED TO MINE.
THIS IS A NEW WORLD. ***REINVENT YOURSELF.***
BUT DON'T DO IT ANYWHERE NEAR ME OR MY PEOPLE.

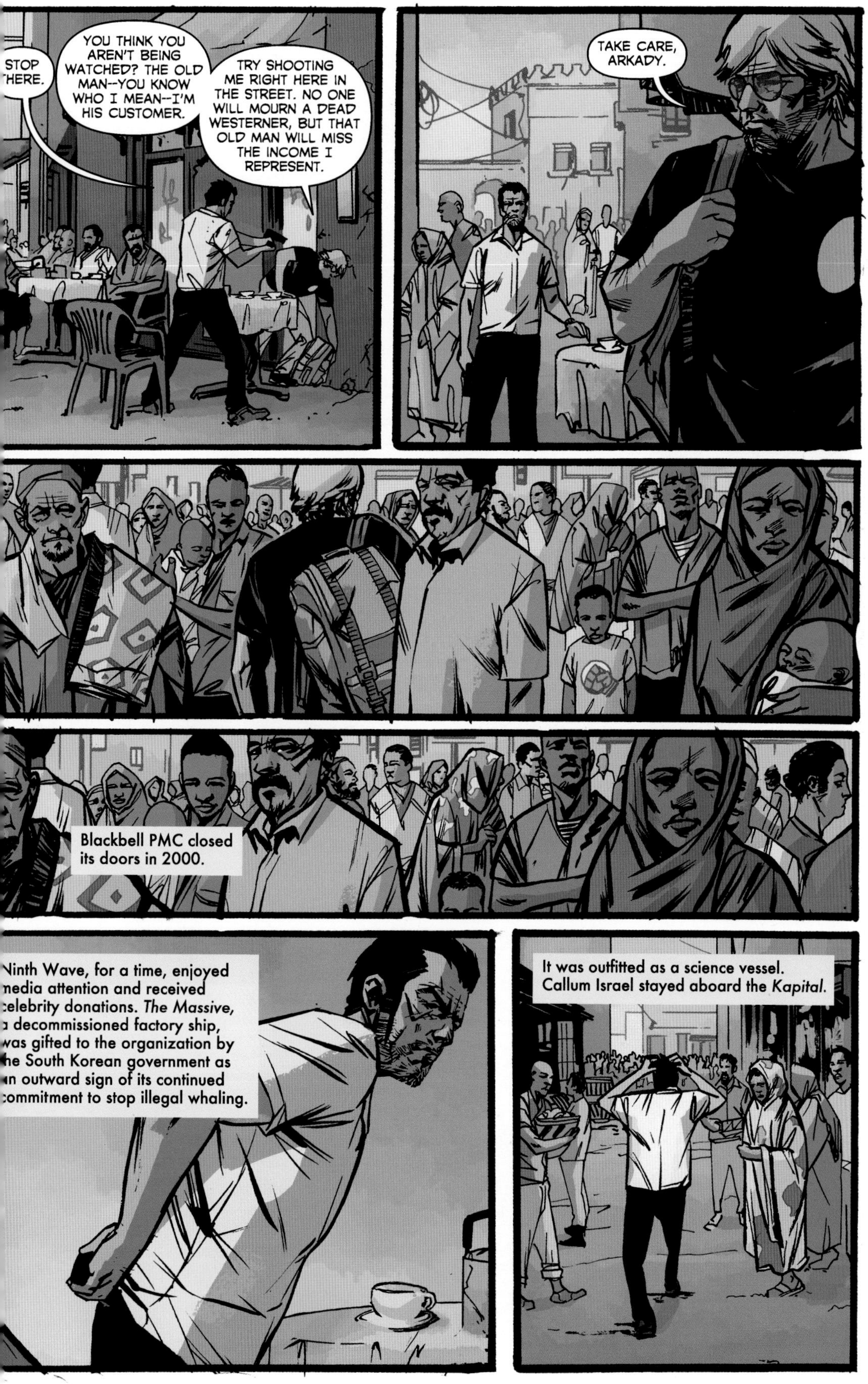
STOP THERE.
YOU THINK YOU AREN'T BEING WATCHED? THE OLD MAN--YOU KNOW WHO I MEAN--I'M HIS CUSTOMER.
TRY SHOOTING ME RIGHT HERE IN THE STREET. NO ONE WILL MOURN A DEAD WESTERNER, BUT THAT OLD MAN WILL MISS THE INCOME I REPRESENT.
TAKE CARE, ARKADY.
Blackbell PMC closed its doors in 2000.
Ninth Wave, for a time, enjoyed media attention and received celebrity donations. *The Massive*, a decommissioned factory ship, was gifted to the organization by the South Korean government as an outward sign of its continued commitment to stop illegal whaling.
It was outfitted as a science vessel. Callum Israel stayed aboard the *Kapital*.

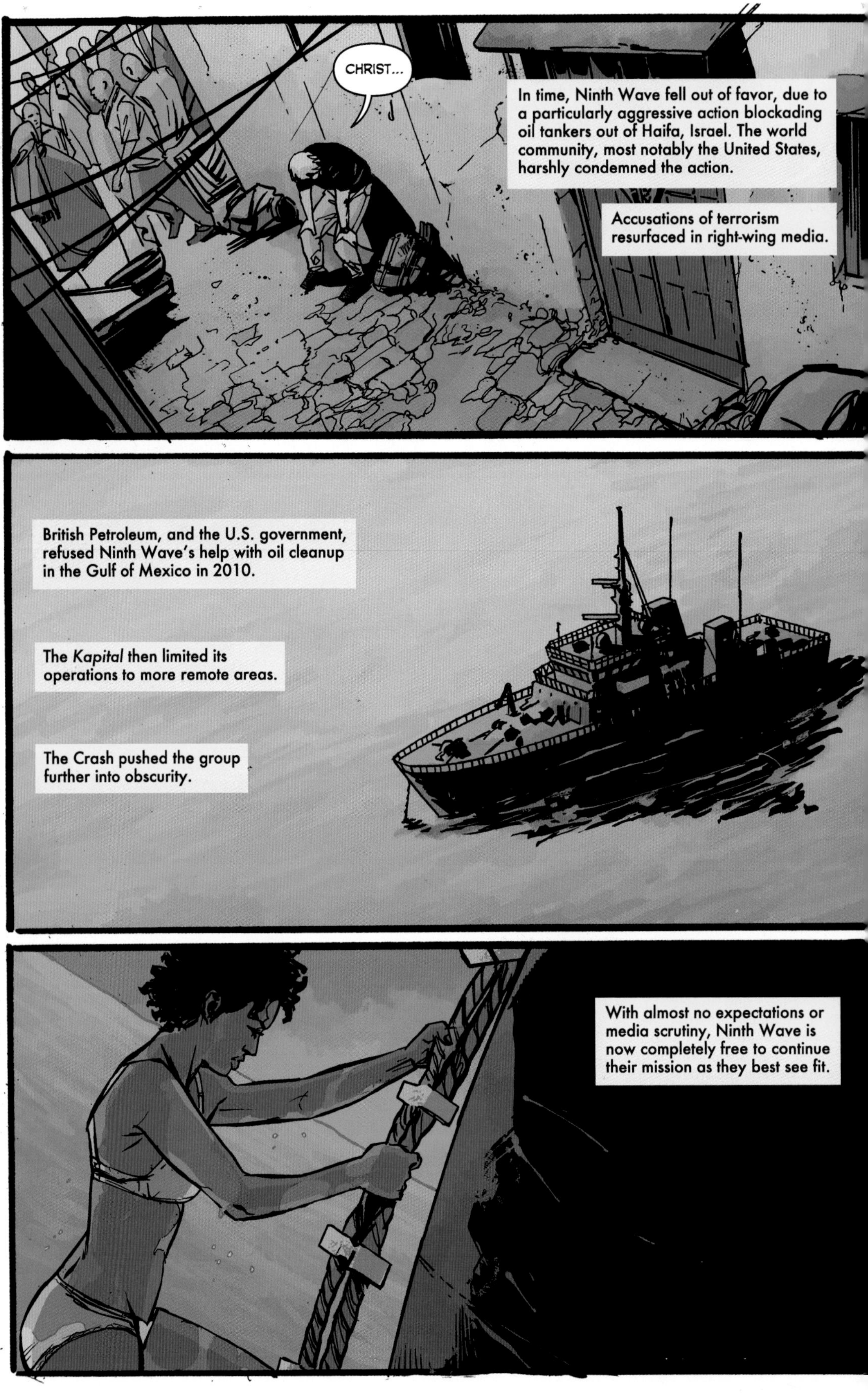
CHRIST...
In time, Ninth Wave fell out of favor, due to a particularly aggressive action blockading oil tankers out of Haifa, Israel. The world community, most notably the United States, harshly condemned the action.
Accusations of terrorism resurfaced in right-wing media.
British Petroleum, and the U.S. government, refused Ninth Wave's help with oil cleanup in the Gulf of Mexico in 2010.
The *Kapital* then limited its operations to more remote areas.
The Crash pushed the group further into obscurity.
With almost no expectations or media scrutiny, Ninth Wave is now completely free to continue their mission as they best see fit.

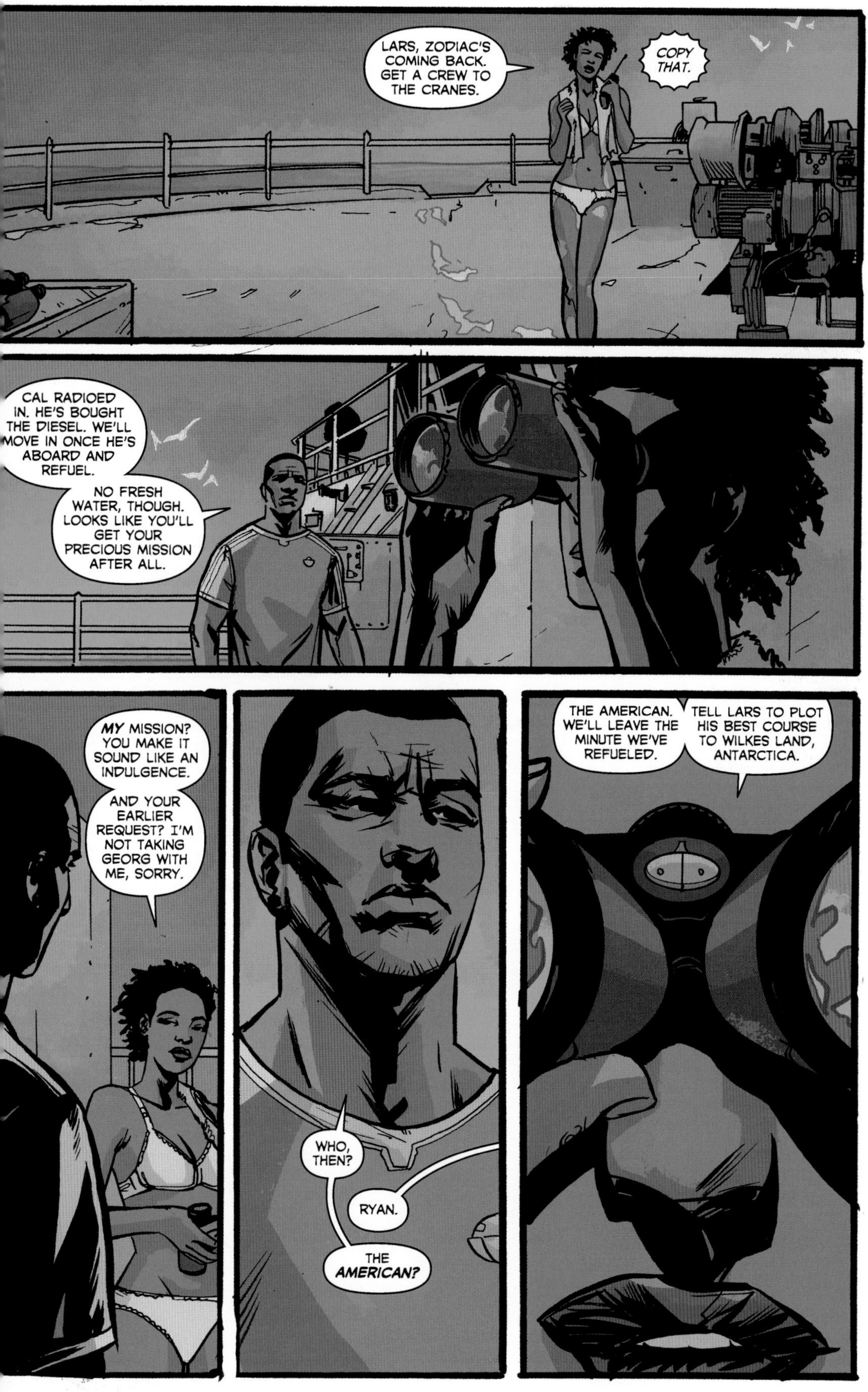
LARS, ZODIAC'S COMING BACK. GET A CREW TO THE CRANES.
COPY THAT.
CAL RADIOED IN. HE'S BOUGHT THE DIESEL. WE'LL MOVE IN ONCE HE'S ABOARD AND REFUEL.
NO FRESH WATER, THOUGH. LOOKS LIKE YOU'LL GET YOUR PRECIOUS MISSION AFTER ALL.
MY MISSION? YOU MAKE IT SOUND LIKE AN INDULGENCE.
AND YOUR EARLIER REQUEST? I'M NOT TAKING GEORG WITH ME, SORRY.
WHO, THEN?
RYAN.
THE AMERICAN?
THE AMERICAN. WE'LL LEAVE THE MINUTE WE'VE REFUELED.
TELL LARS TO PLOT HIS BEST COURSE TO WILKES LAND, ANTARCTICA.

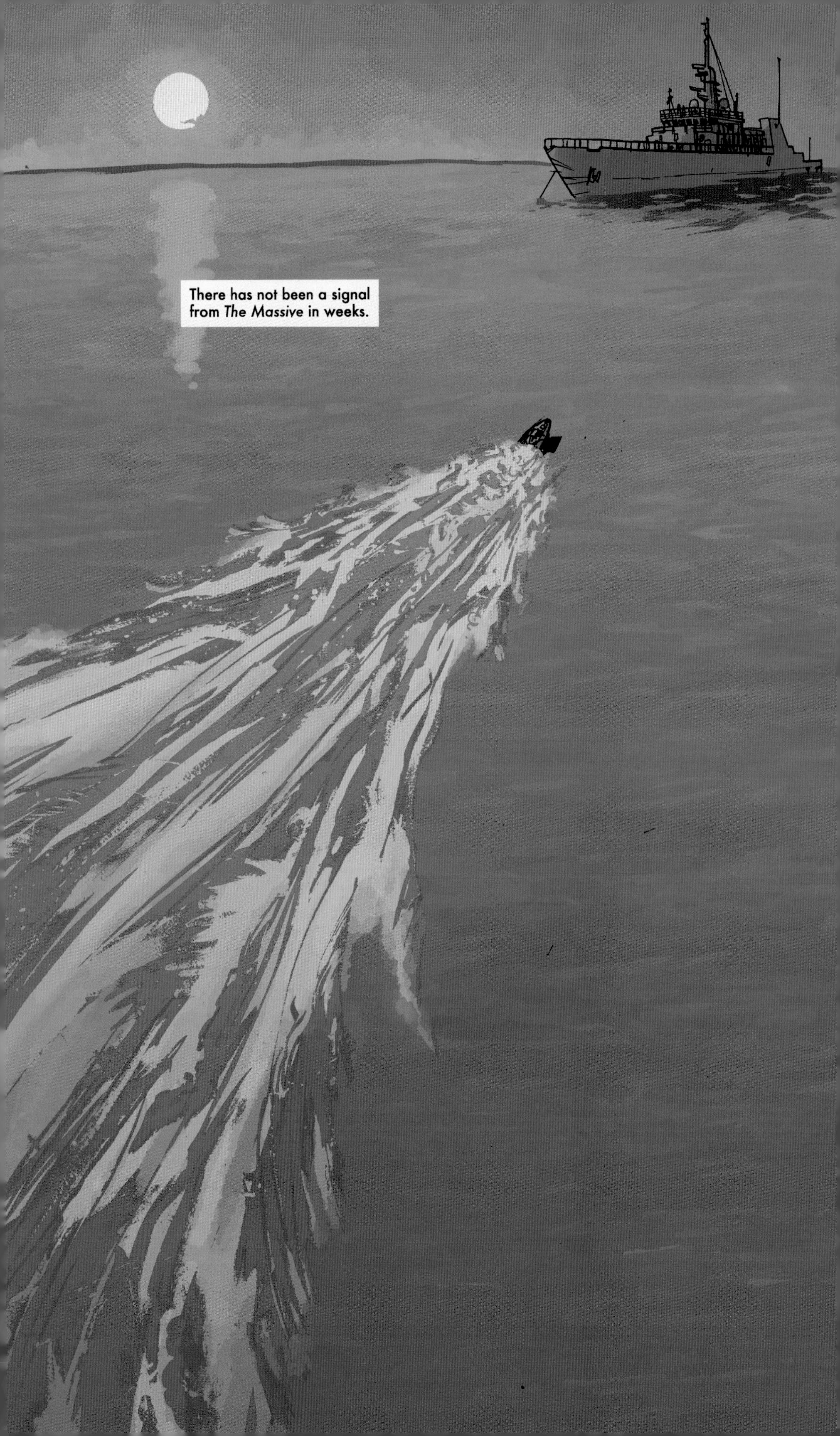
There has not been a signal from *The Massive* in weeks.

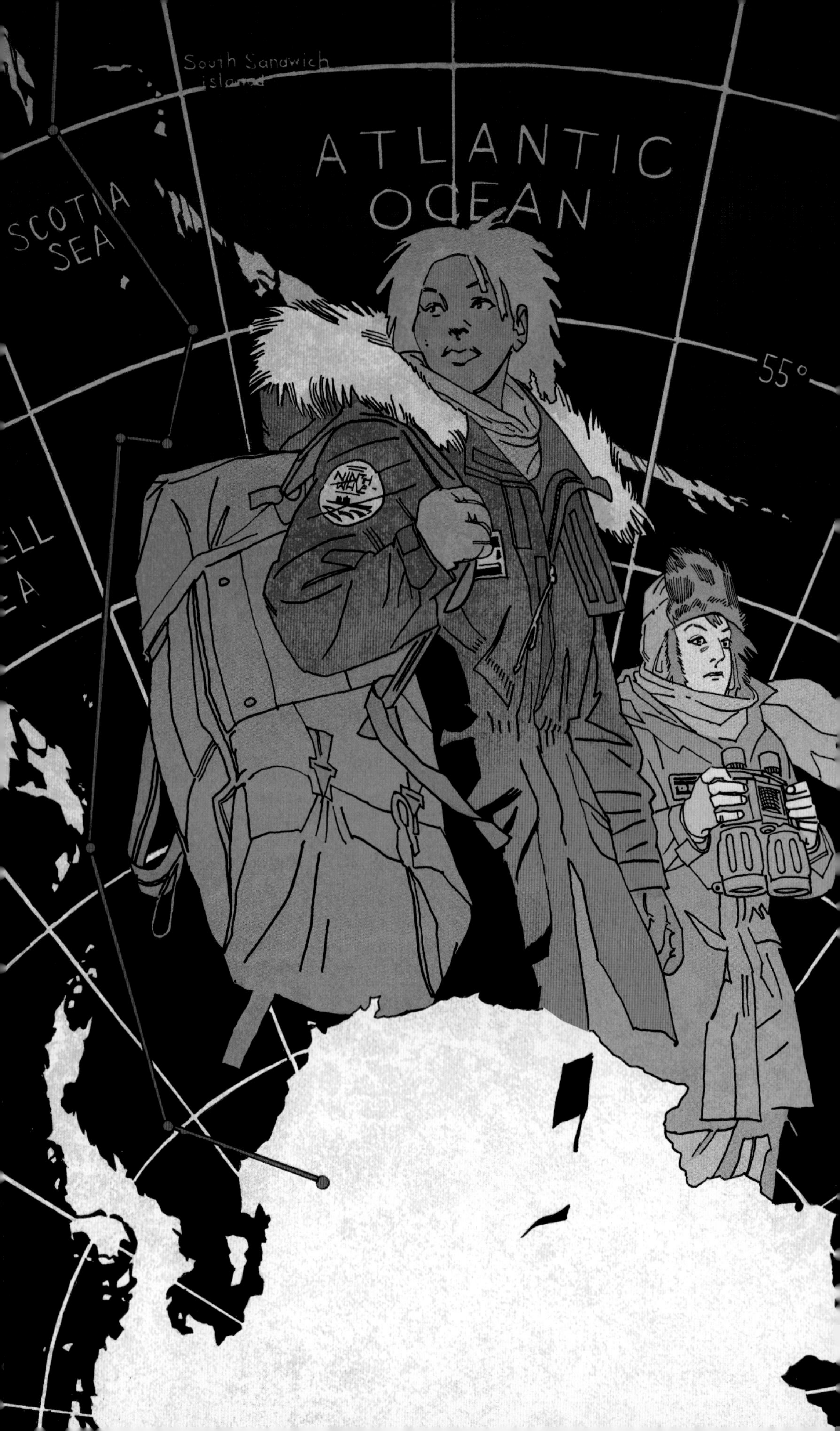
South Sandwich
ATLANTIC OCEAN
SCOTIA SEA
55°

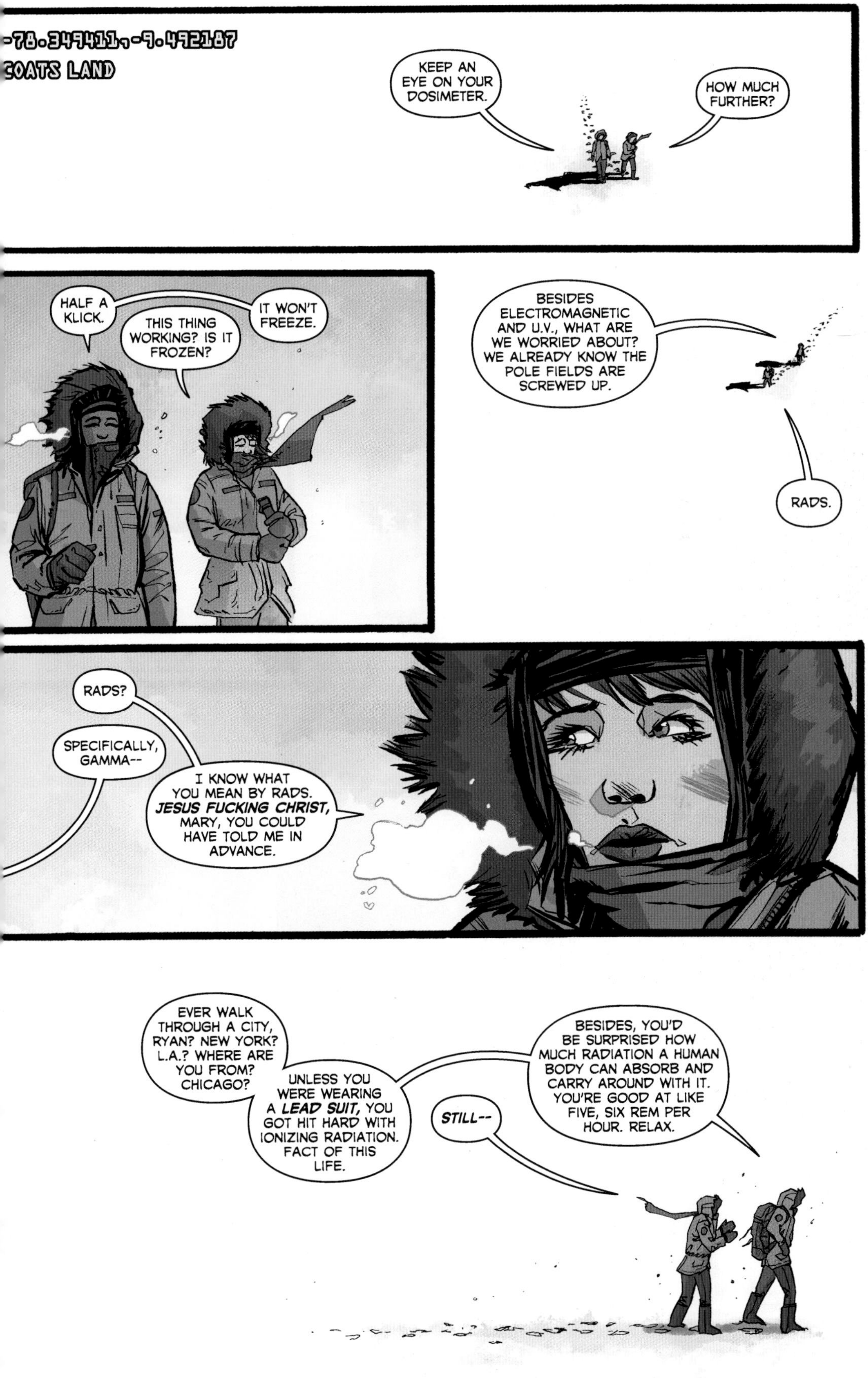
-78.349411,-9.492187
COATS LAND
KEEP AN EYE ON YOUR DOSIMETER.
HOW MUCH FURTHER?
HALF A KLICK.
THIS THING WORKING? IS IT FROZEN?
IT WON'T FREEZE.
BESIDES ELECTROMAGNETIC AND U.V., WHAT ARE WE WORRIED ABOUT? WE ALREADY KNOW THE POLE FIELDS ARE SCREWED UP.
RADS.
RADS?
SPECIFICALLY, GAMMA--
I KNOW WHAT YOU MEAN BY RADS. JESUS FUCKING CHRIST, MARY, YOU COULD HAVE TOLD ME IN ADVANCE.
EVER WALK THROUGH A CITY, RYAN? NEW YORK? L.A.? WHERE ARE YOU FROM? CHICAGO?
UNLESS YOU WERE WEARING A LEAD SUIT, YOU GOT HIT HARD WITH IONIZING RADIATION. FACT OF THIS LIFE.
STILL--
BESIDES, YOU'D BE SURPRISED HOW MUCH RADIATION A HUMAN BODY CAN ABSORB AND CARRY AROUND WITH IT. YOU'RE GOOD AT LIKE FIVE, SIX REM PER HOUR. RELAX.

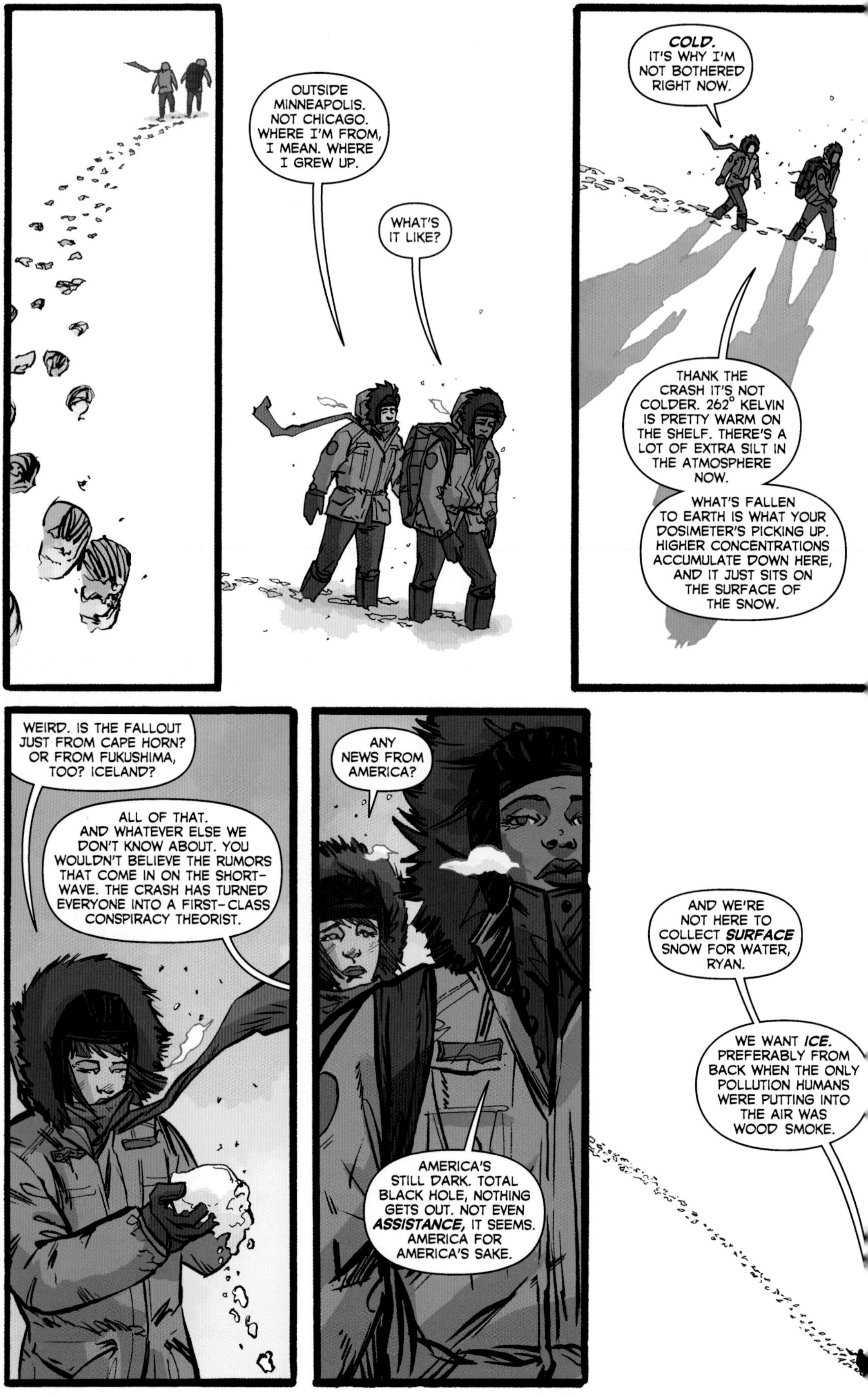
OUTSIDE MINNEAPOLIS. NOT CHICAGO. WHERE I'M FROM, I MEAN. WHERE I GREW UP.
WHAT'S IT LIKE?
COLD. IT'S WHY I'M NOT BOTHERED RIGHT NOW.
THANK THE CRASH IT'S NOT COLDER. 262° KELVIN IS PRETTY WARM ON THE SHELF. THERE'S A LOT OF EXTRA SILT IN THE ATMOSPHERE NOW.
WHAT'S FALLEN TO EARTH IS WHAT YOUR DOSIMETER'S PICKING UP. HIGHER CONCENTRATIONS ACCUMULATE DOWN HERE, AND IT JUST SITS ON THE SURFACE OF THE SNOW.
WEIRD. IS THE FALLOUT JUST FROM CAPE HORN? OR FROM FUKUSHIMA, TOO? ICELAND?
ALL OF THAT. AND WHATEVER ELSE WE DON'T KNOW ABOUT. YOU WOULDN'T BELIEVE THE RUMORS THAT COME IN ON THE SHORT-WAVE. THE CRASH HAS TURNED EVERYONE INTO A FIRST-CLASS CONSPIRACY THEORIST.
ANY NEWS FROM AMERICA?
AMERICA'S STILL DARK. TOTAL BLACK HOLE, NOTHING GETS OUT. NOT EVEN *ASSISTANCE,* IT SEEMS. AMERICA FOR AMERICA'S SAKE.
AND WE'RE NOT HERE TO COLLECT *SURFACE* SNOW FOR WATER, RYAN.
WE WANT *ICE.* PREFERABLY FROM BACK WHEN THE ONLY POLLUTION HUMANS WERE PUTTING INTO THE AIR WAS WOOD SMOKE.

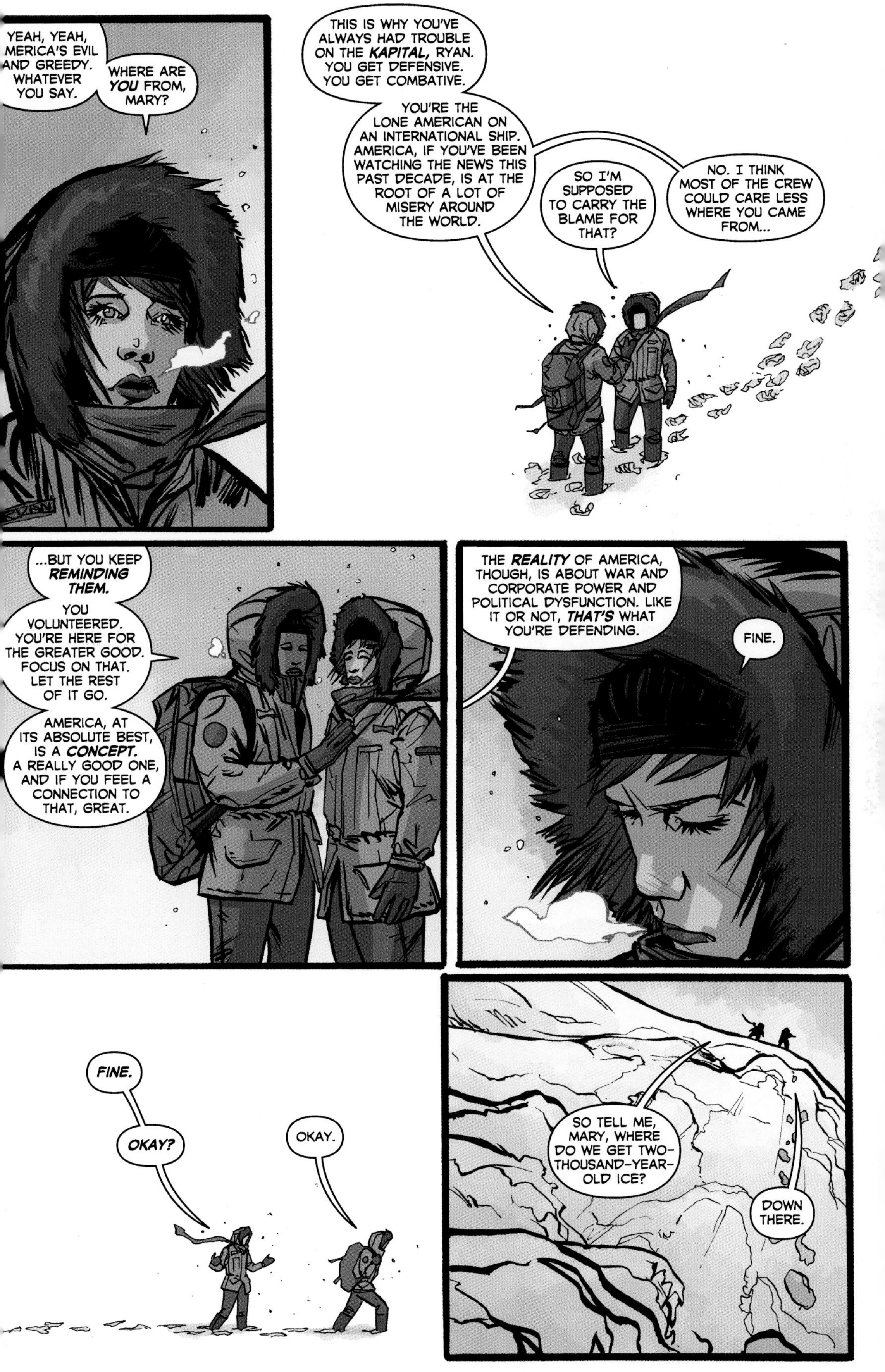

YEAH, YEAH, MERICA'S EVIL AND GREEDY. WHATEVER YOU SAY.
WHERE ARE *YOU* FROM, MARY?
THIS IS WHY YOU'VE ALWAYS HAD TROUBLE ON THE *KAPITAL,* RYAN. YOU GET DEFENSIVE. YOU GET COMBATIVE.
YOU'RE THE LONE AMERICAN ON AN INTERNATIONAL SHIP. AMERICA, IF YOU'VE BEEN WATCHING THE NEWS THIS PAST DECADE, IS AT THE ROOT OF A LOT OF MISERY AROUND THE WORLD.
SO I'M SUPPOSED TO CARRY THE BLAME FOR THAT?
NO. I THINK MOST OF THE CREW COULD CARE LESS WHERE YOU CAME FROM...
...BUT YOU KEEP *REMINDING THEM.*
YOU VOLUNTEERED. YOU'RE HERE FOR THE GREATER GOOD. FOCUS ON THAT. LET THE REST OF IT GO.
AMERICA, AT ITS ABSOLUTE BEST, IS A *CONCEPT.* A REALLY GOOD ONE, AND IF YOU FEEL A CONNECTION TO THAT, GREAT.
THE *REALITY* OF AMERICA, THOUGH, IS ABOUT WAR AND CORPORATE POWER AND POLITICAL DYSFUNCTION. LIKE IT OR NOT, *THAT'S* WHAT YOU'RE DEFENDING.
FINE.
FINE.
OKAY?
OKAY.
SO TELL ME, MARY, WHERE DO WE GET TWO-THOUSAND-YEAR-OLD ICE?
DOWN THERE.

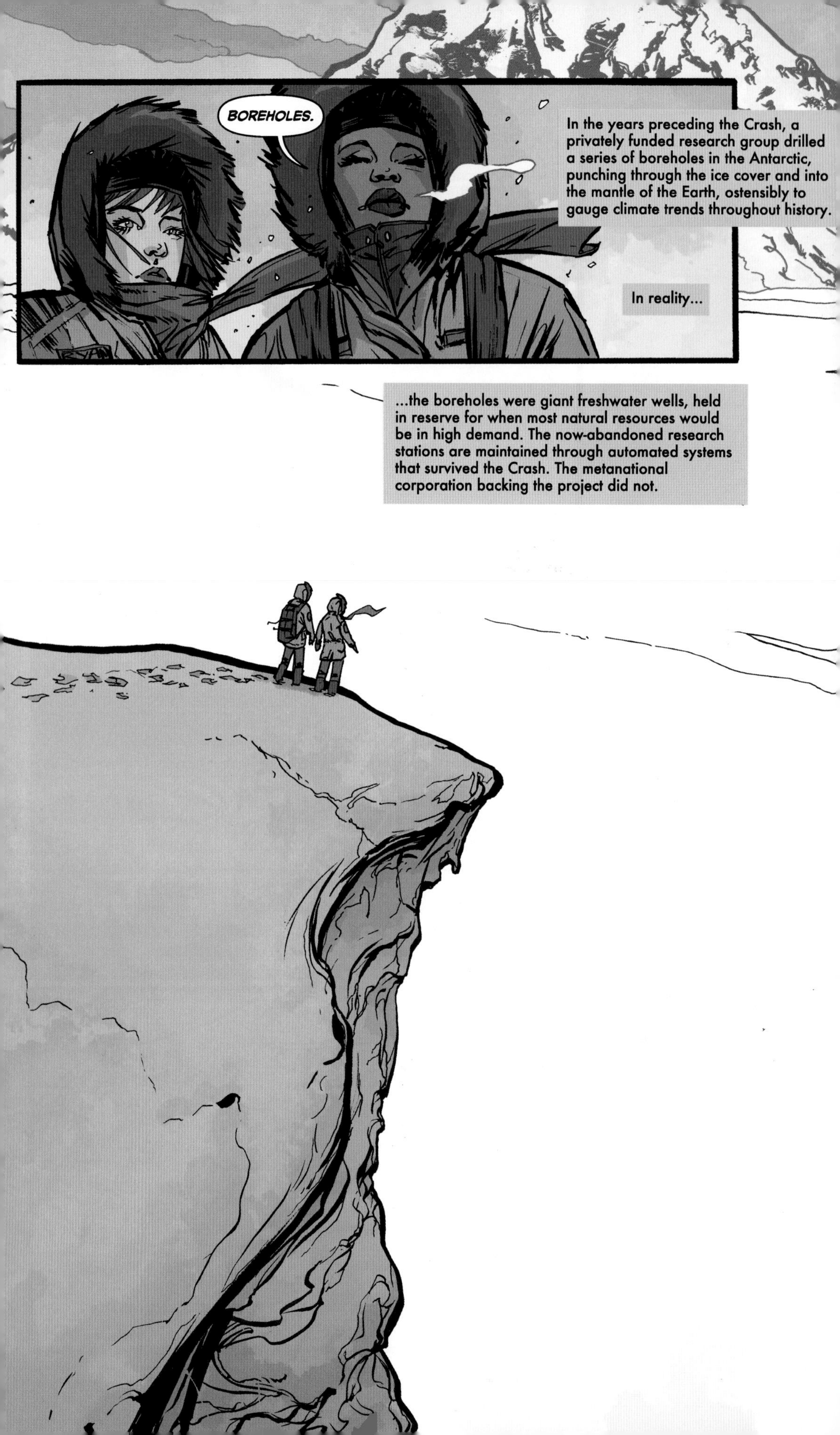
BOREHOLES.
In the years preceding the Crash, a privately funded research group drilled a series of boreholes in the Antarctic, punching through the ice cover and into the mantle of the Earth, ostensibly to gauge climate trends throughout history.
In reality...
...the boreholes were giant freshwater wells, held in reserve for when most natural resources would be in high demand. The now-abandoned research stations are maintained through automated systems that survived the Crash. The metanational corporation backing the project did not.

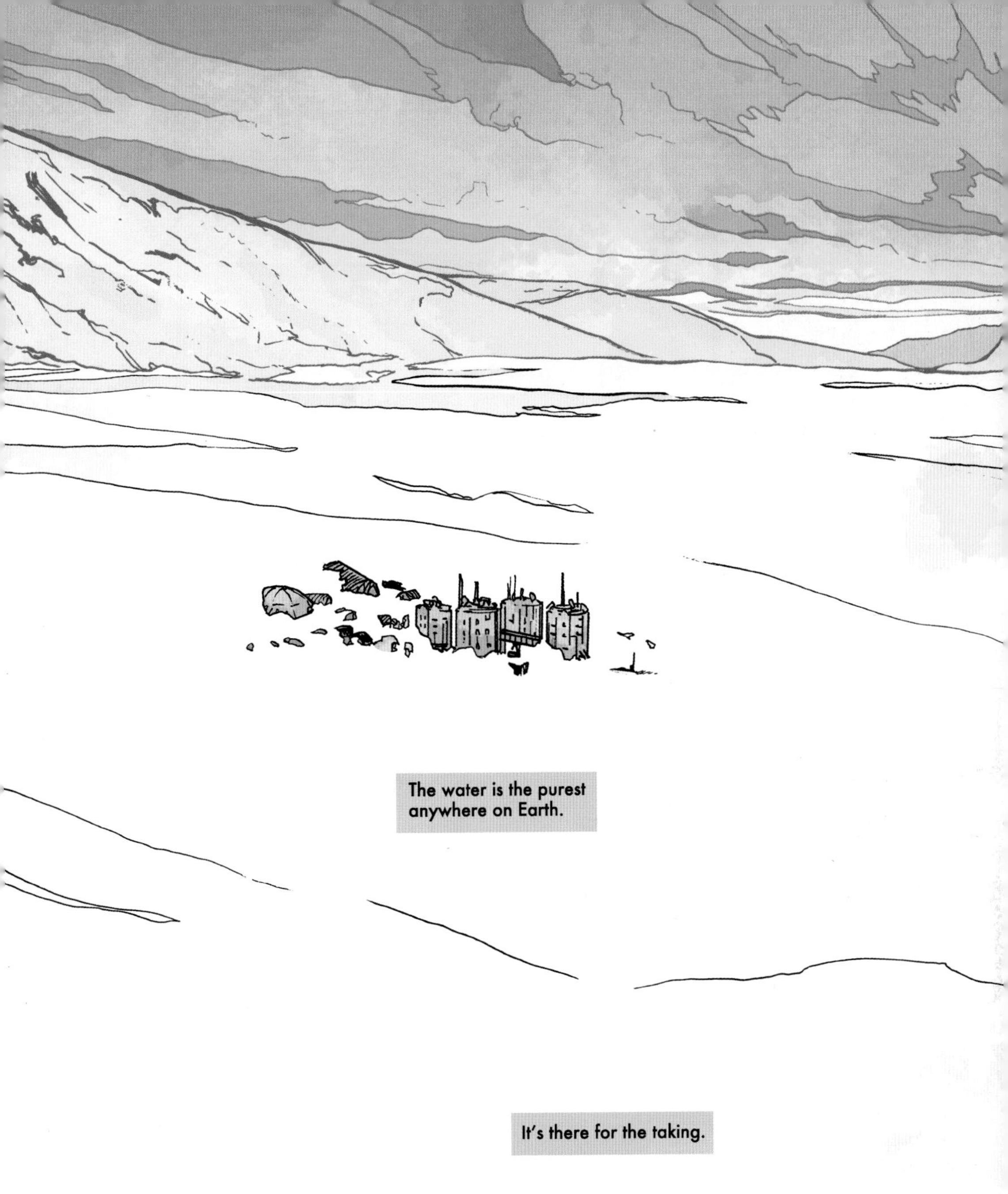
The water is the purest anywhere on Earth.
It's there for the taking.

THE MASSIVE
BLACK PACIFIC: "ANTARCTICA"

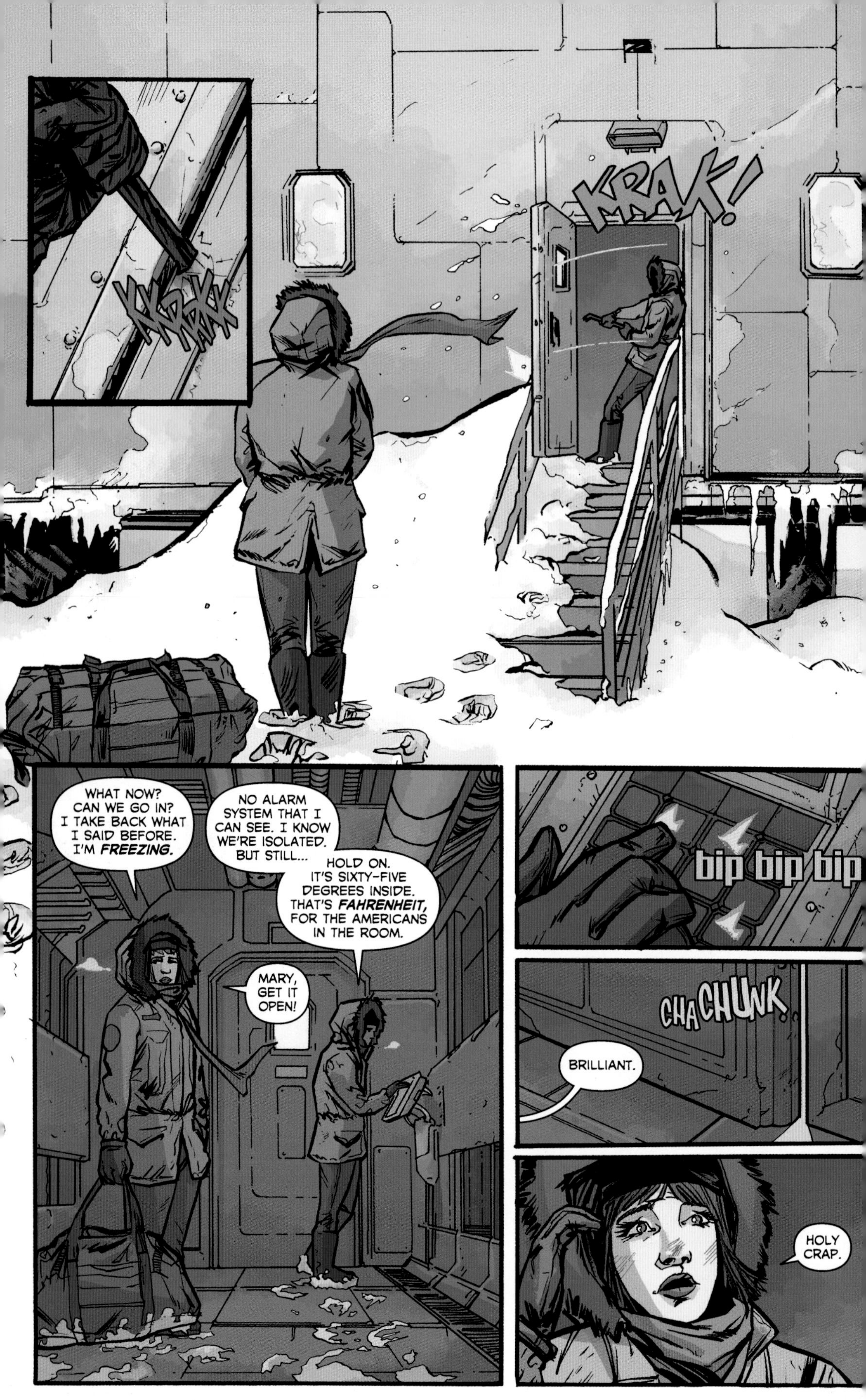
KYRAKK
KRAK!
WHAT NOW? CAN WE GO IN? I TAKE BACK WHAT I SAID BEFORE. I'M *FREEZING.*
NO ALARM SYSTEM THAT I CAN SEE. I KNOW WE'RE ISOLATED. BUT STILL...
HOLD ON. IT'S SIXTY-FIVE DEGREES INSIDE. THAT'S *FAHRENHEIT,* FOR THE AMERICANS IN THE ROOM.
MARY, GET IT OPEN!
bip bip bip
CHACHUNK
BRILLIANT.
HOLY CRAP.

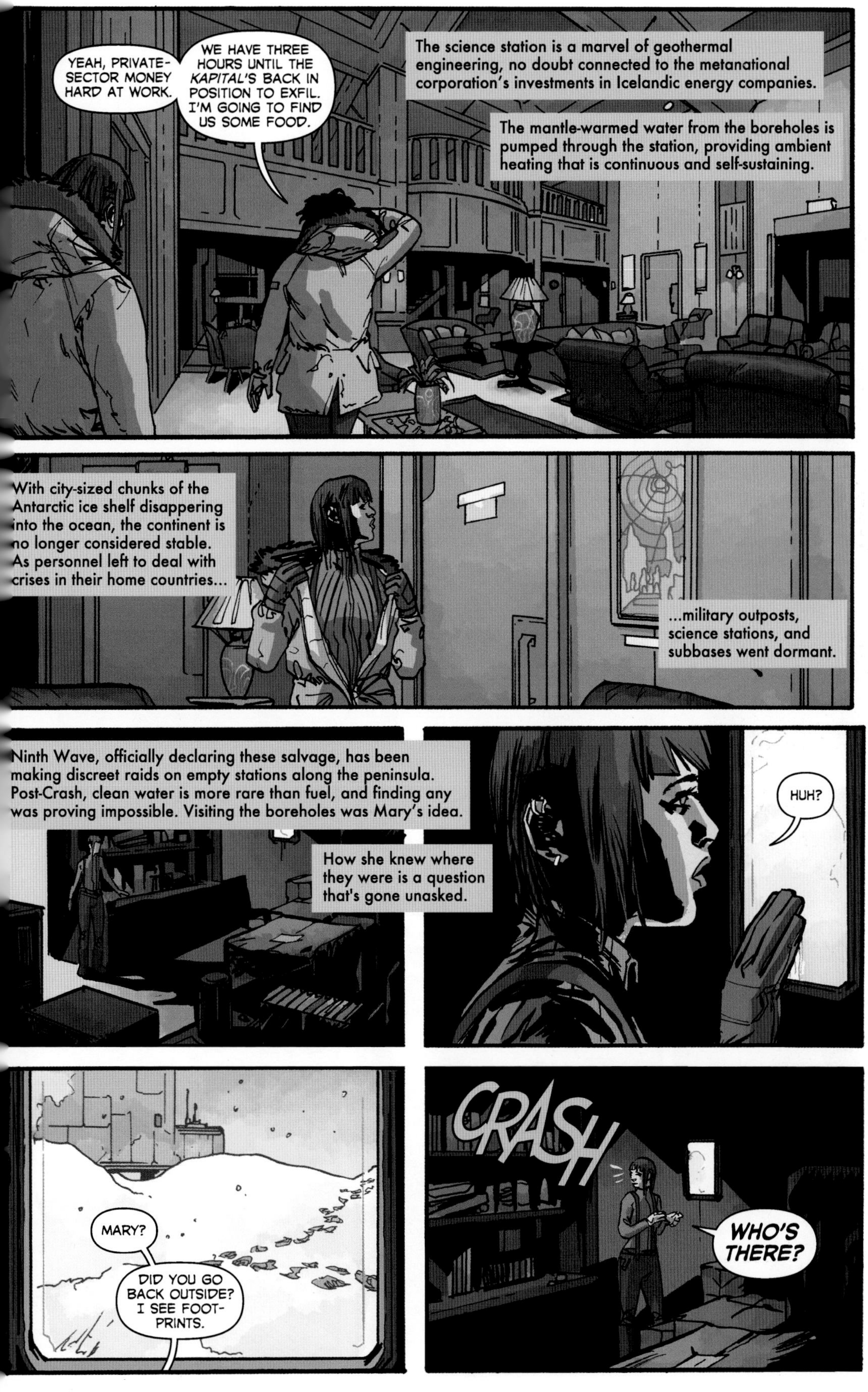
YEAH, PRIVATE-SECTOR MONEY HARD AT WORK.
WE HAVE THREE HOURS UNTIL THE *KAPITAL*'S BACK IN POSITION TO EXFIL. I'M GOING TO FIND US SOME FOOD.
The science station is a marvel of geothermal engineering, no doubt connected to the metanational corporation's investments in Icelandic energy companies.
The mantle-warmed water from the boreholes is pumped through the station, providing ambient heating that is continuous and self-sustaining.
With city-sized chunks of the Antarctic ice shelf disappering into the ocean, the continent is no longer considered stable. As personnel left to deal with crises in their home countries...
...military outposts, science stations, and subbases went dormant.
Ninth Wave, officially declaring these salvage, has been making discreet raids on empty stations along the peninsula. Post-Crash, clean water is more rare than fuel, and finding any was proving impossible. Visiting the boreholes was Mary's idea.
How she knew where they were is a question that's gone unasked.
HUH?
MARY?
DID YOU GO BACK OUTSIDE? I SEE FOOT-PRINTS.
CRASH
WHO'S THERE?

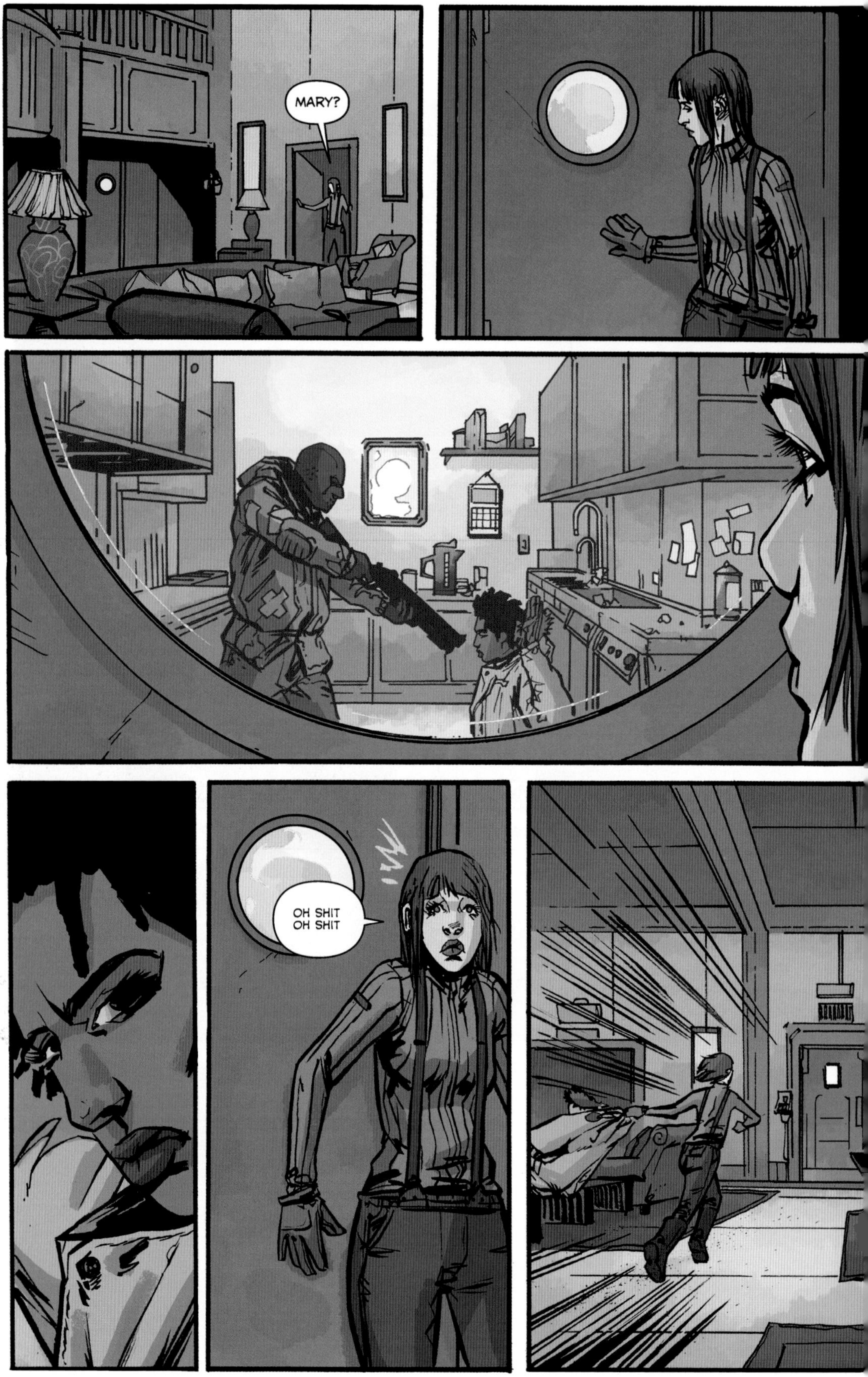
MARY?
OH SHIT
OH SHIT

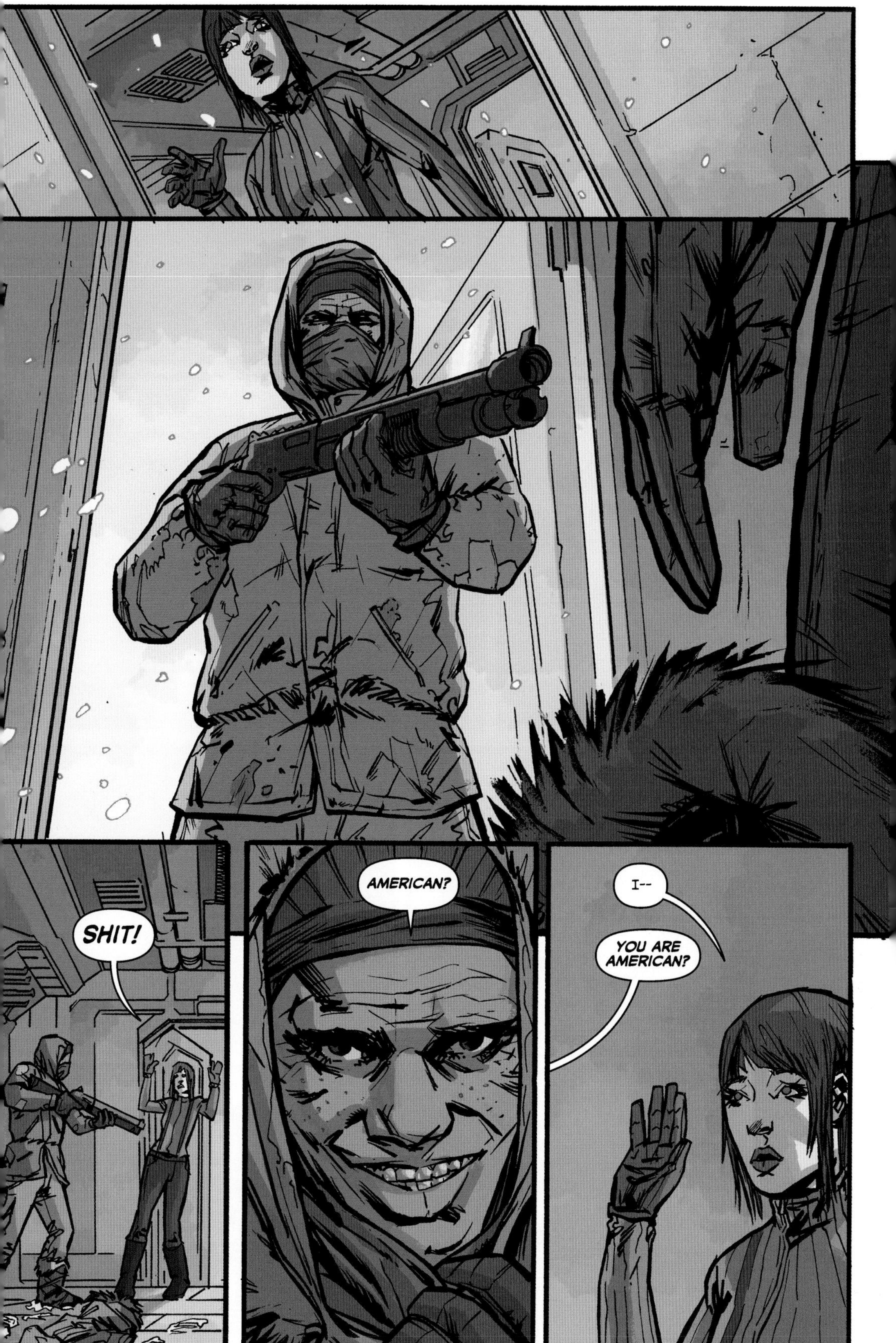
SHIT!
AMERICAN?
I--
YOU ARE AMERICAN?

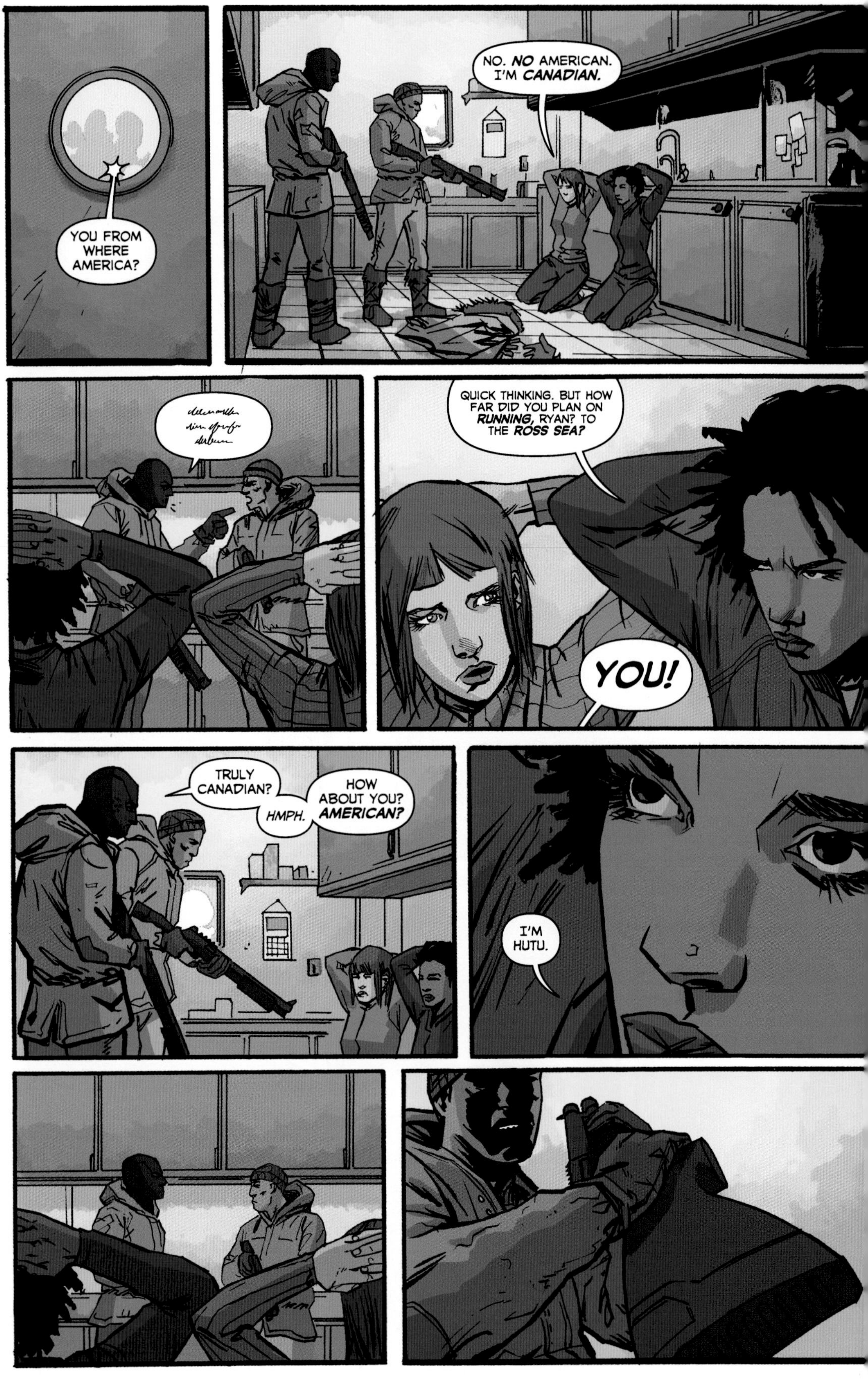
YOU FROM WHERE AMERICA?
NO. NO AMERICAN. I'M CANADIAN.
QUICK THINKING. BUT HOW FAR DID YOU PLAN ON RUNNING, RYAN? TO THE ROSS SEA?
YOU!
TRULY CANADIAN?
HMPH.
HOW ABOUT YOU? AMERICAN?
I'M HUTU.

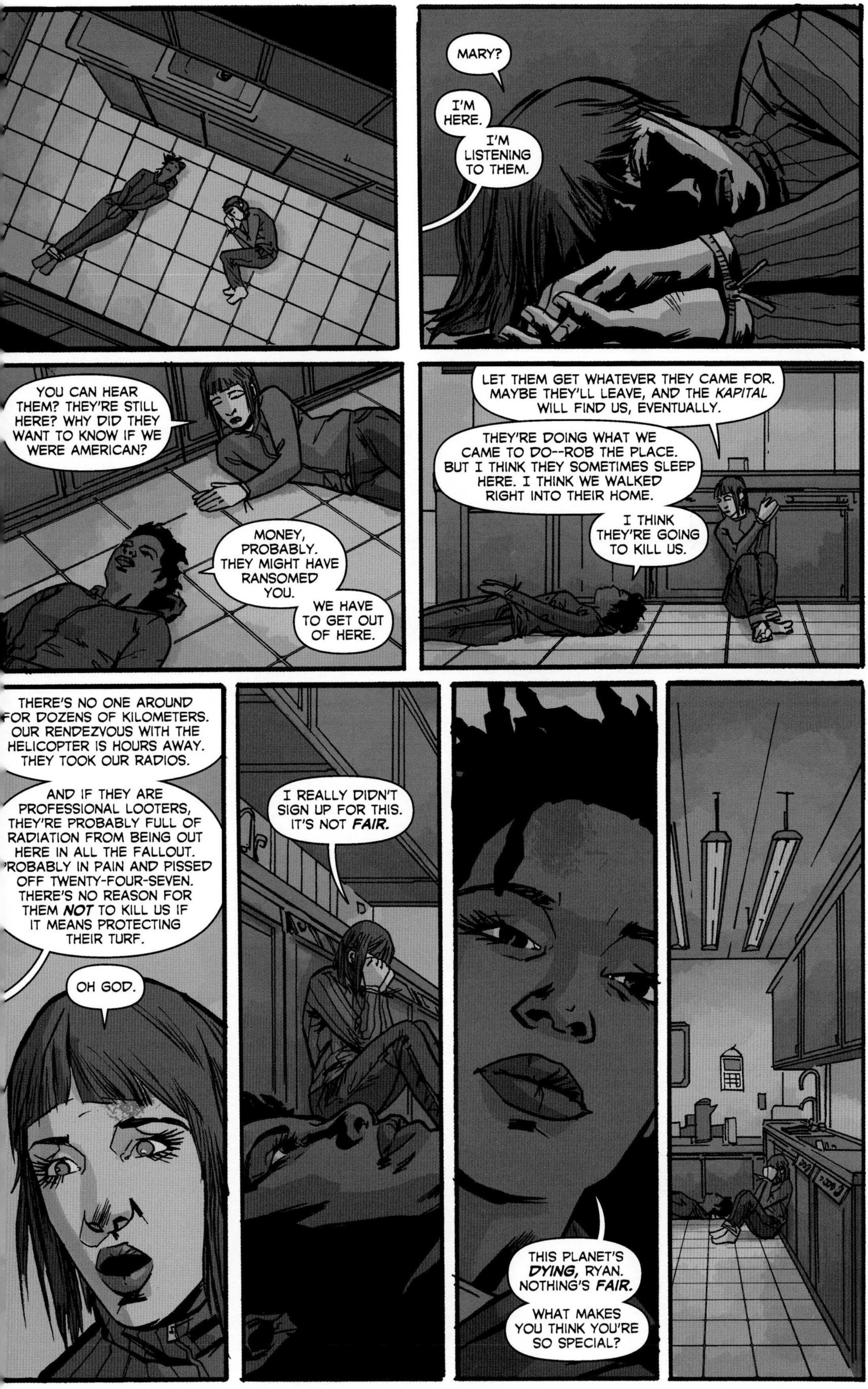
MARY?
I'M HERE.
I'M LISTENING TO THEM.
YOU CAN HEAR THEM? THEY'RE STILL HERE? WHY DID THEY WANT TO KNOW IF WE WERE AMERICAN?
MONEY, PROBABLY. THEY MIGHT HAVE RANSOMED YOU.
WE HAVE TO GET OUT OF HERE.
LET THEM GET WHATEVER THEY CAME FOR. MAYBE THEY'LL LEAVE, AND THE *KAPITAL* WILL FIND US, EVENTUALLY.
THEY'RE DOING WHAT WE CAME TO DO--ROB THE PLACE. BUT I THINK THEY SOMETIMES SLEEP HERE. I THINK WE WALKED RIGHT INTO THEIR HOME.
I THINK THEY'RE GOING TO KILL US.
THERE'S NO ONE AROUND FOR DOZENS OF KILOMETERS. OUR RENDEZVOUS WITH THE HELICOPTER IS HOURS AWAY. THEY TOOK OUR RADIOS.
AND IF THEY ARE PROFESSIONAL LOOTERS, THEY'RE PROBABLY FULL OF RADIATION FROM BEING OUT HERE IN ALL THE FALLOUT. PROBABLY IN PAIN AND PISSED OFF TWENTY-FOUR-SEVEN. THERE'S NO REASON FOR THEM ***NOT*** TO KILL US IF IT MEANS PROTECTING THEIR TURF.
OH GOD.
I REALLY DIDN'T SIGN UP FOR THIS. IT'S NOT ***FAIR.***
THIS PLANET'S ***DYING,*** RYAN. NOTHING'S ***FAIR.***
WHAT MAKES YOU THINK YOU'RE SO SPECIAL?

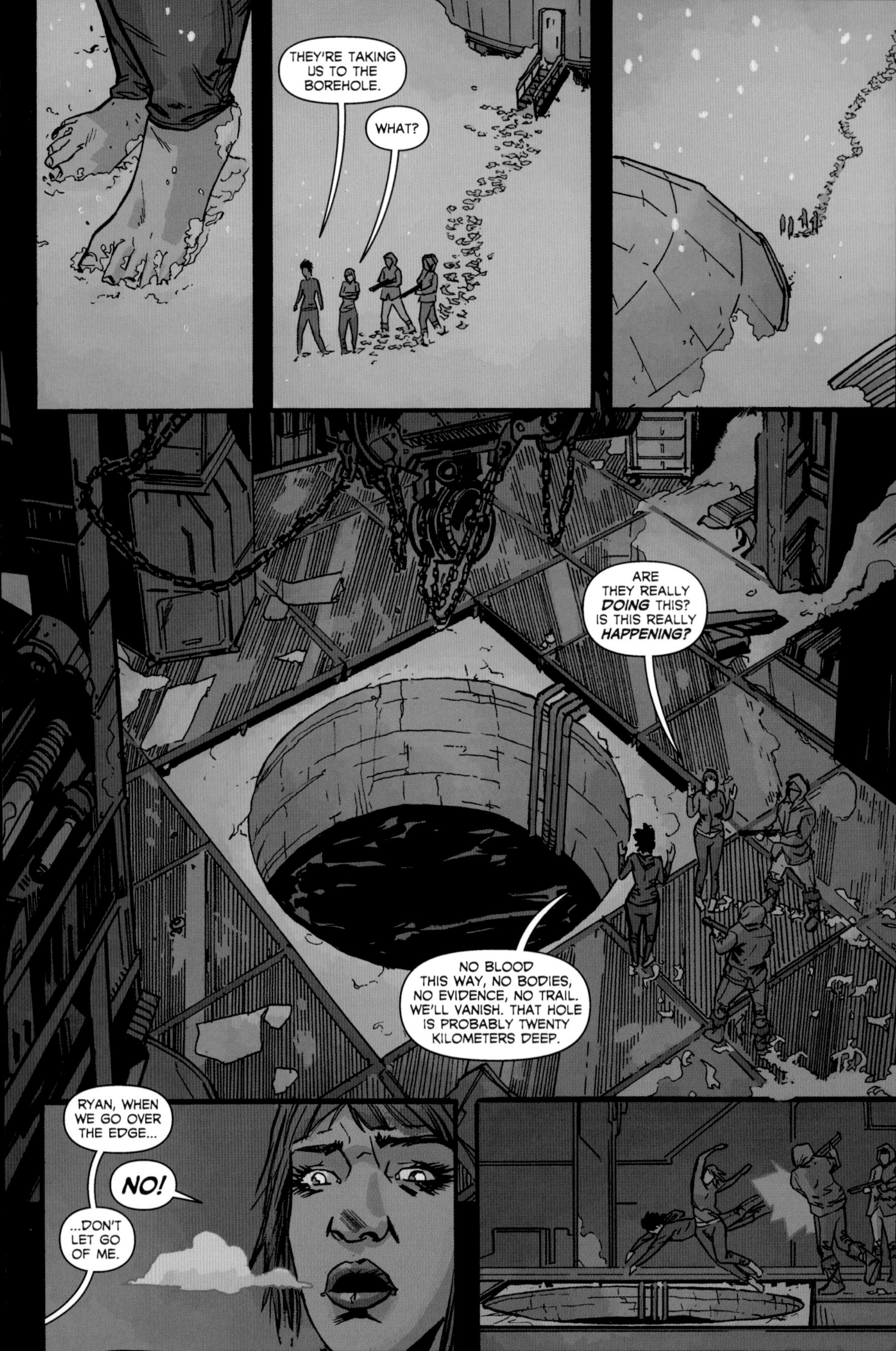
THEY'RE TAKING US TO THE BOREHOLE.
WHAT?
ARE THEY REALLY *DOING* THIS? IS THIS REALLY *HAPPENING?*
NO BLOOD THIS WAY, NO BODIES, NO EVIDENCE, NO TRAIL. WE'LL VANISH. THAT HOLE IS PROBABLY TWENTY KILOMETERS DEEP.
RYAN, WHEN WE GO OVER THE EDGE...
NO!
...DON'T LET GO OF ME.

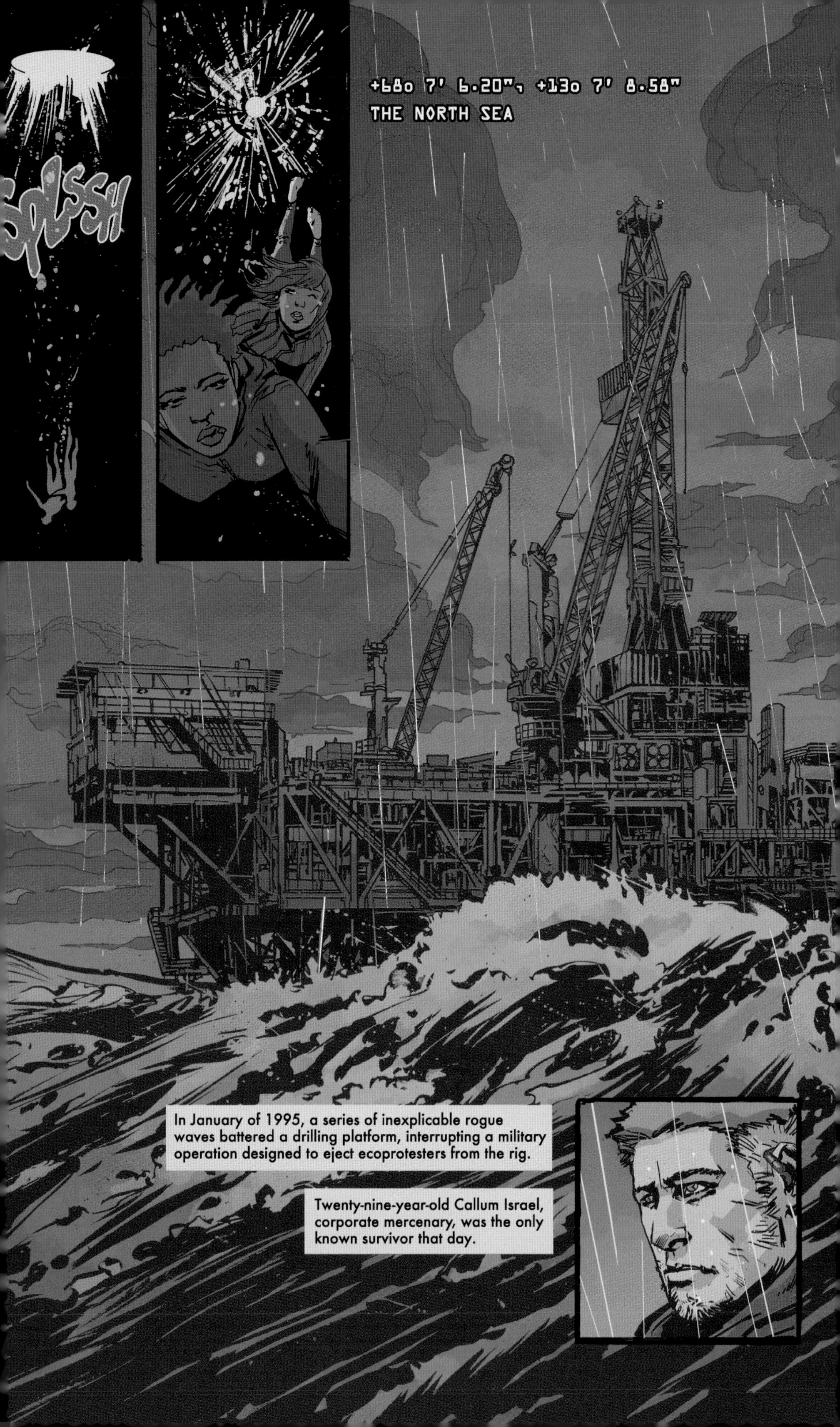
SPLSSH
+68o 7' 6.20", +13o 7' 8.58"
THE NORTH SEA
In January of 1995, a series of inexplicable rogue waves battered a drilling platform, interrupting a military operation designed to eject ecoprotesters from the rig.
Twenty-nine-year-old Callum Israel, corporate mercenary, was the only known survivor that day.

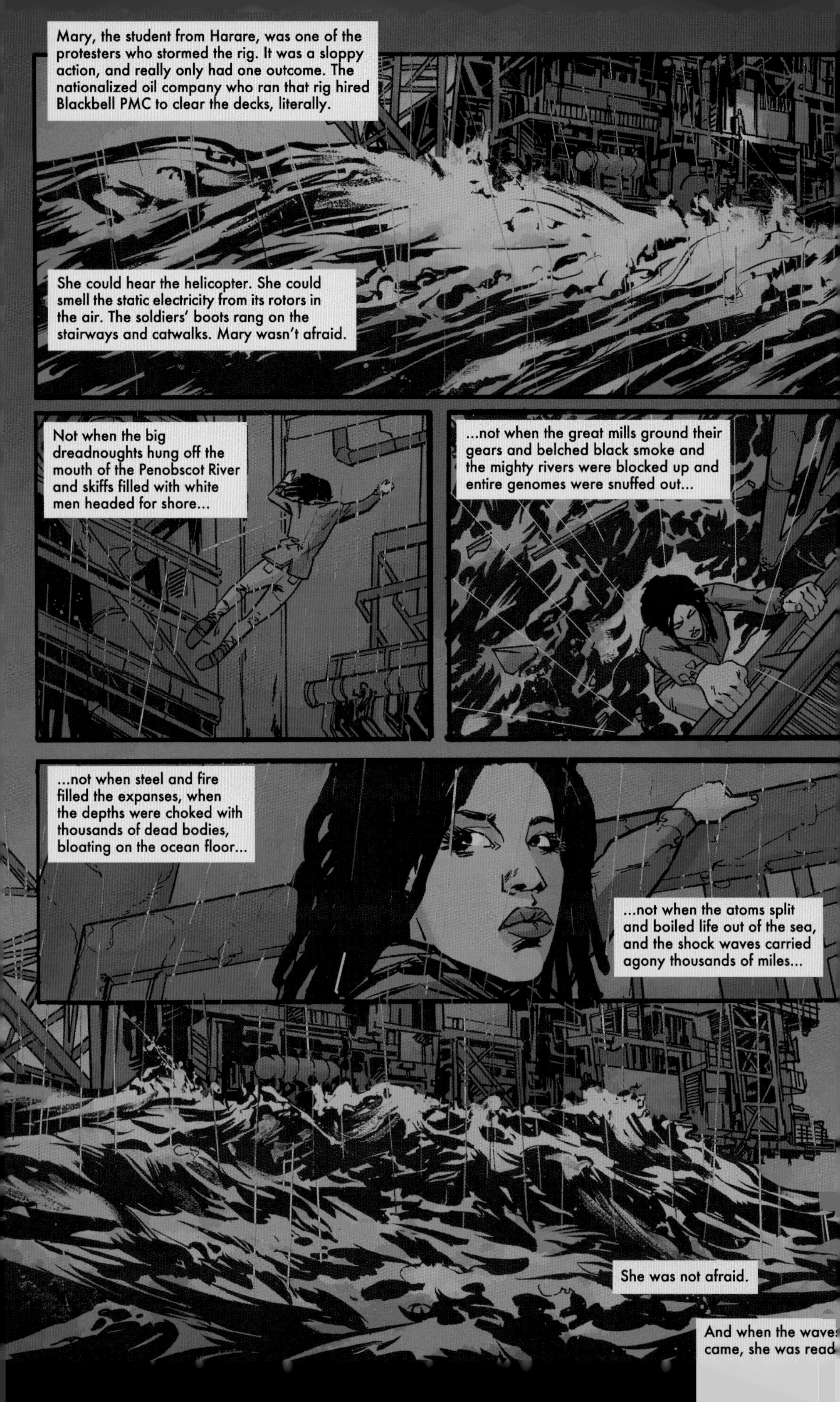
Mary, the student from Harare, was one of the protesters who stormed the rig. It was a sloppy action, and really only had one outcome. The nationalized oil company who ran that rig hired Blackbell PMC to clear the decks, literally.
She could hear the helicopter. She could smell the static electricity from its rotors in the air. The soldiers' boots rang on the stairways and catwalks. Mary wasn't afraid.
Not when the big dreadnoughts hung off the mouth of the Penobscot River and skiffs filled with white men headed for shore...
...not when the great mills ground their gears and belched black smoke and the mighty rivers were blocked up and entire genomes were snuffed out...
...not when steel and fire filled the expanses, when the depths were choked with thousands of dead bodies, bloating on the ocean floor...
...not when the atoms split and boiled life out of the sea, and the shock waves carried agony thousands of miles...
She was not afraid.
And when the wave
came, she was read

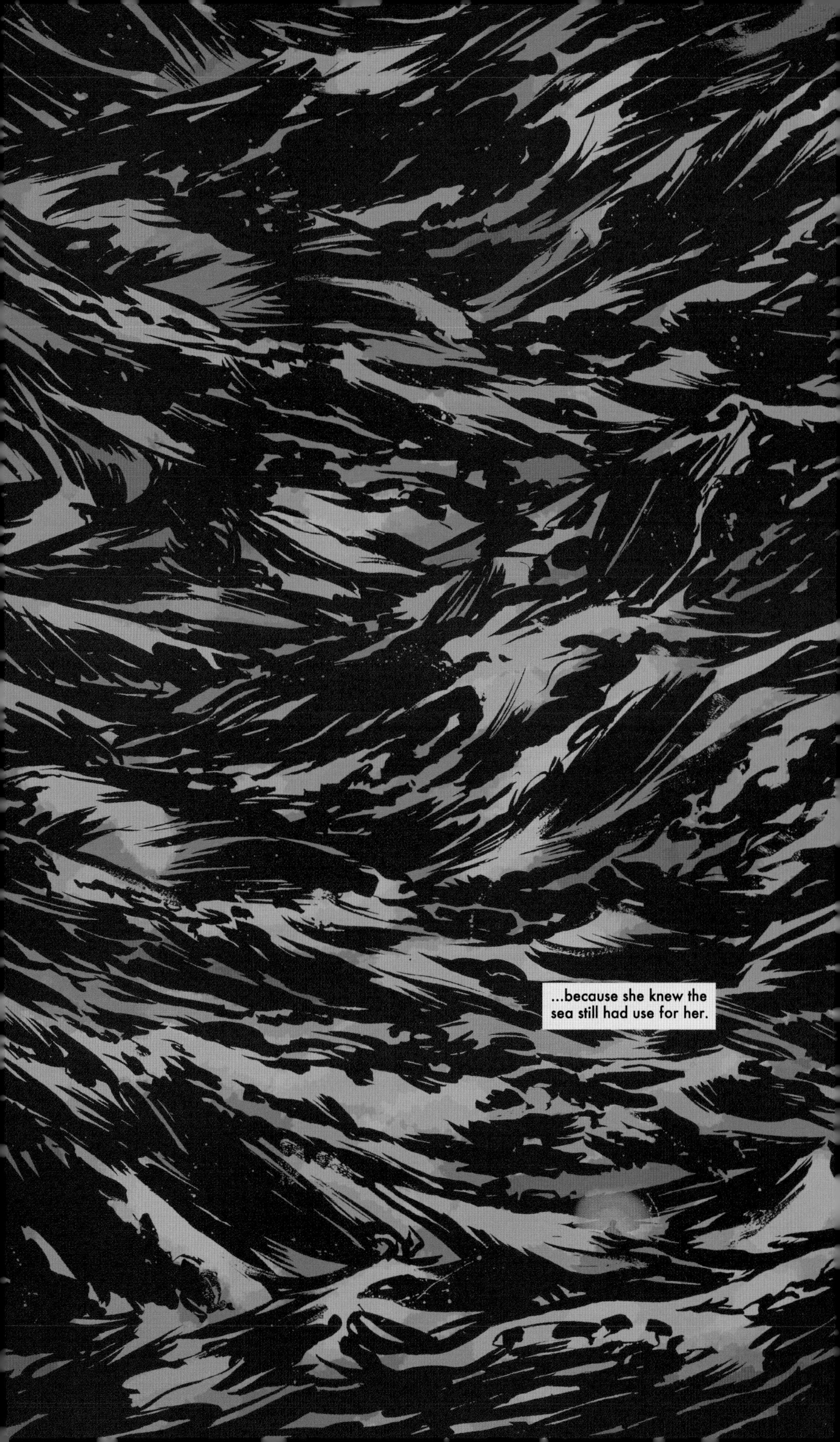
...because she knew the
sea still had use for her.

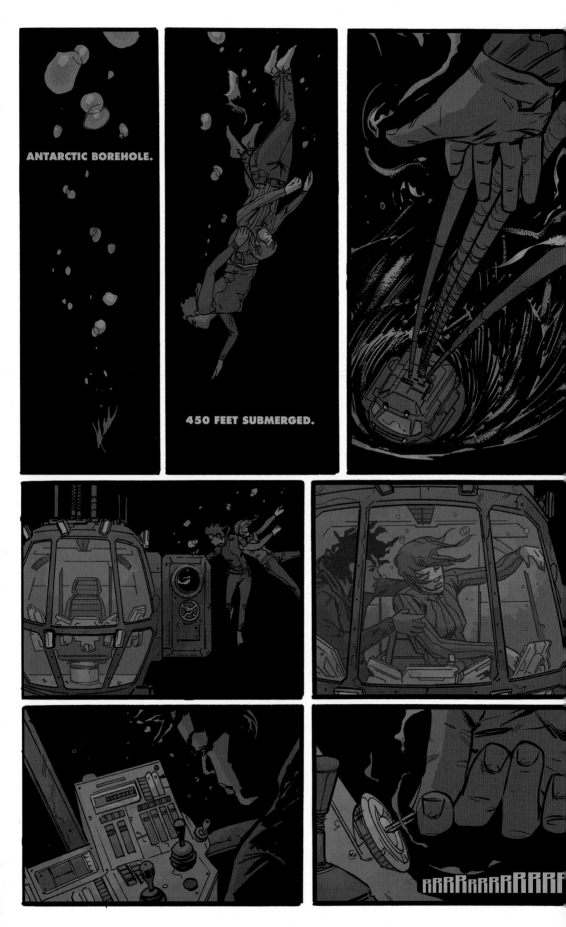

ANTARCTIC BOREHOLE.

450 FEET SUBMERGED.

RRRRRRRRRRR

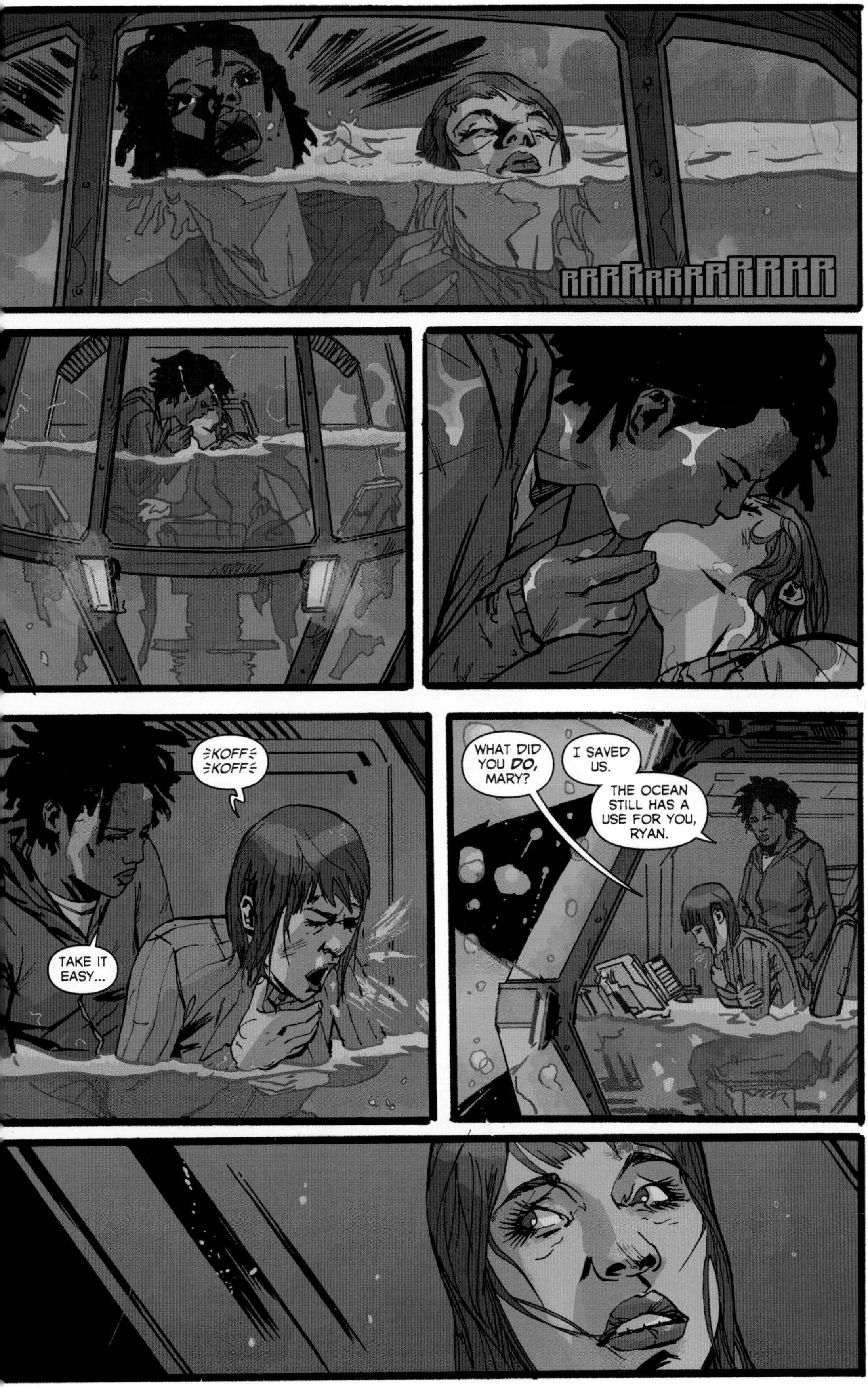
RRRRRRRRRRRR
KOFF KOFF
TAKE IT EASY...
WHAT DID YOU *DO*, MARY?
I SAVED US.
THE OCEAN STILL HAS A USE FOR YOU, RYAN.

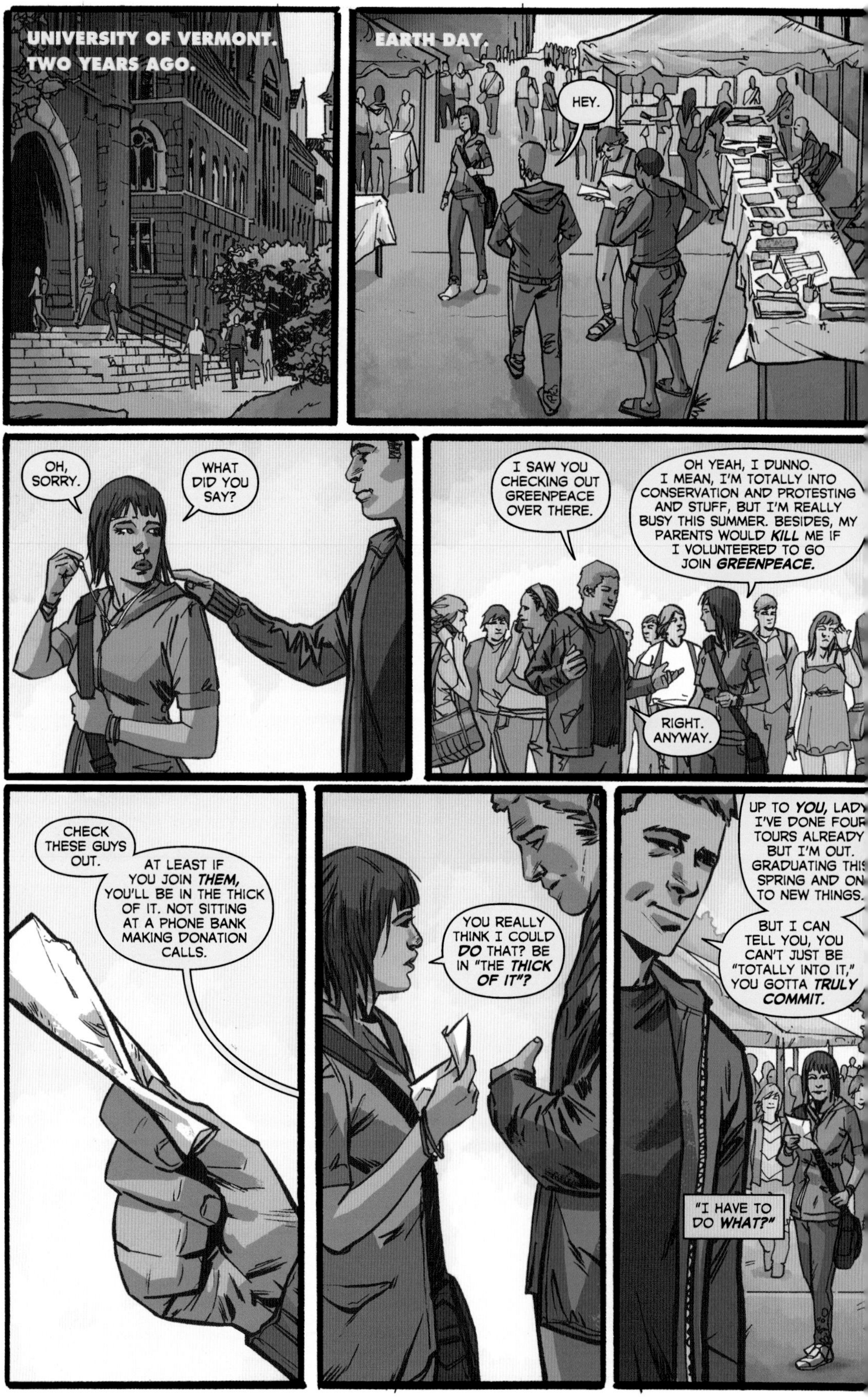
UNIVERSITY OF VERMONT.
TWO YEARS AGO.
EARTH DAY.
HEY.
OH, SORRY.
WHAT DID YOU SAY?
I SAW YOU CHECKING OUT GREENPEACE OVER THERE.
OH YEAH, I DUNNO. I MEAN, I'M TOTALLY INTO CONSERVATION AND PROTESTING AND STUFF, BUT I'M REALLY BUSY THIS SUMMER. BESIDES, MY PARENTS WOULD KILL ME IF I VOLUNTEERED TO GO JOIN GREENPEACE.
RIGHT. ANYWAY.
CHECK THESE GUYS OUT.
AT LEAST IF YOU JOIN THEM, YOU'LL BE IN THE THICK OF IT. NOT SITTING AT A PHONE BANK MAKING DONATION CALLS.
YOU REALLY THINK I COULD DO THAT? BE IN "THE THICK OF IT"?
UP TO YOU, LADY. I'VE DONE FOUR TOURS ALREADY BUT I'M OUT. GRADUATING THIS SPRING AND ON TO NEW THINGS.
BUT I CAN TELL YOU, YOU CAN'T JUST BE "TOTALLY INTO IT," YOU GOTTA TRULY COMMIT.
"I HAVE TO DO WHAT?"

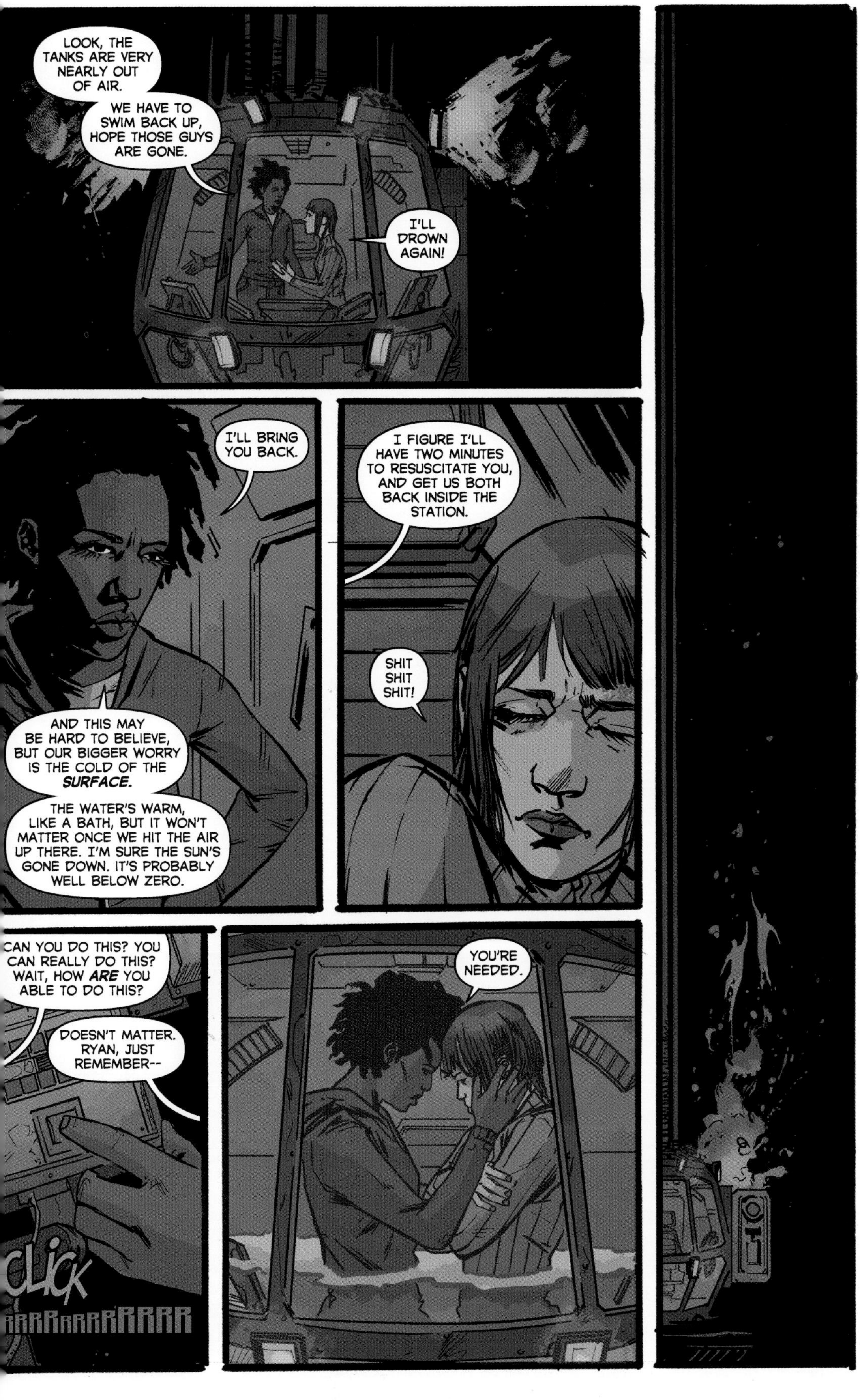
LOOK, THE TANKS ARE VERY NEARLY OUT OF AIR.
WE HAVE TO SWIM BACK UP, HOPE THOSE GUYS ARE GONE.
I'LL DROWN AGAIN!
I'LL BRING YOU BACK.
AND THIS MAY BE HARD TO BELIEVE, BUT OUR BIGGER WORRY IS THE COLD OF THE ***SURFACE.***
THE WATER'S WARM, LIKE A BATH, BUT IT WON'T MATTER ONCE WE HIT THE AIR UP THERE. I'M SURE THE SUN'S GONE DOWN. IT'S PROBABLY WELL BELOW ZERO.
I FIGURE I'LL HAVE TWO MINUTES TO RESUSCITATE YOU, AND GET US BOTH BACK INSIDE THE STATION.
SHIT SHIT SHIT!
CAN YOU DO THIS? YOU CAN REALLY DO THIS? WAIT, HOW ***ARE*** YOU ABLE TO DO THIS?
DOESN'T MATTER. RYAN, JUST REMEMBER--
CLICK
RRRRRRRRRRRR
YOU'RE NEEDED.

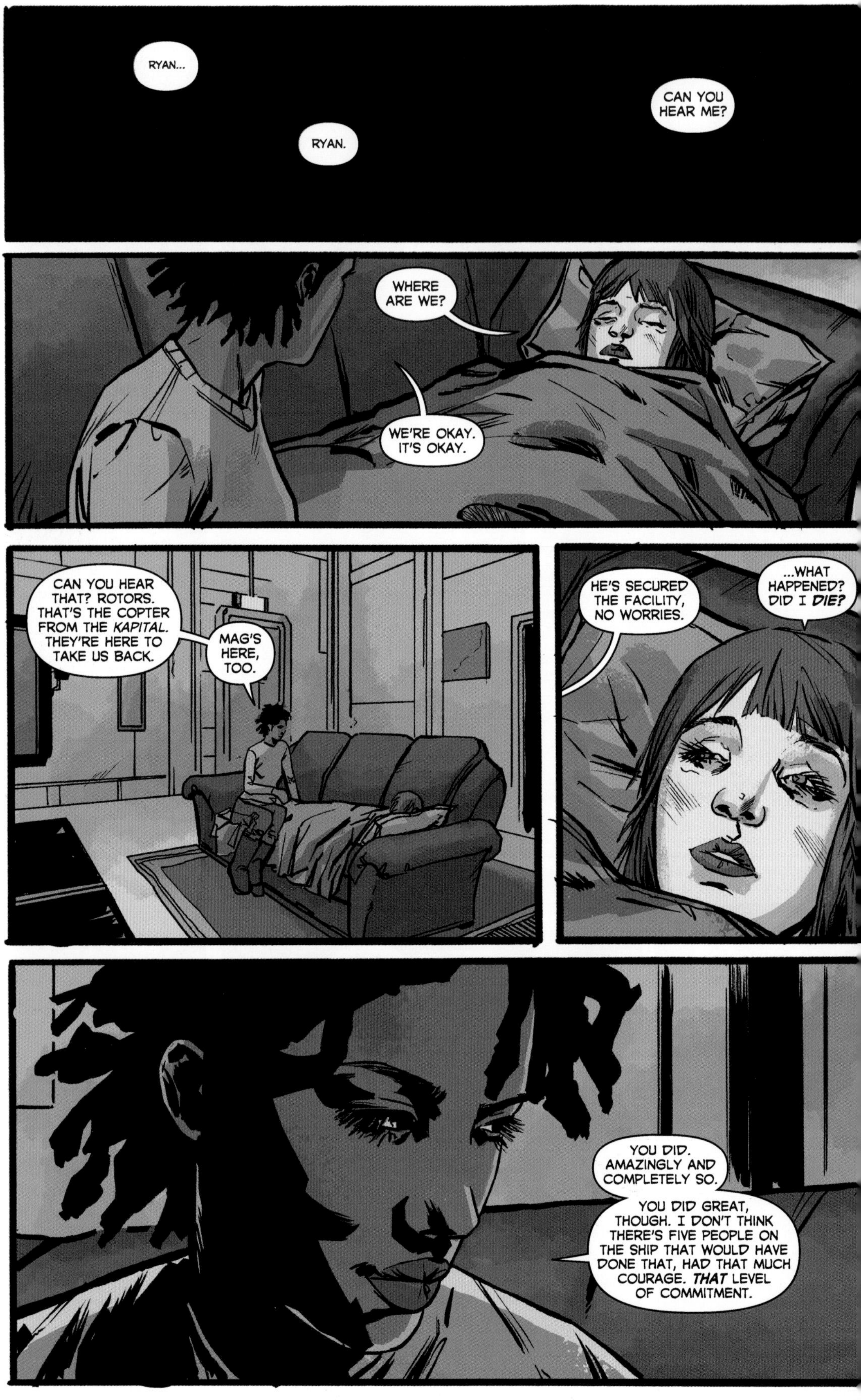
RYAN...
RYAN.
CAN YOU HEAR ME?
WHERE ARE WE?
WE'RE OKAY. IT'S OKAY.
CAN YOU HEAR THAT? ROTORS. THAT'S THE COPTER FROM THE *KAPITAL.* THEY'RE HERE TO TAKE US BACK.
MAG'S HERE, TOO.
...WHAT HAPPENED? DID I ***DIE?***
HE'S SECURED THE FACILITY, NO WORRIES.
YOU DID. AMAZINGLY AND COMPLETELY SO.
YOU DID GREAT, THOUGH. I DON'T THINK THERE'S FIVE PEOPLE ON THE SHIP THAT WOULD HAVE DONE THAT, HAD THAT MUCH COURAGE. ***THAT*** LEVEL OF COMMITMENT.

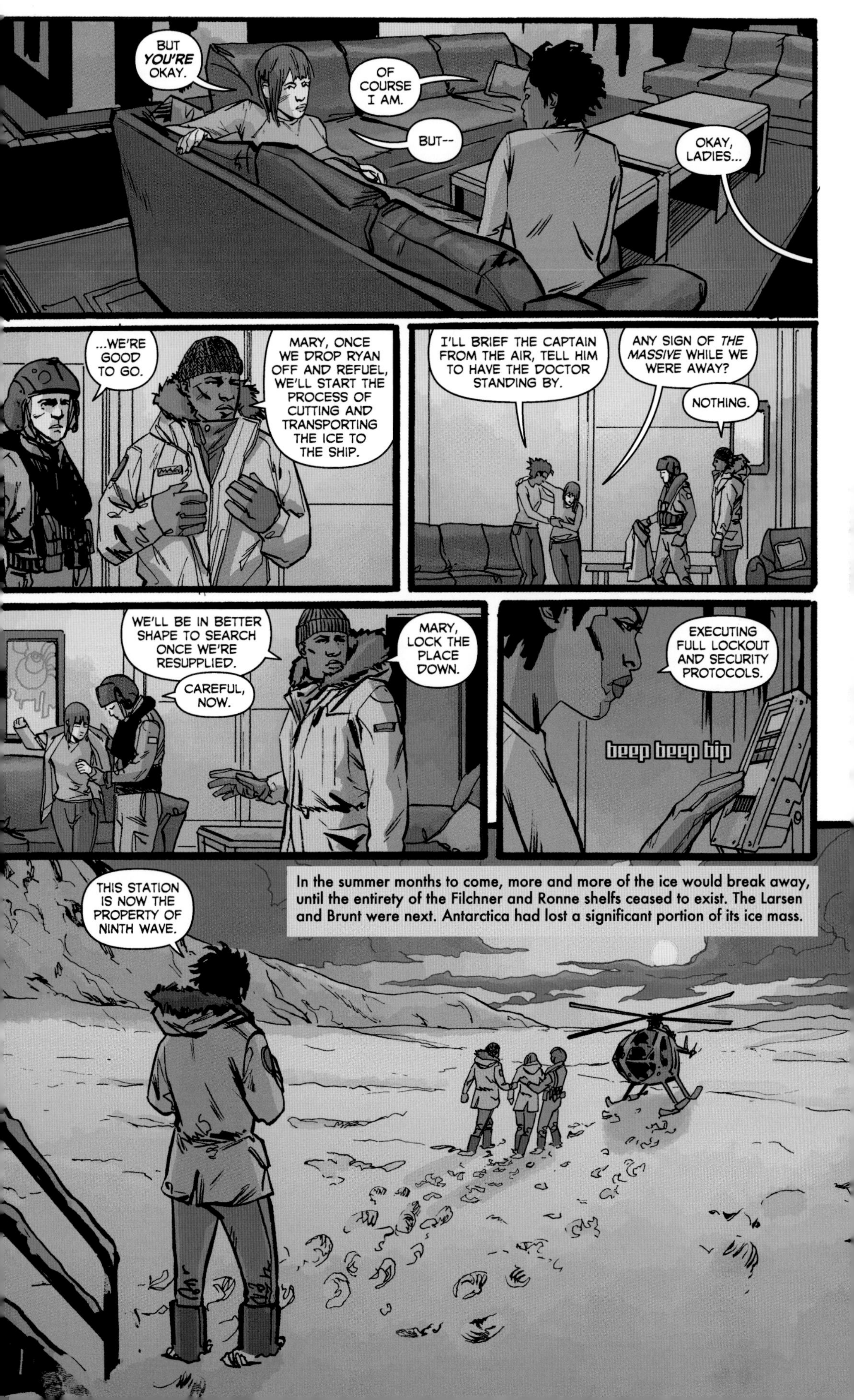
BUT *YOU'RE* OKAY.
OF COURSE I AM.
BUT--
OKAY, LADIES...
...WE'RE GOOD TO GO.
MARY, ONCE WE DROP RYAN OFF AND REFUEL, WE'LL START THE PROCESS OF CUTTING AND TRANSPORTING THE ICE TO THE SHIP.
I'LL BRIEF THE CAPTAIN FROM THE AIR, TELL HIM TO HAVE THE DOCTOR STANDING BY.
ANY SIGN OF *THE MASSIVE* WHILE WE WERE AWAY?
NOTHING.
WE'LL BE IN BETTER SHAPE TO SEARCH ONCE WE'RE RESUPPLIED.
CAREFUL, NOW.
MARY, LOCK THE PLACE DOWN.
EXECUTING FULL LOCKOUT AND SECURITY PROTOCOLS.
beep beep bip
THIS STATION IS NOW THE PROPERTY OF NINTH WAVE.
In the summer months to come, more and more of the ice would break away, until the entirety of the Filchner and Ronne shelfs ceased to exist. The Larsen and Brunt were next. Antarctica had lost a significant portion of its ice mass.

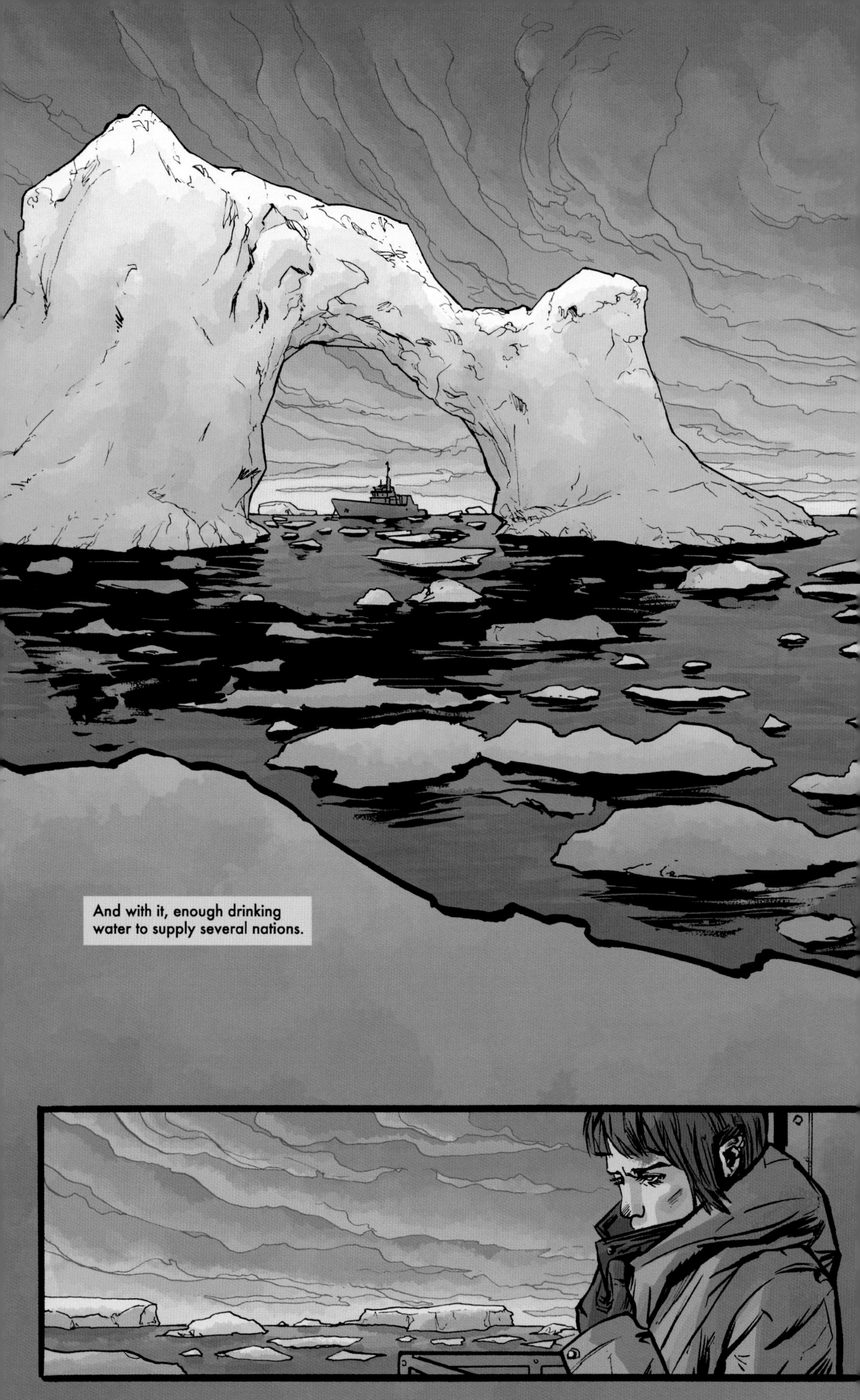
And with it, enough drinking water to supply several nations.

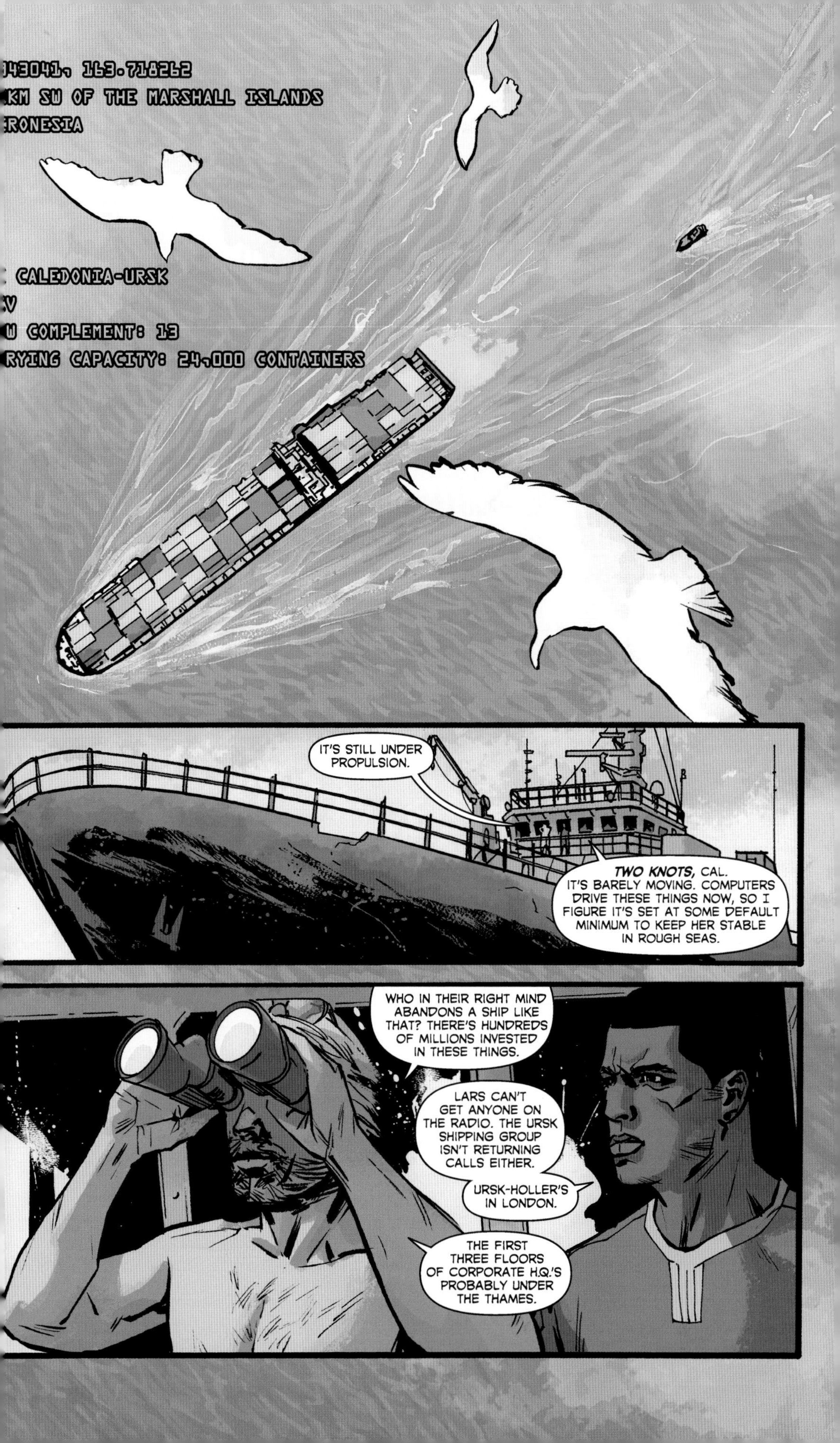

343041, 163.718262
KM SW OF THE MARSHALL ISLANDS
RONESIA
CALEDONIA-URSK
V
W COMPLEMENT: 13
RYING CAPACITY: 24,000 CONTAINERS
IT'S STILL UNDER PROPULSION.
TWO KNOTS, CAL. IT'S BARELY MOVING. COMPUTERS DRIVE THESE THINGS NOW, SO I FIGURE IT'S SET AT SOME DEFAULT MINIMUM TO KEEP HER STABLE IN ROUGH SEAS.
WHO IN THEIR RIGHT MIND ABANDONS A SHIP LIKE THAT? THERE'S HUNDREDS OF MILLIONS INVESTED IN THESE THINGS.
LARS CAN'T GET ANYONE ON THE RADIO. THE URSK SHIPPING GROUP ISN'T RETURNING CALLS EITHER.
URSK-HOLLER'S IN LONDON.
THE FIRST THREE FLOORS OF CORPORATE H.Q.'S PROBABLY UNDER THE THAMES.

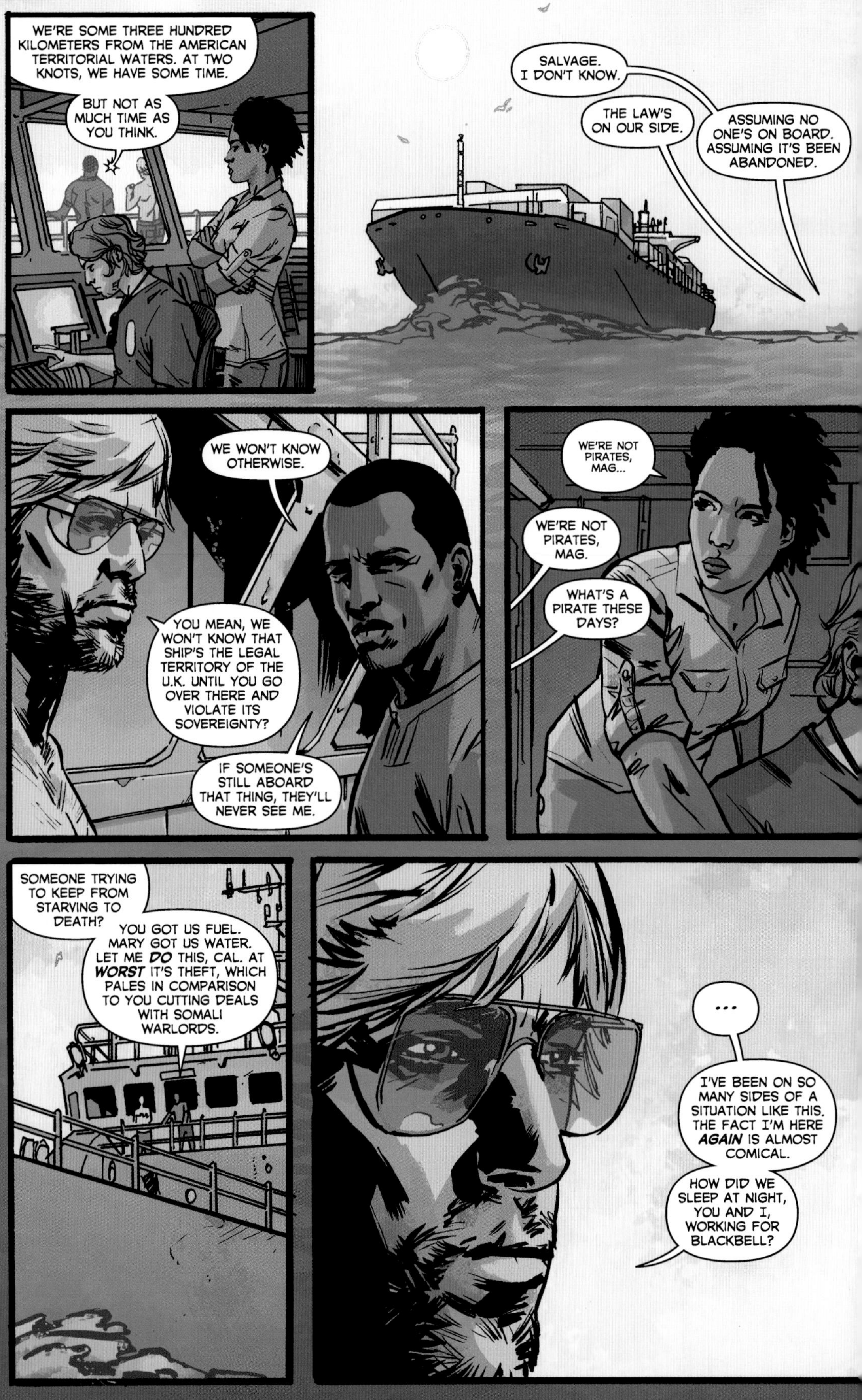
WE'RE SOME THREE HUNDRED KILOMETERS FROM THE AMERICAN TERRITORIAL WATERS. AT TWO KNOTS, WE HAVE SOME TIME.
BUT NOT AS MUCH TIME AS YOU THINK.
SALVAGE. I DON'T KNOW.
THE LAW'S ON OUR SIDE.
ASSUMING NO ONE'S ON BOARD. ASSUMING IT'S BEEN ABANDONED.
WE WON'T KNOW OTHERWISE.
YOU MEAN, WE WON'T KNOW THAT SHIP'S THE LEGAL TERRITORY OF THE U.K. UNTIL YOU GO OVER THERE AND VIOLATE ITS SOVEREIGNTY?
IF SOMEONE'S STILL ABOARD THAT THING, THEY'LL NEVER SEE ME.
WE'RE NOT PIRATES, MAG...
WE'RE NOT PIRATES, MAG.
WHAT'S A PIRATE THESE DAYS?
SOMEONE TRYING TO KEEP FROM STARVING TO DEATH?
YOU GOT US FUEL. MARY GOT US WATER. LET ME DO THIS, CAL. AT WORST IT'S THEFT, WHICH PALES IN COMPARISON TO YOU CUTTING DEALS WITH SOMALI WARLORDS.
...
I'VE BEEN ON SO MANY SIDES OF A SITUATION LIKE THIS. THE FACT I'M HERE AGAIN IS ALMOST COMICAL.
HOW DID WE SLEEP AT NIGHT, YOU AND I, WORKING FOR BLACKBELL?

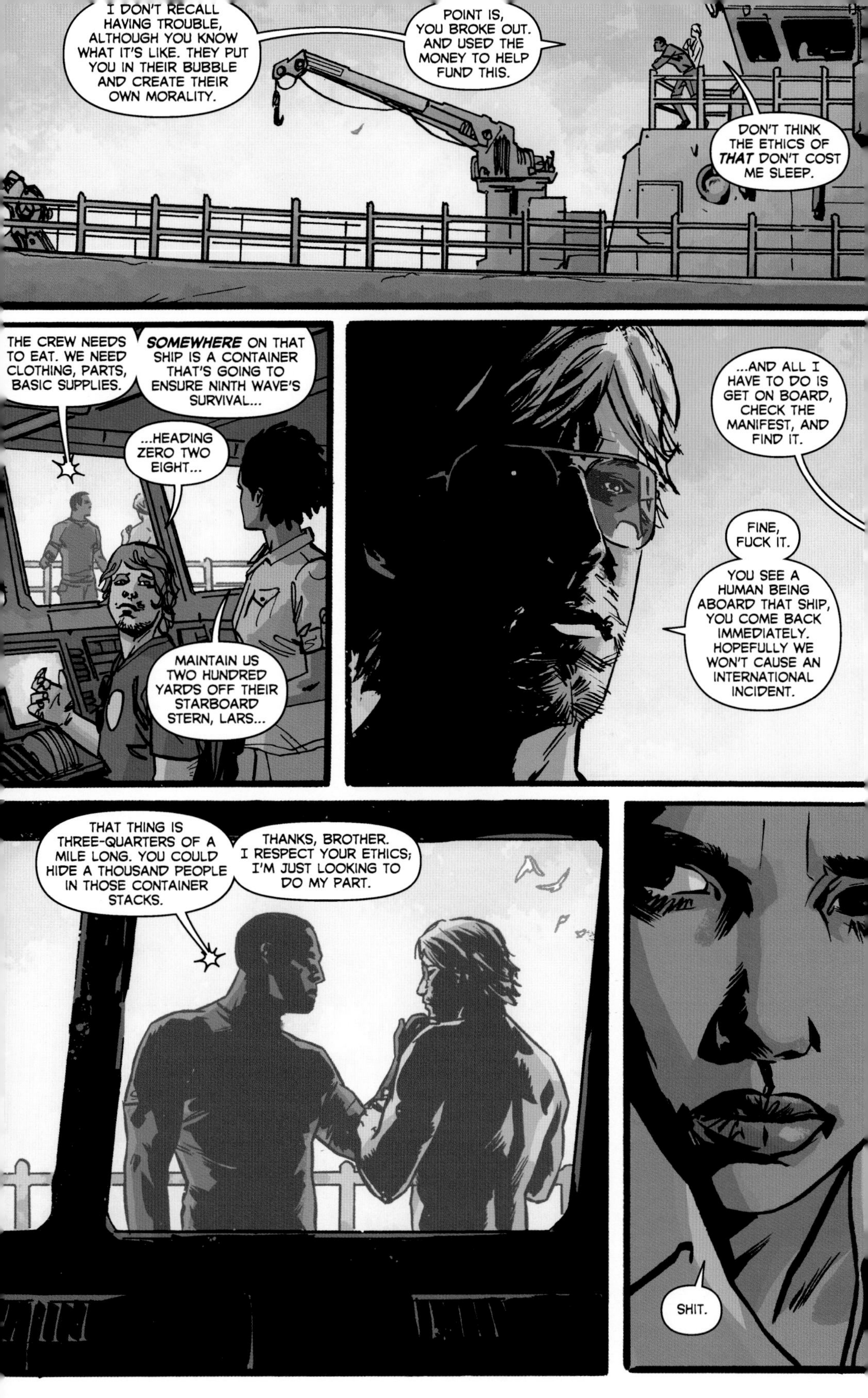
I DON'T RECALL HAVING TROUBLE, ALTHOUGH YOU KNOW WHAT IT'S LIKE. THEY PUT YOU IN THEIR BUBBLE AND CREATE THEIR OWN MORALITY.
POINT IS, YOU BROKE OUT. AND USED THE MONEY TO HELP FUND THIS.
DON'T THINK THE ETHICS OF *THAT* DON'T COST ME SLEEP.
THE CREW NEEDS TO EAT. WE NEED CLOTHING, PARTS, BASIC SUPPLIES.
SOMEWHERE ON THAT SHIP IS A CONTAINER THAT'S GOING TO ENSURE NINTH WAVE'S SURVIVAL...
...HEADING ZERO TWO EIGHT...
MAINTAIN US TWO HUNDRED YARDS OFF THEIR STARBOARD STERN, LARS...
...AND ALL I HAVE TO DO IS GET ON BOARD, CHECK THE MANIFEST, AND FIND IT.
FINE, FUCK IT.
YOU SEE A HUMAN BEING ABOARD THAT SHIP, YOU COME BACK IMMEDIATELY. HOPEFULLY WE WON'T CAUSE AN INTERNATIONAL INCIDENT.
THAT THING IS THREE-QUARTERS OF A MILE LONG. YOU COULD HIDE A THOUSAND PEOPLE IN THOSE CONTAINER STACKS.
THANKS, BROTHER. I RESPECT YOUR ETHICS; I'M JUST LOOKING TO DO MY PART.
SHIT.

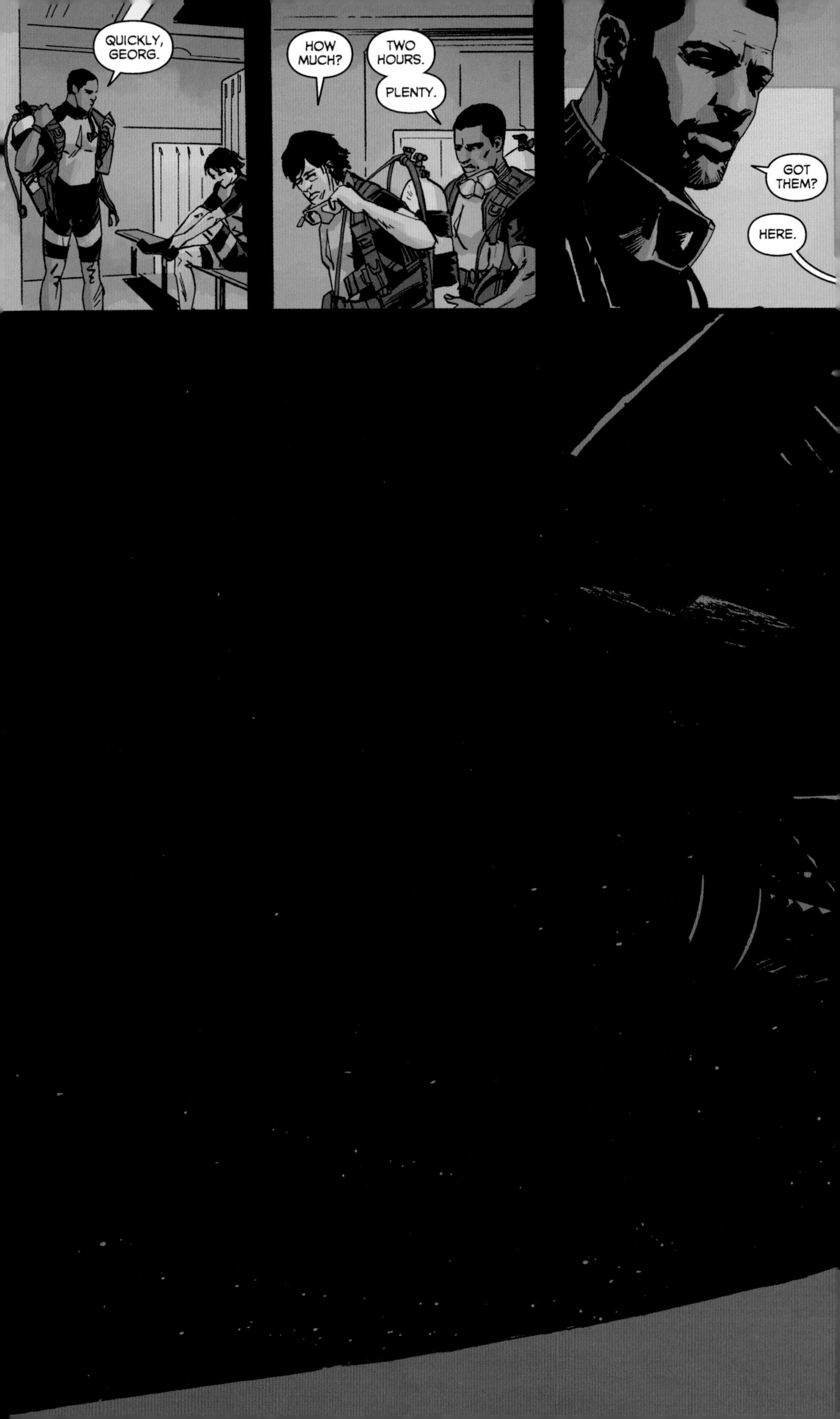
QUICKLY, GEORG.
HOW MUCH?
TWO HOURS.
PLENTY.
GOT THEM?
HERE.

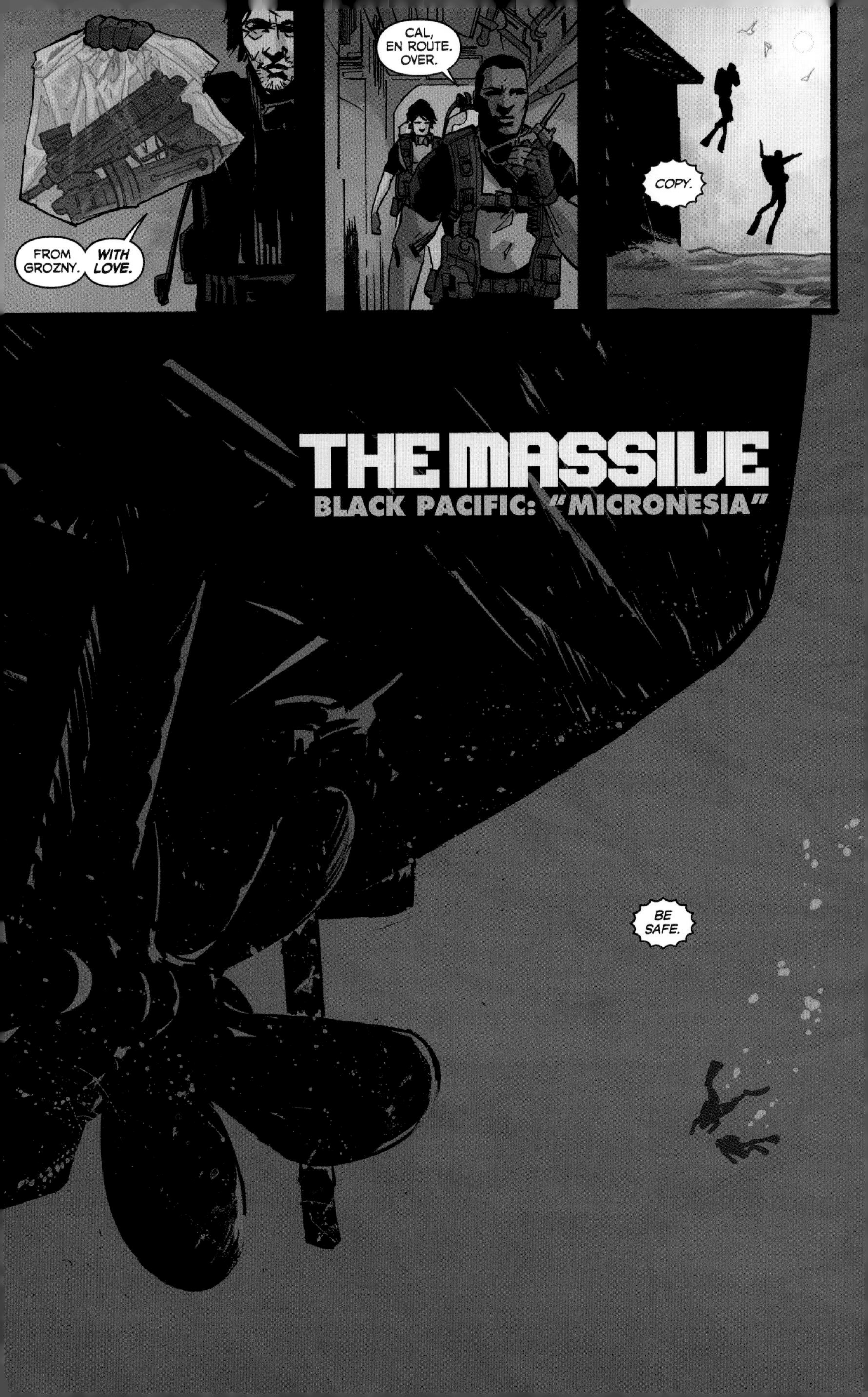
FROM GROZNY.
WITH LOVE.
CAL, EN ROUTE. OVER.
COPY.
THE MASSIVE
BLACK PACIFIC: "MICRONESIA"
BE SAFE.

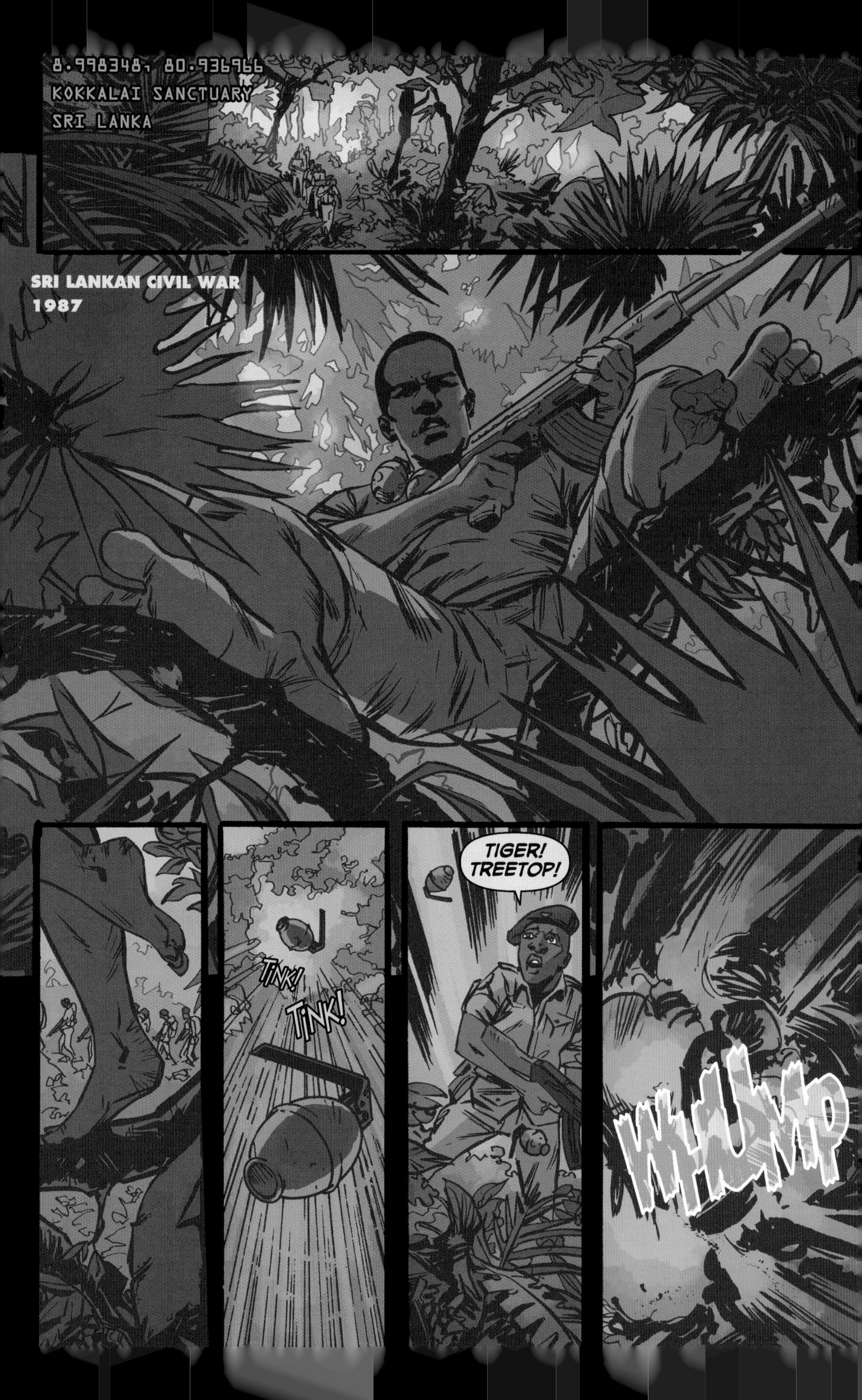
8.998348, 80.936966
KOKKALAI SANCTUARY
SRI LANKA
SRI LANKAN CIVIL WAR
1987
TINK!
TINK!
TIGER! TREETOP!
WHUMP

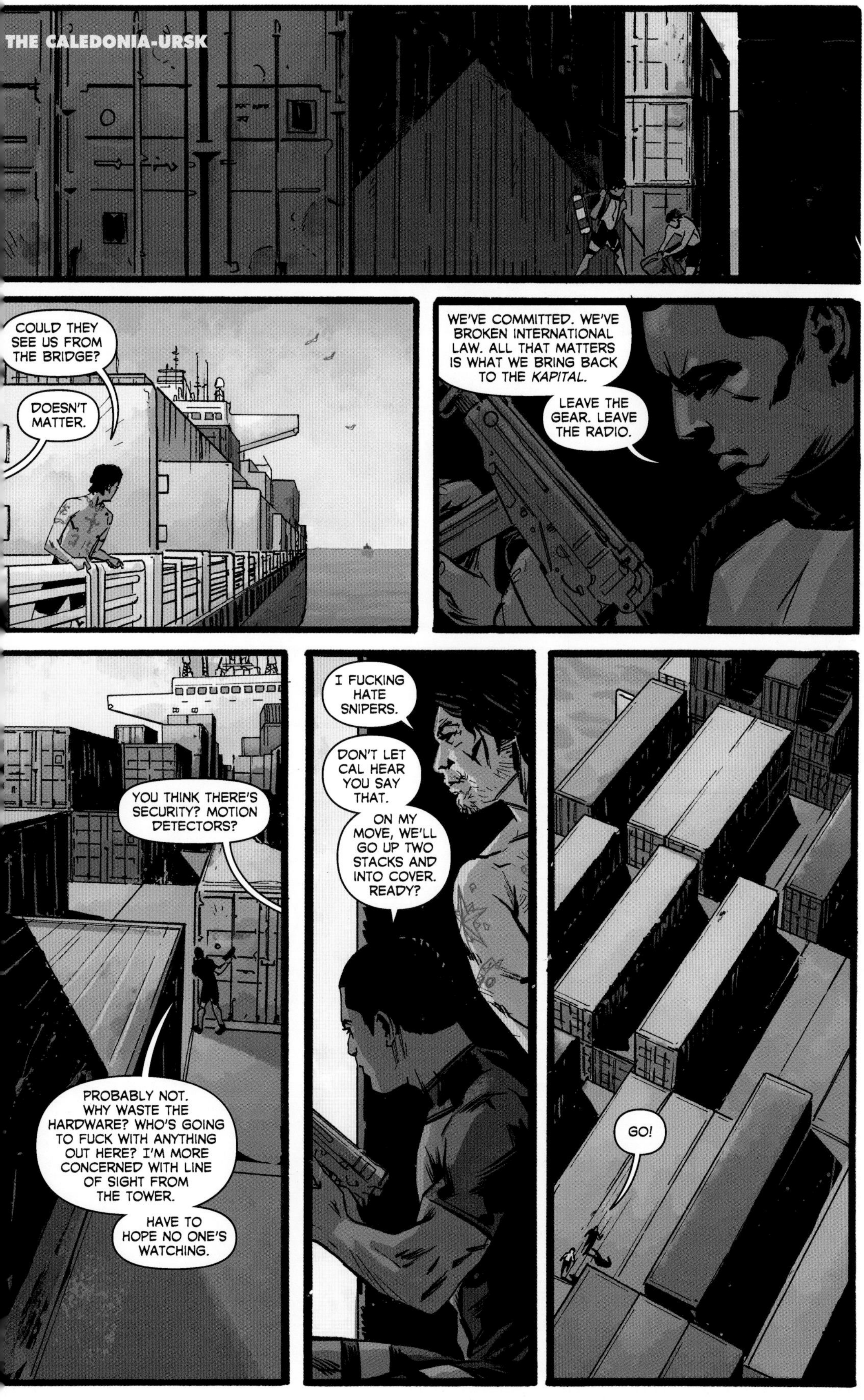
THE CALEDONIA-URSK
COULD THEY SEE US FROM THE BRIDGE?
DOESN'T MATTER.
WE'VE COMMITTED. WE'VE BROKEN INTERNATIONAL LAW. ALL THAT MATTERS IS WHAT WE BRING BACK TO THE *KAPITAL.*
LEAVE THE GEAR. LEAVE THE RADIO.
YOU THINK THERE'S SECURITY? MOTION DETECTORS?
PROBABLY NOT. WHY WASTE THE HARDWARE? WHO'S GOING TO FUCK WITH ANYTHING OUT HERE? I'M MORE CONCERNED WITH LINE OF SIGHT FROM THE TOWER.
HAVE TO HOPE NO ONE'S WATCHING.
I FUCKING HATE SNIPERS.
DON'T LET CAL HEAR YOU SAY THAT.
ON MY MOVE, WE'LL GO UP TWO STACKS AND INTO COVER. READY?
GO!

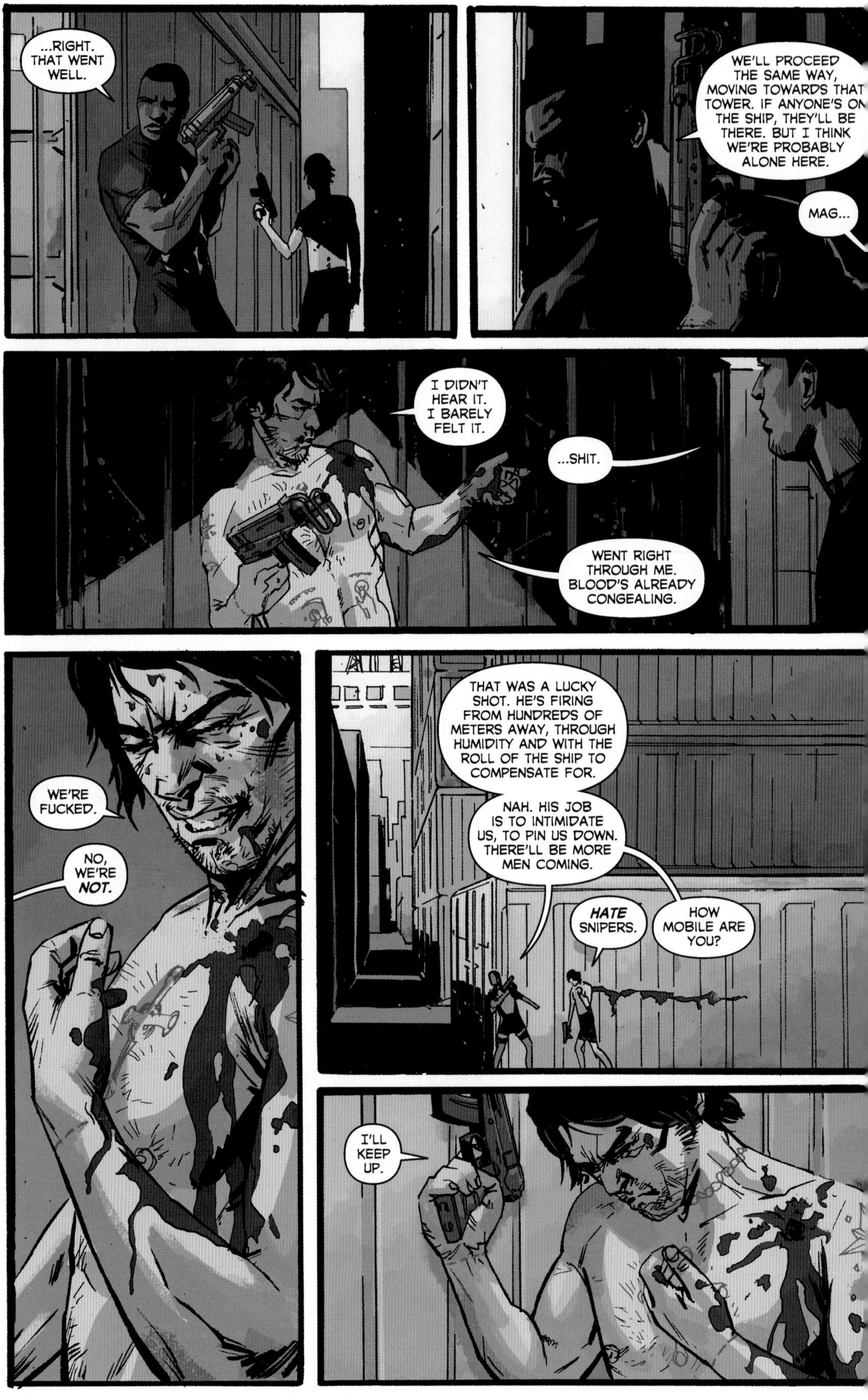

...RIGHT. THAT WENT WELL.
WE'LL PROCEED THE SAME WAY, MOVING TOWARDS THAT TOWER. IF ANYONE'S ON THE SHIP, THEY'LL BE THERE. BUT I THINK WE'RE PROBABLY ALONE HERE.
MAG...
I DIDN'T HEAR IT. I BARELY FELT IT.
...SHIT.
WENT RIGHT THROUGH ME. BLOOD'S ALREADY CONGEALING.
WE'RE FUCKED.
NO, WE'RE *NOT.*
THAT WAS A LUCKY SHOT. HE'S FIRING FROM HUNDREDS OF METERS AWAY, THROUGH HUMIDITY AND WITH THE ROLL OF THE SHIP TO COMPENSATE FOR.
NAH. HIS JOB IS TO INTIMIDATE US, TO PIN US DOWN. THERE'LL BE MORE MEN COMING.
HATE SNIPERS.
HOW MOBILE ARE YOU?
I'LL KEEP UP.

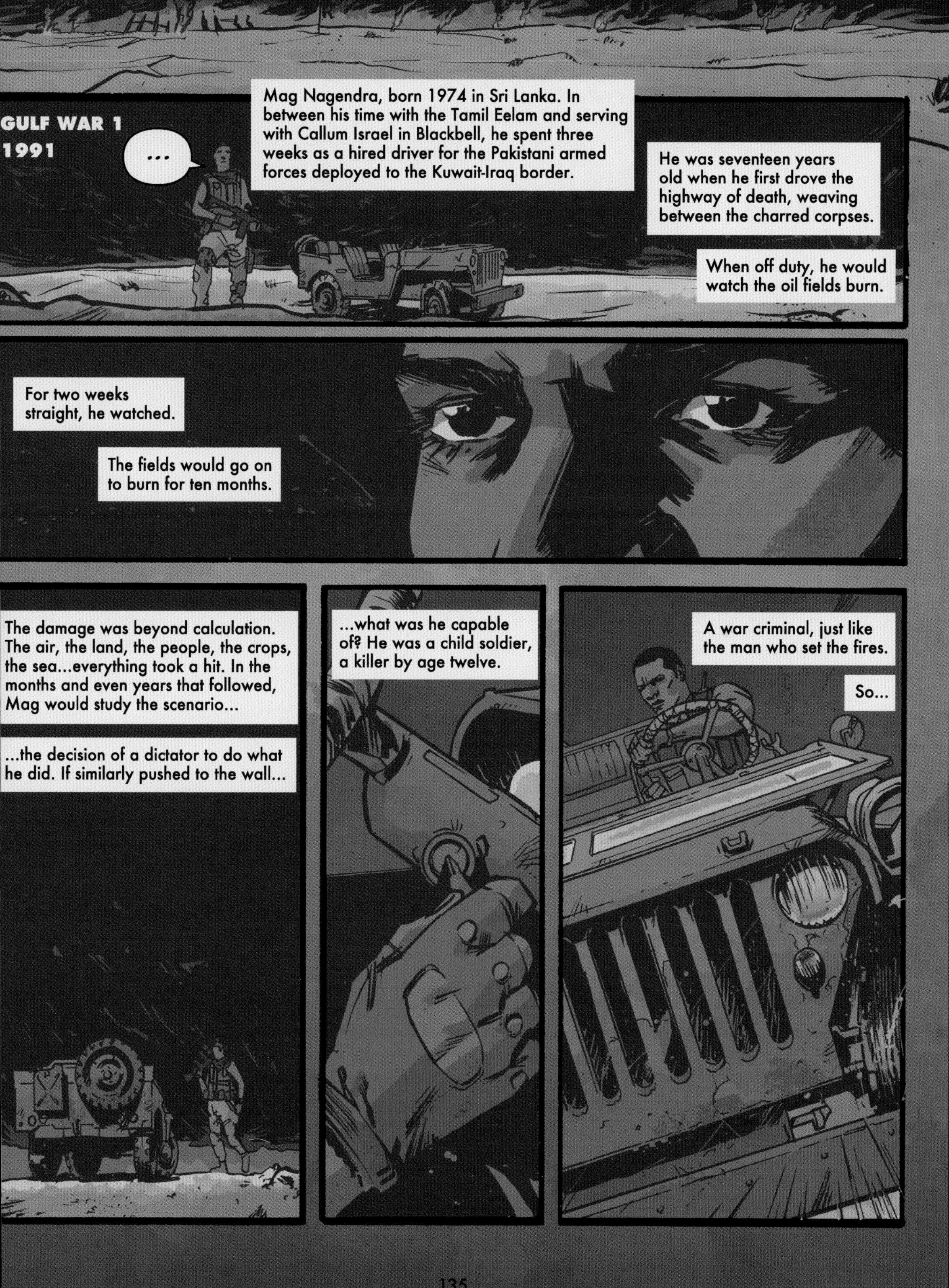
GULF WAR 1
1991
...
Mag Nagendra, born 1974 in Sri Lanka. In between his time with the Tamil Eelam and serving with Callum Israel in Blackbell, he spent three weeks as a hired driver for the Pakistani armed forces deployed to the Kuwait-Iraq border.
He was seventeen years old when he first drove the highway of death, weaving between the charred corpses.
When off duty, he would watch the oil fields burn.
For two weeks straight, he watched.
The fields would go on to burn for ten months.
The damage was beyond calculation. The air, the land, the people, the crops, the sea...everything took a hit. In the months and even years that followed, Mag would study the scenario...
...the decision of a dictator to do what he did. If similarly pushed to the wall...
...what was he capable of? He was a child soldier, a killer by age twelve.
A war criminal, just like the man who set the fires.
So...

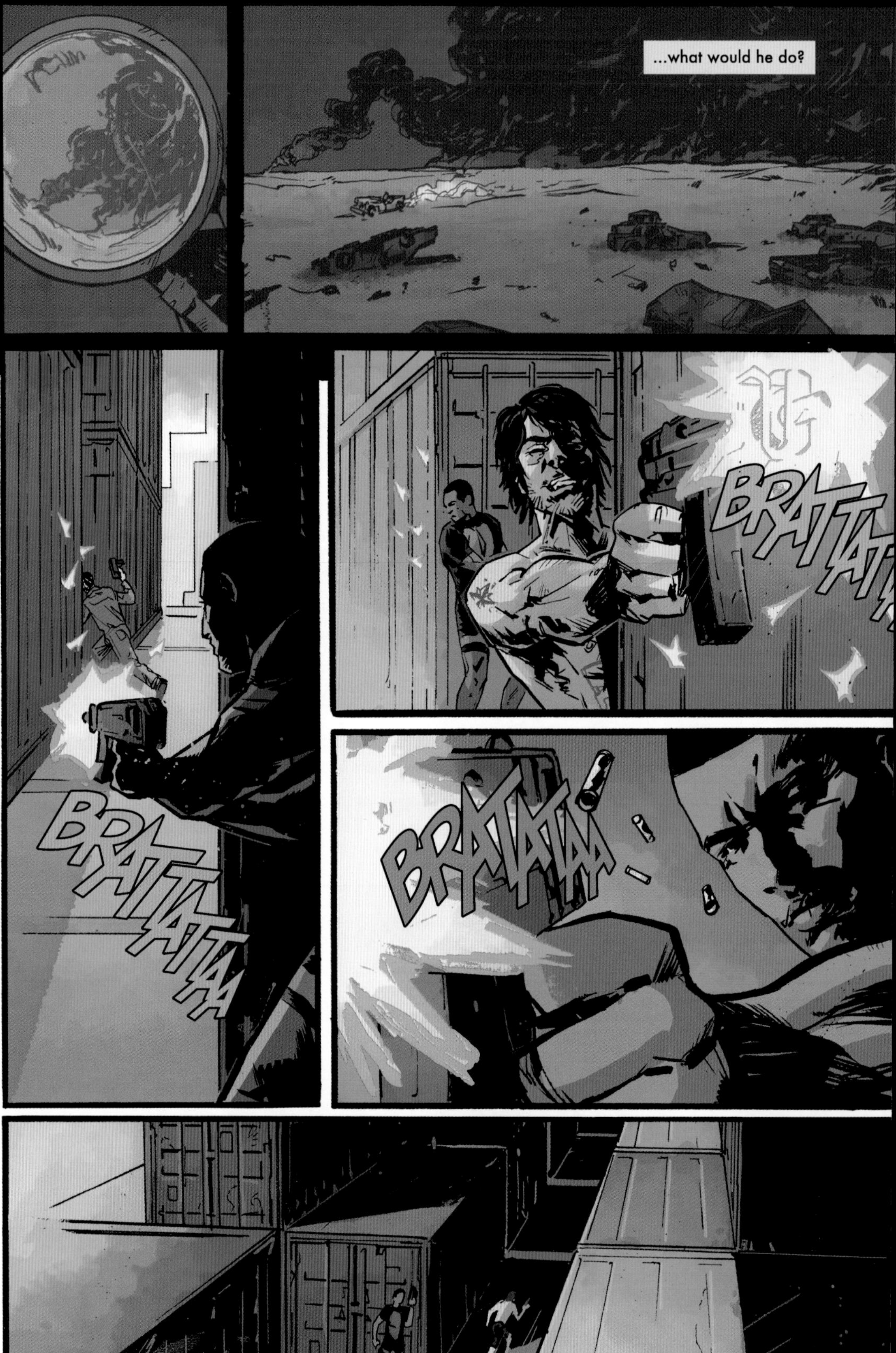
...what would he do?
BRATATA
BRATATATAA
BRATATAA

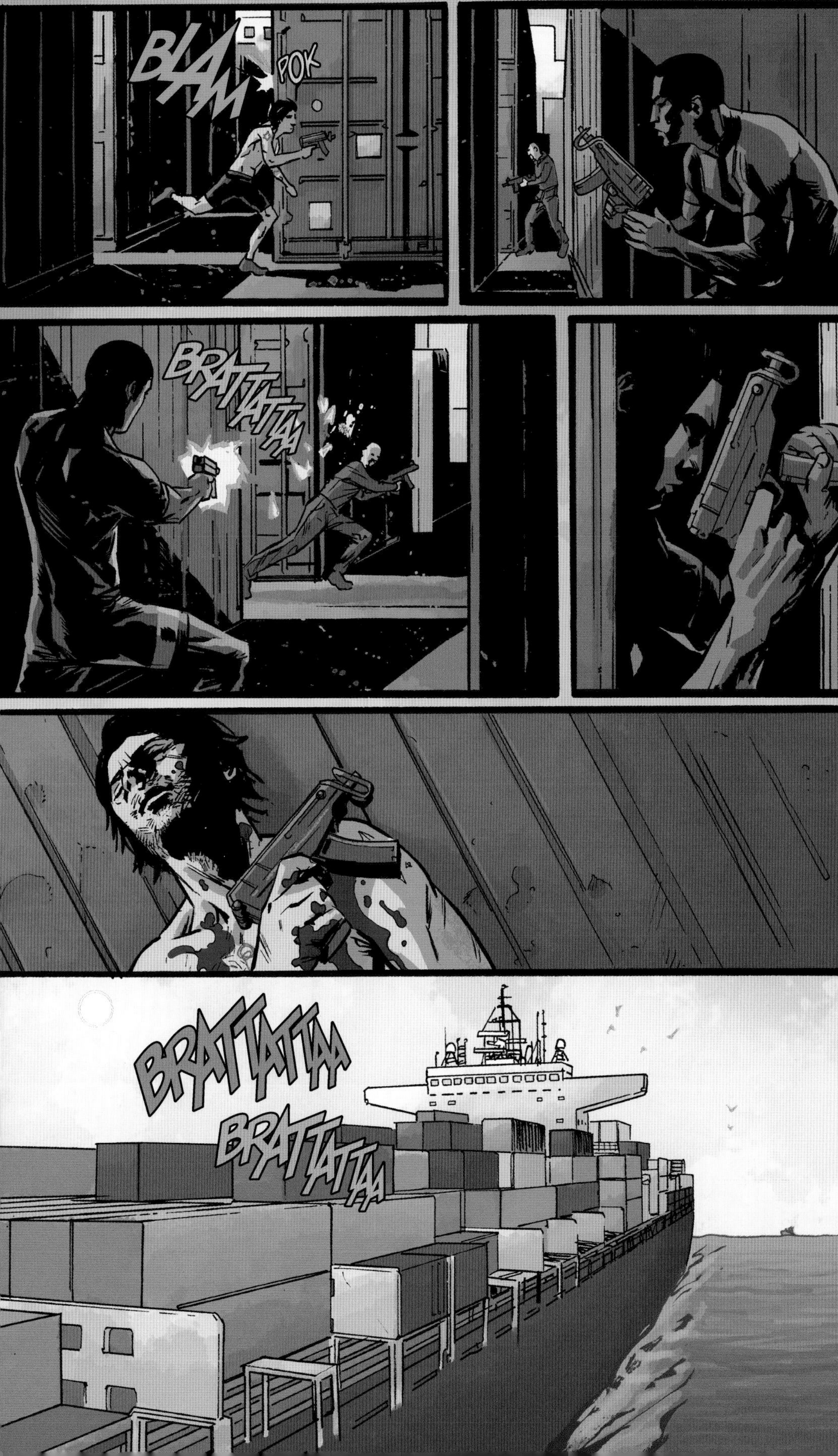
BLAM
POK
BRATTATTAA
BRATTATTAA
BRATTATTAA

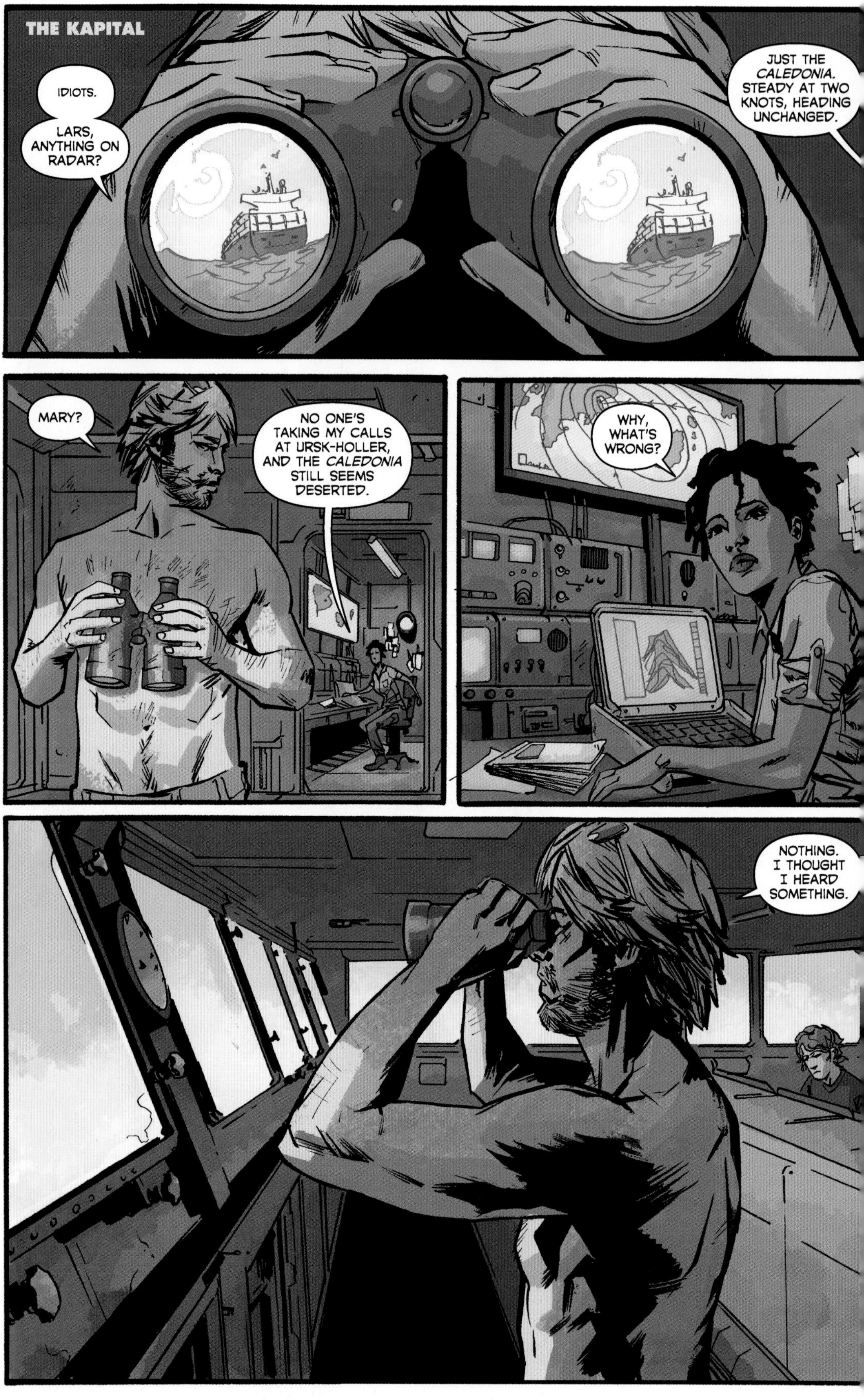

THE KAPITAL
IDIOTS.
LARS, ANYTHING ON RADAR?
JUST THE *CALEDONIA*. STEADY AT TWO KNOTS, HEADING UNCHANGED.
MARY?
NO ONE'S TAKING MY CALLS AT URSK-HOLLER, AND THE *CALEDONIA* STILL SEEMS DESERTED.
WHY, WHAT'S WRONG?
NOTHING. I THOUGHT I HEARD SOMETHING.

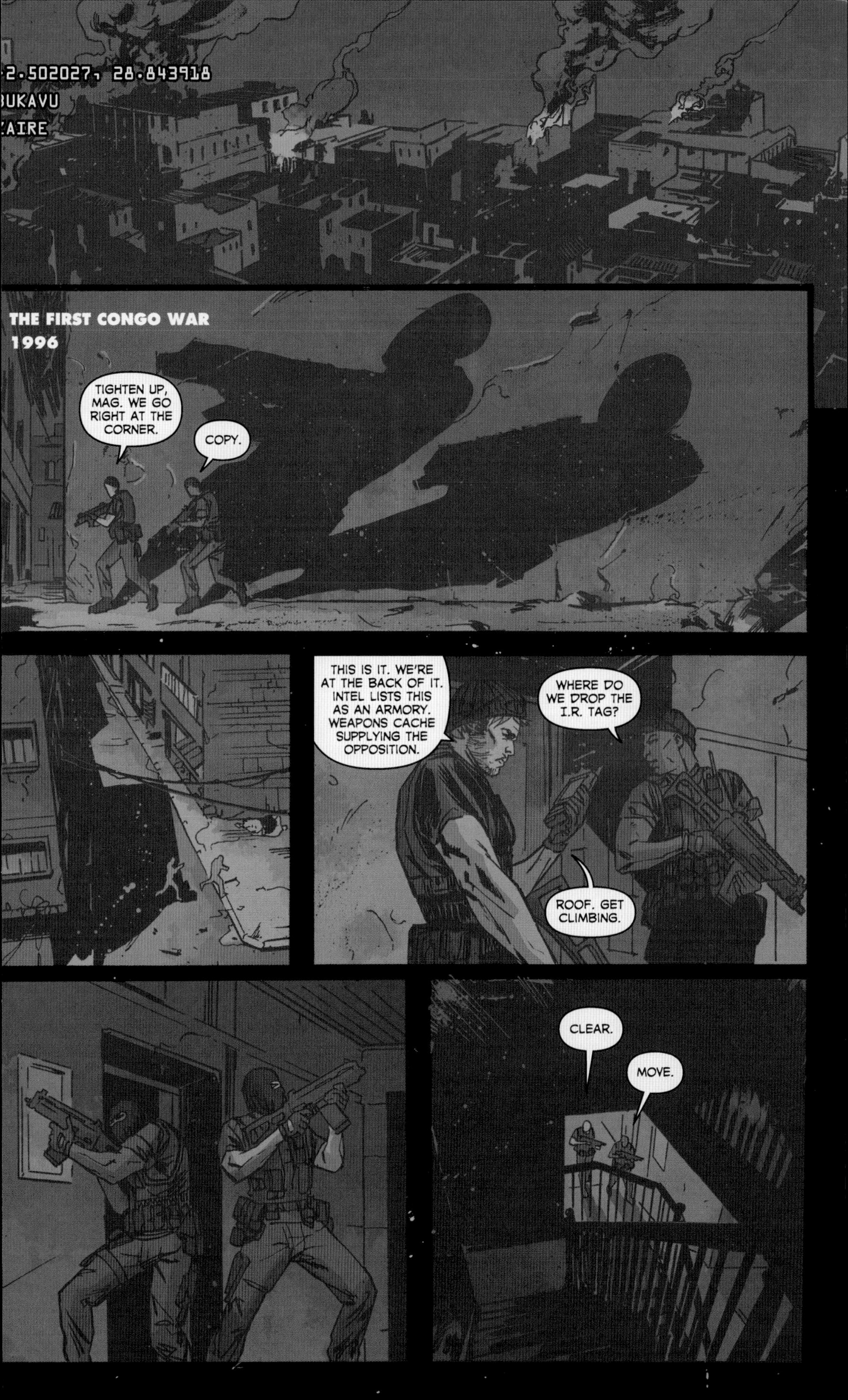
-2.502027, 28.843918
BUKAVU
ZAIRE
THE FIRST CONGO WAR
1996
TIGHTEN UP, MAG. WE GO RIGHT AT THE CORNER.
COPY.
THIS IS IT. WE'RE AT THE BACK OF IT. INTEL LISTS THIS AS AN ARMORY. WEAPONS CACHE SUPPLYING THE OPPOSITION.
WHERE DO WE DROP THE I.R. TAG?
ROOF. GET CLIMBING.
CLEAR.
MOVE.

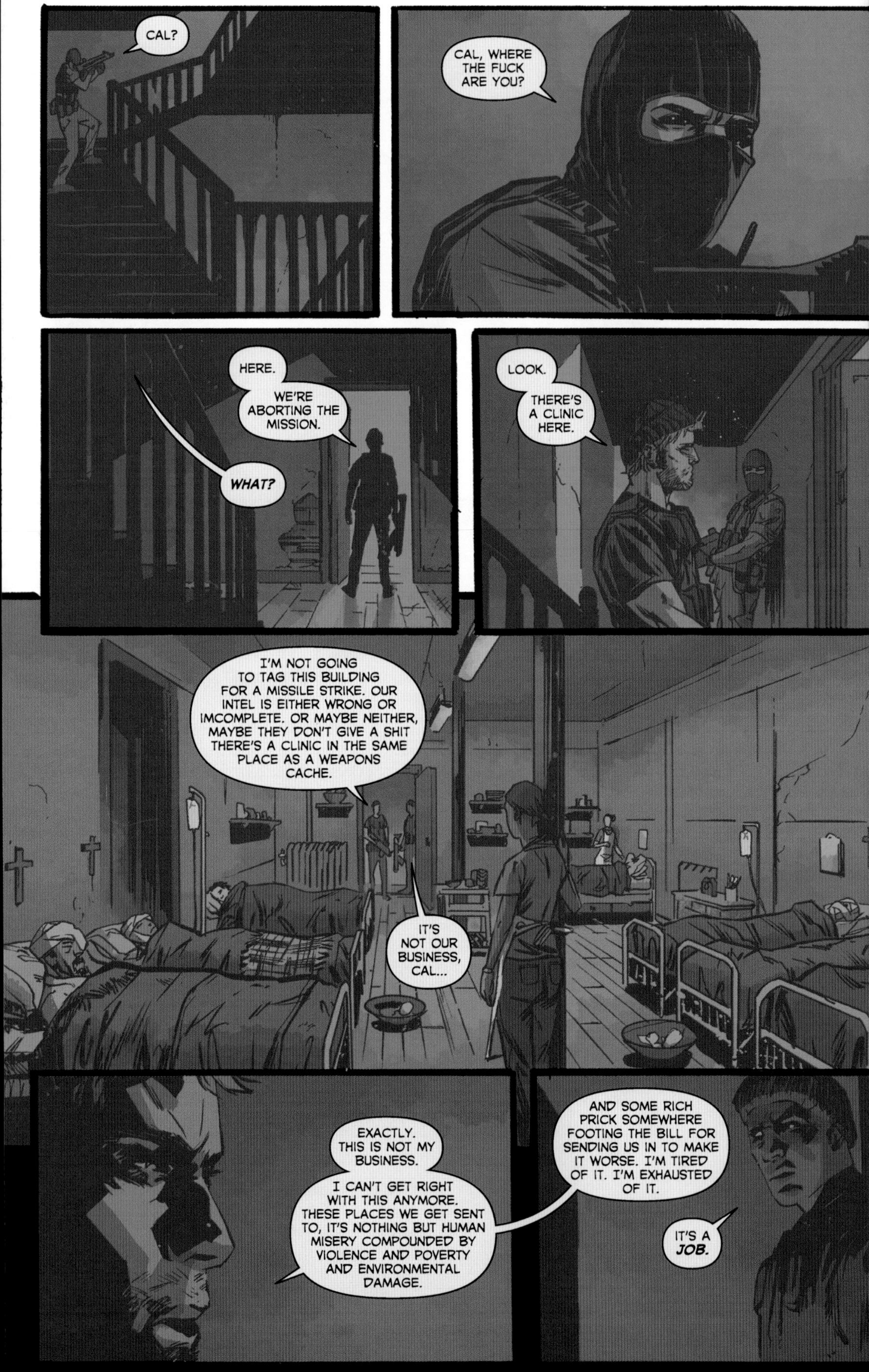
CAL?
CAL, WHERE THE FUCK ARE YOU?
HERE.
WE'RE ABORTING THE MISSION.
WHAT?
LOOK.
THERE'S A CLINIC HERE.
I'M NOT GOING TO TAG THIS BUILDING FOR A MISSILE STRIKE. OUR INTEL IS EITHER WRONG OR IMCOMPLETE. OR MAYBE NEITHER, MAYBE THEY DON'T GIVE A SHIT THERE'S A CLINIC IN THE SAME PLACE AS A WEAPONS CACHE.
IT'S NOT OUR BUSINESS, CAL...
EXACTLY. THIS IS NOT MY BUSINESS.
I CAN'T GET RIGHT WITH THIS ANYMORE. THESE PLACES WE GET SENT TO, IT'S NOTHING BUT HUMAN MISERY COMPOUNDED BY VIOLENCE AND POVERTY AND ENVIRONMENTAL DAMAGE.
AND SOME RICH PRICK SOMEWHERE FOOTING THE BILL FOR SENDING US IN TO MAKE IT WORSE. I'M TIRED OF IT. I'M EXHAUSTED OF IT.
IT'S A JOB.

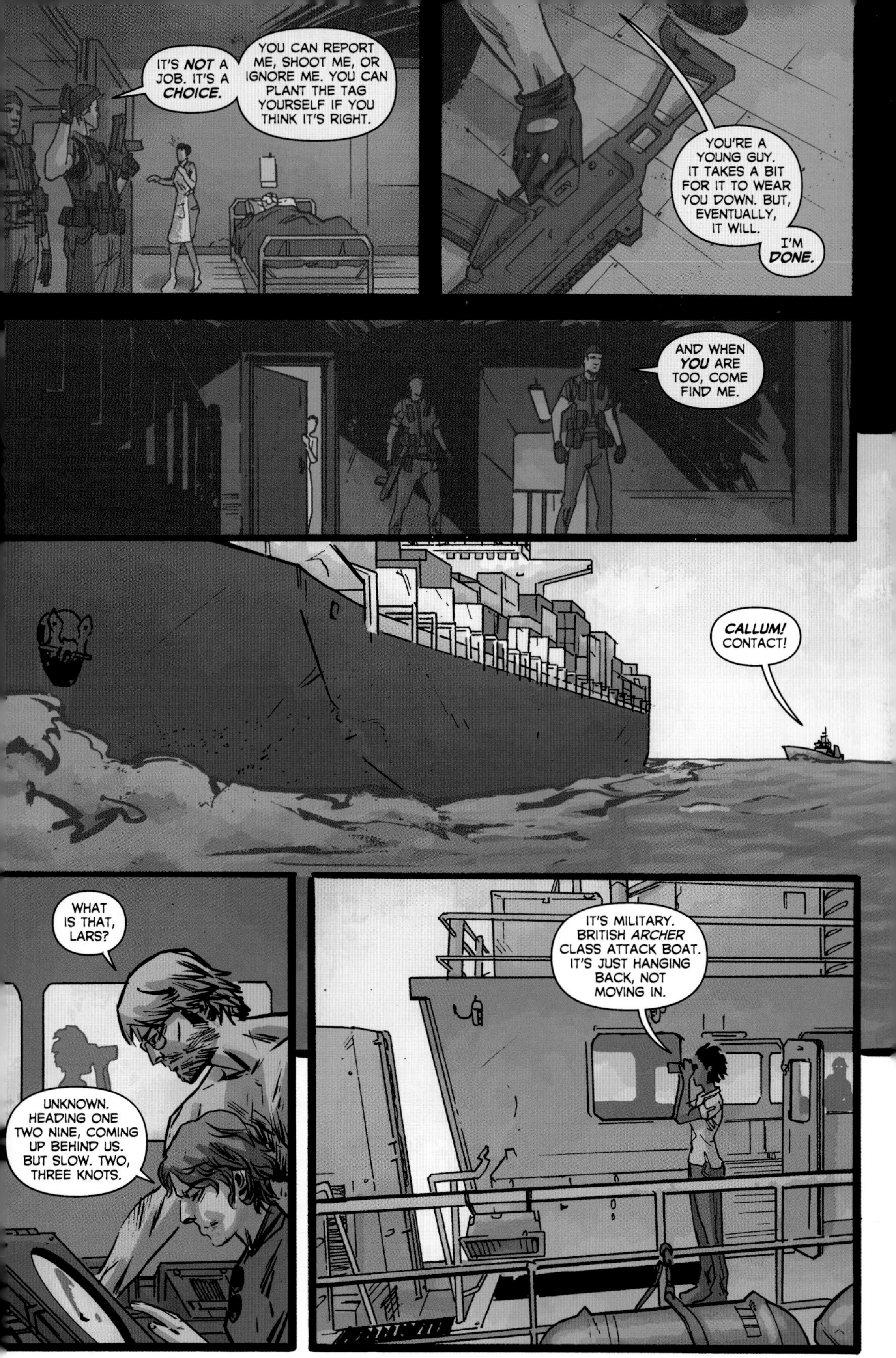
IT'S **NOT** A JOB. IT'S A ***CHOICE.***
YOU CAN REPORT ME, SHOOT ME, OR IGNORE ME. YOU CAN PLANT THE TAG YOURSELF IF YOU THINK IT'S RIGHT.
YOU'RE A YOUNG GUY. IT TAKES A BIT FOR IT TO WEAR YOU DOWN. BUT, EVENTUALLY, IT WILL.
I'M ***DONE.***
AND WHEN ***YOU*** ARE TOO, COME FIND ME.
CALLUM! CONTACT!
WHAT IS THAT, LARS?
UNKNOWN. HEADING ONE TWO NINE, COMING UP BEHIND US. BUT SLOW. TWO, THREE KNOTS.
IT'S MILITARY. BRITISH *ARCHER* CLASS ATTACK BOAT. IT'S JUST HANGING BACK, NOT MOVING IN.

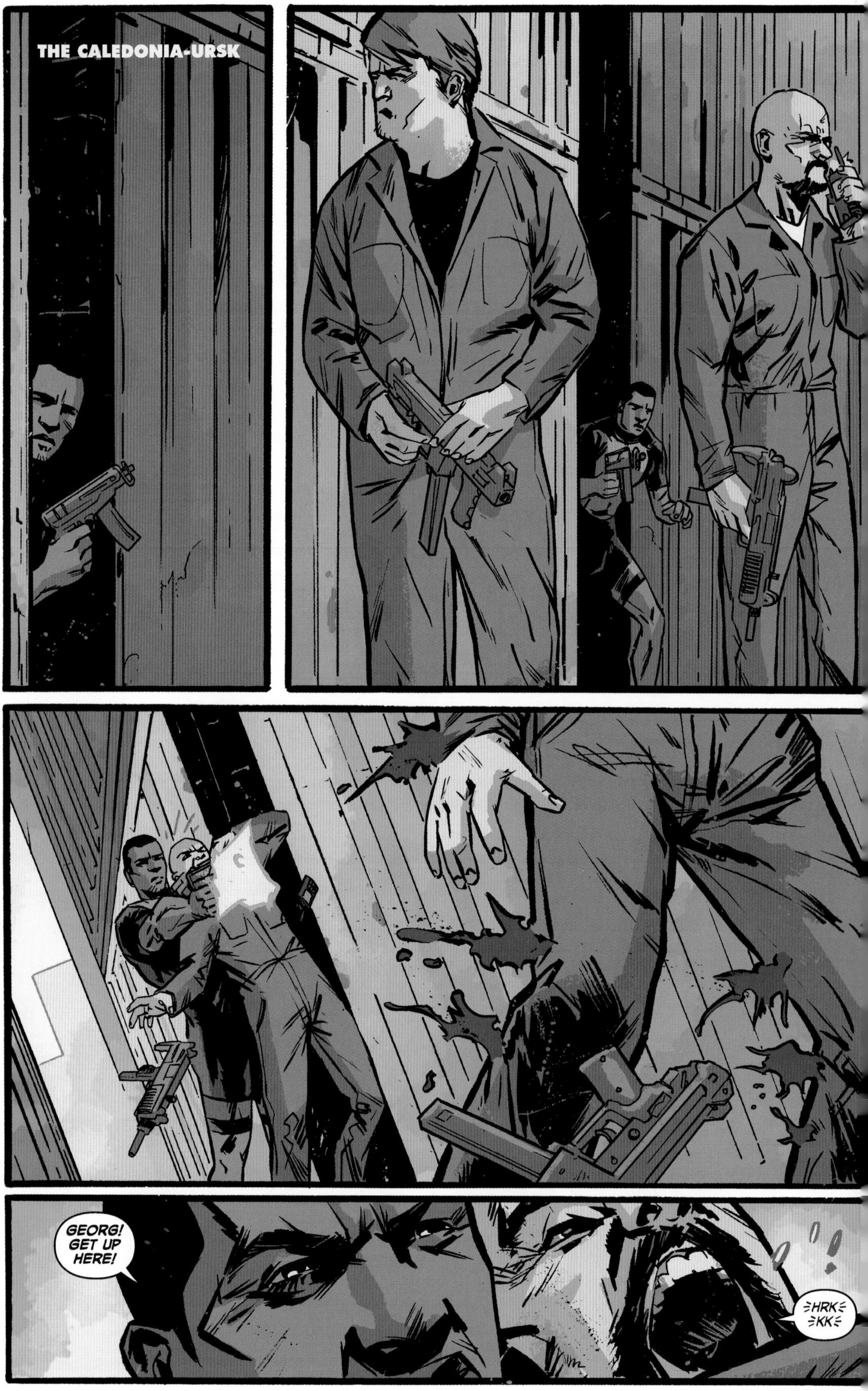
THE CALEDONIA-URSK
GEORG! GET UP HERE!
HRK KK

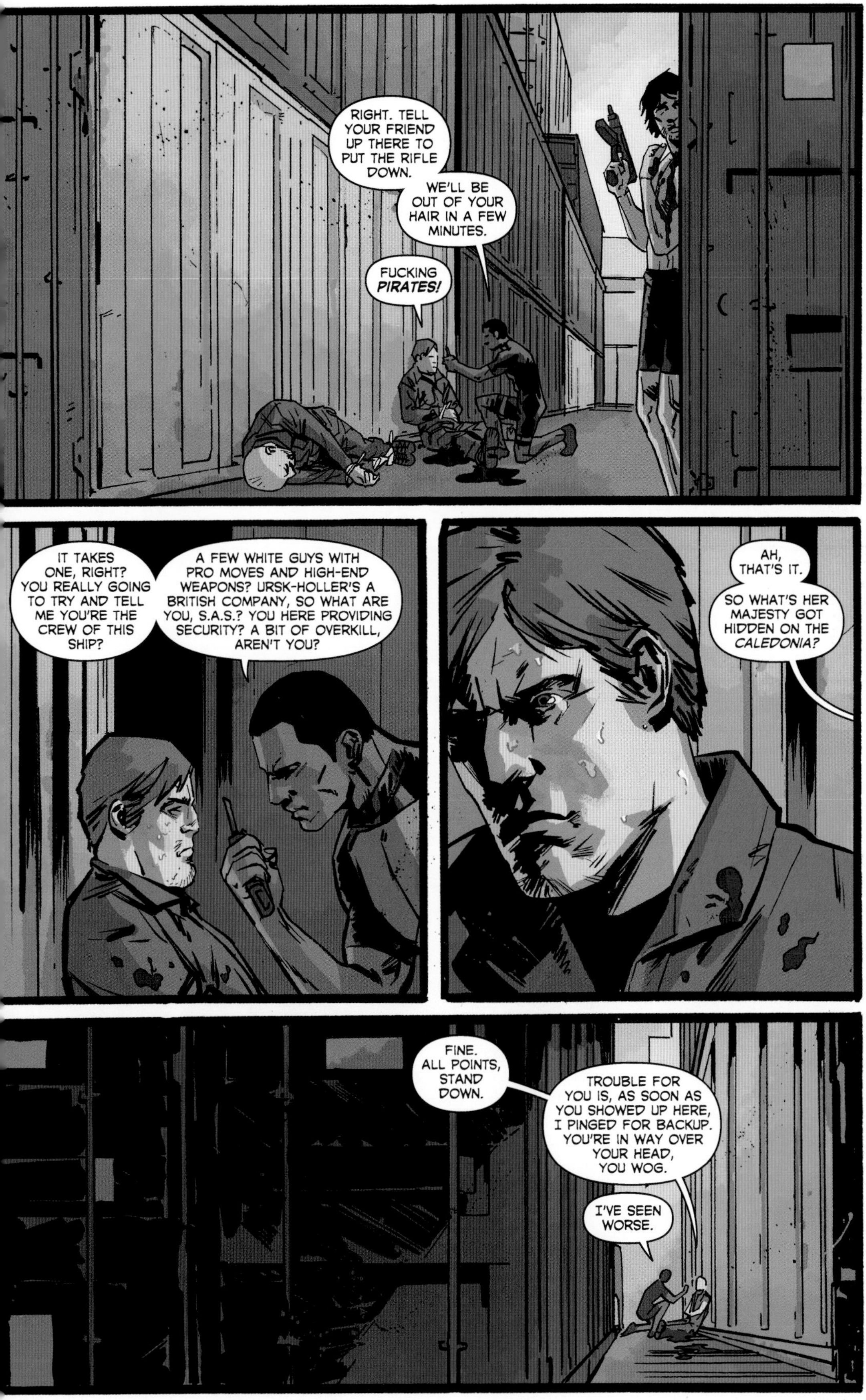
RIGHT. TELL YOUR FRIEND UP THERE TO PUT THE RIFLE DOWN.
WE'LL BE OUT OF YOUR HAIR IN A FEW MINUTES.
FUCKING *PIRATES!*
IT TAKES ONE, RIGHT? YOU REALLY GOING TO TRY AND TELL ME YOU'RE THE CREW OF THIS SHIP?
A FEW WHITE GUYS WITH PRO MOVES AND HIGH-END WEAPONS? URSK-HOLLER'S A BRITISH COMPANY, SO WHAT ARE YOU, S.A.S.? YOU HERE PROVIDING SECURITY? A BIT OF OVERKILL, AREN'T YOU?
AH, THAT'S IT.
SO WHAT'S HER MAJESTY GOT HIDDEN ON THE *CALEDONIA?*
FINE. ALL POINTS, STAND DOWN.
TROUBLE FOR YOU IS, AS SOON AS YOU SHOWED UP HERE, I PINGED FOR BACKUP. YOU'RE IN WAY OVER YOUR HEAD, YOU WOG.
I'VE SEEN WORSE.

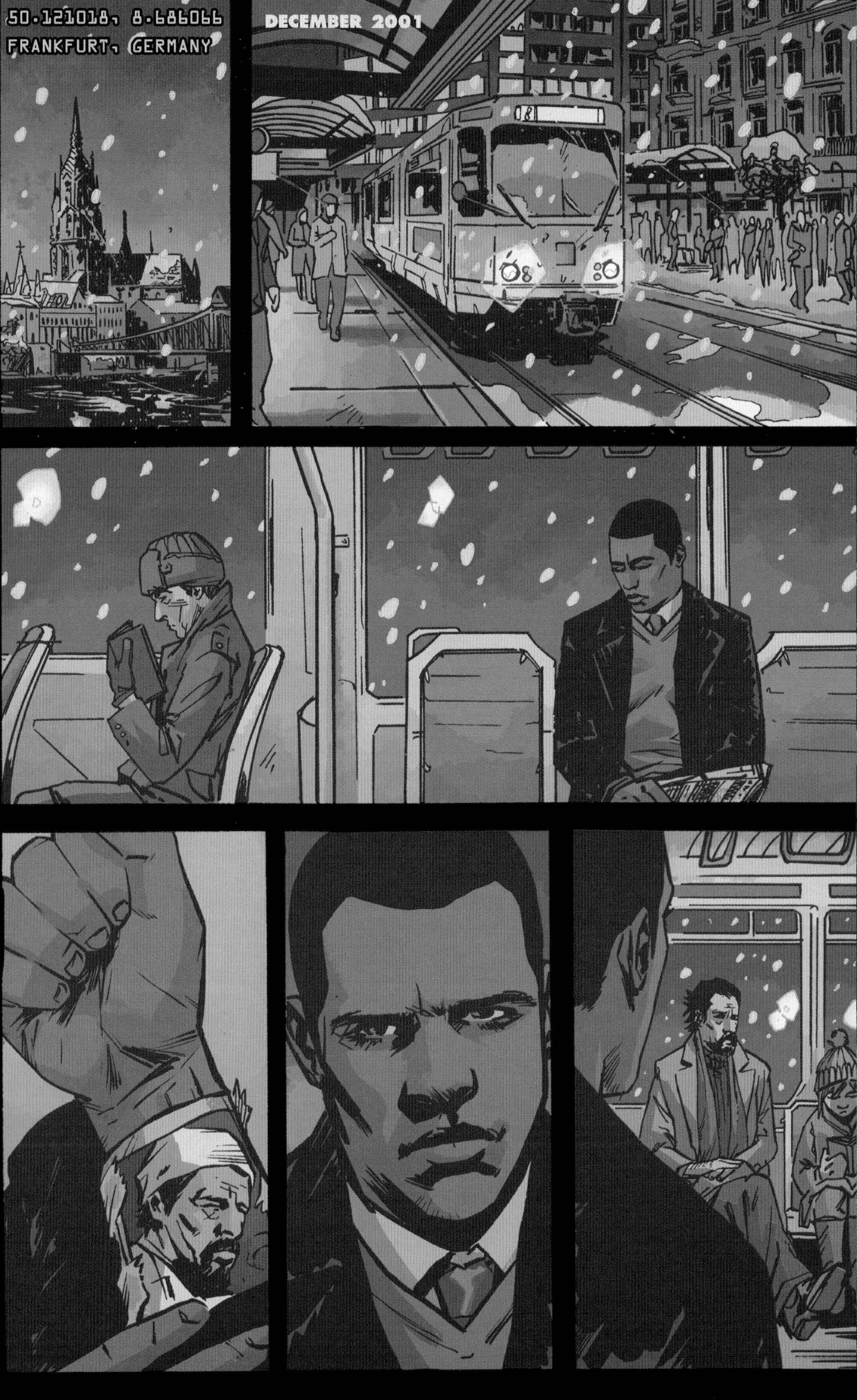
50.121018, 8.686066
FRANKFURT, GERMANY
DECEMBER 2001

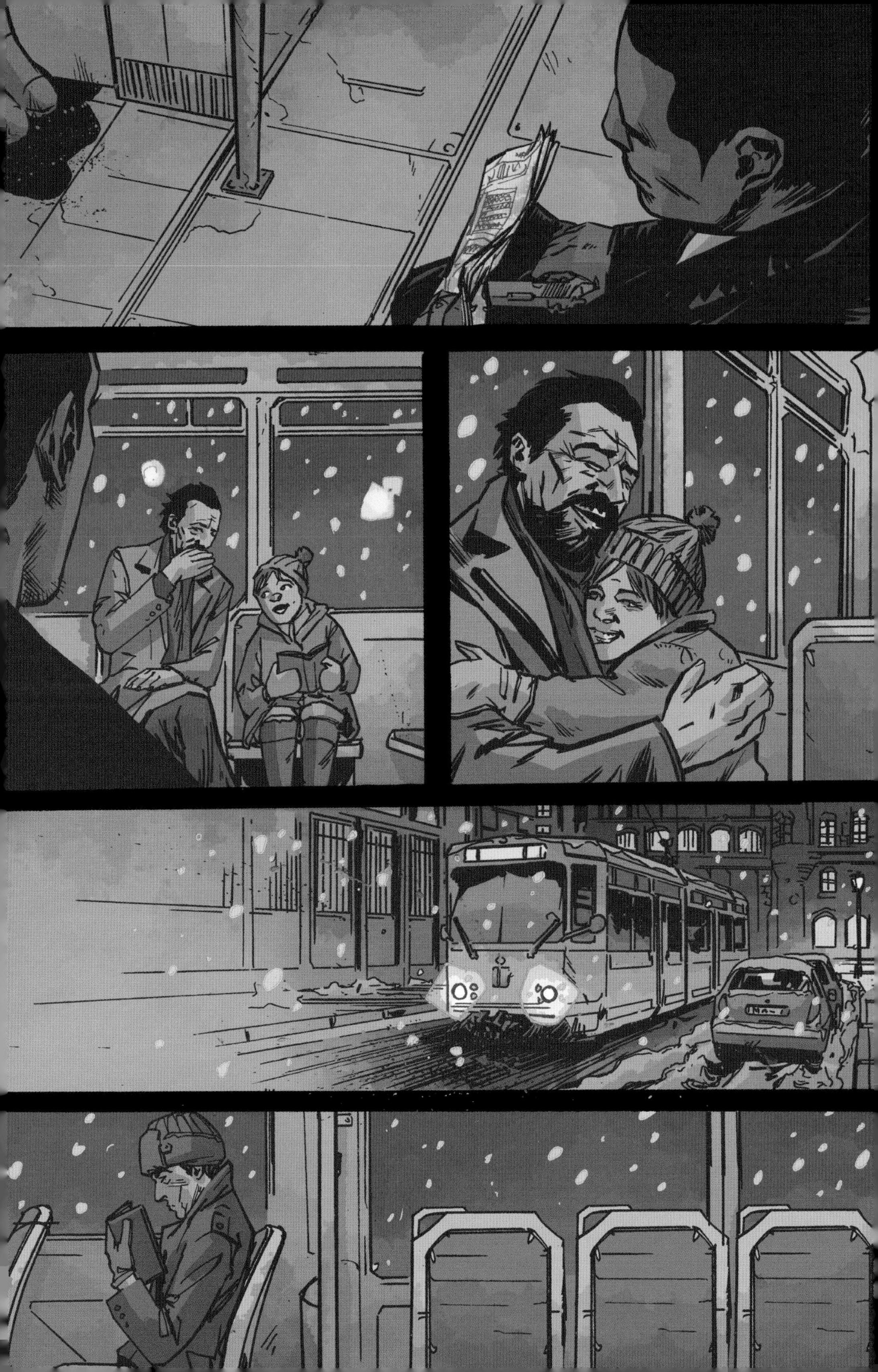

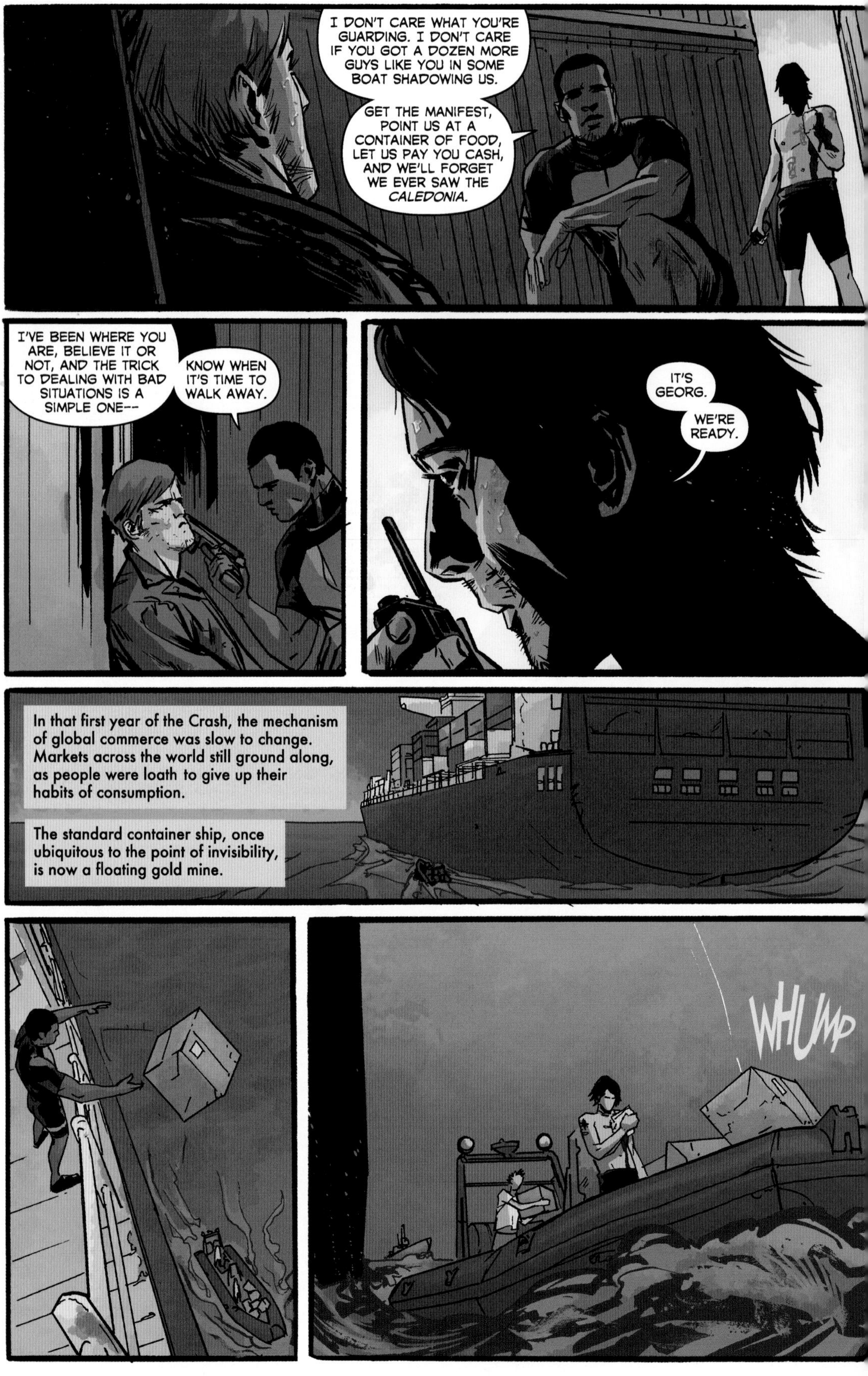
I DON'T CARE WHAT YOU'RE GUARDING. I DON'T CARE IF YOU GOT A DOZEN MORE GUYS LIKE YOU IN SOME BOAT SHADOWING US.
GET THE MANIFEST, POINT US AT A CONTAINER OF FOOD, LET US PAY YOU CASH, AND WE'LL FORGET WE EVER SAW THE *CALEDONIA*.
I'VE BEEN WHERE YOU ARE, BELIEVE IT OR NOT, AND THE TRICK TO DEALING WITH BAD SITUATIONS IS A SIMPLE ONE--
KNOW WHEN IT'S TIME TO WALK AWAY.
IT'S GEORG.
WE'RE READY.
In that first year of the Crash, the mechanism of global commerce was slow to change. Markets across the world still ground along, as people were loath to give up their habits of consumption.
The standard container ship, once ubiquitous to the point of invisibility, is now a floating gold mine.
WHUMP

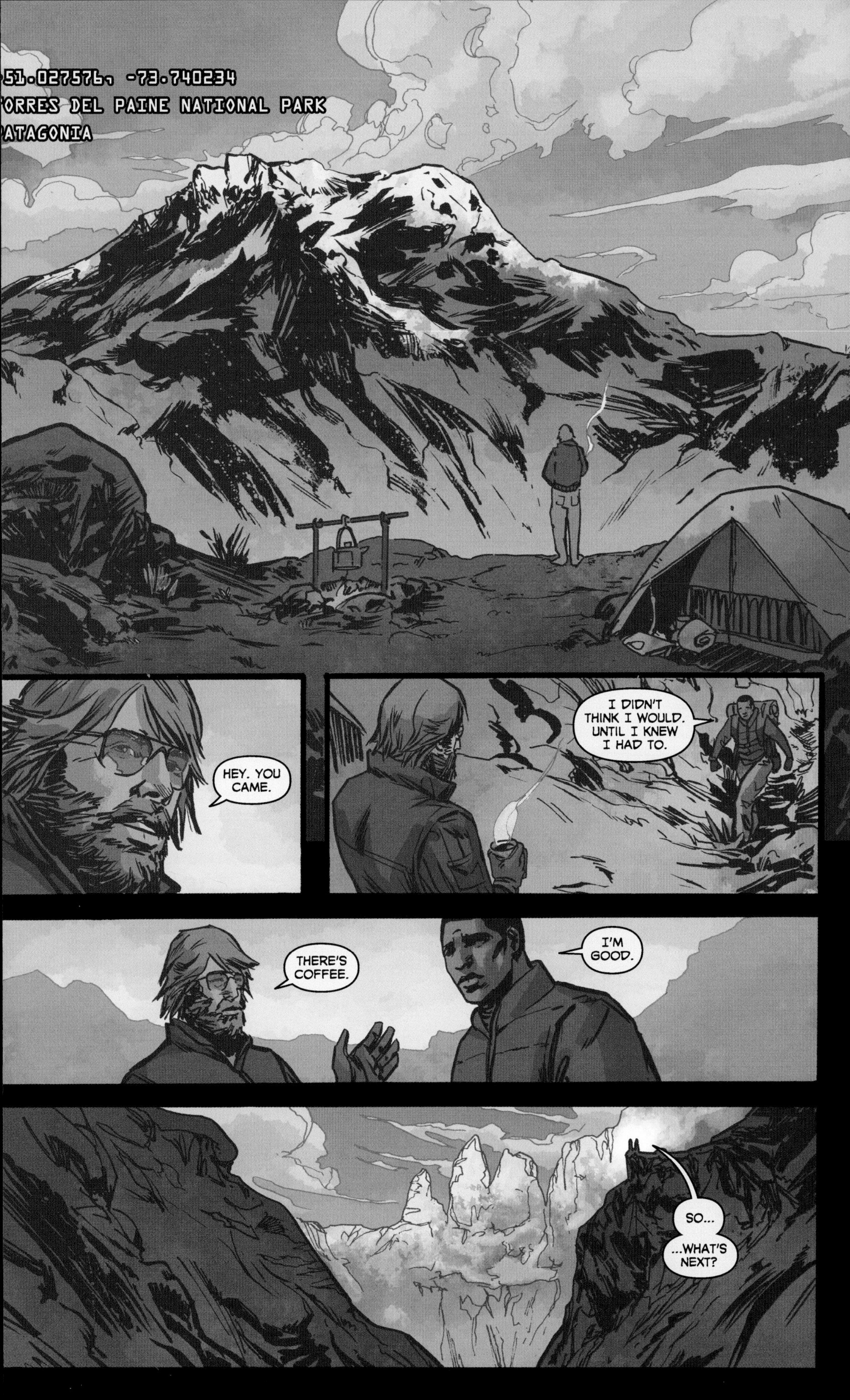
-51.027576, -73.740234
TORRES DEL PAINE NATIONAL PARK
PATAGONIA
HEY. YOU CAME.
I DIDN'T THINK I WOULD. UNTIL I KNEW I HAD TO.
THERE'S COFFEE.
I'M GOOD.
SO...
...WHAT'S NEXT?

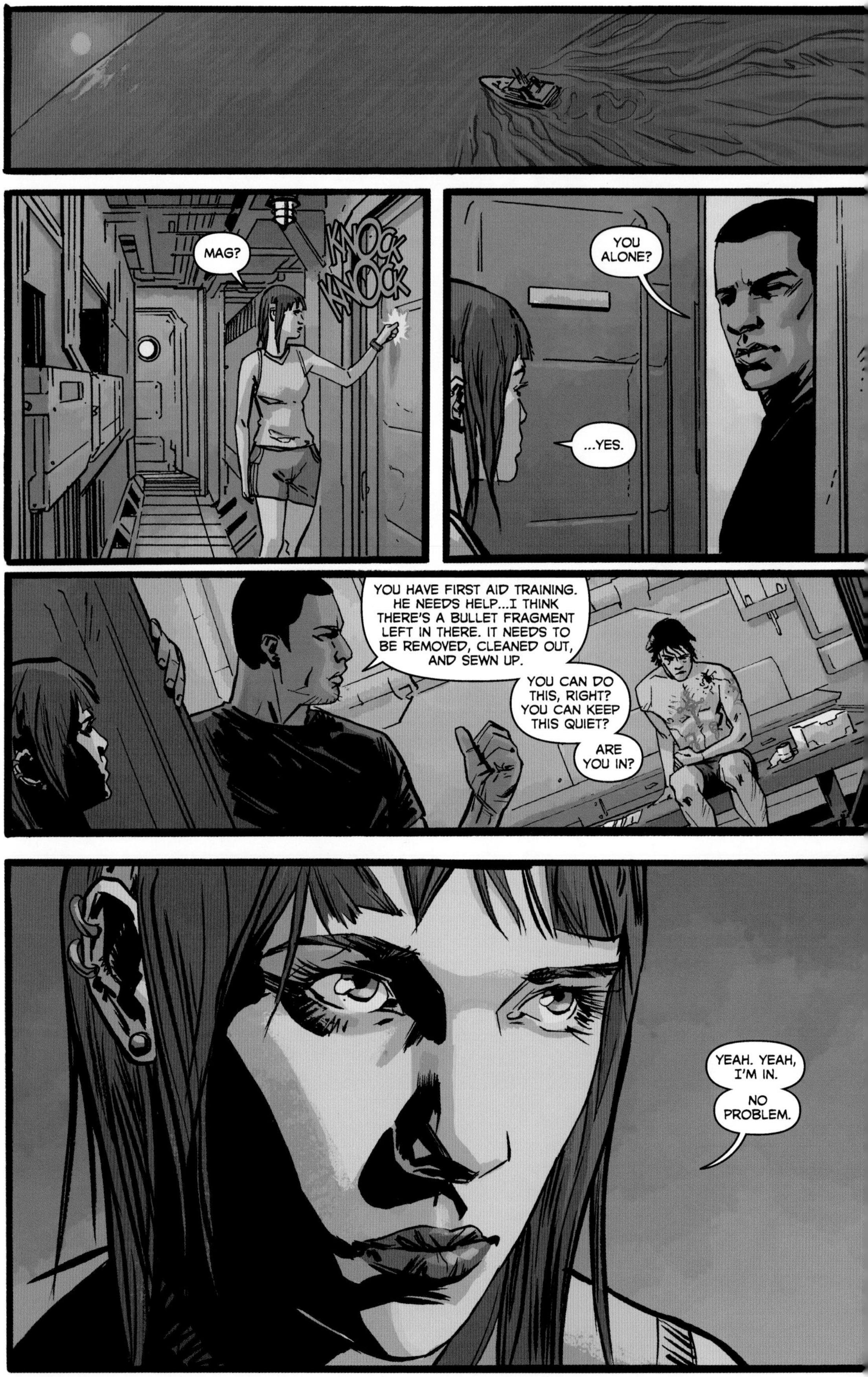
MAG?
KNOCK KNOCK
YOU ALONE?
...YES.
YOU HAVE FIRST AID TRAINING. HE NEEDS HELP...I THINK THERE'S A BULLET FRAGMENT LEFT IN THERE. IT NEEDS TO BE REMOVED, CLEANED OUT, AND SEWN UP.
YOU CAN DO THIS, RIGHT? YOU CAN KEEP THIS QUIET?
ARE YOU IN?
YEAH. YEAH, I'M IN.
NO PROBLEM.

The following pages feature three eight-page stories that appeared in the anthology *Dark Horse Presents*. Focusing on scenes from the histories of Callum, Mag, and Mary, these stories—which were published before issue #1—were readers' first introduction to *The Massive*.

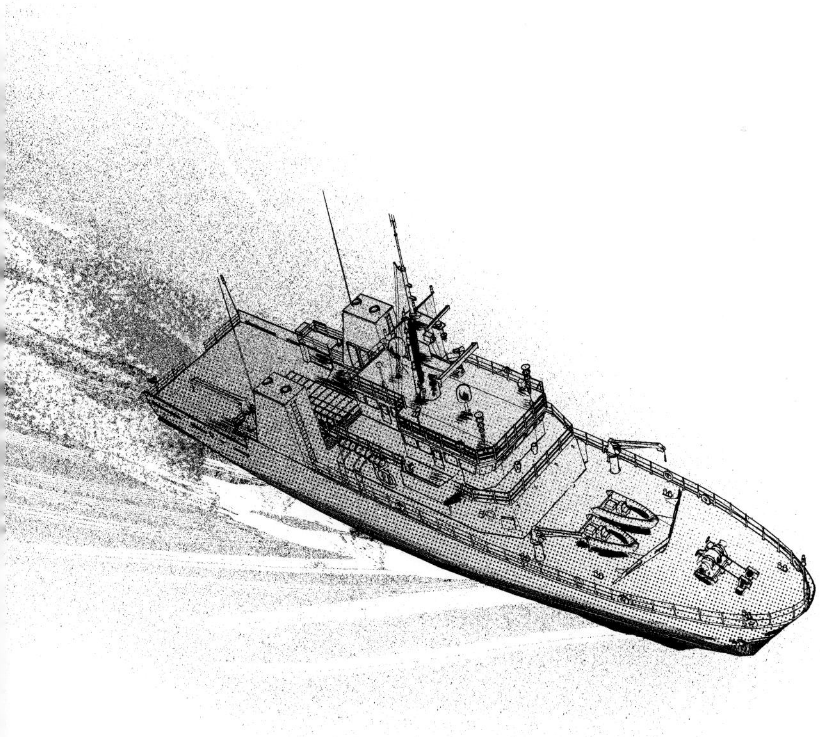

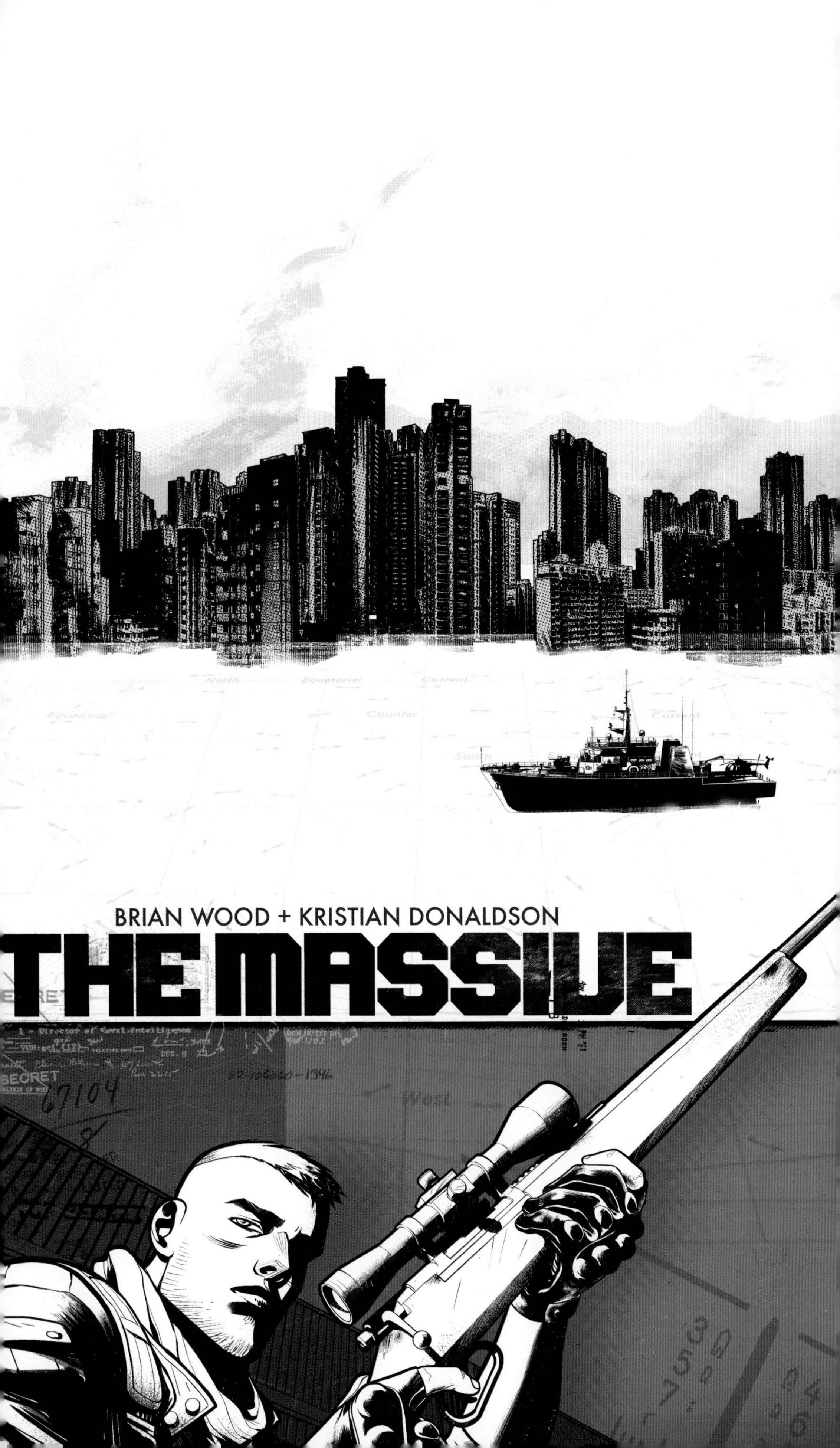
BRIAN WOOD + KRISTIAN DONALDSON
THE MASSIVE

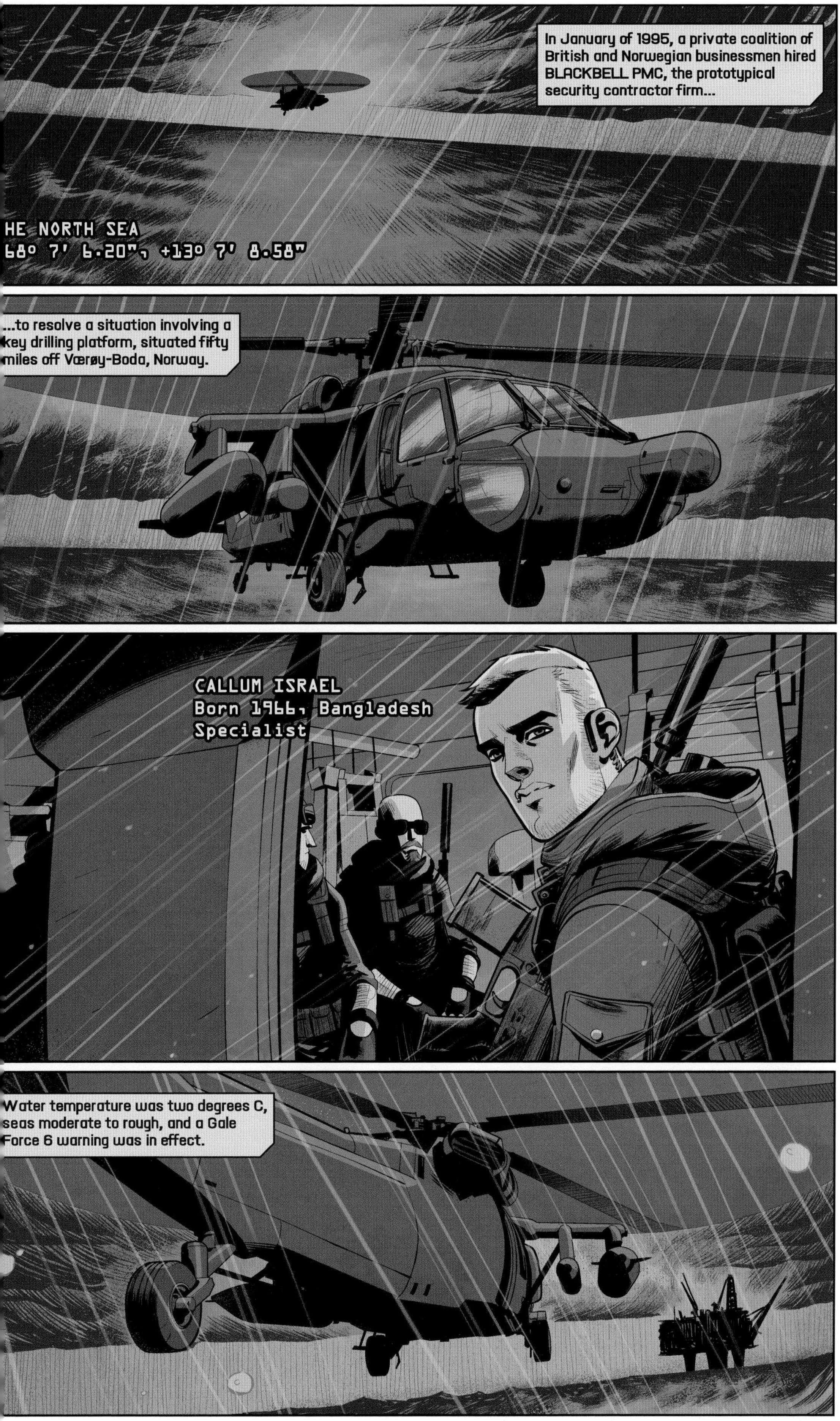
In January of 1995, a private coalition of British and Norwegian businessmen hired BLACKBELL PMC, the prototypical security contractor firm...
HE NORTH SEA
68° 7' 6.20", +13° 7' 8.58"
...to resolve a situation involving a key drilling platform, situated fifty miles off Værøy-Boda, Norway.
CALLUM ISRAEL
Born 1966, Bangladesh
Specialist
Water temperature was two degrees C, seas moderate to rough, and a Gale Force 6 warning was in effect.

Seas nine to thirteen feet, wind speed 25 knots.
The pilot reported no trouble inbound, no cause for concern. Our mission was a go.
THE MASSIVE
NORTH SEA-1995

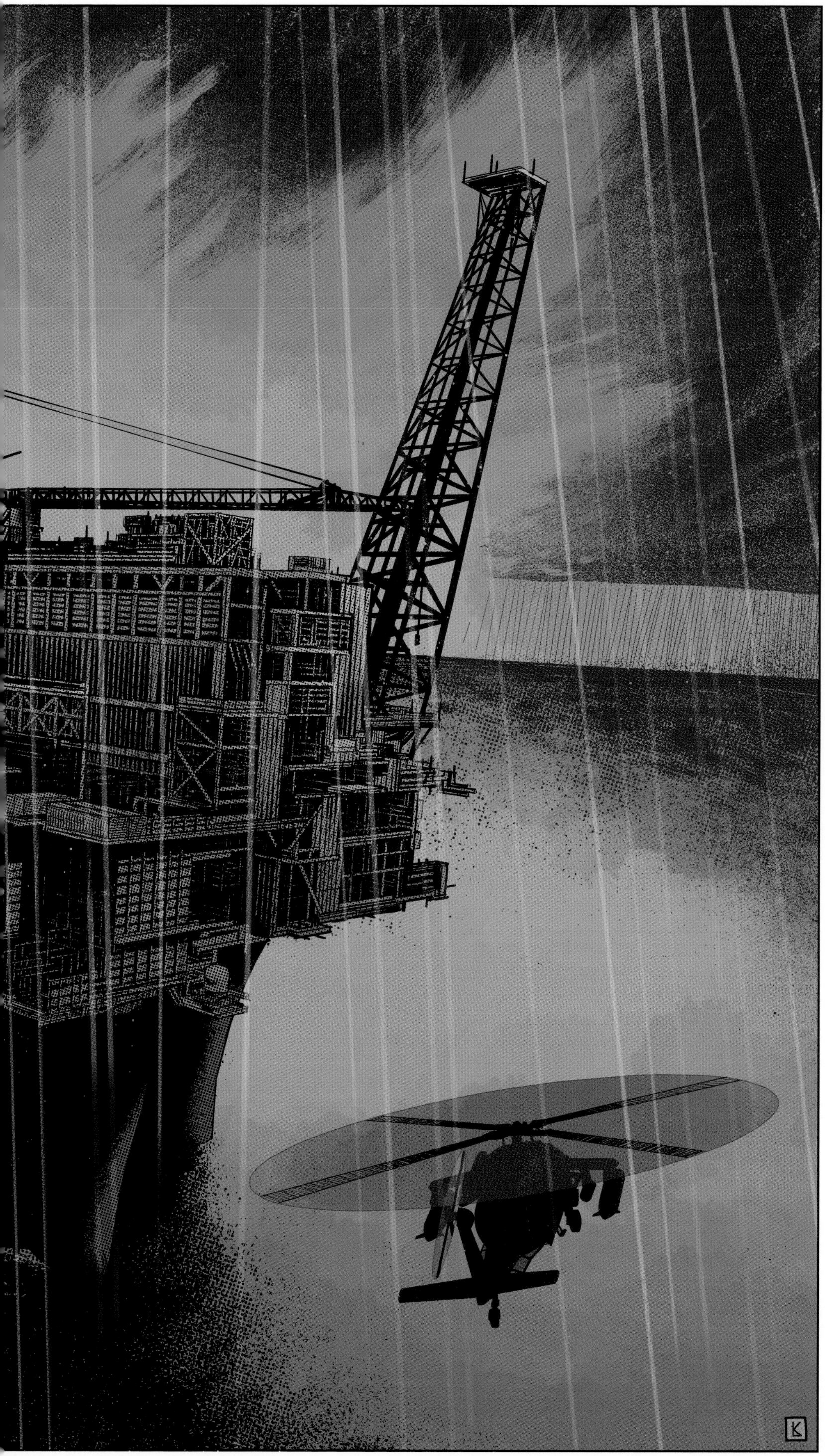

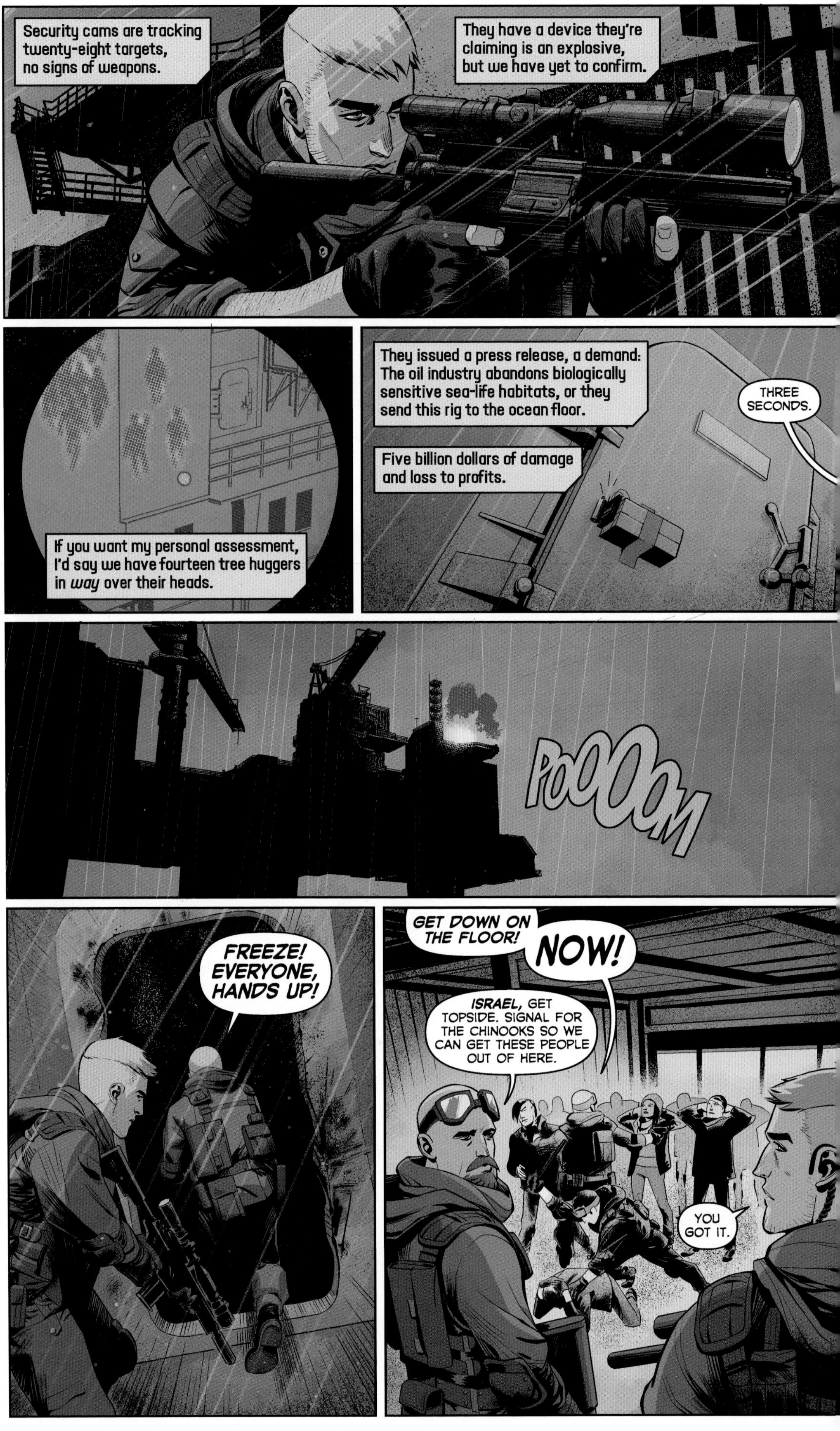
Security cams are tracking twenty-eight targets, no signs of weapons.
They have a device they're claiming is an explosive, but we have yet to confirm.
If you want my personal assessment, I'd say we have fourteen tree huggers in *way* over their heads.
They issued a press release, a demand: The oil industry abandons biologically sensitive sea-life habitats, or they send this rig to the ocean floor.
Five billion dollars of damage and loss to profits.
THREE SECONDS.
POOOOOM
FREEZE! EVERYONE, HANDS UP!
GET DOWN ON THE FLOOR!
NOW!
ISRAEL, GET TOPSIDE. SIGNAL FOR THE CHINOOKS SO WE CAN GET THESE PEOPLE OUT OF HERE.
YOU GOT IT.

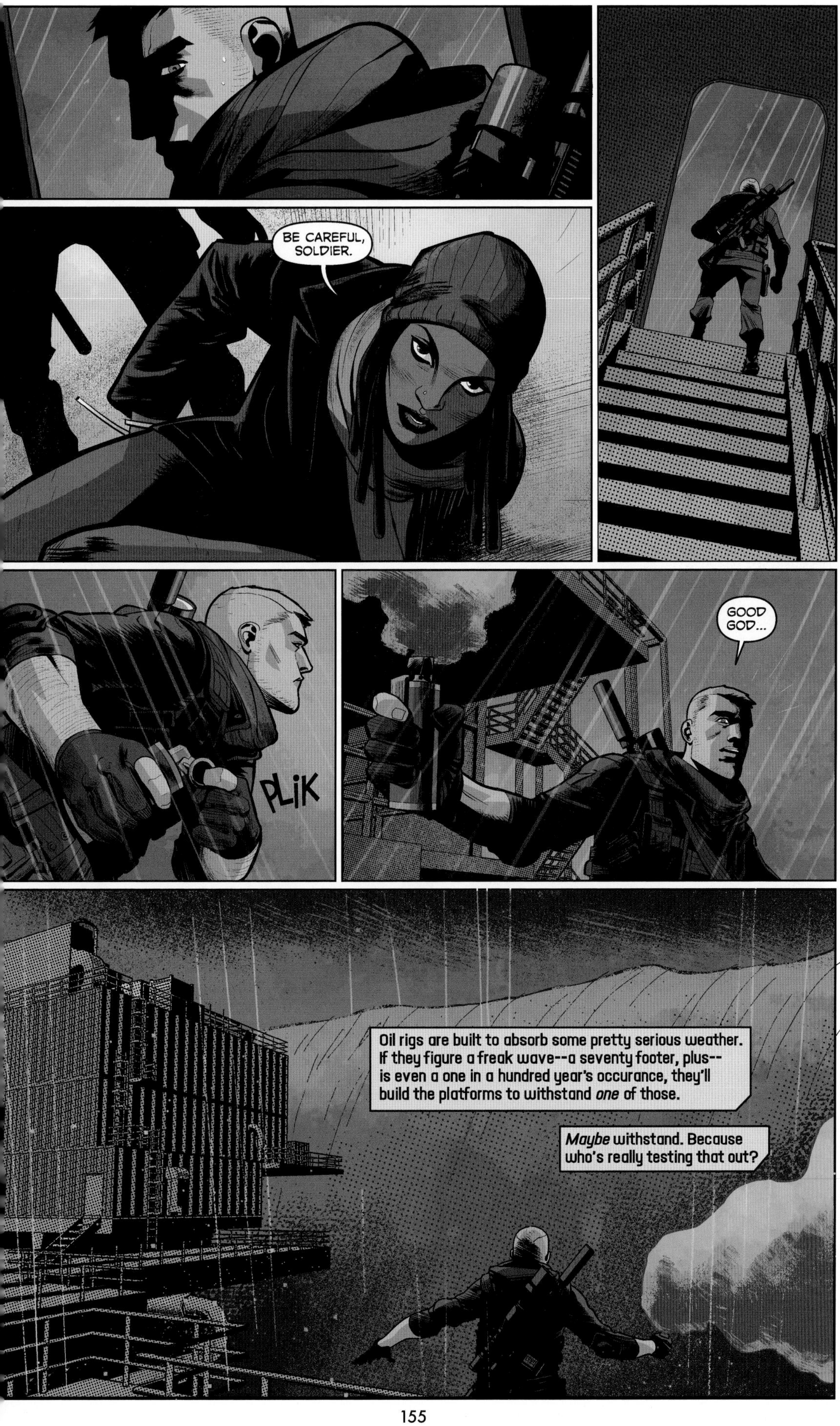
BE CAREFUL, SOLDIER.
PLIK
GOOD GOD...
Oil rigs are built to absorb some pretty serious weather. If they figure a freak wave--a seventy footer, plus--is even a one in a hundred year's occurance, they'll build the platforms to withstand *one* of those.
Maybe withstand. Because who's really testing that out?

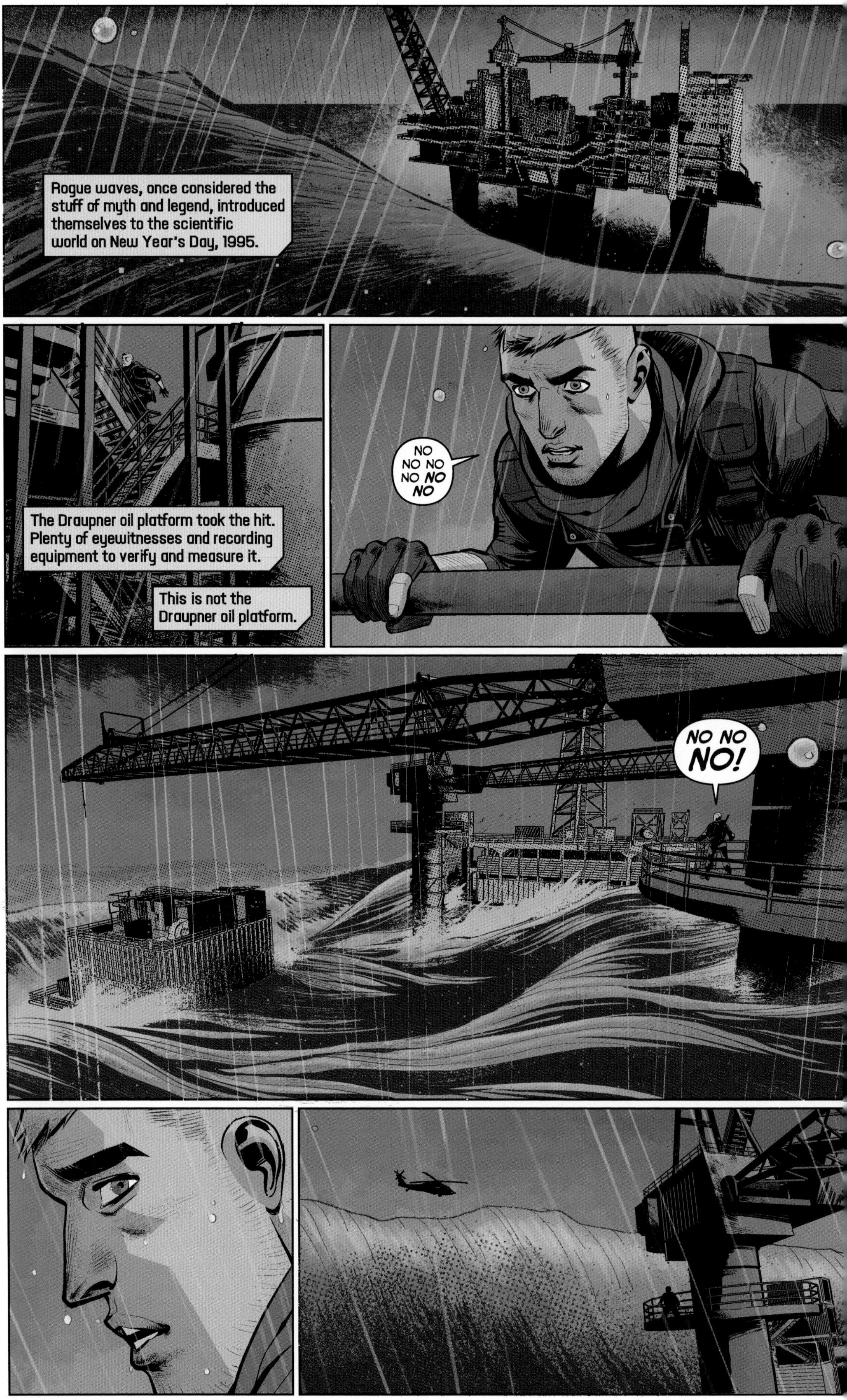
Rogue waves, once considered the stuff of myth and legend, introduced themselves to the scientific world on New Year's Day, 1995.
The Draupner oil platform took the hit. Plenty of eyewitnesses and recording equipment to verify and measure it.
This is not the Draupner oil platform.
NO NO NO NO NO NO
NO NO NO!

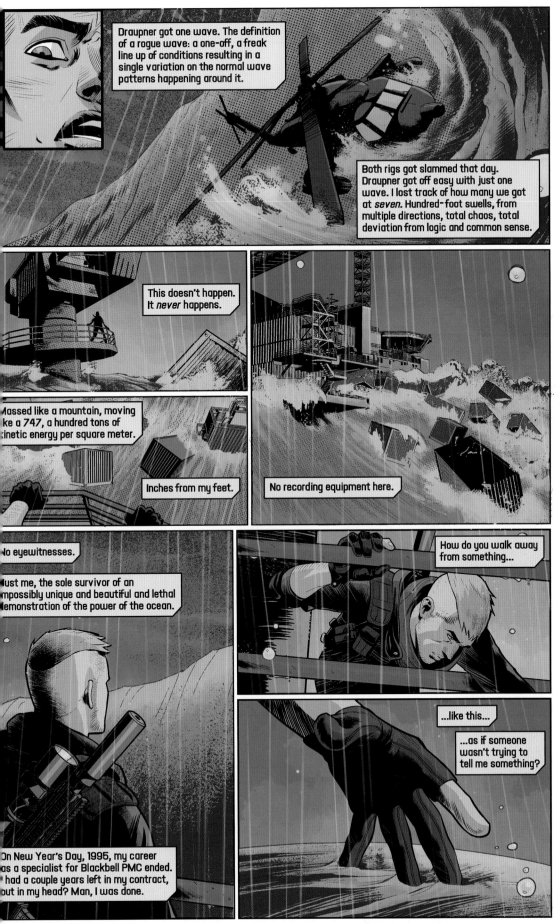

Draupner got one wave. The definition of a rogue wave: a one-off, a freak line up of conditions resulting in a single variation on the normal wave patterns happening around it.

Both rigs got slammed that day. Draupner got off easy with just one wave. I lost track of how many we got at *seven*. Hundred-foot swells, from multiple directions, total chaos, total deviation from logic and common sense.

This doesn't happen. It *never* happens.

Massed like a mountain, moving like a 747, a hundred tons of kinetic energy per square meter.

Inches from my feet.

No recording equipment here.

No eyewitnesses.

Just me, the sole survivor of an impossibly unique and beautiful and lethal demonstration of the power of the ocean.

How do you walk away from something...

...like this...

...as if someone wasn't trying to tell me something?

On New Year's Day, 1995, my career as a specialist for Blackbell PMC ended. I had a couple years left in my contract, but in my head? Man, I was done.

157

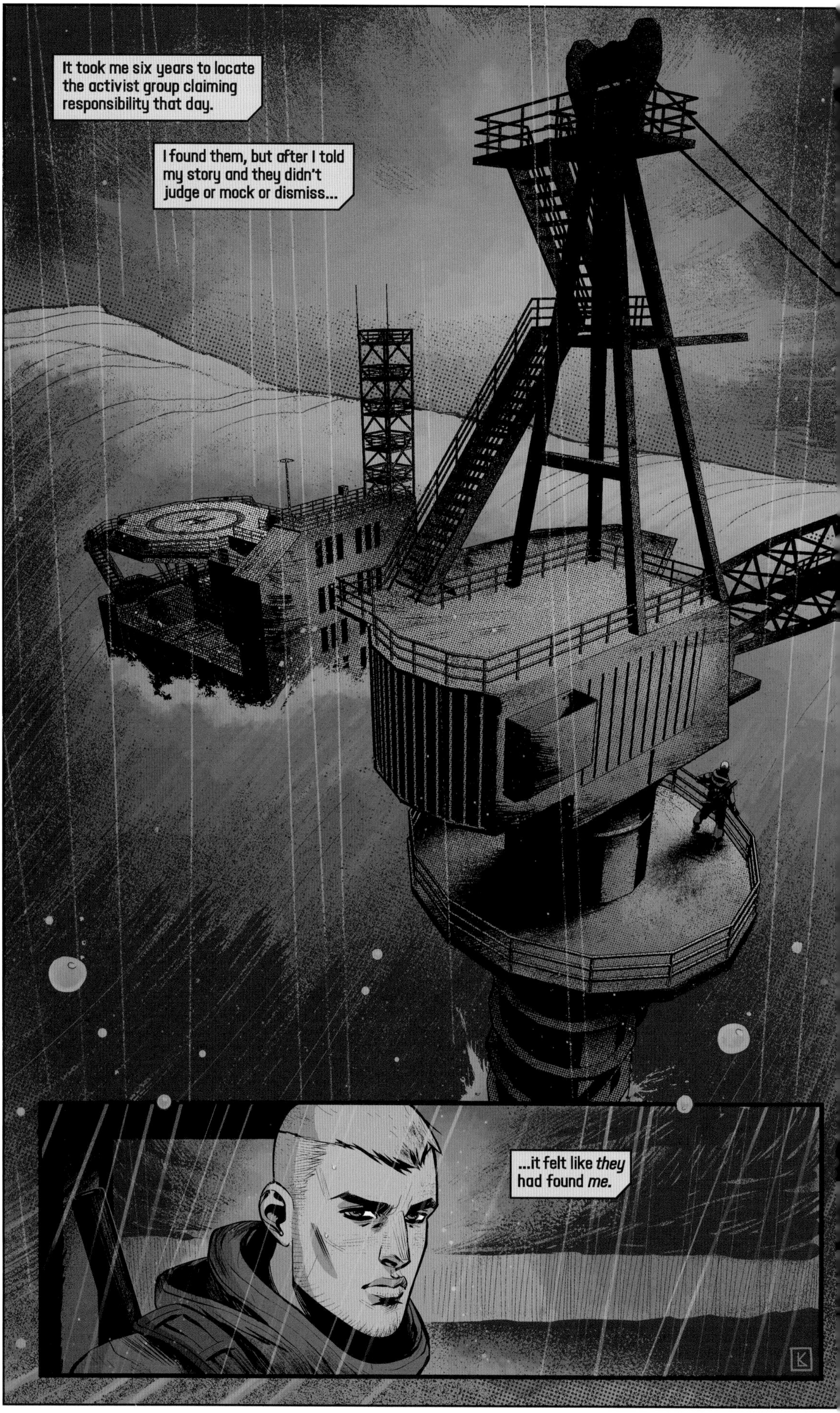
It took me six years to locate the activist group claiming responsibility that day.
I found them, but after I told my story and they didn't judge or mock or dismiss...
...it felt like *they* had found *me.*

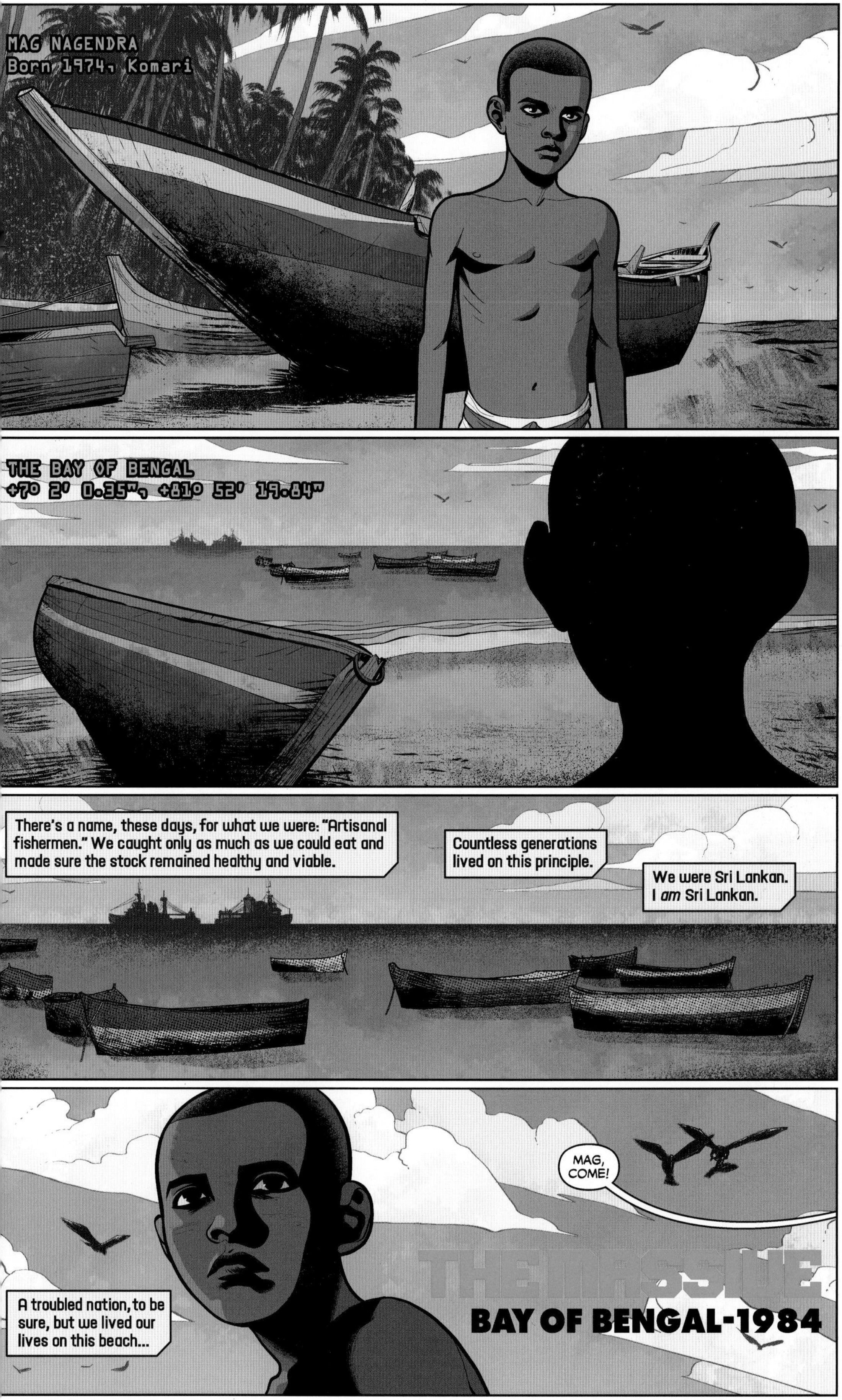

MAG NAGENDRA
Born 1974, Komari
THE BAY OF BENGAL
+7° 2' 0.35", +81° 52' 19.84"
There's a name, these days, for what we were: "Artisanal fishermen." We caught only as much as we could eat and made sure the stock remained healthy and viable.
Countless generations lived on this principle.
We were Sri Lankan. I *am* Sri Lankan.
A troubled nation, to be sure, but we lived our lives on this beach...
MAG, COME!
THE MASSIVE
BAY OF BENGAL-1984

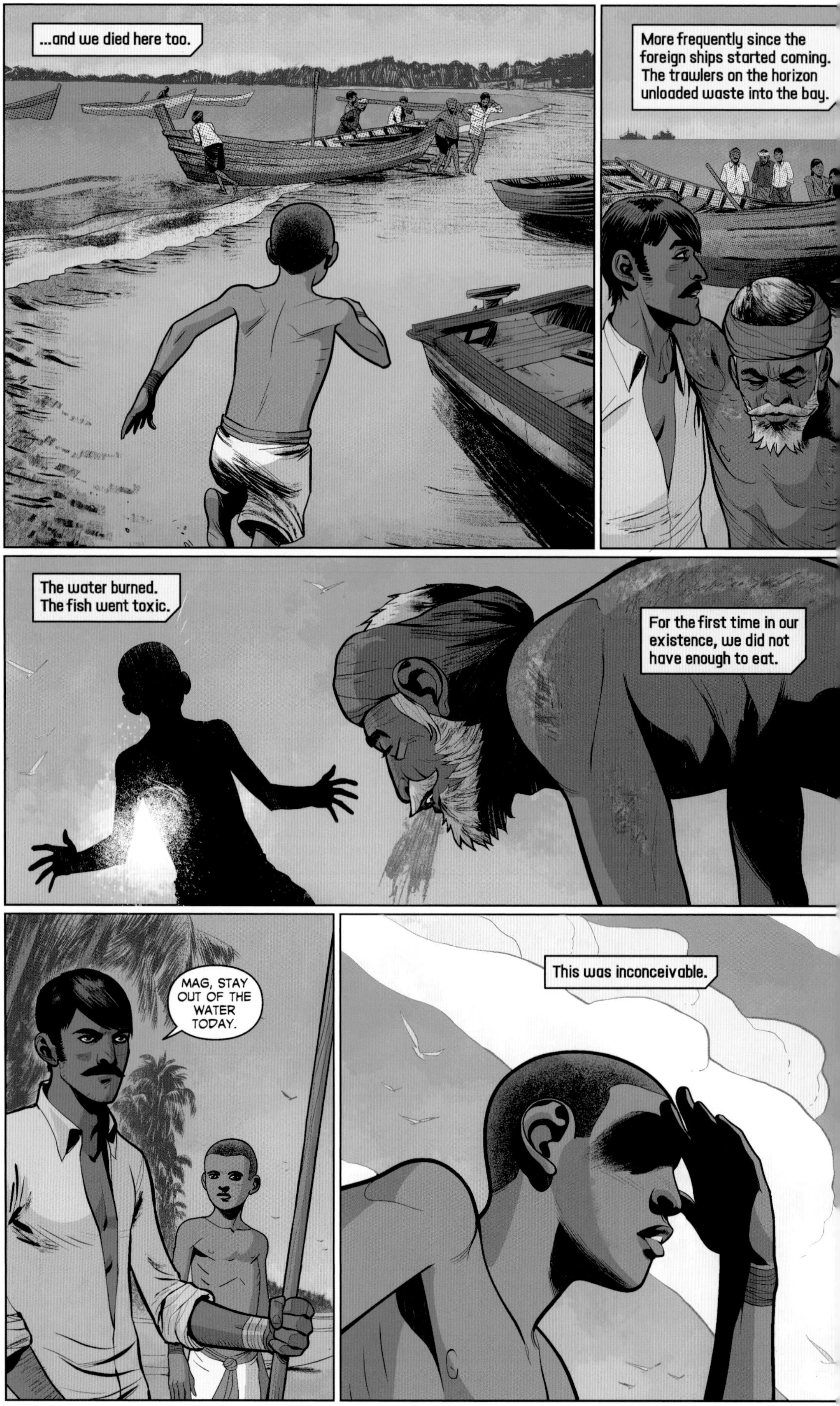
...and we died here too.
More frequently since the foreign ships started coming. The trawlers on the horizon unloaded waste into the bay.
The water burned. The fish went toxic.
For the first time in our existence, we did not have enough to eat.
MAG, STAY OUT OF THE WATER TODAY.
This was inconceivable.

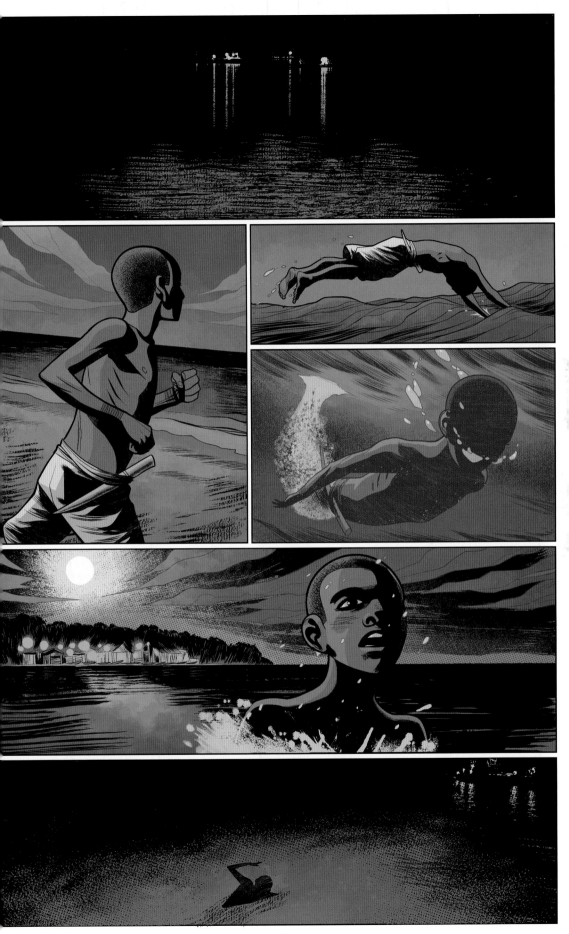

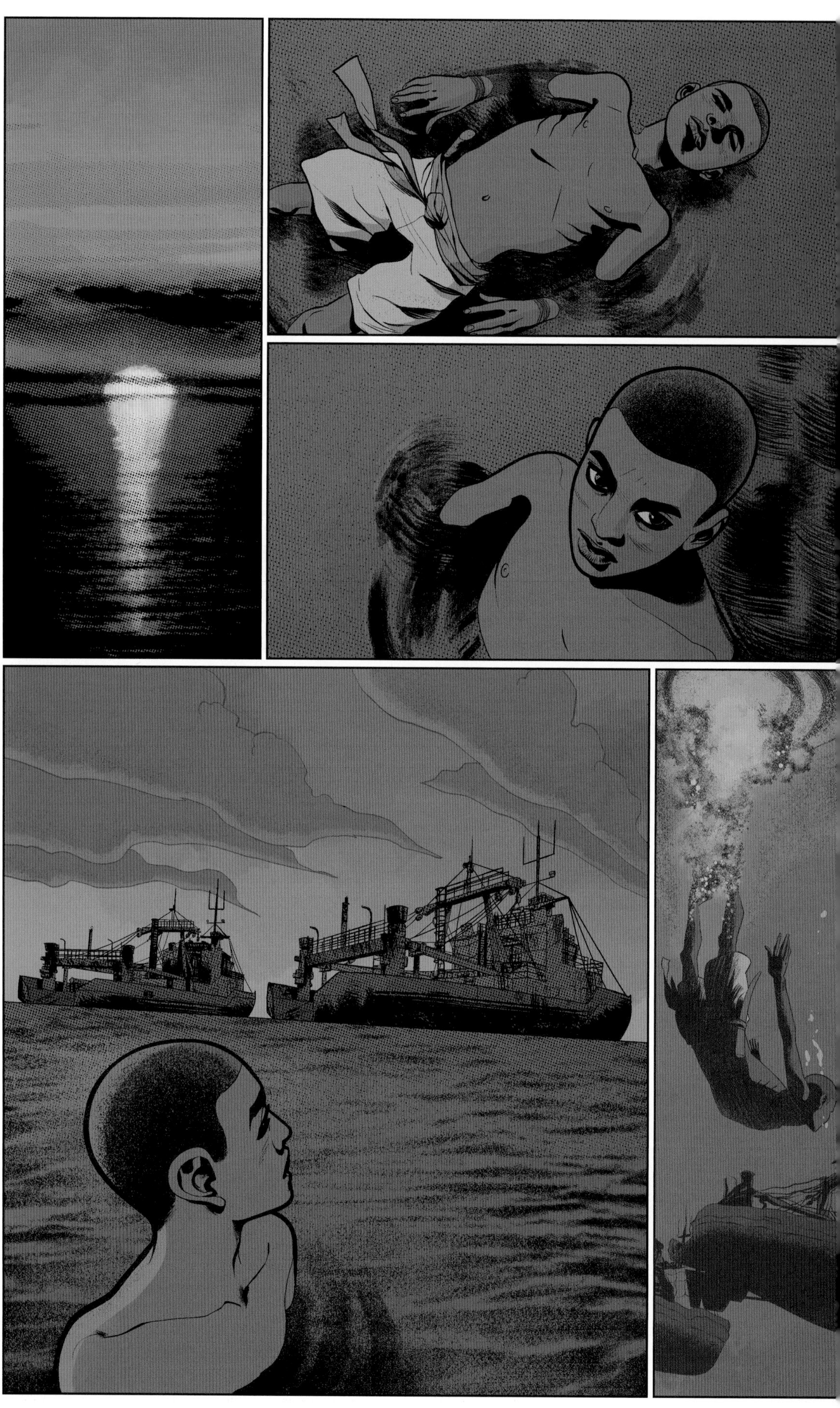

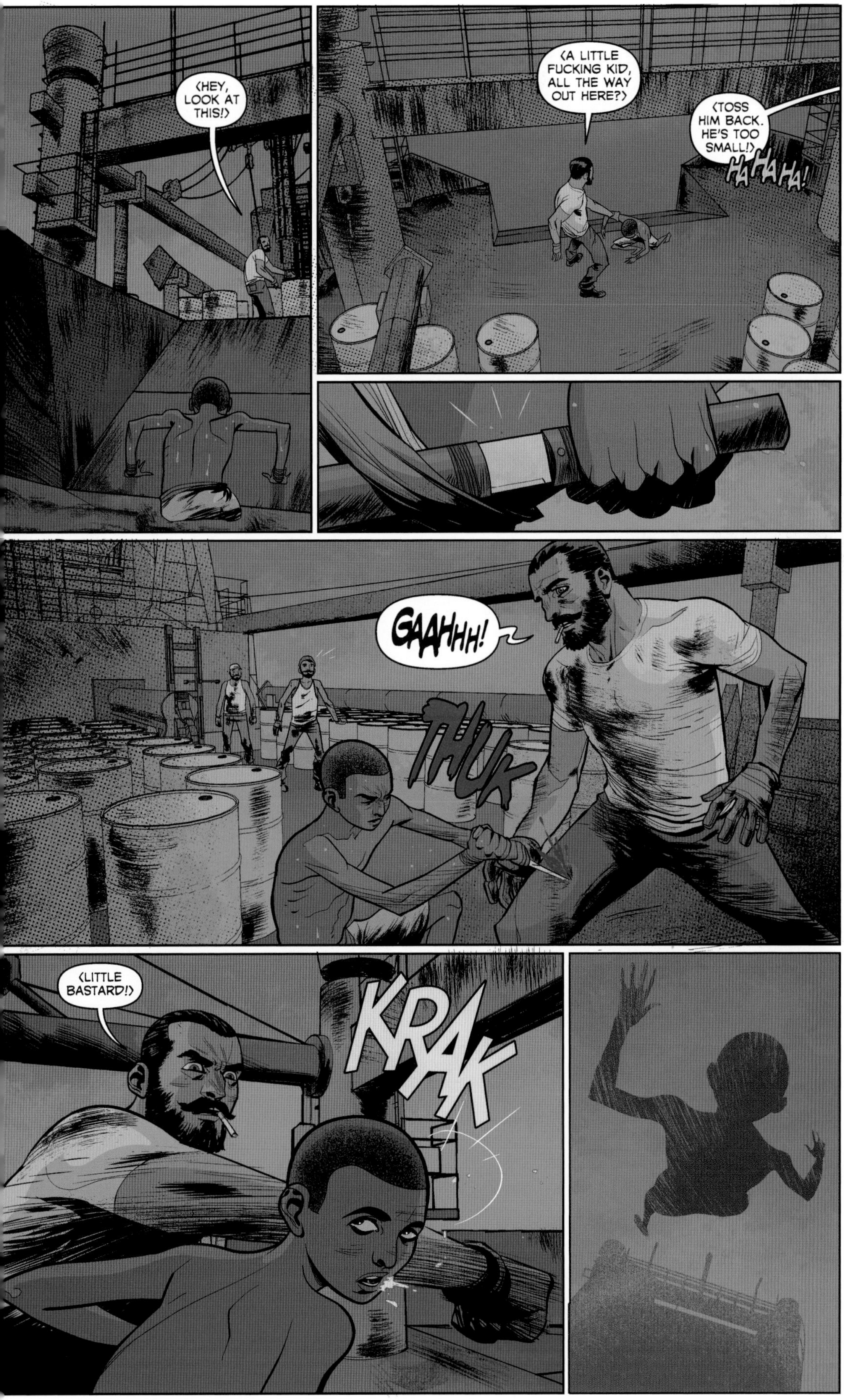

<HEY, LOOK AT THIS!>
<A LITTLE FUCKING KID, ALL THE WAY OUT HERE?>
<TOSS HIM BACK. HE'S TOO SMALL!>
HA HA HA!
GAAHHH!
THUK
<LITTLE BASTARD!>
KRAK

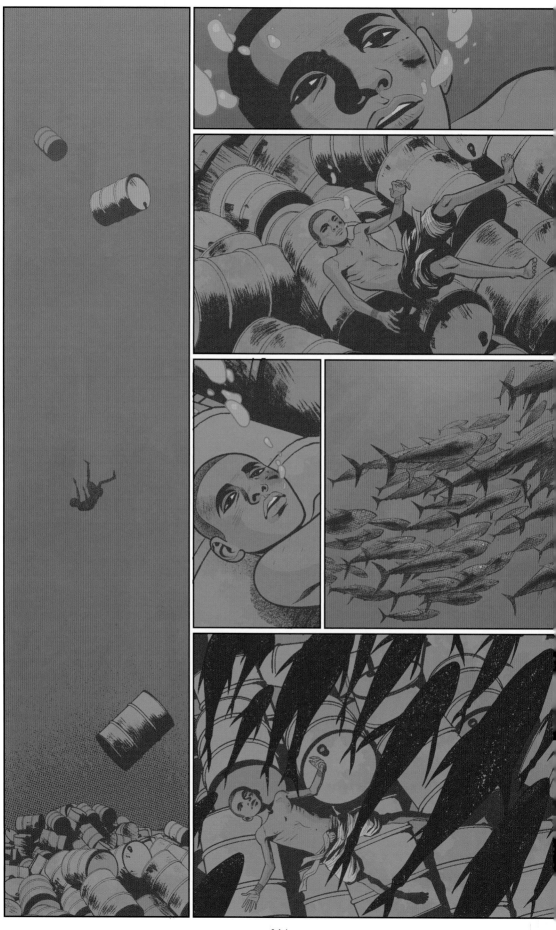

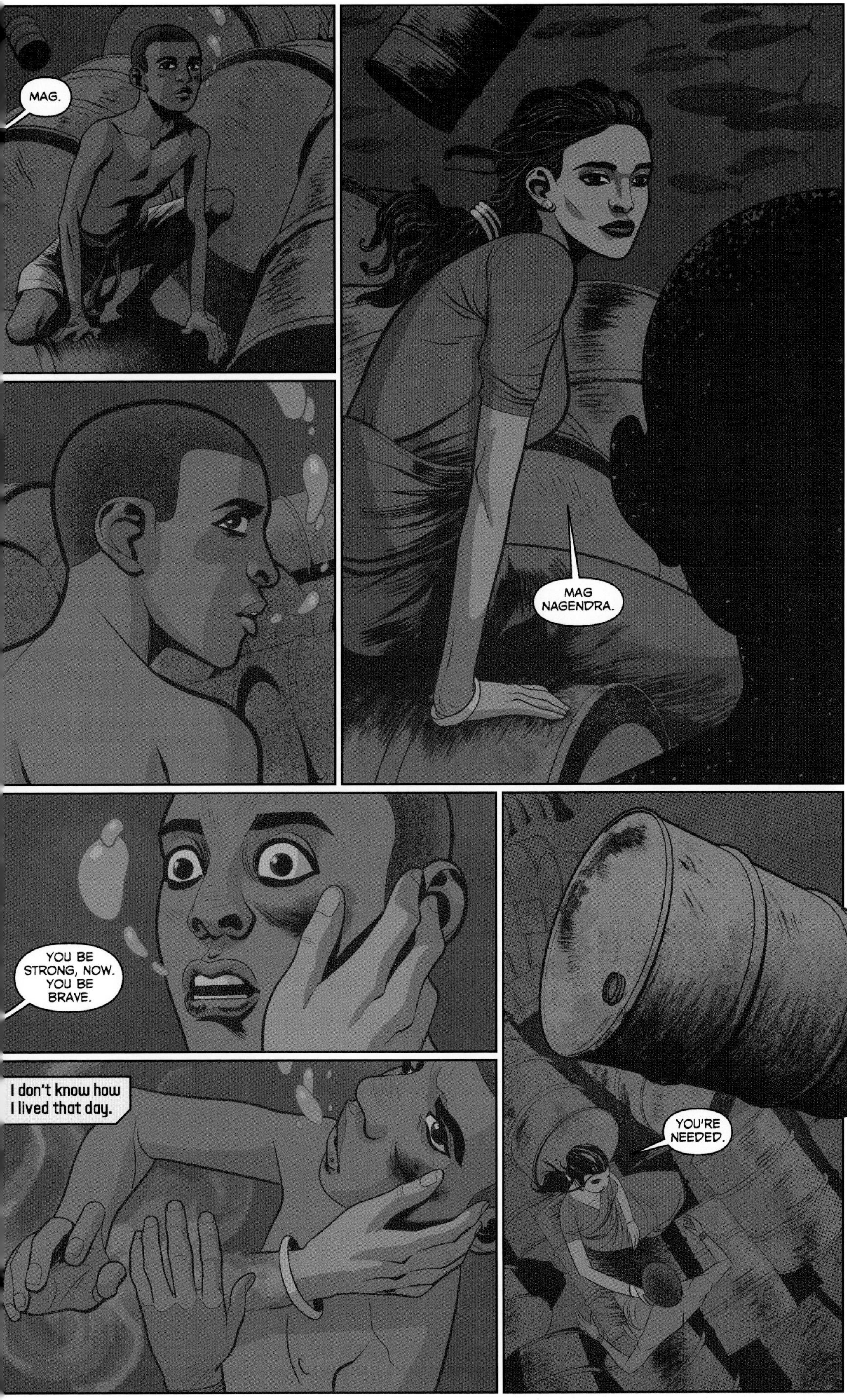
MAG.
MAG NAGENDRA.
YOU BE STRONG, NOW. YOU BE BRAVE.
I don't know how I lived that day.
YOU'RE NEEDED.

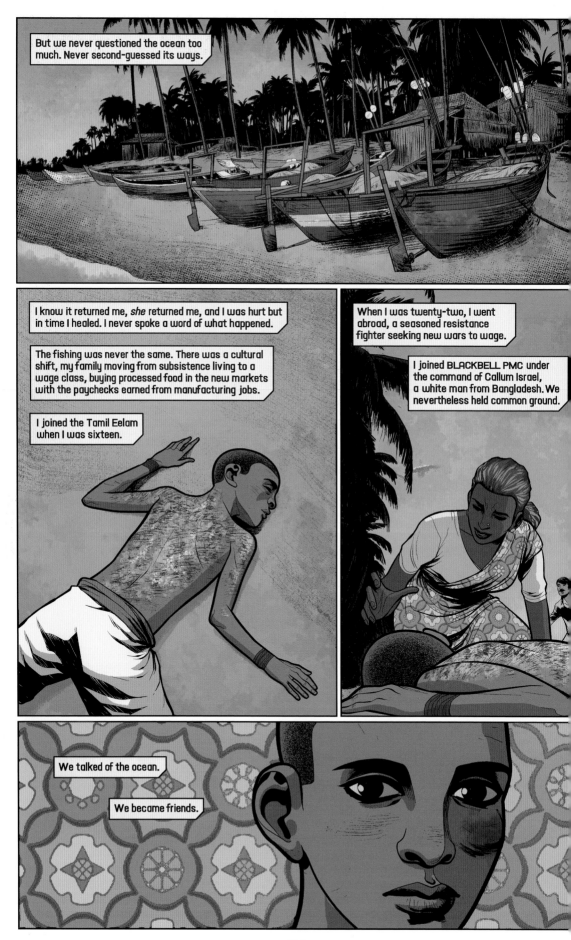

But we never questioned the ocean too much. Never second-guessed its ways.

I know it returned me, *she* returned me, and I was hurt but in time I healed. I never spoke a word of what happened.

The fishing was never the same. There was a cultural shift, my family moving from subsistence living to a wage class, buying processed food in the new markets with the paychecks earned from manufacturing jobs.

I joined the Tamil Eelam when I was sixteen.

When I was twenty-two, I went abroad, a seasoned resistance fighter seeking new wars to wage.

I joined BLACKBELL PMC under the command of Callum Israel, a white man from Bangladesh. We nevertheless held common ground.

We talked of the ocean.

We became friends.

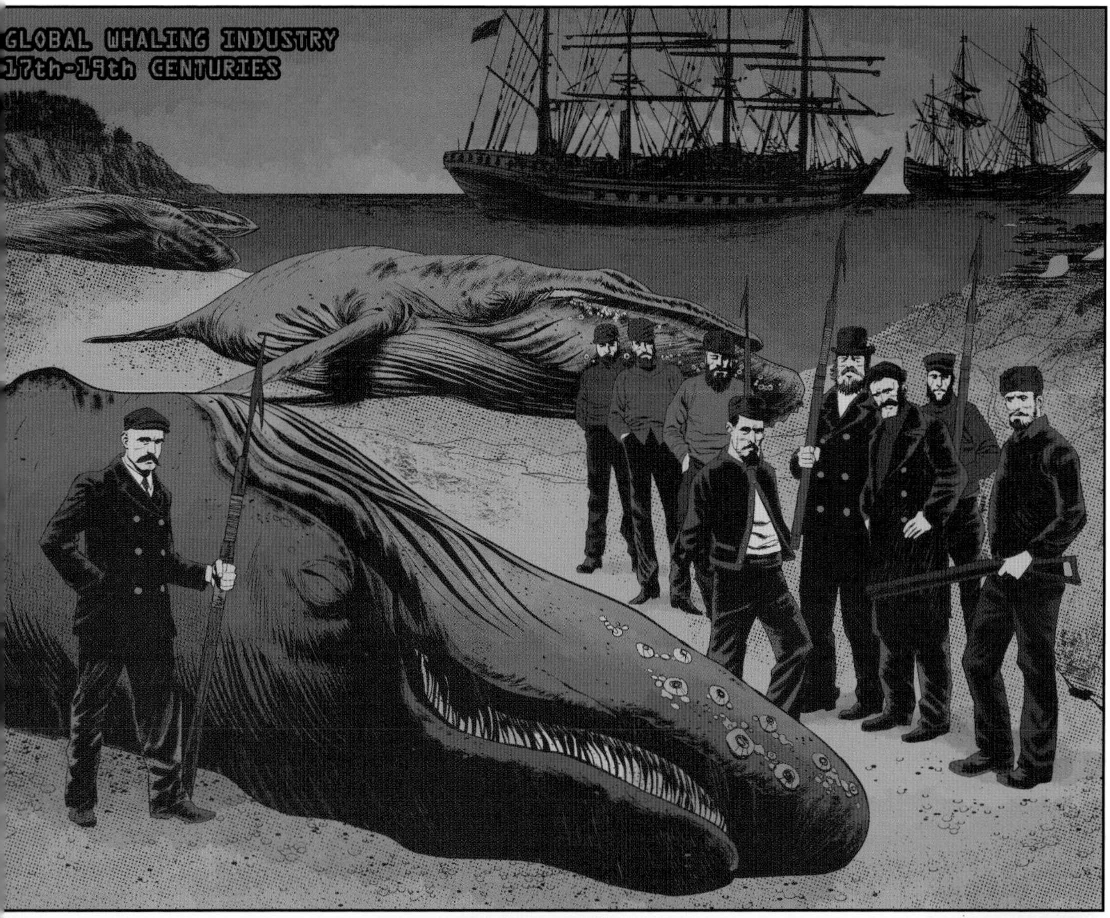
GLOBAL WHALING INDUSTRY
17th-19th CENTURIES

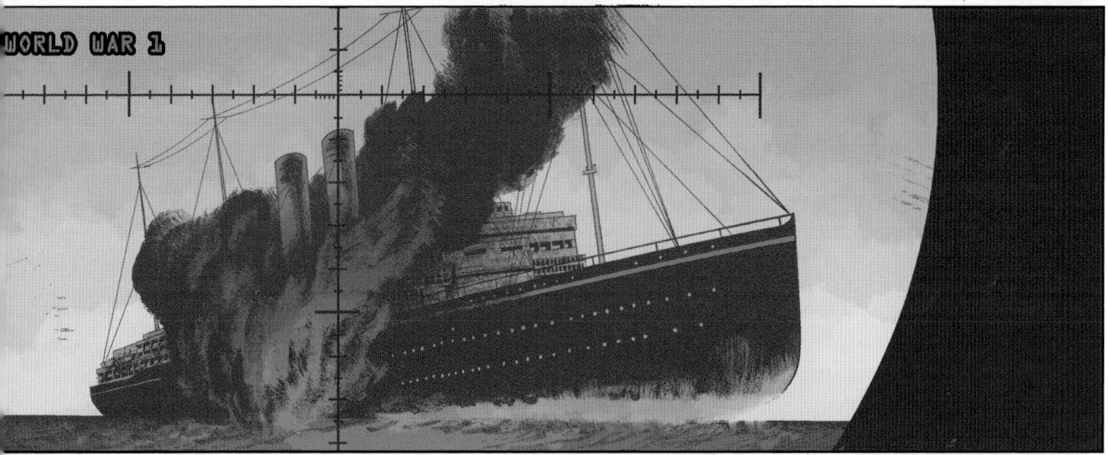
WORLD WAR 1

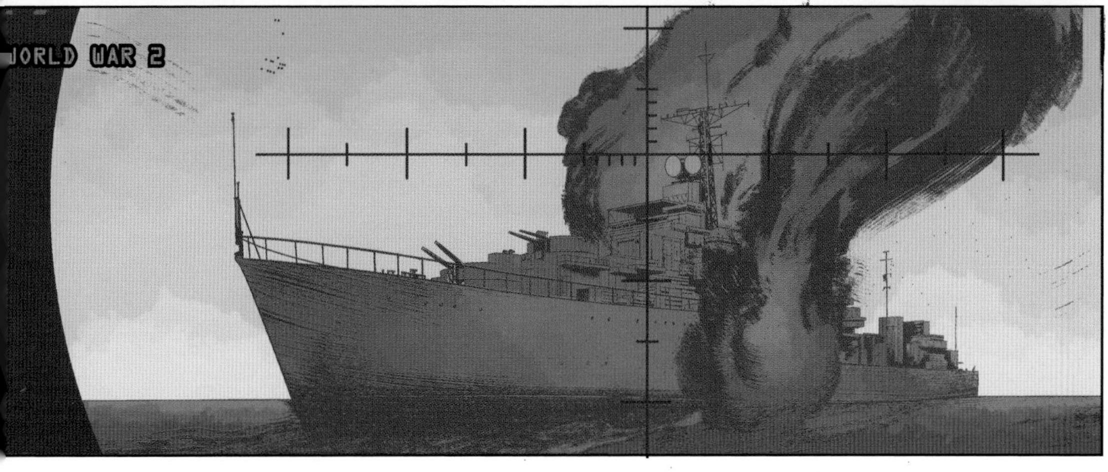
WORLD WAR 2

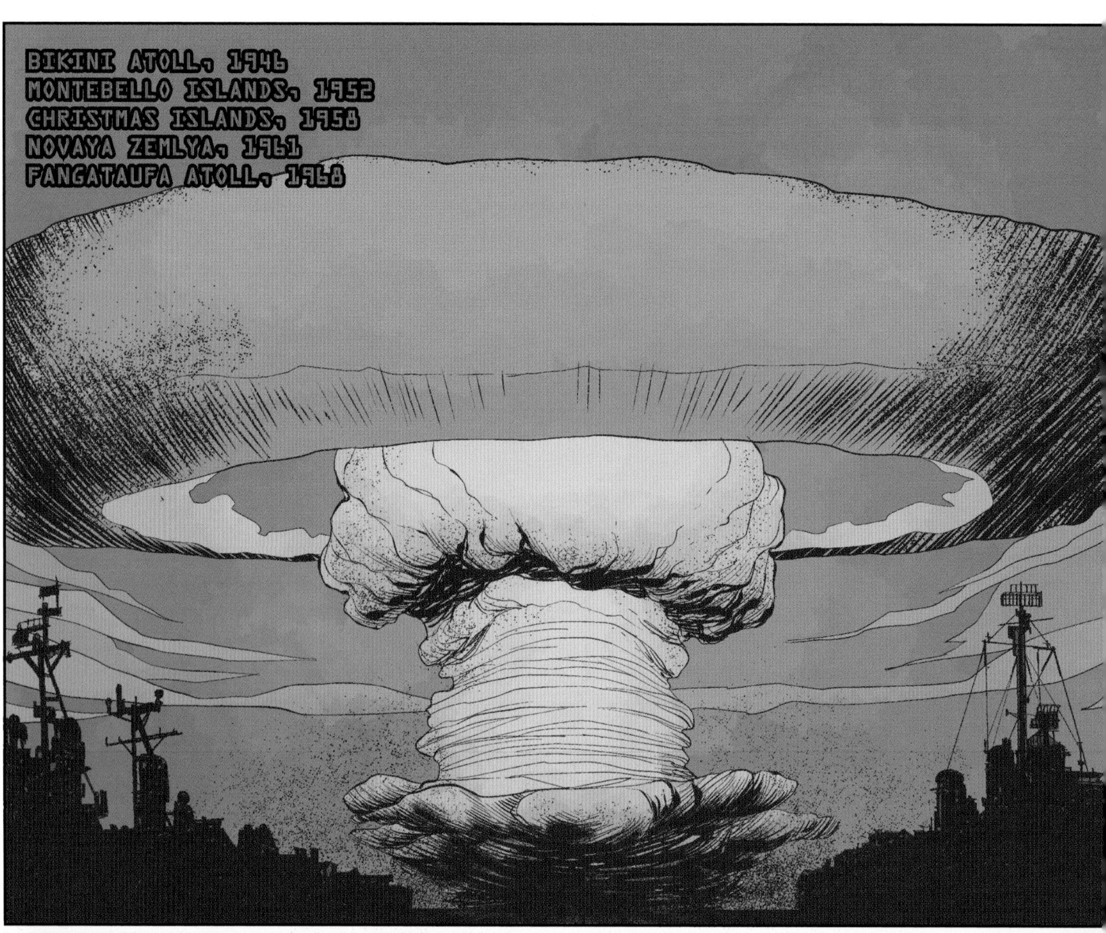
BIKINI ATOLL, 1946
MONTEBELLO ISLANDS, 1952
CHRISTMAS ISLANDS, 1958
NOVAYA ZEMLYA, 1961
FANGATAUFA ATOLL, 1968

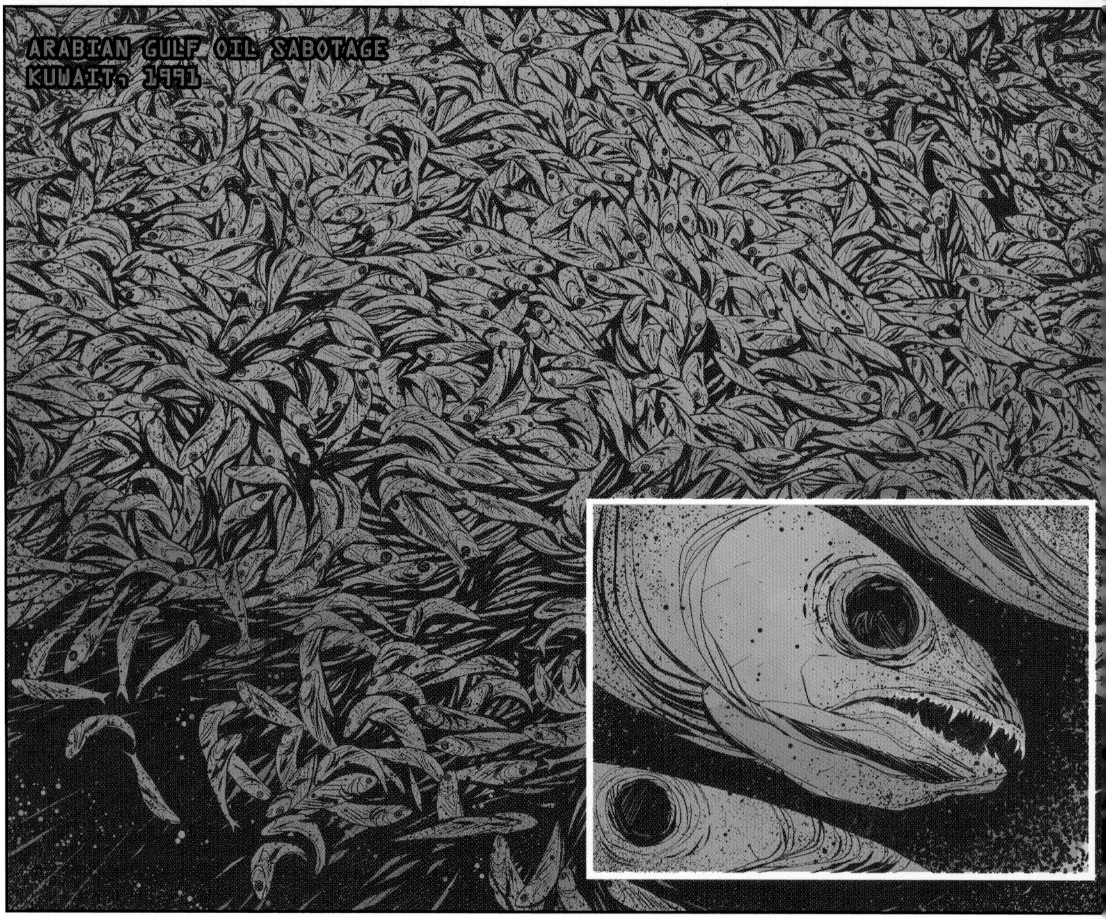
ARABIAN GULF OIL SABOTAGE
KUWAIT, 1991

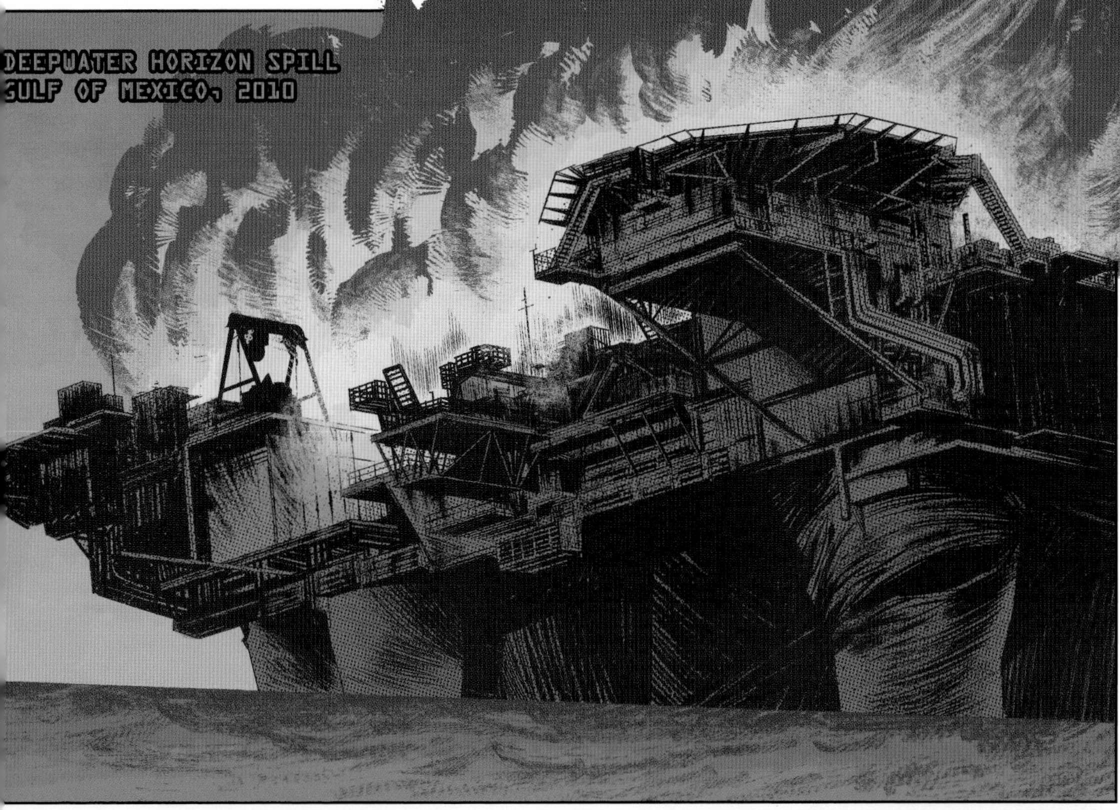
DEEPWATER HORIZON SPILL
GULF OF MEXICO, 2010

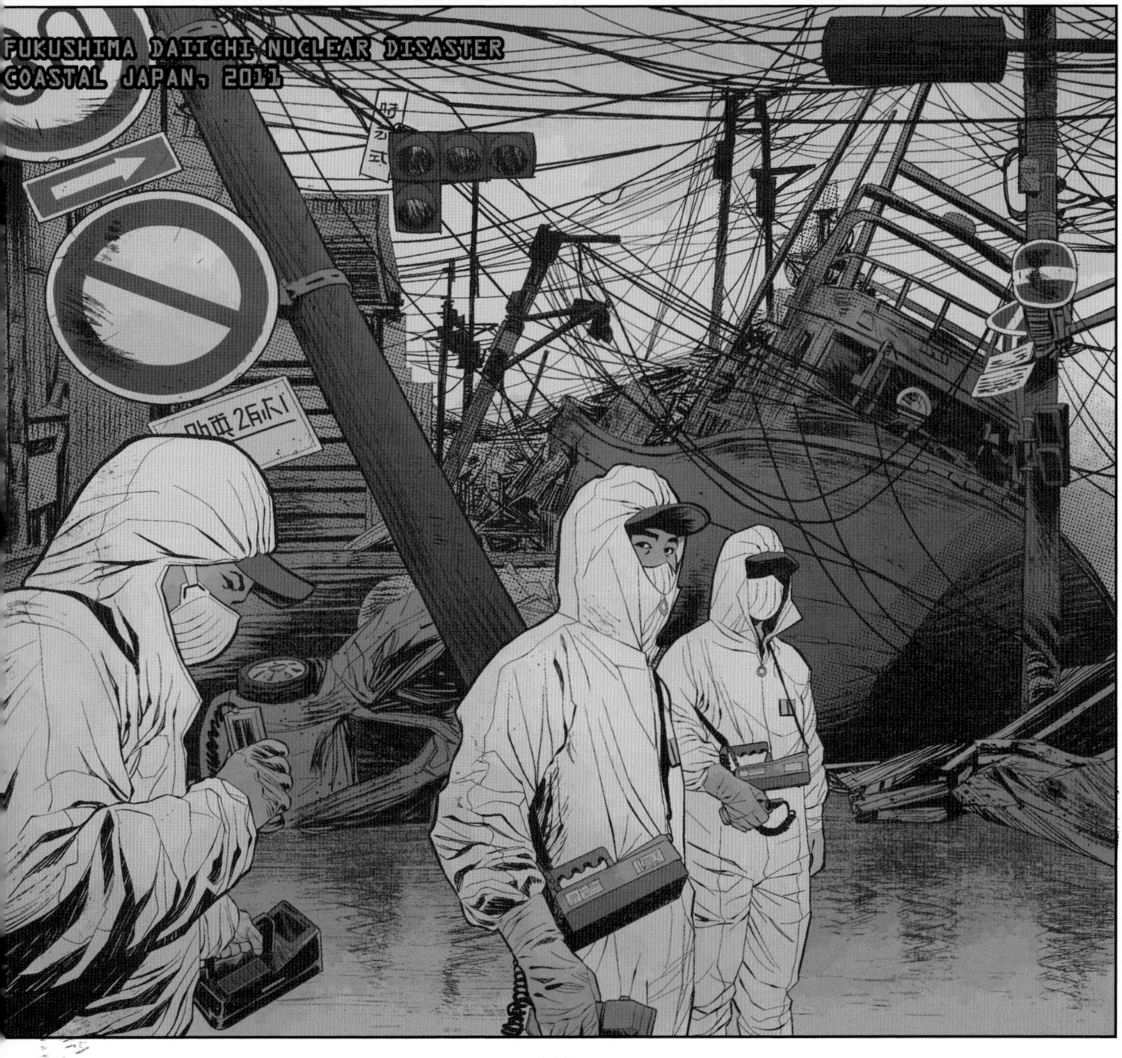
FUKUSHIMA DAIICHI NUCLEAR DISASTER
COASTAL JAPAN, 2011

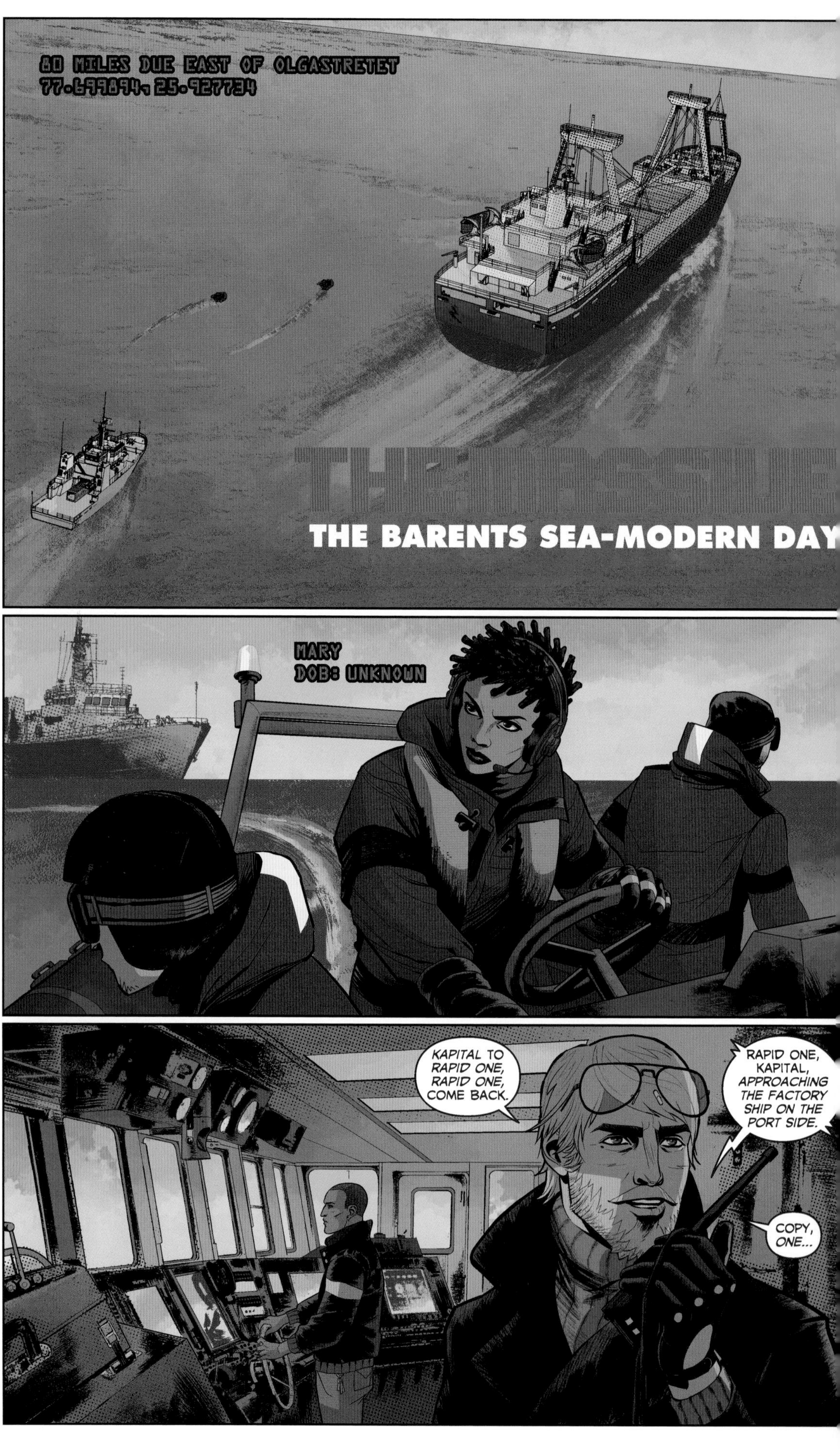
80 MILES DUE EAST OF OLGASTRETET
77.699894, 25.927734
THE BARENTS SEA-MODERN DAY
MARY
DOB: UNKNOWN
KAPITAL TO RAPID ONE, RAPID ONE, COME BACK.
RAPID ONE, KAPITAL, APPROACHING THE FACTORY SHIP ON THE PORT SIDE.
COPY, ONE...

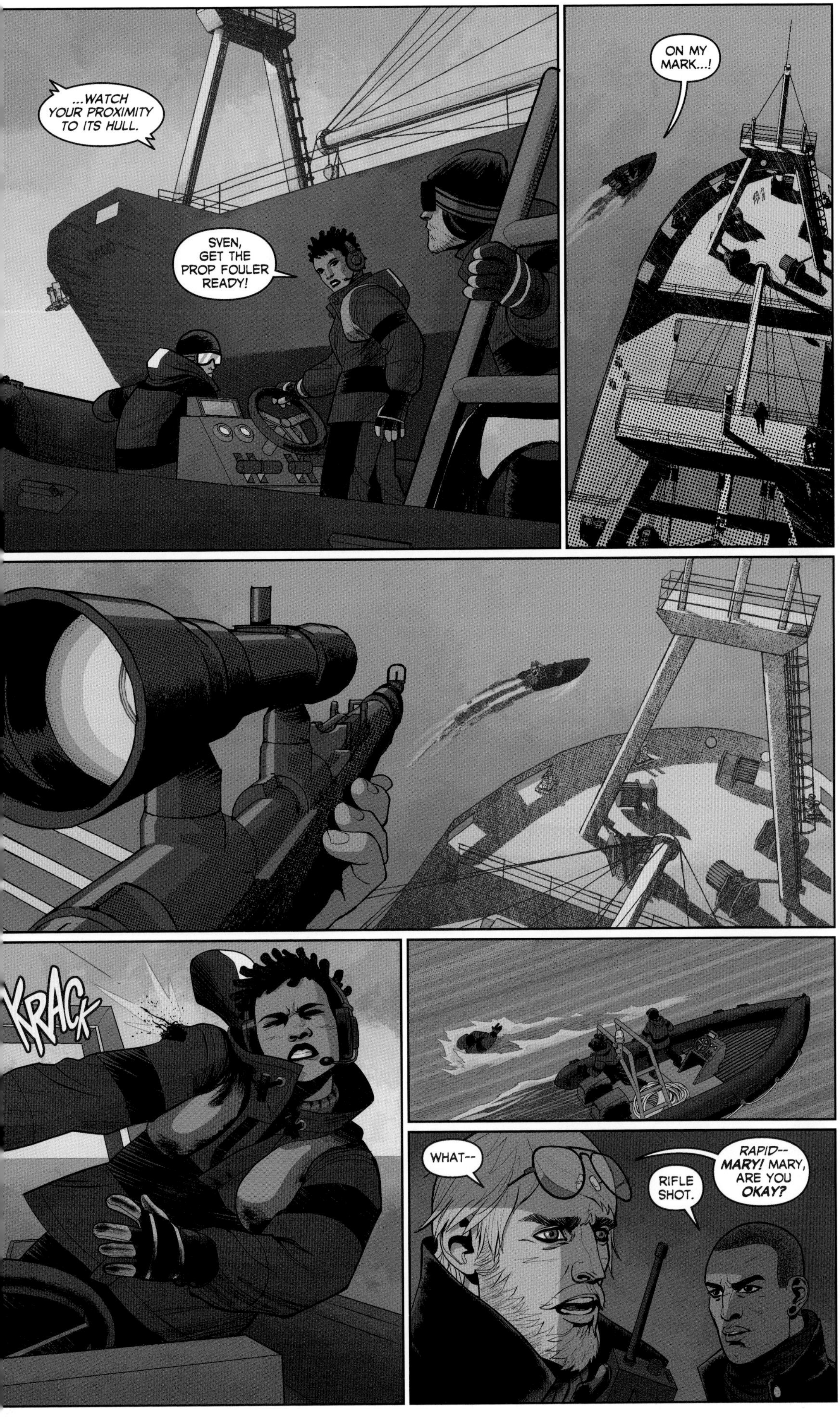
...WATCH YOUR PROXIMITY TO ITS HULL.
SVEN, GET THE PROP FOULER READY!
ON MY MARK...!
KRACK
WHAT--
RAPID-- MARY! MARY, ARE YOU OKAY?
RIFLE SHOT.

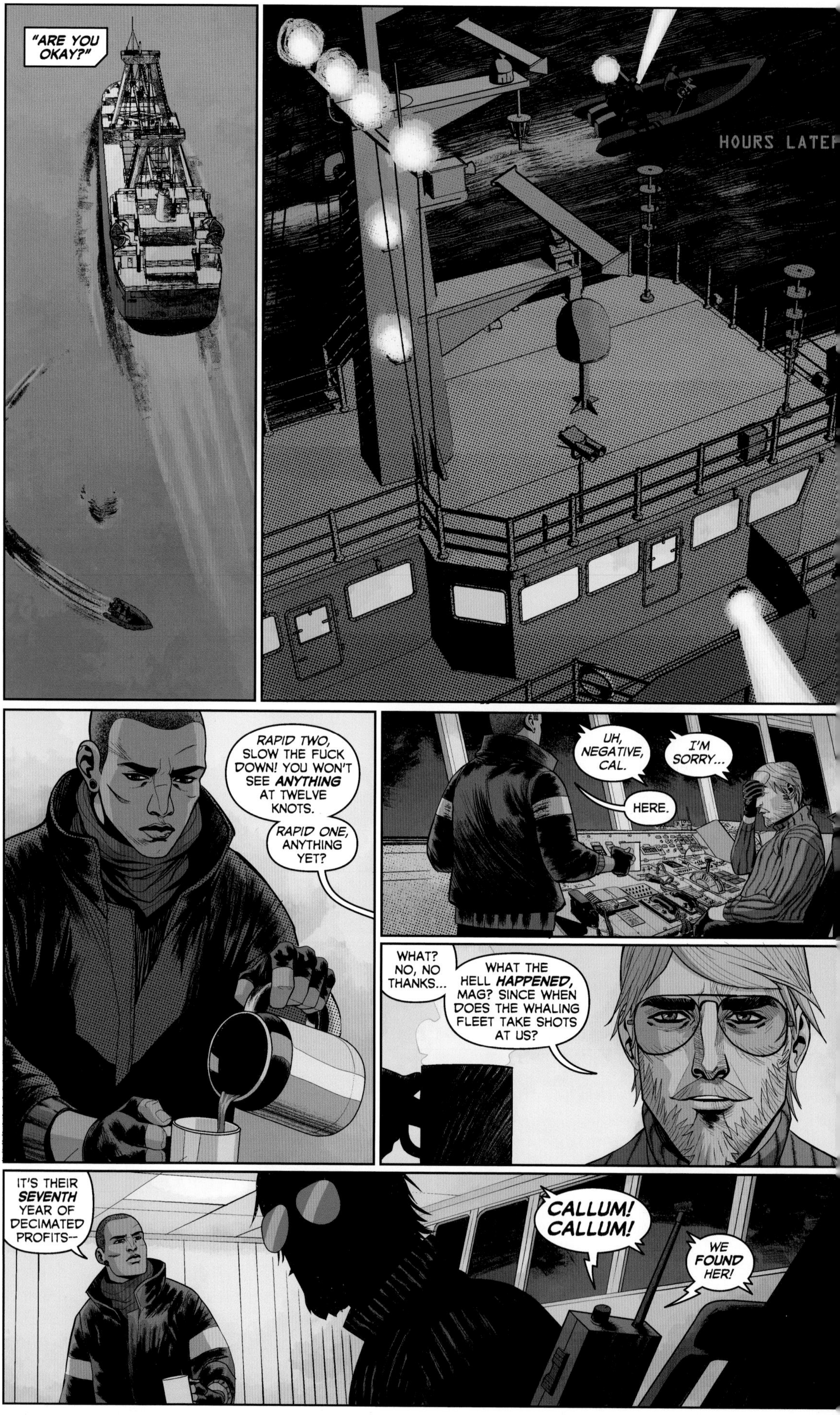
"ARE YOU OKAY?"
HOURS LATER
RAPID TWO, SLOW THE FUCK DOWN! YOU WON'T SEE ANYTHING AT TWELVE KNOTS.
RAPID ONE, ANYTHING YET?
UH, NEGATIVE, CAL.
I'M SORRY...
HERE.
WHAT? NO, NO THANKS...
WHAT THE HELL HAPPENED, MAG? SINCE WHEN DOES THE WHALING FLEET TAKE SHOTS AT US?
IT'S THEIR SEVENTH YEAR OF DECIMATED PROFITS--
CALLUM! CALLUM!
WE FOUND HER!

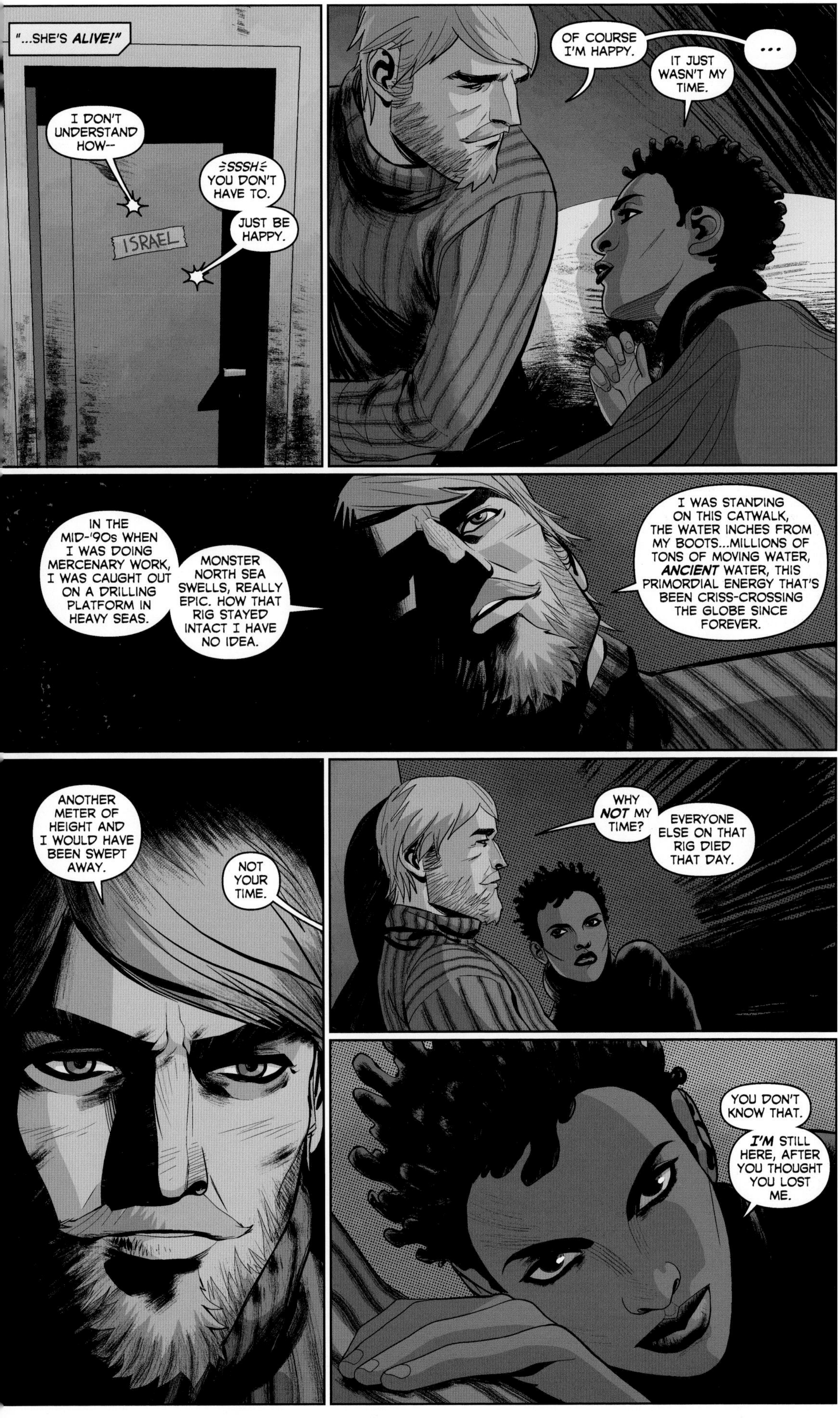
"...SHE'S *ALIVE!*"
I DON'T UNDERSTAND HOW--
SSSH YOU DON'T HAVE TO.
JUST BE HAPPY.
ISRAEL
OF COURSE I'M HAPPY.
IT JUST WASN'T MY TIME.
...
IN THE MID-'90s WHEN I WAS DOING MERCENARY WORK, I WAS CAUGHT OUT ON A DRILLING PLATFORM IN HEAVY SEAS.
MONSTER NORTH SEA SWELLS, REALLY EPIC. HOW THAT RIG STAYED INTACT I HAVE NO IDEA.
I WAS STANDING ON THIS CATWALK, THE WATER INCHES FROM MY BOOTS...MILLIONS OF TONS OF MOVING WATER, *ANCIENT* WATER, THIS PRIMORDIAL ENERGY THAT'S BEEN CRISS-CROSSING THE GLOBE SINCE FOREVER.
ANOTHER METER OF HEIGHT AND I WOULD HAVE BEEN SWEPT AWAY.
NOT YOUR TIME.
WHY *NOT* MY TIME?
EVERYONE ELSE ON THAT RIG DIED THAT DAY.
YOU DON'T KNOW THAT.
I'M STILL HERE, AFTER YOU THOUGHT YOU LOST ME.

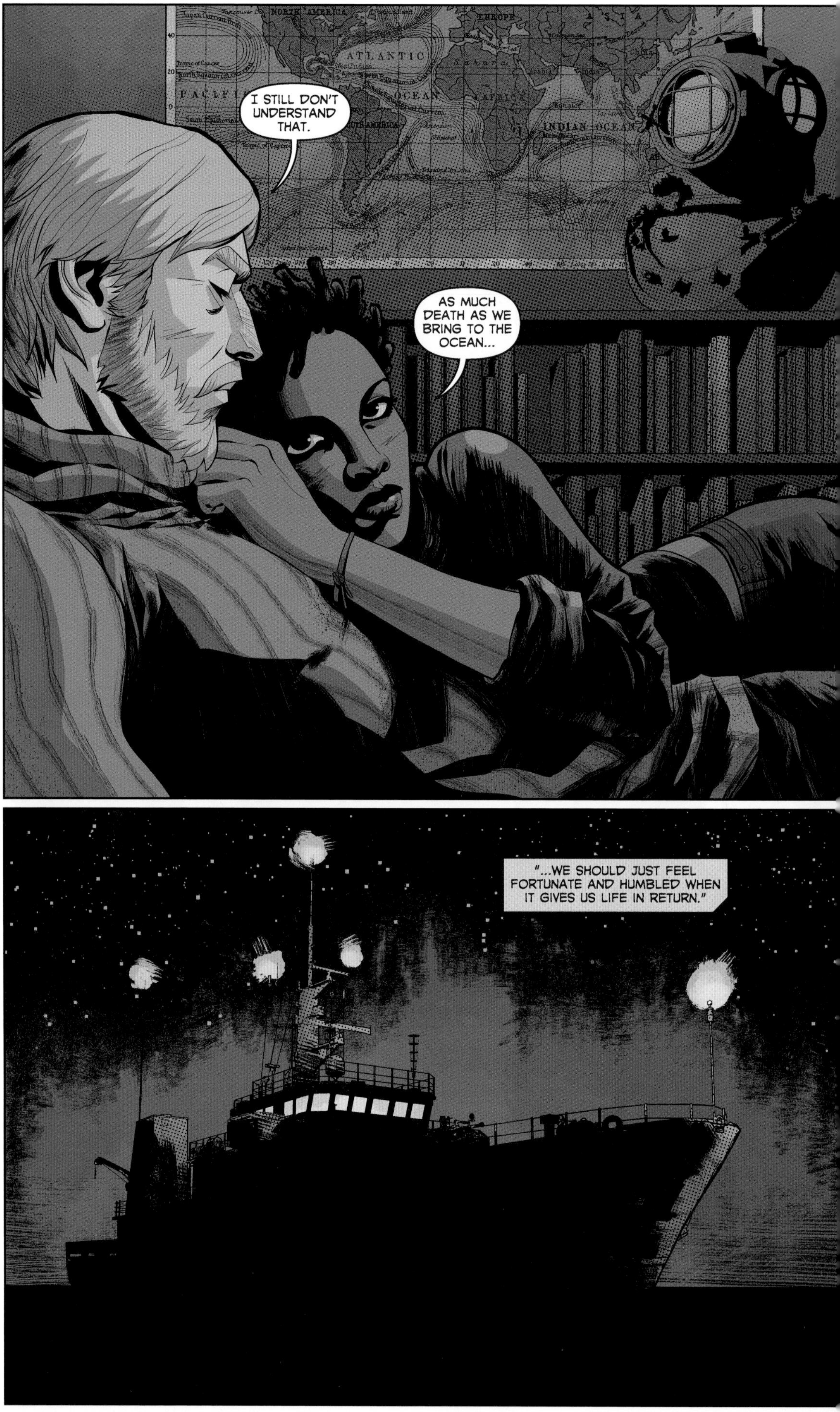
I STILL DON'T UNDERSTAND THAT.
AS MUCH DEATH AS WE BRING TO THE OCEAN...
"...WE SHOULD JUST FEEL FORTUNATE AND HUMBLED WHEN IT GIVES US LIFE IN RETURN."

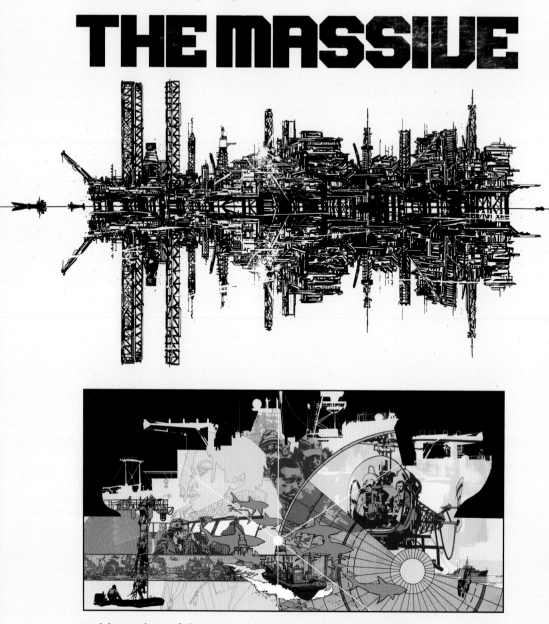